CLASSICAL CIVILIZATION
Greece

THE HEPHAESTEUM, OR SO-CALLED "THESEUM." (See page 306). The Hephæsteum is the most perfectly preserved Doric temple in Greece.

CLASSICAL CIVILIZATION

HERBERT NEWELL COUCH
DAVID BENEDICT PROFESSOR OF CLASSICS
BROWN UNIVERSITY

AND

RUSSEL M. GEER
W. R. IRBY PROFESSOR OF CLASSICAL
LANGUAGES, THE TULANE UNIVERSITY
OF LOUISIANA

GREECE
H. N. COUCH

Second Edition

NEW YORK : 1951
PRENTICE-HALL, INC.

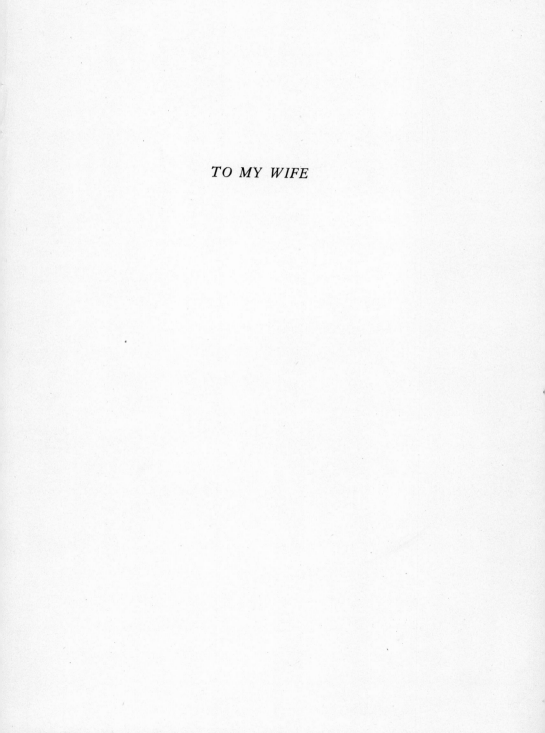

TO MY WIFE

PREFACE TO THE SECOND EDITION

In the preparation of the second edition of this book the entire text has been subjected to close scrutiny and revision. Without abandoning the essential features of the original plan of presentation, many changes have been made to attain greater clarity. Chapters have been subdivided, sections added, details that seemed unnecessary eliminated, and subjective judgments modified and elaborated in the light of experience. Approximately one quarter of the illustrations have been changed. It has thus been possible to take account of archæological work renewed in Greece since the close of World War II and to include more recent pictures of some ancient sites. The section on the technical details of Greek architecture has been retained and a simplified ground plan of the Parthenon added; at the same time the discussion of the Greek temples as creative works of art has been considerably expanded and appropriate illustrations included. A guide to the pronunciation of proper names and technical terms has been incorporated into the index.

In the chapters on literature variety has been sought by including the verse translations of a number of different scholars, whose names are mentioned in the text. Several passages, especially from the Homeric poems, have been taken from a little book by the author entitled *Beauty and Parting; Translations from the Greek Poets.* Wherever the translator of an extract, whether in verse or prose, has not been identified, it may be assumed to be the version of the author.

Warm appreciation is due to many scholars who have been kind enough to offer suggestions for the revised edition, either through reviews, by personal letters, or through communication with the publisher. I am particularly indebted to one scholar, who preferred not to disclose his name, for a long and thoughtful list of detailed criticisms. All suggestions have been carefully weighed and in the great majority of cases it has been possible to include them in the second edition. My greatest debt continues to be that which I owe to my wife, whose judgment and encouragement show no signs of flagging. Finally, I wish to express again my thanks to the Editorial Department of Prentice-Hall, Inc., for their skill and patience in the process of producing the present volume.

HERBERT NEWELL COUCH

PREFACE TO THE FIRST EDITION

This book has grown out of the desire to present a proportioned picture of the enduring qualities of ancient Greek civilization. For a study of this nature the reader should be able to reflect on the artistic and literary endeavors of the Greeks against a background of their political and social history. To attain such continuity and cohesion of thought, the discussion of art and literature has not been planned as material incidental and correlative to the history of Greece, but rather the chapters on historical themes have been interspersed as a necessary background to the study of cultural topics.

The spelling of proper names has presented the usual problem of steering a middle course between the Scylla of inconsistency and the Charybdis of pedantry. In general, a Latinized form has been preferred, but wherever another spelling has been sanctioned by English literary usage or where it seemed more familiar to modern eyes, it has been adopted even at the cost of consistency. Such a form as *Cnossus* or *Cnidus* may be employed with composure, but to alter the sacred *Delos* to *Delus* would be impossible. The opposite policy, namely, to transliterate all Greek names, is likewise beset with difficulties, for to designate the enchantress who metamorphosed the companions of Odysseus into swine as *Kirke* rather than *Circe* would remove the magic from her name, if not the wand from her hand. Occasionally, as with *Peisistratus* and *Polycleitus,* the spelling has been adopted as an aid in pronunciation. Greek technical terms, when transliterated, have, in general, been italicized the first time and not thereafter.

The literary passages in translation have been freely rendered, with some omissions and some brief interpolations to clarify the meaning, but, except in one or two instances, the appearance of the page has not been marred by the repeated insertion of dots. Every care has been taken to avoid altering the meaning of an ancient author.

The outbreak of war in Europe just as the illustrations were being assembled necessitated certain omissions. It was possible, however, to make proportionately greater use of the excellent material in American museums, and this fact may well prove of definite value to the reader, who will in many cases have the opportunity to consult the objects himself. I wish to express my thanks to all those who have coöperated so generously in gathering the photographs.

My debt to the standard handbooks and lexicons, the larger political, literary, and art histories, as well as to the journals and to the many excellent shorter manuals in the field of Greek studies has been great and is no less sincerely appreciated because specific acknowledgment is not possible.

Many colleagues in my own and other institutions have aided my work with their criticisms. In particular it is a pleasure to mention Professor B. C. Clough, of Brown University, at whose instigation the book was originally undertaken; Professor Russel M. Geer, of The Tulane University, with whom it has been my privilege to work; Dr. Frank P. Jones, of Brown University, who, from his experience with a class in Greek Civilization at Pembroke College, has offered many valuable suggestions; Professor John H. Monroe, of Brown University, who has given expert assistance in the preparation of the index; and Professor M. N. Wetmore, of Williams College, who has read the manuscript with great care. Above all, the dedication of the book to my wife is an acknowledgment of the untiring assistance that she has given at all times. The skill and care of the Editorial Department of Prentice-Hall, Inc., have contributed much to the consistency and accuracy of the final form.

HERBERT NEWELL COUCH

TABLE OF CONTENTS

[xi]

TABLE OF CONTENTS

[xii]

TABLE OF CONTENTS

[xiii]

TABLE OF CONTENTS

The decline of art in the post-Mycenæan period. The awakening of genius. The law of frontality. The archaic smile. Types of archaic statues. The standing undraped male figure. The standing draped female figure. The seated draped figure. Modifications and variations from the common types. The Acropolis Maidens. Decorative sculpture. The temple sculptures of the western colonies. Materials and techniques. Genuine works and Roman copies. A summary of the qualities of archaic art.

Poetry and society. The didactic epic. The *Works and Days*. The precept. Pandora's Box. The conviction of decadence. Other poems of Hesiod.

Varieties of poetry. The inspiration of the poetry of the archaic age. Classification.

Callinus. Tyrtæus. The exhortation to battle. Contrast between Callinus and Tyrtæus. Solon. Versatility of Solon. The Seven Sages. Theognis.

Mimnermus. Phocylides and Demodocus. Alcæus and his political associations. The ship of state. Sappho, her fame in antiquity. The life of Sappho. The poems of Sappho. The later estimate of Sappho. Anacreon and the *Anacreontics*.

Archilochus. His personal character. The high regard for Archilochus. Hipponax. Semonides of Amorgos.

Alcman. Later lyric poets; Pindar. The renown of Pindar. An ode to Megacles. An ode to Psaumis. Simonides of Ceos. Danaë and Perseus in the chest. The scolion. *The Swallow Song*.

TABLE OF CONTENTS

TABLE OF CONTENTS

TABLE OF CONTENTS

[xvii]

TABLE OF CONTENTS

TABLE OF CONTENTS

[xx]

TABLE OF CONTENTS

TABLE OF CONTENTS

LIST OF ILLUSTRATIONS

LIST OF ILLUSTRATIONS

LIST OF ILLUSTRATIONS

LIST OF ILLUSTRATIONS

LIST OF ILLUSTRATIONS

CLASSICAL CIVILIZATION
Greece

ANCIENT GREECE
(HELLAS)

Dorians
Ionians
Aeolians
Modern Coast Line
Messene Founded or renamed after 371 B.C.

SCALE OF STATUTE MILES
0   10   20   30   40   50   60

THERMOPYLAE
480 B.C.
SCALE OF MILES
0   1   2   3   4   5
The route of the Persians
over the mountains·····

CRETA

Hammond's 8 x 11 Map of Ancient Greece, (Hellas)
Copyright, 1917, by C.S. Hammond & Co., N.Y.

CHAPTER I

THE LAND OF GREECE;
ITS NATURE AND RESOURCES

The civilization of the ancient Greeks commands thoughtful attention primarily for two reasons. One is the inherent beauty and worth of their achievements, the other is the profound influence that has been exercised by their culture on European and American life. The literature and art, the science and philosophy of the Western world go back to Greek origins. In the stresses and strains of politics also, whether on the national scale or between conflicting world ideologies, a study of ancient Greek civilization will immeasurably heighten the understanding of the motives and purposes of men. The Greeks were humanists; everything pertaining to the fortunes of man in his environment was of absorbing interest to them. As a result, the story of Greek life and activity can be viewed as a pattern in miniature of many of the subsequent experiences through which the world has passed, even to this day.

The Communities of Greece. In a study of Greek civilization, it will be well to recognize at once that Greece, or Hellas, must be broadly interpreted as embracing all the lands and islands of the Mediterranean area in which the Greek, or Hellenic, peoples lived and worked. Neither in antiquity nor in modern times has Greece long remained a country with static and readily definable borders. In antiquity the numerous separate and independent Greek city-states guarded their sovereignty with zealous watchfulness, although at times the pressure of external danger forced them into temporary alliances, or even federations, with each other. Even within the past century, the borders of Greece have expanded and contracted with the fortunes of war and diplomacy.

But the roots of Hellenic culture spread widely, and thus it will be found that the center of the earliest pre-Hellenic civilization lay, not on the Greek mainland, but on the island of Crete, that epic poetry and philosophy developed first in Asia Minor, and that the period of organized colonization in the eighth to sixth centuries before Christ saw the settlement of true Greek communities from the Black Sea to southern France and Spain. Some of those colonies, notably Syracuse in Sicily, had, by the latter part of the fifth century, grown richer and more powerful than the mother cities of Greece, from which the colonists had gone forth five or six generations earlier. From these peoples, often forming a small unit of free society amid hostile barbarian neighbors, there flowed back into the current of Greek achievement a contribution to science, letters, and art vastly greater, especially in the early years of endeavor, than their mere numbers ever warranted.

The Small Scale of Ancient States. In thinking of Greece as something other than a single consolidated country, it is important to modify the inevitable modern concept of large political units like the United States and to picture clearly the miniature geographic scale on which the drama of politics, war, trade, and alliance was played in the ancient Hellenic world. The modern phenomenon of vast territories constituting nations or empires, peopled with millions of inhabitants, makes it difficult to adjust one's thought to a region so much smaller in area and so much more intense in local loyalties and convictions. The Greek peninsula was less in size than many of the states of the American Union, and it was subdivided into scores of tiny communities entirely independent of one another. They maintained their own laws, their private coinage, and their own armies and navies, which they were ready to use on all too slight provocation to annihilate their neighbors with a

[2]

ferocity that is strangely out of harmony with the spiritual sensitiveness of Greece.

The Geographical Limits. The mainland of Greece itself is a short, deeply cut peninsula jutting down into the Mediterranean Sea toward its eastern end. Snow-capped Mount Olympus stands as a northerly landmark of continental Greece, and the southerly limit of the peninsula is Cape Taenarum in the Peloponnese. The distance between these two points is some two hundred and fifty miles, and Marathon and Acarnania, marking the eastern and western extremities respectively, are about one hundred and eighty miles distant one from the other. The total area of the country, as thus delimited, is somewhat less than that of the state of Maine. Attica, with its great city of Athens, was smaller than Rhode Island, and the free and active population of Athens probably never rose above five hundred thousand. On the other hand, the Greeks were not troubled by smallness, either in size or numbers. The sense of individual freedom was strong, and they were more interested in the development of ideas than in the enlargement of national boundaries.

No part of the land of Greece was rich in the products of agriculture or in the raw materials of wealth. There were, moreover, areas in the west of Greece that were almost totally unproductive, wild mountain states that had little or no part in the commercial and cultural development of the city states that looked toward the East for traffic in wares and ideas. To an Athenian, facing the Ægean Sea, the city life of the islands that were visible to him on the horizon and the distant Hellenic communities on the coast of Asia Minor were more real and important than the fortunes of his physically closer but spiritually more remote neighbors of the mainland. The cultural activities of the Greek dwellers on the islands and in Asia Minor compensated in large measure for the undeveloped areas of Greece itself.

The Influence of Physical Geography on Life. The location of Greece in relation to the other countries of the Mediterranean area, and the physical properties of the country itself, exerted certain influences on the social relations of the people, and consequently on the development of Greek civilization. It is easy to exaggerate the significance of these external influences, yet some of them should unquestionably be pointed out. The peninsula itself, with Crete as a proximate link, forms one of three natural lines of communication between Europe and Africa; similarly the Italian peninsula is linked through Sicily to Carthage, and the Spanish coast comes close to Morocco. Through seafaring, whether inspired by commerce, piracy, or adventure, the men of Africa and Asia, with their more advanced cultures, early came in contact with their vigorous but less developed European neighbors. Similarly, the closely dotted islands of the Ægean Sea tempted cautious mariners, to whom the compass was unknown, to feel their way from port to port until they reached Corinth, Megara, or the Piræus on the eastern coast of Greece. In addition to the stimulus of all wider contacts, one result of this acquaintance with her eastern and southern neighbors was that Greece, in the period of her intellectual awakening, started with the advantage of having observed peoples who had already mastered certain of the techniques of art and letters. It was the salvation of Greece that she was then able to profit by the inspiration of the achievements of others without falling into the mental bondage that imitation would have engendered.

The Gulf of Corinth. The long inlet of the Corinthian Gulf from the west gave to Phocis, Bœotia, and Ætolia, as well as to the entire north coast of the Peloponnese, an outlet to the sea; but the commerce of these ports was necessarily with the as yet undeveloped regions of Italy, Sicily, and western Europe. On the other hand, the culture of the Phœnicians and Lydians filtering across the islands of the Cyclades, touched the eastern Greek cities facing the Ægean Sea or located but slightly inland, such as Athens, Corinth, Megara, Sicyon, and Thebes, and quickened their intellectual growth. The Corinthians had little reason to deplore the existence of the isthmus for, situ-

[4]

ated strategically at the narrowest point, they controlled the unloading of cargoes from the East and their reloading in smaller boats on the other side, or the dragging of ships on skids across the isthmus; and upon all the traders, whether they stopped by choice or compulsion, tribute was levied, until, by Biblical times, Corinth had grown famous for her wealth and her iniquity. Unhappily, her contribution to art and literature was not commensurate with her prosperity.

The Isthmus of Corinth. This narrow strip of land, which on the east links the southern half of the country, the Peloponnese, to northern Greece, affected the political relations of the different states. The almost complete physical separation of the Peloponnesians from their neighbors of the northern mainland, with a consequent imagined immunity from foreign invasion, contributed to the development among the Peloponnesian states of a narrow and insular point of view that came close to altering the course of the Persian Wars. Yet, conversely, the very fact of the existence of the narrow isthmus dictated the military policy of the Spartans during the Peloponnesian War, when year by year they led their troops up this natural pathway to ravage Attica and to drive the inhabitants of that state to take refuge within the walls of Athens.

The barrier presented by that same little strip of land shut out from the cities of western Greece the ships of the Orient and delayed for three hundred years the development of Italy. Had there been no isthmus, and had the Peloponnese been, in fact as well as in name, an island, the cargo-laden ships from Asia would then have sailed freely through a safe and land-locked strait to the western shores of Greece and on to the Italian peninsula; Corinth would have lost her reason for existence; Sparta, or some other Peloponnesian city, would of necessity have cultivated naval armaments; and the centers of Hellenic activity would have been very different from those that we have come to know. Merchants would have been freed alike from the inconvenience and expense of transshipment at the isthmus and from the danger of rounding Cape Malea to the south—a region so hazardous that in later times it became a proverb for destruction—and, as a consequence, they would have carried their arts and their wealth without hindrance to the cities of the central and western Mediterranean areas. Had a small waterway existed in antiquity, the fortunes of Italian and other European nations would have developed along widely different lines. A tiny isthmus, three and a half miles

Photograph by Alinari

FIGURE 1. THE CORINTH CANAL. The stratification of the rock may be observed. The canal, closed by bombing in World War II, has since been restored to service.

in width, which the Corinthian tyrant Periander, Julius Cæsar, and Nero in turn thought to cut through with a canal, could thus hold back the wave of eastern enterprise so long. Yet the speculation on what might have been in other circumstances scarcely belongs to a positive evaluation of any society. The consideration of the isthmus of Corinth may, therefore, be dismissed with the observation that in 1893 a French company completed the construction of the canal that had been so often projected in antiquity, and now all but the largest steamers can avoid the stormy voyage around Cape Taenarum and Cape Malea to the south. The scarped walls of the canal afford an

[6]

excellent opportunity to study the peculiar twisted geological formation of the isthmus.

The Islands. The numerous islands in Greek waters played a significant part in the economy of ancient life—a fact that was not always appreciated in antiquity. The unvarying determination of the Greeks to view society in terms of small and isolated communities rendered it inevitable that they should consider the islands as separate entities, which a fickle chance had marked off by surrounding waters instead of by the more familiar surrounding mountains and which were, as a matter of course, to pursue their separate political and economic paths. They did not recognize the relationship of the islands to the development of the eastern Mediterranean area as a whole. It could scarcely have been otherwise, for minds that could not grasp the common destiny of such states as Athens, Thebes, and Megara were not likely to spare a thought for any plan of unified action in which the insignificant islands of Seriphus, or Peparethus, or Ephyra might be included.

Nevertheless, the facts of physical geography do not depend on the narrow view of man; the islands, large and small, took their places in the turbulent interplay of Hellenic life, and it is in their environment that we must assess their importance. The strategic and economic significance of some of the larger islands and more important groups becomes apparent on thoughtful consideration.

Crete. Crete, the largest and most important of all the islands, reached the peak of its civilization during the pre-Hellenic period. Its early and close association with the other communities of Greece is attested by the account in the *Iliad* of Homer of the presence among the warriors at Troy of the hero Idomeneus with his stout squire Meriones, and their Cretan warriors, who came with eighty black ships to join their Hellenic comrades from the mainland. This literary testimony to the important place of Crete in the earlier story of Greece is amply corroborated by the rich material evidence that has been revealed by the many archæological missions that

[7]

have worked on the island. In a subsequent chapter the story of Cretan civilization will be considered in detail.

Ithaca. Quite different from Crete, but no less significant for its literary association is Ithaca, celebrated by Homer as the far-distant, rugged home of Odysseus in the Ionian Sea. "It is an island," as Telemachus explains to Menelaus, "with no wide driving ways for horses, and no fertile ploughland. Only pasturage for goats may be found thereon, for not one of the islands that lie softly on the sea is fitted to the driving of horses or fair in meadowland, and Ithaca least of all, though lovelier far to its native sons are the stern shores of Ithaca than all the level horse-breeding plains of Greece." So faithful is the Homeric description to the contours of the Ionian islands that the exploring archæologist is inclined to identify them all as Ithaca. Caution must always be exercised in making over-hasty identifications of modern sites with ancient cities.

The Ægean Islands. The islands that dot the Ægean Sea between Greece and the Asia Minor coast gradually assumed an importance in the growth of Greek culture that was no less real for the fact that it was not widely or frequently acknowledged in antiquity. In the shadowy past of legend, some of these insular communities found a place. Tradition had it that the tiny island of Delos was the birthplace of Apollo and Artemis, the children of Leto; in historical times, the worship of Apollo was fostered on the site, and a festival of gymnastics and music drew visitors from all parts of Greece to honor the kindred deities. So important did Delos become that it lent unity to the surrounding islands, which were called the Cyclades, or circling, islands. To ancient sailors the islands offered a tempting path, for, sailing without a compass, they found it comforting to steer for a definite destination, and in the lee of the sheltering rocks of their shores a ship might ride out a storm as it made its way from Asia to Greece, freighted with its material treasures and its intangible cargo of thought. It will presently be seen that the earliest development of critical philosophy and of lyric poetry took place in the cities of Asia

[8]

Minor or on the eastern islands of the Ægean, and only later, and over the highway marked by the islands, did this culture find its way to the cities of the Greek mainland. By the middle of the fifth century before Christ the islands had largely served their great mission as a route of thought.

The Strategic Danger of the Islands. From the strategic point of view, it is clear that the islands, especially those located near the shore, were viewed essentially as a nuisance and a menace. Salamis, lying close to the port of Piræus, was so vital to an aspiring naval power that Athens and Megara had to settle by bloodshed their rival claims to its possession before the former state could embark on her policy of expansion. It was in the straits of Salamis that the last decisive naval battle between the Greeks and Persians was bought in 480 B.C., and in the shelter of Salamis the naval base of the modern kingdom of Greece is located. Ægina, the larger island lying within sight of Athens, though a little farther distant, afforded so obvious a menace that Pericles was accustomed to term it "the eyesore of the Piræus." Chilon of Lacedæmon, one of the Seven Sages, looked with like apprehension on the goodly island of Cythera to the south of the Peloponnese, and declared that it were better for Sparta if the island had been sunk beneath the sea. So also the tiny island of Sphacteria, on the western coast of Greece to the south of Pylos, was to prove, for strategic reasons, the site of the most startling surrender of armed Spartan soldiers in the proud history of that military city.

When islands were so located that they could not be disregarded by a powerful state, they were a source of danger and anxiety rather than of security, for the spirit of separatism, which was basic to the political philosophy of classical Greece, usually made it impossible to incorporate them as loyal and enthusiastic members of a state.

The Rivers. Somewhat different from the influence of gulfs, the isthmus, or neighboring islands on the historical growth of the country was the effect of the physical configuration of the land itself. The rivers, the mountains, the coastline, and the sea have left their mark in the story of Greece. The rivers impeded the normal course of life and served few useful purposes. Following a night of torrential spring or autumn rains, an inconsequential stream, over which one had hitherto stepped with ease, became a raging torrent, carrying houses, vineyards, trees, and flocks in its short tempestuous flight down the steep slopes of the mountainside to the sea. The thundering rumble of such torrents became part of the yearly experience of the people of Greece. It affords an effective simile for armed conflict to Homer, when he describes two mountain streams that mingle their tumultuous waters as they fall from the mighty crests into a hollow ravine, while far off in the mountains a shepherd hears the dull roar. Many a modern sojourner in Greece has wakened to just such a rumble of waters as the Homeric shepherd heard. In Greek mythology, and later, in the extension of mythology to the coin engraver's craft, a river was sometimes represented as a bull, the embodiment of reckless and ferocious power.

While in spate the stream was difficult to cross for either man or beast, and it was impracticable to bridge a watercourse which varied in width with the seasons from a few feet to an eighth of a mile. Nor were the rivers of value for the movement of men or goods, for they were not navigable either as streams trickling over the pebbles or as swollen torrents. A Greek had to travel to other lands, as Herodotus did, to observe with naïve enthusiasm boats actually afloat on the Euphrates or the Nile.

Though the rivers were, therefore, a positive hindrance to the free course of travel, and were usually too muddy if not too uncertain even to serve as a water supply, one or two practical advantages may be credited to them. They carried down from the mountains silt, which was deposited in the valleys to form some of the few fertile plains of a barren and unproductive country, and this led, in turn, to the settlement of the valley and the not infrequent founding of a town beside the river.

[10]

So, too, although men might not travel on the rivers, they sometimes found it easier to follow the dry bed of a stream during the rainless season, or to mark a footpath by its banks, where the water ran by the easiest passes through the mountains. A few Greek rivers have attained immortality in literature, as the Ilissus and Cephissus of Athens; a few have been symbolically represented in sculpture, as the Alpheius and the Peneius of Olympia.

Springs and Fountains. The unsatisfactory contribution of the rivers to the universal need for water was balanced by the abundance of natural springs throughout the land, which in notable instances were led into artificial fountains to serve the needs of a community. The Enneakrounos, or Nine-Spouted Fountain, of Athens was adapted to meet the requirements of a city that had grown too large to be served by more casual methods of securing water. Poetic associations grew up about the springs of Greece, and the transference of literary allusions to our own language has familiarized modern readers with such names as Hippocrene, or Horse-Spring, the fountain on Mount Helicon that gushed forth at the spot where Pegasus, the winged horse of Bellerophon, stamped his hoof, or Castalia, the spring at Delphi that conveyed to those who drank of it the gift of poetry, or with fair-flowing Callirrhoë, Dirce, Aganippe, or Peirene. Nor will one forget the "warm gates" of Heracles at Thermopylae, named for the hot springs located at the Pass. In somewhat the same manner as the rivers led to the founding of cities, so the springs facilitated and motivated by their presence the establishment of communities or the foundation of shrines.

The Mountains. The mountains constitute the most important single feature of Greek geography for they are of the warp and woof of Greek life. They, too, deterred travel, but, instead of being regarded for that reason simply as a seasonal nuisance, they contributed more than any other physical factor to the development of the city-state organization, which, wise or unwise, was to prove the foundation of Greek political

[11]

theory to the end of freedom. One need not refer to obscure poetical passages or to doubtful sculptural allegory to illustrate the national importance of the mountains. Their names have become a part of English poetry almost as much as of Greek. Mount Olympus, the highest and noblest summit of them all, covered the year round with snow, was a fit home for Zeus and the galaxy of gods. Mount Helicon was the home of the Muses. Hymettus, famed for its honeybees, threw a friendly shelter around Athens, contributing with its trees and its flowers to the purple haze of the city. One will think, too, of Parnes, Parnassus, Pentelicus, Pelion, and Ossa of literary allusion, not to mention the long spine of Euboea and the islands of the Ægean Sea that are the unsubmerged peaks of mountain ranges, some of them extinct craters. Many of the mountain names come from a pre-Greek language, and in that very fact there is interesting linguistic testimony to the infiltration into Greece of successive hordes of invaders in the prehistoric past.

In the *Agamemnon* of Æschylus there is a dramatic passage in which Clytemnestra, whose husband has been fighting for ten years before Troy, describes the beacon fires flashing the news of the capture of Troy from mountain peak to mountain peak until it is seen by the watchman on the palace roof of Argos. Seven beacon fires, according to the tale, relayed the message of Troy's capture, and in spite of geographical difficulties, which a study of the Æschylean passage in relation to the map will suggest, there is romantic plausibility in the story of the use of mountain peaks in speeding the long-awaited message, for there is not a square mile of land in Greece on which a man might stand and find himself beyond the view of some mountain range or summit.

The mountains are everywhere, so that, with the exception of Mount Olympus, they do not convey the impression of great height, but rather of universality. They are marked by features so distinctive that they have given to the poets a recognized series of descriptive adjectives. *Many-gladed, many-*

[12]

fountained, gleaming, snowy, lofty, overhanging are terms that inevitably come to mind, and if it be thought that these are words that might spring to the lips of any man in any land, surely it was reserved to the Greek poets to invent such terms as *aigilips,* "where even a goat might not stand," or *elibatos,* "trodden only by the sunbeams," if such in truth be their meanings.

The Sea and the Shore. The coastline of Greece, like that of Maine, multiplies itself many fold with its deep bays and inlets. The scarped and varied outline twists and turns as it follows the devious contour of the mountainside. The long Gulf of Corinth and the Saronic Gulf, which all but make an island of the Peloponnese, have already been mentioned. The seas that surround Greece are scarcely less arresting than the mountain ranges themselves, both in the beauty of clear waters and in the boundaries provided by numerous inlets, which the Greeks were quick to seize upon as logical delimitations for their city-states. To the Greeks, however, the waters of the Ægean were not an "unplumb'd, salt, estranging sea," for the sea lanes served also to unite the scattered dwellers of Greece, who were normally isolated both by natural boundaries and by their own inclination. To the colonists on the islands, on the Euxine Sea or the Propontis to the north, in Italy, or Sicily, the sea was the connecting link with the homeland. Independent and liberty-loving though the Greeks were, they prided themselves on their common Hellenic origin, their language, religion, and name; and the sea was the one practical highway for the transmission of new ideas, of compositions in literature, of new techniques in art, as well as for the visiting of national shrines and national festivals. As the Greeks made use of the sea, which lay so close to their lives, they came to know it and cherish it in all seasons and moods, whether in the sparkling beauty of a summer sun or in the storms of winter, "when the snow falls in thick flakes on a winter's day, after Zeus the Counsellor has stirred himself to snow, and it snows steadfastly until the crests of the high mountains are

[13]

covered and the distant headlands, and the fertile plains and rich steadings of men; and over the harbors and shores of the gray sea the drifts are piled, and only the wave of the sea rolling in keepeth off the snow."

The sea played its part also in the economic and military life of the people. Not only was it a source of fish, a food not too highly favored, at least in Homeric times, but, more important, Athens depended for her continued prosperity at the period of her greatest power on keeping open the lines of trade with her colonies and with the ports of the East. Food and timber, gold and ivory were brought to her markets with increasing abundance; but when sea power was wrested from her, decline was swift and certain.

The Effects of Physical Environment. To summarize, one finds in Greece a country that consists in large part of barren mountains with the thinnest and poorest of soil, capable of nourishing little more than the grape and the olive, with rivers famed in poetry but of little practical use, with a coastline that twists and winds about the mountains, and with the sea serving both to separate and to unite the scattered cities. Some brief estimate of the relationship between the environment of the people and their intellectual growth must be attempted. It is easy to argue from results back to plausible causes. Thus one may, by way of contrast, point to the unimaginative monotony of peasant life in Egypt and to the comparative immobility of Egyptian art and find in this a natural reflection of a flat, sandy land that owes its lifeblood to a single element of nature, the Nile River. On the other hand, one may recall how Greece, with its checkered pattern of mountains, torrents, valleys, and sea inlets, produced a people of amazing versatility and imagination. But analogy is a deceptive instrument of logic, and such reasoning is not altogether true, for human genius has blossomed in all climes and under all conditions, and the later Greeks themselves, not to mention Albanians, Goths, Franks, and Turks, have dwelt on the same mountains and sea coasts

[14]

and beneath the same skies without finding in their environment the key to preeminent intellectual activity.

The Flowering of Genius. Human history, viewed from sufficient perspective, reveals a series of peaks, each preceded and followed by a lower level of achievement. In the long tale of man's advance, Greece of the classical centuries occupies a great and noble place. The years of her highest attainment were brief, but in the fifth century the varied intellectual creations of the Greeks combined to produce one of the rare and splendid periods in history, such as occur again during the Italian Renaissance or in Elizabethan England, when one part of the human race taps a new spring of mental capacity and sets its seal on the thoughts of man. No amount of explanation bearing on the influence of beautiful scenery on an imaginative people, or on their contact with more spectacular if less abiding civilizations in the east and south, or on an advantageous location resulting in the impact of the trading Phœnicians with their enterprise and their alphabet, can tell more than part of the story of Greek achievement. Greece was poor in material resources of farm and mine, but her people surmounted poverty or, more accurately, thrust it from their consciousness in the pursuit of their goals of life. The Greeks developed a superb intellectual attitude that centered primarily in an interest in man; that, at its best, fostered an exquisite artistry and, at the same time, a veneration for harmony and restraint—a magnificent heritage from which little less than perfection could be expected.

The Adaptation to Environment. Uncritical admiration will not, however, prove a satisfactory substitute for dispassionate inquiry into the evidence available, and certain very definite results in Greek political and economic history can be attributed to the physical features of the land. It will be seen at once that, apart from the sea lanes of traffic, the facilities for travel in so small a country were extraordinarily circumscribed. With the exception of a Homeric reference to a wagon road from Pylos to Sparta over which Telemachus traveled in search of his father Odysseus, the testimony of ancient literature and archæology tells of a country almost innocent of long carriage roads. When necessity took a Greek from place to place on the mainland, mules, horses, or donkeys were the alternative to travel on foot, and only through isolated passes was it physically possible to reach many of the remote settlements.

The Growth of the City-States. Inducements to travel were neither common nor powerful. Nature itself seems to have imposed on this land the principle, which the people adopted with entire satisfaction, of life in isolated communities. There is no more basic principle of Greek political theory than the city-state, by which is meant a small plain or valley bounded by enclosing mountains and dominated by a walled city or acropolis in which all inhabitants took refuge in time of danger. Athens was the fortress of Attica, with such communities as Eleusis, Thoricus, and Zoster finding their political life in it as the principal city; Sparta was the center of Laconia, Corinth of Corinthia, and thus the list might be prolonged. Above any conception of a common loyalty to Hellas, each citizen cherished the self-sufficiency of his own state. Socially and politically the states were separate; the difficulties of communication made isolation inevitable, and the restrictions on trade, foreign residence, and foreign marriage furthered the tendency to separatism arising from geographical accident. Occasionally individuals influenced by political exile, or treachery, or even by an ideological loyalty, left their home states and sought careers elsewhere. One thinks of Tyrtæus, the Athenian who became a citizen of Sparta, of Themistocles, who sought refuge in Persia, or of Xenophon, who was received in Lacedæmon, but such instances are rare. Normally the citizens of a Greek community lived and died within its borders.

The sheer mountain walls, with narrow and tortuous passes, offered natural facilities for defense against foreign aggression. At the Pass of Thermopylae a small number of Greek defenders were able to hold the hordes of Asia at bay until the enemy were shown the mountain path by which they came upon the Spartans from the rear. In contrast, the Greek cities of the Asia Minor coastal plain, located in a flat and fertile region, were overcome with comparative ease by the Lydians and the Persians in turn. Yet the momentary advantage of defense afforded by the mountains of the mainland was outweighed in the long run by the constant and inexorable pressure that they exercised against unity of action among the city-states, thus helping to produce the incurable division that was to be, in the end, the ruin of the country.

This saddening result, in addition to the multiplication beyond all reason of independent city-states and the assumption by the first critical political scientists that small separate communities are an axiomatic prerequisite of civilization, has given to the divisional organization in Greece an importance that transcends a similar though less intensive development in Italy, Sicily, Spain, Gaul, and elsewhere. In Greece, the city-state is one of the vital political institutions, but its origin and persistence are due to a geographical phenomenon.

The Beauty of the Countryside. It would be a mistake to leave the impression that Greece, though harsh and poor in the extreme, was an unlovely country. On the contrary, there are few parts of the world more beautiful, and the loveliness ranges over all notes of beauty, whether it be the serene and matchless dignity of Mount Olympus, a flock of sheep grazing in a stony pasture with the mountains rising beyond, or a peasant ploughing with his oxen against the soft and dusty background of an olive grove. When one stands on the ancient ruins of Delphi and looks down the breathtaking mountain slopes and away to the port of Itea, or up to the glistening rocks, where the vultures circle overhead as they did in antiquity, when, as Euripides tells, they seized the meat offerings from the altars, one cannot but feel that the site was marked out from the beginning of time to be an oracular shrine of Apollo. The overpowering beauty of the scene takes possession of one's senses. Or again in the spring, when the poppies redden the

[17]

fields of the Peloponnese, and the peasant women, eternally spinning, smile quietly at the passing traveler, there are combined in modern days the handicraft and the tranquillity of antiquity.

The Greek Interest in Man. In ancient Greek literature, especially of the fifth and fourth centuries, there is little direct and objective description of landscape. When it does occur, as,

Photograph by Eunice Burr Couch

FIGURE 2. SHEEP GRAZING IN ARCADIA. Flocks of sheep or goats are typical of the Greek countryside.

for instance, in the beautiful choric passages of the tragedies, it is usually as a background to human action. This is due to two factors—the primary interest of the Greeks in mankind and the fact that the writing of landscape poetry always awaits the passing of intensity in national life into a period dominated by a reflective mood. Some wingèd words—"the wine-dark sea" of Homer, or "violet-crowned Athens" of Pindar—bear witness to the observation in antiquity of nature as it can still be seen in Greece by those who have eyes to see.

The Effect of Climate on Society. A country so small as

[18]

Greece could not offer very pronounced climatic variety as a result of differences of latitude. The peculiarities of location, however, and of physical geography combined to produce an astonishing differential of climate over the peninsula, which, in turn, modified the pursuits and aptitudes of the people. The most striking characteristic of the Greek climate as a factor in social life is the change of the weather with the seasons and its consistent performance within fixed periods. Through the late spring, summer, and early fall, from April to September, rain is virtually unknown in Attica, and ancient life moved on the reasonable assumption that dry, hot, dusty days would follow one another with unvarying persistence. It is difficult, in a modern society of universal communication and of well-nigh universal disregard of the elements in the pursuit of war or commerce, to understand the importance of the weather in the social and political life of Greece, and yet Thucydides arranged his history of the Peloponnesian War by summer and winter seasons as the most reasonable and natural division of time in that struggle.

With the beginning of the warm, dry season, military projects, which had been interrupted the previous fall (unless such a man as Philip of Macedon chose to disregard the established rules of decent warfare and press his campaign in winter) were resumed again, the appropriate tasks in the fields were performed, the sheep and goats were driven by the shepherds to the mountains to find greener vegetation through the parching summer months, and ships plied the sea now freed from storms. The social implications of such logical adaptation to the elements were considerable. Shepherds from neighboring but isolated states would meet with their flocks on the mountain crests; disputes over pasturage rights would arise; and with their solution early treaties of mutual forbearance and cooperation would follow.

Every autumn, when the signs of winter filled the air, the pleasant outdoor life of Greece came to an end. Ships hurried to harbor, shepherds drove their flocks down from the mountains, and the Greeks prepared to endure the season in discomfort, though not in idleness or distress. Now other interests claimed attention. In Athens there were dramatic festivals to attend, plays to judge, and lawsuits, suspended with the spring, to be prosecuted again to the vast entertainment of the large and litigiously-minded Athenian juries. Material comforts were scarce in Greece almost to the point of nonexistence, for rich and poor alike. The ancient Greeks lived with the scantiest food and clothes, in the sorriest of dwellings, lacking both ventilation and sanitation, under conditions of the most severe privation and discomfort. Yet it was a poverty of external resources only, which courted no pity, for it felt the need of none. The zest of endeavor was maintained unimpaired through it all. It is not that the Greeks welcomed hardship. They counted that man disgraced who made no effort to avoid poverty, and they believed in the enjoyment of all that life could offer, including that which could be purchased by money. On the other hand, they had learned that things of the mind must not wait on material resources. Poverty and achievement walked hand in hand.

Greece was warmed by the hot breezes of Africa and the southern Mediterranean Sea, but she escaped the persistent and debilitating sirocco, which plagued Rome each autumn. From the north the cold winds of Thrace came down in the winter, and there are months of the year in northern Greece that are not appreciably warmer than the same season in southern New England. The result was an invigorating climate during part of the year at least, nor was there any prolonged period so unbearably hot as to stultify ambition or to drive a wedge between thought and action. For this reason the philosophy of Greece was always predicated on action, in contrast to the passive introspection of Persian or Indian thought. Their own climate appeared admirable to the Greeks, although, as a people, they largely lacked self-consciousness regarding their natural surroundings. It is, therefore, the more remarkable to find Herodotus praising the superior climate of Greece as compensation for the comparative poverty of the land in material resources.

It is perhaps worth noting that modern science, after elaborate research, has reached the conclusion that the vigor and vitality of human life are promoted by relatively low temperatures, and that the comfort of overheated homes and vehicles is more than likely to sap the strength of society. The Greek was the beneficiary of such wisdom, not because he reached it by science, but because he could not do otherwise.

Agricultural Products. Variations of altitude between mountain ranges and valleys modified the temperature and enabled the land of Greece to sustain a great variety of products for a country so small. Subtropical fruits, such as olives, could be grown in the valleys, and wheat and barley, native to the temperate zone, flourished on higher ground. Flax and wool provided the principal stuff of garments when the skins of hares or other animals were not used. Cotton, too, was known, but was largely imported from Egypt. Scientific agriculture was not found, although the Greeks knew something of the rotation of crops, and, from watching the signs of the heavens, they built up an empirical science of seasonal planting that, in turn, gave rise to calendars of lucky and unlucky days, such as that preserved in Hesiod's *Works and Days.*

Two products were of predominant importance to the country, the grape and the olive. Viticulture flourished practically everywhere, and the wine of Chios, Samos, and many another community has retained its fame from antiquity until the present. The Greeks treated their wine with resin, imparting to it a characteristic pine-tree taste and adding to the thirst-quenching properties of the drink. The olive, which also took kindly to the soil, was the staff of Greek life. Olives were processed to afford oil for the lamps, soap for the toilet, and a liniment for the use of athletes; a handful of olives and a piece of bread have always been an acceptable meal to a Greek workman. Olive oil was almost the only agricultural product of which Athens succeeded in manufacturing an exportable

[21]

surplus. The prevalence and importance of the product are attested by the symbolic olive twig that appears on the coins of Athens.

Of domestic animals, the goat was the most important, with the sheep perhaps second. Not only can these ruminants snatch a living from scanty vegetation, but they can live on the hillsides and range over steep paths of the mountains, whereas most pasturage areas of Greece were too precipitous to permit the browsing of so cumbersome a creature as a cow. Goats and sheep will flourish on a wide variety of vegetation, often poor and limited in quality, that would be quite inadequate for cows, though the latter were by no means unknown in Greece. Horses, too, demand space, and only in comparatively few places, notably the plains of Thessaly and Argos, were they successfully reared. The horses of ancient Greece were distinctly smaller than at present. This may be observed in the comparative sizes of horses and riders on the Ionic frieze of the Parthenon.

Imports. Athens was one of the few great importing states of antiquity, for she built up through her industry a population greater than could be sustained by the fertility of her own soil. Grain was brought to feed the population of the city from widely scattered places, from Sicily, the Euxine, southern Russia, and Thrace, with the result that in the fifth century Athens could boast of her self-sufficiency, the economic ideal of every Greek state, only with the mental reservation that such self-sufficiency could last just so long as her navy kept the Piræus open to the commerce of the world. When she lost her fleet, threatening starvation brought her empire to an end.

There are some few products ordinarily associated with Greece that were unknown in antiquity, such as currants, which take their name from Corinth, silk, tobacco, and opium. These belong to mediæval or modern economy.

The Utilization of Natural Resources. Whatever resources the land afforded were adapted by a quick combination of perception and initiative to the needs of man. The clay of

[22]

Greece was well suited to the manufacture of pottery, and there arose the art of vase painting, with its exquisite delicacy of design and beauty of ancient draughtsmanship. Certain mountains of Greece contained marble, and the Greeks used it to build their temples and carve their statues. Mount Pentelicus, which can be seen from Athens, provided a beautiful gleaming marble that was admirably adapted for construction; it is from this source, as we learn from building inscriptions, that the marble was secured for the Parthenon and the Stadium, as well as for other buildings of ancient Athens. The islands of Paros and Naxos likewise produced marbles of peculiar excellence; from Hymettus a stone of bluish tinge was secured.

The mineral deposits of Greece were slight. The rich gold work of the Mycenæan sites is a testimony to the extent of pre-Hellenic trade and not to native wealth, for Greece was dependent on extraneous sources for the precious metal. Silver was found in greater quantity, especially in the mines of Laurium at the tip of the Attic peninsula, and it provided the raw material out of which grew the great circulating medium of coinage.

Copper was more plentiful. From Homeric times and throughout the historical period, copper and bronze were freely used for armor as well as for implements of peace. Iron, too, was known, both on the Greek mainland and on some of the islands, and with the growth of civilization, the smelting and purification of metals opened new fields of power, especially in war.

There is an immediacy of life in Greece that is admirably illustrated by the full and understanding use of the available native resources of the land, whether base or precious, as vehicles for the expression of thought and purpose. Those same qualities of the people also made possible and desirable the very simple domestic economy that was universally observed, with the women carding and spinning the wool and weaving the clothing and bedding for the family.

Summary. The description of the physical geography of Greece has been limited largely to the land itself and to the islands and communities over which Greek culture spread. The Greek viewed geography in these terms, for neither the restless urge for travel nor an inclusive interest in other lands was characteristic of the Greek people. Distant seas suggested dangers more fearsome than the advantages that were likely to accrue from their penetration, and the narrow channels of the Hellespont, or the Bosporus, or the Straits of Gibraltar were noted more for the difficulties they presented to the navigator than as the gateways to new areas of adventure or commerce.

A similar attitude marked the view of every physical aspect of life entertained by a Greek. He accepted and utilized the gifts of nature, but he adapted himself to the requirements of soil and climate with a readiness that made unlikely any co-operative effort to better his lot by scientific inquiry. The life of the mind was his delight. Nature had provided the means of subsistence but never dulled the senses by lavish and unearned excess.

CHAPTER II

THE PEOPLE OF GREECE;
THEIR FESTIVALS

The Inhabitants of Greece. In the long history of human occupation in Greece and the Greek islands, a variety of peoples flourished from age to age. A Neolithic culture was superseded by the Bronze Age, and the Ægean peoples who built their distinctive civilization in the third and second millennia before Christ presently declined and were driven from their holdings or merged with invading tribes from the north. There was little uniformity in the resulting communities, but, according to their varying needs and temperaments, and always with a powerful instinct toward individualism, they launched themselves on the program of thought and work from which the Greek states of historical times were to emerge.

The Ethnic Groups. The separatism of the city-states has already been mentioned, and will recur constantly in the story of Greek civilization. In addition to the city-states, there were certain ethnic groups whose origins, though actually to be found in the waves of invasions from the north, extend back in their mythological ramifications to a Greek legend that parallels the Biblical story of the flood. Zeus, growing angered at the iniquity of mankind, resolved to destroy the human race with a deluge, and he might have succeeded had it not been for the continuing solicitude of Prometheus, who had already preserved men by stealing fire for them from Heaven and teaching them the handicrafts of communal society. When the

[25]

threat of flood was perceived by Prometheus, he warned his son Deucalion, who built a boat in which he and his wife, Pyrrha, rode out the deluge, until the craft came to ground on Mount Parnassus. They were then counseled by the Delphic oracle to throw "their mother's bones" over their shoulders. Recognizing the bones to be the stones of Earth, the universal mother, they acted accordingly, and from the stones thrown by Deucalion and Pyrrha, respectively, men and women sprang to life. The eldest son of Deucalion and Pyrrha was Hellen, who was to give his name to the Hellenes, the people of Greece. Hellen in turn had three sons, Dorus, Xuthus, and Æolus. Dorus became the progenitor of the Dorian Greeks and Æolus of the Æolian Greeks, while Xuthus, through his adopted son, Ion, became the founder of the Ionian Greeks.

The Ionians and the Dorians. Two of these groups in particular, the Dorian and the Ionian, assumed major importance in the history of the Greek people. The Dorians, to which ethnic group the Lacedæmonians, among others, belonged, were a dull and stolid people, who lived in rigid conformity to unchanging institutions, while the more volatile Ionian culture, to which the Athenians belonged, was conducive to greater genius and initiative. On the whole, these divisions made for further disunity, although each ethnic group did include, without any formal organization, a number of ancient cities, which acknowledged the sentimental ties of a common ancestry. Thus, on the basis of kinship, the cities of Ionia in Asia Minor, on revolting from the Persians in 499 B.C., asked for and received military assistance from Athens, as did Segesta in Sicily when she was attacked by the Dorian city of Syracuse in 415 B.C. Sparta, on the other hand, was a Dorian city, and to the same group belonged Corinth, Thebes, Megara, and various other states of the Peloponnese and the colonies. Although it was not unknown for cities within the same ethnic group to engage in war one against the other, group allegiance often afforded a basis for alliance or concerted action.

The Æolians. The Æolians, though they inhabited an area

larger than that occupied by both the Dorian and Ionian peoples, were confined largely to the central and western parts of Greece, where geographical and other hindrances retarded their cultural development, with the result that much less is heard of the Æolians in the tale of Greek achievement than of the other ethnic groups. In the progress of formal colonization the various ethnic groups expanded in approximately parallel lines across the Ægean Sea, so that the coast lands of Asia Minor were occupied by Æolians toward the north, Ionians to the center, and Dorians toward the south. The unpredictable vagaries of human volition, however, did more at all times to scatter than to concentrate ancient Greek communities and more to foment differences than to effect harmony in this internal cultural development.

Pride in a Common Ancestry. Nevertheless, though recognizing all the influences that made for individualism, it is with some justification that all the peoples of Greece and of the colonies are designated as Hellenes, for whatever the differences of clans, cities, and ethnic groups might be, they were all profoundly conscious of the common tie of kinship in their descent from the mythical hero, Hellen. Those nations beyond the confines of Hellas were "barbarians," whether Persians, Egyptians, or Thracians. In that distinction, which was maintained with a bland and complacent assurance of the sufficiency of Greece, "barbarian" meant little other than "foreign." Even in classical times a Greek did not feel the need of other cultures; he rarely troubled to learn another language, a prime requisite of a modern curriculum; and in time, "barbarian" came to signify to him an inferior civilization.

A Common Religion. In addition to the ties of mythical ancestry, the Greeks of historical times shared also a veneration of common gods and the right of appeal to the shrines and oracles of the land, and in these mutual interests are found some of the few elements of unity. Though various gods and goddesses were recognized as having a particular connection with certain cities, as Athena with Athens or Apollo with

[27]

Delphi, this association did not imply an exclusive right on the part of the citizens of such communities to the services and cult of their patron deities. In the *Iliad* even the Trojans are represented as praying to gods whom they shared with their Hellenic foemen. This identity of religious interest, and above all the acknowledgment of Zeus as the father of gods and men, was a constant reminder of a common heritage, which was never entirely forgotten. It resulted sometimes in the growth of religious federations or *amphictyonies,* from which, however, political expediency was not entirely absent. The Greek was always too much of an individualist, and too concrete in his thinking, to pray for abstract justice with dispassionate objectivity. He knew what he wanted from the gods no less than from his fellow men, and he was not hesitant in pressing his petitions.

Common Beliefs and Practices. In addition to similar religious practices and cults, there were certain universal qualities, which, when viewed in the light of contemporary life in other parts of the ancient Mediterranean world, seem to justify the Greek conviction of common ancestry. In spite of the superficial differences between a cultivated Athenian and a mountain shepherd of Acarnania or Epirus, each held in some measure to the Hellenic balance of physical and mental training, each revered the ancestral gods, and each rejected with repugnance the grosser concepts of religious rites that demanded human sacrifice, self-torture, or the mutilation of the body.

The Delphic Oracle. No factors, however, contributed more forcefully and directly to the unification of Greece than the oracular shrines, the sacred sites, and the great festivals, for to visit these was at once the duty and the delight of the Greeks, wherever they might live. No important enterprise, whether national or civic or personal, was undertaken without first consulting the priestess at Delphi, who, under the inspiration of Apollo, pronounced his riddling responses. The voice of the god is usually to be heard in the background of important

[28]

events of antiquity. Crœsus, the king of Lydia, undertook a disastrous military expedition against Cyrus, the Persian, because of a mistaken interpretation of the advice of Apollo, who had declared that by so doing he would destroy a mighty empire; the Athenians entrusted their fate to their ships, and fought the Battle of Salamis, because the god promised salvation in the wooden walls; and Socrates, though convinced of

Photograph by Alinari

FIGURE 3. SITE OF DELPHI. Note the theater, left, and the foundations of the Temple of Apollo, right foreground. The road winds around the base of the mountain.

his own ignorance, devoted his life to the search after wisdom, because the Delphic oracle had said that there was no man living wiser than Socrates.

The site of Delphi has been excavated, and much has been revealed that throws light on the practices of those who came to make offerings to the god or to seek counsel. The literary sources, however, are more enlightening than the somewhat puzzling archæological ruins for the reconstruction of the ritual that was followed in connection with the oracular responses. The priestess, who was called the Pythia, seems to have sat upon a tripod, from whence, under the hypnotic influence of fumes that issued from a crevice in the rock, she gave utterance to the wisdom of the god. Her confused words were, in turn, cast in verse form by a priest and passed on to the suppliant. A number of the verses have survived, and they are frequently susceptible of at least two meanings. If the inquirer came upon misfortune as a later consequence, his piety was usually strong enough to lead him to place the blame on his own faulty interpretation rather than on the perfidy of the god, although Crœsus sought and obtained permission from his conqueror to visit the shrine again for the express purpose of upbraiding Apollo. The god, however, was able to justify his answer. There were, moreover, occasions when the Delphic oracle could not be considered politically neutral.

In matters pertaining to foreign enterprises, and especially to projected colonization, the advice of the oracle was often sound and disinterested, for the confluence at Delphi of people from every part of the ancient world afforded an excellent opportunity for the pooling and weighing of knowledge. Ethically and religiously, too, the advice of the oracle was on the side of moderation and integrity, and its influence was normally for good. Nevertheless, it would be idle to deny that there was much that was ignorant and frivolous in the oracular responses. The essential thing about the Delphic oracle, as it pertains to the people of Greece, is their own trust in it, and their constant recourse to its facilities. If the inherent conservatism of religion delayed intellectual growth in the prophetic shrine itself, at least the exchange of ideas promoted expansion in virtually every other area of thought.

The oracular shrine of Apollo at Delphi attracted the Hellenes at all times of the year when travel from their several homes was feasible by land or water. The visits were motivated by the needs of the individual or the exigencies of domestic politics, rather than by the desire to take part in the specific functions occurring at Delphi itself. In this respect the attraction of the Delphic oracle differed from that of the regularly recurring athletic or religious festivals of the Greek cities, which attained to varying degrees of celebrity.

Courtesy of the Metropolitan Museum of Art

FIGURE 4. RECONSTRUCTION IN MINIATURE OF BUILDINGS WITHIN THE ALTIS AT OLYMPIA. The large Temple of Zeus appears in the center; the smaller Heræum to the upper left; the Treasuries of various Greek cities in a row at the upper center. The square buildings to the lower center and left belong to the Roman period.

The Athletic Festivals. There were many public festivals throughout the land, but four in particular gained national significance. These were the Olympian, Pythian, Nemean, and Isthmian games, and of these the Olympian festival quickly attained preeminence. Like so many of the sacred sites of Greece, Olympia was remote from frequently traveled paths. It lies in the northwest portion of the Peloponnese, and the attribution of the first games to be celebrated there to Pelops or Heracles is evidence of the antiquity of the site. The later, though still legendary, date of 776 B.C., when the first festival is said to have occurred, is associated with the revival of the games by the Spartan lawgiver, Lycurgus. In this year, according to tradition, the name of the winner in the foot race at Olympia was first inscribed, and there followed the celebration in four-year cycles of the Olympian festival, sacred to Zeus, the father of gods and men. From that time, too, began the practice of dating events of Greek history by reference to the first, second, third, or fourth year of a certain Olympiad, the name given to each four-year period between the observance of the games.

The Olympic Games. By the time of its comparative maturity, the Olympian festival had assumed enormous importance, for in these games was embodied the Greek ideal of physical and mental perfection. The needs of a society that depended on the physical prowess of its citizen soldiers for the maintenance of its tradition of city-state independence here found public expression. From childhood, training in athletic pursuits, such as running, jumping, or discus throwing, was recognized as an integral part of the development of the youth of the community. This type of physical training, which was carried out as a matter of pleasure and necessity everywhere in Greece, was quickly regularized in conformity with the Greek temperament. The important place of religion, the love of competition, and a natural interest in neighboring states, combined to foster the rise of a national festival, where contestants from many different communities might come together to match their strength and skill under the ever-present influence of the gods. The Olympian festival was devoted very largely to athletic contests, but opportunities were also afforded to those who would recite their compositions in prose, verse, or music; competitions were held for heralds and trumpeters; even the more frivolous competitions in drinking or beauty were not unknown. The athletic contests were carried out

[32]

under the most careful supervision. Victory in a race brought glory and preferment to the contestant and honor to his city; sculptors perpetuated the features of the runners in marble or bronze, and poets celebrated their fame. Thus the festival became a focus of art and letters, no less than of physical accomplishment.

The Olympian festival recurred often enough to induce men to begin their training for the forthcoming contest practically from the day on which the previous one had come to an end. Moreover, in order that men might gather from the farthest colonies of the Euxine, or from Magna Græcia, a sacred truce of three months was declared, and under this assurance of peace, a varied throng of contestants and spectators poured into the quiet valley and overflowed the sacred Altis of Olympia. There it may be supposed that not all remained quiet and reverent, for improvised quarters were set up, feasting and hilarity marked the reunion of friends, bargains were driven, poets recited their verses, and historians read their compositions to the always curious crowds, who were everywhere on hand to see and hear and learn something new.

Then, after five brief days of festival, men scattered on their homeward journeys, which might occupy as many weeks. The *ekecheiria,* or holy truce, would come to an end, and the forces of separatism would again be in the ascendant. Citizens of neighboring communities, who had met in friendly rivalry at Olympia, would resume their wars in Thessaly, or Sicily, or Colchis.

The Conduct of the Games. The Olympian festival embodied the practices of most of the other athletic assemblies of Greece, and at the same time enjoyed a prominence and respect that transcended them. Its history over twelve centuries reflects all the changes of Greek character from the noble and disinterested pursuit of athletic prowess as a service to the state, when the victor was content with a crown of olive leaves for his reward, to the days of more bitter and commercialized rivalry, when material gain was the stimulus to effort. The

[33]

finest days of the festival lie in the fifth century, when the Greek genius was at its height.

The festival had been established for a period of five days by the legendary founder, Heracles, and religious conservatism maintained the same span in classical times. Certain of these days, perhaps the first and the last, were given over to the sacrifices and ceremonial offerings, the most important among which was the hecatomb, or sacrifice of a hundred oxen,

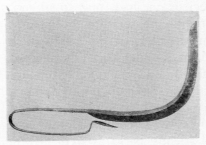

Courtesy of the Museum of Fine Arts, Boston

FIGURE 5. ATHLETE'S STRIGIL. These instruments, usually of bronze, were part of the athlete's equipment.

dedicated to Zeus by the people of Elis, in whose land Olympia lay. Feasting, too, had an undisputed part in any gathering of the early Greeks, and not least in those in which the gods were included. The healthy and hearty banquets of the Homeric heroes, in striking contrast to the meager fare of the later Greeks, afford some idea of the practice at the festivals.

The Events of the Games.

The games included a number of athletic contests open to men and boys. All arrangements in connection with the conduct of the festival were entrusted to the *Hellanodicæ,* a board of stewards, who were charged with responsibility for determining both the fitness and the integrity of the competitors, and for supervising their rigorous training according to the rules. Of the athletic contests, the stade race, which corresponds to the modern two-hundred-and-twenty-yard dash, was perhaps the most ancient and celebrated. Other foot races for men and boys, wrestling, boxing, and the sometimes brutal pancratium, in which wrestling and boxing were combined, with few restraining rules, were followed with keen interest. A race in armor seems to have been introduced late in the history of the festival. The pentathlon was, as the name indicates, a five-fold

[34]

contest in wrestling, jumping, running, discus throwing, and javelin throwing, and success in this exacting series of tests proclaimed the all-round athlete. Chariot racing and horse racing also had their place, but in a land ill adapted to horse breeding and among people of meager resources, the contenders were necessarily limited to the wealthy. The names of the tyrants of Sicily or the kings of Macedon are more frequently met with in this connection than are the names of the citizens of Athens or any other democratic community.

The long history of Greek athletics not only is preserved in the legends of the ancient founding of the Olympian festival, but also permeates the literature from the earliest times, having its fullest descriptive treatment in the Funeral Games of Patroclus in the *Iliad*. The Greek devotion to athletics is even more strikingly reflected in sculpture. In fact, the beautifully proportioned human forms that are the rule in all branches of art indicate the universality of athletic training.

The Pythian Games. Many other festivals of varying degrees of importance were held in different cities of Greece. Three of these, the Pythian, the Isthmian, and the Nemean, may be briefly described. It was nearly two centuries after the traditional date of the founding of the Olympian games that the old musical festival of Delphi was reorganized in the form of the Pythian games, which were held once in four years to celebrate the victory of Apollo over the Python, the great serpent that had been his predecessor in the oracular shrine. The Pythian games took place in the third year of each Olympiad. Although athletic contests were introduced on the model of those practiced at Olympia, they never attained so distinctive a place, for the early musical tradition of the Pythian festival continued to dominate the scene. The Pythian games, however, like the Olympian, drew to a sacred site dwellers from all the outposts of Hellenism. Pindar has left in his *Pythian Odes* a record of some of the achievements of the competing athletes.

The Isthmian Games. The two other Pan-Hellenic festivals, occurring at two-year intervals, served each in its way to continue the tradition of competition and to foster intercommunication. One of these was the Isthmian festival, held in honor of Poseidon at the Isthmus of Corinth in the second and fourth years of each Olympiad. The commercial importance of Corinth drew traders and travelers to the isthmus, and the ease of access from Athens, both by land and sea, made this festival one of special interest to the Athenians. Socrates tells on one occasion that apart from the duties of military service, the only time that he left Athens was to visit the Isthmian games. The presence of the philosopher at the festival is an indication of the universal appeal that such gatherings aroused.

The Nemean Games. The Nemean festival, conducted under the auspices of Argos, began, as did so many others, in a small and local way and only gradually assumed a Pan-Hellenic character, with the customary combination of athletic and musical contests. Heracles is credited with the dedication of the games to Nemean Zeus. Less is known about this festival than any of the others.

Other Festivals. To the national celebrations, others in the several states must be added, which varied in their grandeur from the great Panathenaic festival of Athens to the most modest ritual of the tiny demes, or political subdivisions of Attica. The festivals arose in every instance from deep-rooted religious or racial customs, and their scrupulous observance was dictated by conventional piety. The commingling of people at the festivals offers one of the few persisting counter-influences against the instinct toward local self-sufficiency that is so characteristic of the communities of Greece.

The Forms of Unity and Isolation. In summary, the similarities of religion, manners, and customs, and the absence of savagery in ritual differentiated the Greeks from the barbarians, so that, despite variations in dialect, government, and membership in ethnic groups, a certain Hellenic solidarity was evolved. Politically the theory of isolation remained unchanged. An Athenian found scope for his loyalty in the Acropolis, in the cult of local gods, in the Theater of Dionysus,

[36]

in the free assembly of citizens—in short, in all that went to constitute his city. Had a Greek wished to express in his language what is now meant by "a civilized people," he would probably have said "those who dwell in cities."

One cannot but deplore the excess to which the Greeks carried their exclusive devotion to a single city, for it obliterated a larger loyalty to Hellas that might have carried the genius of the race further into the future, but it must be recognized also that such speculation involves the inherent danger of comparing the known evils of historical fact with all the imagined benefits of an alternate course. As it was, when a Greek boy grew to manhood, there were no distant industrial cities and no national or federal enterprises to tempt him from his native community with the illusion of larger opportunity. His own hills and sea coast and countryside and the institutions of his own city were to offer the only outlet for his talents that he would ever know. As a consequence, the natives of a city-state developed an attitude of enthusiastic participation in the object of the moment. The individual citizen identified himself instinctively and completely with the fortunes of a state that was small enough to make possible his intimate understanding of it.

CHAPTER III

CRETE AND THE MINOAN CULTURE

The Pre-Hellenic Period

Both in the centuries that lay before the beginnings of recorded history and in those for which abundant documentation is available, it is possible in the study of Greek civilization to establish fairly definite periods. This orderly development is due to the fact that the Greeks were not building over older areas of cultural achievement, but rather were originating new forms in art, literature, and politics.

Two Cultures, Prehistoric and Classical. In Greece there were two different civilizations, widely separated in time and with distinctive cultures. The earlier, which may be called Ægean, rose, was subjected to varying fortunes, declined, and was followed by a period of several centuries during which cultural activity lay dormant, before a new and vigorous civilization developed. In the interval, successive waves of migration from the north had brought new peoples into the peninsula, who amalgamated with the previous inhabitants instead of displacing them. This infiltration gave a new vitality to the ancient genius and ultimately produced the flowering of the classical centuries in Greece. The Ægean civilization is pre-Hellenic in the sense that it preceded the age of the Hellenes; it is prehistoric in the sense that it is to be dated in the period for which no written records have been preserved. Fortunately, archæological excavations have uncovered abundant material

[38]

evidence from which the nature of life in those early centuries may be determined.

The Transition from the Neolithic Age. The earliest discoveries in Greece indicate the residence of man in the peninsula or on the islands during the Neolithic Age, which commenced several thousand years before the Ægean civilization arose. The culture was characteristically that of the New Stone Age: the implements and weapons were made of chipped stone, and the vessels were crude, hand-worked pottery. Concerning the Neolithic folk little more need be said. Lacking any stimulus to progress, they continued their existence millennium after millennium, without appreciable change, as the evidence of excavation demonstrates. About the year 3500 B.C., the spark destined to kindle another culture was struck by the discovery that a proper mixture of tin, brought probably by the Phœnicians in their trading vessels from the distant British Isles, with copper, native to Greece, would produce a remarkably malleable and useful alloy, bronze. With that discovery, the long dormant genius awoke; the Bronze Age commenced; and the resulting civilization, which flourished for more than two thousand years, is the Ægean culture.

At the turn from the nineteenth to the twentieth century, an English archæologist, Sir Arthur Evans, commenced excavations on the hill of Cnossus, which rises about four miles inland from the north central coast of the island of Crete. These were not the first excavations of prehistoric sites in Greece, as will shortly be made clear, but they were dramatic and significant in their impact on scholarship. In an amazingly short time, the excavators had brought to light the great Palace of Minos, heart and center of a civilization that had, some four thousand years ago, built up a naval power, extended its dominion over the islands of the Ægean Sea, and compelled Athens to pay yearly tribute.

The discoveries at Cnossus were followed by further excavations on the island of Crete, especially as Phæstos, Haghia Triada, Gournia, and Pachyammos. Similar excavations on

[39]

the Ægean islands, at Mycenæ and Tiryns in Greece, and at Troy in Asia Minor, to mention but a few of the sites, have resulted in a fresh conception of the early history of Europe. This pre-Hellenic society represents the earliest culture in Europe that rose above the level of the Neolithic people, for the Egyptian and Phœnician cultures belong to Africa and Asia.

Since decipherable documents are lacking, the history of the period must be reconstructed from archæological material. Fortunately, this type of evidence is rich and abundant, and from it a reasonable history of the daily life of the people, their games, amusements, art, religion, their physical type and stature, dress, industry, methods of warfare, political organization, and homes may be reconstructed.

The Legends. It must not be thought, however, that all indication of the existence of a pre-Greek culture waited on the excavations. The legends of the Greeks themselves, which are to be found in the Homeric poems and in later literature, embraced the stories of Helen, the fairest of Greek women, of Odysseus, the man of unfailing devices, of Theseus, who slew the Minotaur, of Dædalus and Icarus, who devised the first means of human flight, and a host of others. Legends are rarely constructed without some basis of fact, and, though scholarship was slow to seize the connection, the evidence nevertheless remained. Furthermore, not all the monuments of the Ægean age had been so completely covered over as had the Palace of Minos. At Mycenæ and Tiryns the great *beehive* tombs, the city walls, and the corbel arches, built with converging stones but without keystones, had been known and used by the peasants through the Middle Ages and into modern times.

Schliemann's Researches. Moreover, the earliest organized investigations of prehistoric remains in Greece had occurred a generation before the excavations of Sir Arthur Evans in Crete, for to Heinrich Schliemann, a German boy without formal education, belongs the credit for first insisting on the germs of truth in the Homeric tales, and for vindicating his conviction. His own romantic story, in which truth and fiction have been freely mingled, tells how, as a boy, he listened with delight as his father told him the Greek fables, from which he learned how Paris had come to Menelaus at Sparta, and had taken the fair Helen back to Troy, and how Agamemnon, lord of Mycenæ, had marshaled the Greek chieftains for the ten-year struggle that was to lay waste Troy and recover Helen. All this Schliemann accepted with implicit faith. The story goes that a drunken miller came one day to the shop where the young Schliemann was working, and recited verses from Homer. The enchanted boy spent his money freely on *Schnapps* to keep the stranger pleasantly intoxicated, so that he might continue his recital. Schliemann in the end learned Greek, entered business, assembled a fortune, partly in America, and in his maturity went to Greece, married a Greek girl who could recite Homer from memory, and set out to prove the conviction of his childhood. From 1868 until his death in 1890, he was engaged in his excavations and publications on the prehistoric sites of Greece. He went first to Hissarlik, the modern site of Troy, in Asia Minor, and there commenced his work. He found the walls of ancient peoples but not the city of the *Iliad,* as he supposed.

The Interpretation of Levels. In Schliemann's excavations at Troy, as in those of practically all prehistoric sites that have been inhabited either continuously or intermittently over many centuries, the different levels of habitation were clearly to be traced. It is difficult for the inexperienced student to understand how an ancient city could be completely covered over, but the process of burying usually came about in one of two ways. If the city had been destroyed, by either fire or pillage, the inhabitants, before rebuilding, might deliberately level off and cover up the site in order to start anew, and if the city were abandoned for a time, the stones, tiles, and the crumbling mud-brick walls of houses would very quickly be cast down by the action of the weather. Consequently, when a trench is cut through an ancient site, it is comparatively easy to interpret a stratum of charred embers or a leveled stratum of building material as evidence of the end of one period of habitation and the beginning of another.

Evidence from Potsherds. Pottery is also an important source of information about an ancient people. Vases are known from the beginning to the end of civilization in Greece, and, though they may be shattered, the broken sherds are practically indestructible by fire or the elements, and almost as valuable as the perfect pots in determining the type of manufacture and art. Furthermore, they do not tempt pillagers to carry them away as do objects of metal, and the evidence remains. Complete specimens of vases are found as a rule only in unopened tombs, but when an excavation is made on a prehistoric site, broken potsherds are found in the lowest level in which there are signs of human habitation.

When a pit is dug on a prehistoric site, it is necessary to study the objects found at the lowest level first, in order to preserve a proper chronology. In other words, we must work backward, as though we were digging from the bottom of the pit to the surface, and thus a well-conducted excavation demands an intricate system of filing and classification. In the very lowest stratum just above virgin soil lie rude, undecorated fragments of pots of the Neolithic Age, which were handmade and hardened in an open fire or cured in a crude potter's kiln. A few meters nearer the surface, above an accumulation of debris that may represent several thousand years in the Neolithic Age, sherds bearing evidences of decoration begin to appear. On these pots geometric lines were incised while the clay was still soft, and then filled with a chalky substance. There are, also, pots that have been polished to a shiny surface by rubbing with a bone. Very rapidly now, that is, rapidly in terms of meters as one ascends, though hundreds of years may mark the progress of evolution, new ideas in decoration come to light. The polish on the potsherds is heightened and thrown into relief by an undulating surface made with a blunt instrument while the clay is still soft. The uneven surface is intended perhaps to represent the gentle ripples of the sea. The

[42]

incised geometric lines are sometimes shaped into the semblance of a leaf or a twig.

At the time of Schliemann's excavations there was little comparative evidence by which to date the successive levels, and it is small wonder that he sometimes erred both in dating and in interpretation. From Troy, Schliemann went to Mycenæ and Tiryns, and there discovered visible evidence of the Homeric stories whose scenes lie on the Greek mainland. The excavations established the historical existence of the Mycenæan civilization, which is now known to have flourished from about 1400 B.C. to 1100 B.C. To Schliemann, in spite of his lack of scientific methods of excavation, belongs the credit for having laid the foundation of modern prehistoric research in the Mediterranean area. On all the sites that he originally examined, careful and more scientific archæological work has subsequently been done to the great enrichment of scholarship.

Pre-Hellenic Chronology. The varying dates and the different places at which excavations have been carried on in modern times should, however, not be allowed to confuse the proper sequence of ancient chronology. Crete is the location of the pre-Hellenic civilization in its oldest form. It was a natural center toward which travel from the mainlands of Greece, Asia Minor, and Egypt converged. Its coastline was rocky and indented, offering safe harbors for timid mariners, and the land itself was rich and fair. It is not unnatural that a great culture should early have arisen there. When excavations were first conducted at Cnossus, there were no records by which absolute dates could be determined. This difficulty was quickly rectified when it became evident that the ancient Cretans and Egyptians had been in fairly close commercial contact. The history of Egypt was familiar, and, when some object of Egyptian manufacture of a known and dated dynasty was found with Cretan works of art or in a Cretan tomb, a fixed date was established. So, too, Cretan articles found in Egypt added their weight of evidence (Figure 6), until by the assembling of all contributory facts, by an appraisal of artistic development in Crete, and by the exercise of enormous scholarly patience, a consistent and convincing story of pre-Hellenic chronology has been built up.

The pre-Hellenic culture of Crete lasted from the beginning of the Bronze Age in 3500 B.C. until its decline and final destruction about 1100 B.C. Some convenient method of designating the historical vicissitudes of those twenty-four hundred

Courtesy of the Metropolitan Museum of Art

FIGURE 6. LATE MINOAN I VASE. Reproduction. Original in Marseilles. This vase was found in Egypt, indicating ancient commerce between that country and Crete.

years had to be found, and the archæologists turned to the verses of Homer, in which he says: "In Crete is Cnossus, a goodly city, and in it King Minos, the bosom friend of mighty Zeus, reigned for nine seasons." The nine seasons of epic fancy have been translated into the nine divisions of Cretan prehistory, or, as it will be called hereafter, Minoan civilization, for the name has been adopted from King Minos himself. About the year 1400 B.C., the Minoan culture began to decline, but on the Greek mainland a pre-Hellenic civilization was rising to take its place. Its center was the city of Mycenæ, where for another three hundred years a rich pre-Hellenic culture flourished. The civilization that centered in and about Mycenæ is known as Mycenæan, and the period as the Mycenæan Age.

No subject has been the cause of more animated disagreement than the dates of the pre-Hellenic periods, and each new discovery adds to, or subtracts from, or otherwise modifies the sum of evidence on which the chronological story has been

[44]

built. A table is offered, without dogmatism, as one that will give the student an approximate idea of what is meant when reference is made in works on pre-Hellenic culture to a discovery belonging in Middle Minoan II, or Late Minoan I, or some other period. It will be observed that Late Minoan III and the Mycenæan Age are contemporaneous. Other terms, too, will be found in reading, such as Helladic and Cycladic. The intricacies of dating in these periods need not be elaborated, but the following definitions may prove useful. *Minoan* refers to the pre-Hellenic culture as it is found on the island of Crete, *Mycenæan,* in general, as it is found between fixed dates in and about Mycenæ, *Helladic,* in general, as it is found elsewhere on the Greek mainland, especially in the less developed regions, and *Cycladic* as it is found on the islands of the Cyclades.

The table follows:

Early Minoan I
Early Minoan II   } . . . . .3500—2300 B.C.
Early Minoan III

Middle Minoan I   . . . . .2300—1900 B.C.
Middle Minoan II   . . . . .1900—1700 B.C.
Middle Minoan III   . . . . .1700—1600 B.C.

Late Minoan I   . . . . .1600—1500 B.C.
Late Minoan II   . . . . .1500—1400 B.C.
Late Minoan III   . . . . .1400—1100 B.C.

Mycenæan Age   . . . . .1400—1100 B.C.

MINOAN CIVILIZATION

The foregoing brief statement of fact and chronology is almost entirely derived from archæological discoveries, which may best be discussed under separate categories, such as architecture, fresco painting, vases, sculpture, and private life. Though Cnossus in Crete and Mycenæ in Greece are the two cities from which evidence has principally been drawn, it

[45]

should be borne in mind that other centers of Minoan and Mycenæan civilization are also of very great importance. Nor is the story yet completed, for the resumption of archæological work in Greece since the close of World War II is constantly revealing new evidence of the extent and importance of the preclassical civilization.

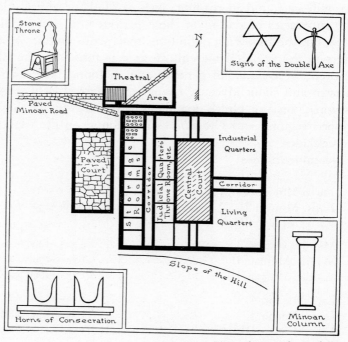

Drawn by Dorothy I. Chubb

FIGURE 7. SIMPLIFIED SCHEMATIC PLAN OF THE PALACE OF MINOS AT CNOSSUS. Note the fourfold division of the main palace building about the central court; also, the theatral area and the outer paved court. The inserts at the corners illustrate typical features of Minoan art.

Architecture. The most conspicuous remains of pre-Hellenic life are architectural. The enormous walls and the huge beehive tombs of the Mycenæan sites and the spreading labyrinthine palaces of Crete were seemingly the product of an

[46]

abundance of cheap labor, an impulse toward grandeur, and a very practical concern for protection. In Cnossus, located strategically some four miles from the Cretan coast to prevent sudden piratical raids, there was built the Palace of Minos, the greatest of all the Minoan palaces, embracing within itself divisions of government, justice, industry, and entertainment, as well as the living quarters of the ruling dynasty. It was planned with amazingly detailed attention to light, sanitation, water supply, and drainage. The careful interpretation of the evidence, as revealed in the exhaustive reports of the original excavators and in subsequent studies, indicates the ultimate growth of a civilization in which utility had made room for comfort, and the useful had welcomed the beautiful.

The Palace of Minos. The palace was not the product of an architect's plan or the creation of a single monarch. The foundation seems to have been laid in the early part of the Middle Minoan I Period, but any study of the palace becomes a study of the modification, enlargement, and rebuilding that went on through the whole life of the structure, until the decline of the civilization itself. Many changes in the plan of the palace have been assigned to the latter half of the period to which its original building belongs. Earthquakes occurred with considerable frequency, and each shock brought reconstruction and change in its wake.

The palace in its early form probably resembled a number of more or less separate buildings. In the Middle Minoan II Period, these were united, further necessary construction was undertaken, and for the first time the confused labyrinth that resulted became in some sense a single unit. It was at this period that the domestic quarter to the east of the central court was built.

At the end of the Middle Minoan II Period, a major earthquake destroyed many sites in ancient Crete, and the rebuilding of the palace in the Middle Minoan III Period resulted in substantially the structure that has been excavated in modern times, although repairs and changes never ceased to be made.

[47]

In the Late Minoan I Period, extensive plastering of the walls was undertaken, and to the Late Minoan II Period belongs the exceedingly interesting Throne Room. The close of this period is marked by the virtual demolition of the palace, although the site continued to be inhabited and the Hall of the Double Axes, an area dedicated to religious rites, belongs to the Late Minoan III Period.

It is not surprising, therefore, that the palace became a sym-

Photograph by M. Alison Frantz

FIGURE 8. THE HALL OF THE DOUBLE AXES AT CNOSSUS. The restoration affords an interesting illustration of a detail of the Palace of Minos in relation to the Cretan landscape.

bol for confusion in antiquity. The detailed plans of the palace and the discussion of the variations in form that it underwent from one period to another must be studied in the works devoted to Minoan archæology. The basic division of the palace, however, is comparatively easy to understand, as may be seen from the simplified sketch (Figure 7).

The Plan of the Palace: the Western Half. The palace, as it has now been uncovered, measures about four hundred feet square, and covers an acreage larger than that occupied by the Library of Congress in Washington. It was built on a hillside that slopes to the east, and there appear to have been more floors on the eastern side than on the west. In the center was a great court, about one hundred and ninety feet long from north to south and about ninety feet in width, with a passage-way across the northern and southern ends. The western half of the palace was divided by a corridor running from north to south, and still to the west of this corridor lay a succession of passages, or magazines. Along the walls of the magazines stood huge jars, or *pithoi,* as tall as a man, and, in the floor, pits, called *kaselles,* were dug. These receptacles were filled with oil or grain, carefully sealed to prevent theft or mould, and maintained against a day of necessity. The *kaselles* were lined with lead, and traces of valuable objects, notably gold leaf, have been found within them, lending credence to the suggestion that they may have served as repositories for the protection of the most valued possessions of the rulers of the palace. To the right of the long dividing corridor was an area for the adjudication of legal cases, as well as for local government, and included in it was the room for the meeting of the king with his councillors. The stone throne itself, the most ancient royal throne of Europe, is still in place, and about the walls of the room ran the stone benches for the councillors to sit upon. The royal council chamber is the more impressive since it is an actual example of such a room as that to which an Homeric king may be thought to have repaired with his court to deliberate on the affairs of his kingdom. In this section, too, shrines and ritual objects were found.

The Theatral Area. To the northwest of the palace and beyond its walls was a paved theatral area with low rising steps of stone, and immediately to the west of the palace lay a paved court for the gathering of the people. The theatral area inevitably suggests the dancing place that Dædalus, the skilled artisan, is said by Homer to have constructed for Ariadne, the fair but faithless daughter of King Minos, who was to betray

[49]

the secret of the labyrinth to Theseus. From the theatral area there ran off an ancient forked road (Figure 9), the pavement of which is still intact after four thousand years.

Living Quarters: the Eastern Half. The portion of the palace to the east of the central court was divided by a corridor running from east to west, and the lower or southeastern section was devoted to the living quarters of the men and the women. These are sometimes referred to as the Men's Mega-

Photograph by Eunice Burr Couch

FIGURE 9. ANCIENT CRETAN PAVED ROAD. Note the precision with which the blocks are laid as the two forks join.

ron and the Queen's Megaron. To the living quarters one descended over a great processional staircase, which is still in an admirable state of preservation. Five flights of stairs have been preserved, with broad low treads, over which processions or pageants could pass in dignified review. The northeastern quarter of the palace was given over to the wine and olive presses, the rooms of the potters, the studios of artists and gemcutters, the kitchens, and the schoolroom. In fact, the palace, like a mediæval castle, embraced a largely self-sustained life within its spreading area.

The Exterior of the Palace. The walls of the palace, as well as the door jambs and parts of the floors, were made of gypsum, a stone that disintegrates quickly when exposed to the elements, and for that reason they were covered with plaster. Paint was used over this to some extent for decoration, but, aside from the occasional relief of color, the building must have presented a dazzling expanse of white. The focus of life in the palace was on the central court. Such windows as were let into the outer walls of either palaces or private homes were small and high above the ground (Figure 10). Light wells descended like empty elevator shafts to illuminate the lower floors, and toward the eastern side, where the hill dropped away, the roof may have been stepped to facilitate lighting. A further ingenious engineering feat was the piping of water from the hills through the palace, with the provision of drains to carry the waste from the

Courtesy of the Metropolitan Museum of Art

FIGURE 10. MINIATURE FAÏENCE MODELS OF CRETAN HOUSE FAÇADES. Reproductions. Originals in Candia. The high windows are characteristic of houses which looked to interior courts.

lowest area in the southeastern corner. The rate of flow of the water was controlled by a very cleverly devised system of parabolic curves in the aqueduct. The pipes were made in sections, constructed with collars at one end for ready fitting and thus permitting easy adaptation to the physical setting much as drains are laid in modern times.

Vases. In the excavations at Cnossus the Neolithic pottery indicates that the area of settlement of the city had reached

[51]

very considerable proportions toward the end of the Stone Age, and the gradual raising of the level of the hill through the accumulated debris of many generations proves that the site was continuously occupied over a period of thousands of years.

These earliest strata are succeeded by a very significant level. It is that at which bronze was first introduced and which is now known to belong about 3500 B.C. Here the Neolithic Age is left behind and the Minoan civilization begins. A curious thing is noticed in the potsherds, for the promise of artistic development shown in the last designs of the Neolithic pottery is arrested and even declines. The explanation is that the more

Courtesy of the Metropolitan Museum of Art

FIGURE 11. TYPICAL MIDDLE MINOAN POTTERY. The designs are adapted to the shapes of the vases.

skilled workers turned with enthusiasm to bronze, the new medium of manufacture, and clay was left to the less experienced craftsmen. In similar manner a new invention in present-day society, such as the radio, may cause a temporary decline in phonographic recordings, only to be followed by greater technical and artistic excellence in the former field when the public reasserts its right to a choice of entertainment. Thus the setback in ceramic art was only temporary, for improved techniques of firing presently produced more satisfactory results in hardening the clay. Paint also was discovered, and it was baked on the pots. The results were not at first very striking, for they produced only a lusterless black background on which the Neolithic incised chalk lines were

[52]

imitated in white paint. But with time the skill of the workers developed and the new technique proved its worth.

As the work of excavation continues upward through the strata at Cnossus, another remarkable change is observed in the pottery belonging to the Middle Minoan I Period. Vases are now made of the most deli-cate texture, thin as eggshell, and one realizes that the potter's wheel, introduced from Egypt, has given the artists a new mastery over their material. They imitate the fineness of metal. This technique persisted, and the best eggshell ware is found in the Middle Minoan II Period.

Presently, too, the angular geometric lines give place to graceful curves and spirals as the brush is developed and replaces the fine incising tool. New color pigments are found, and in place of the lusterless black the artists exploit their wares in a garish polychrome, with orange,

Courtesy of the Metropolitan Museum of Art

FIGURE 12. PITHOS OF THE MIDDLE MINOAN PERIOD. The rope pattern is typical of these large storage vases.

white, red, and crimson splashed on a black background. There are a number of types of pottery, which are characteristic of certain pre-Hellenic divisions of time. Kamares ware, of egg-shell type, so named because of its discovery in the Kamares cave, is a delicately fashioned pottery of the Middle Minoan Periods. It is sometimes made in the shape of modern teacups, though much of it is also in the form of low bowls with spouts. The great storage pithoi of this period are decorated with two characteristic designs, one representing circling ropes, and the

[53]

other, known as the "trickle pattern," tracing about the mouth flowing lines of paint to represent an accidental overflow of oil. Barbotine ware, characterized by raised or applied globules

Courtesy of the Metropolitan Museum of Art

FIGURE 13. VASE OF THE LATE MINOAN II PERIOD. Reproduction. Original in Candia. The decoration of this vase illustrates the skilful adaptation of plant designs and spirals to the curving surface of the vase.

arranged in a decorative motif on the vase, begins in the Middle Minoan I Period and runs a comparatively brief course, for it was crowded out in the Middle Minoan II Period by the more facile work that was made possible through the potter's

[54]

wheel. In the Middle Minoan III Period, however, this persistent, though not particularly artistic, technique was revived, and artists decorated their vases by applying in the barbotine manner moulded pellets in the form of shells, fish, or plants. Technical skill began to show a tendency to outrun good taste.

Meanwhile ornamentation had been going through a normal and rapid evolution. The ripple and twig patterns of geometric inspiration in the Neolithic Age were supplanted by designs derived from spirals, leaves, foliage, fish, shells, weeds, water lilies, rocks, and, perhaps most successfully of all, from the octopus, whose circling tentacles were admirably adapted to either a schematic or a naturalistic treatment on the curved surface of a vase. Human figures and also animals were represented on the later pottery. It is in this period that many incidental evidences of the course of life in a pre-Hellenic society are revealed in dress, ornaments, attributes, and activities that appear in connection with the human figures. There is little reason to believe that the artist is drawing on his imagination; he is clearly portraying something that he has seen and understood.

Evidence of Decline. At some of the levels it is possible to observe signs of abrupt changes in the centuries of civilization, such as a great fire, a time of pillage, or a devastating earthquake like that which must have shaken the ancient Ægean world after the volcanic eruption that tore the island of Thera apart. These catastrophes have been made the basis for divisions of pre-Hellenic archæology, since after each, to some extent the nature of art and life changed. During the Late Minoan II Period, there is evidence that the city of Cnossus came to a sudden and violent end. The disaster is reflected in the vase designs, which after that time became stiff, spiritless, and conventional. No longer did the artist look with enthusiasm to nature itself for plant and animal designs. Degeneration continued, and during the Late Minoan III Period, the vase painter was content merely to avail himself of the implements that once stimulated his art—the wheel and the brush—and to sit holding the latter against a revolving pot, while a mechanical line was traced. The spirit of art had gone from Crete.

FIGURE 14. BOXER VASE. Late Minoan I Period. Reproduction. Original in Candia. The vase is made of steatite, a black substance of soapy texture.

Other Uses of Clay. In addition to vases, other objects were made from clay. The water pipes were so constructed; sarcophagi were made and decorated in much the same style as vases; lamps, tables, hardware, and building material were also, among a great variety of other utilitarian articles, manufactured from clay.

Steatite Vases. A number of vases cut in soft stone, or steatite, and dating in the Late Minoan I and Late Minoan II Periods are decorated with lively and forceful figures cut in relief on the black surface. The steatite vases are frequently, though not invariably, cut in the shape of a conical rhyton, or vase with an opening at the bottom. One such stone vase from Haghia Triada in Crete is divided into four panels (Figure 14), on three of which scenes from boxing are shown, while on the remaining panel, the second from the top, the subject is bull baiting, which recalls in its motif a fresco from Cnossus and in its execution the *repoussé,* or hammered-out, work on the gold cups from Vaphio (Figure 30). The scenes on various steatite vases afford significant evidence for the customs and the dress of the Minoan people. Military and ceremonial processions may be seen, while, for an understanding portrayal in animal sculpture, there are few pieces better

[56]

than the carving in the shape of a bull's head (Figure 15), or the lid of a vase on which a dog is stretched at ease (Figure 16). The delineation of scenes on the steatite vases reaches its peak, however, in the fragment known as the Harvester Vase (Figure 17), in which peas-ants are shown singing lustily as they return from the fields with their forks carried over their shoulders, while one man shakes an Egyptian musical rattle called a *sistrum*.

Frescoes. Objects of every nature and from all sources, both within and beyond the borders of Crete, have con-tributed to the interpreta-tion of pottery from the successive levels, just as pot-tery in turn has helped to explain further archæolog-ical discoveries. Frescoes have been found in con-siderable abundance. Bril-liant colors were used—red ochre, yellow, black, and blue—to adorn the outer walls of the Palace of Minos and the inner corridor walls, as well as the *megara,* or great halls, with large,

Courtesy of the Metropolitan Museum of Art

FIGURE 15. STEATITE BULL'S HEAD FROM CNOSSUS. Late Minoan I Period. Reproduction. Original in Candia. The adornment of horns, eyes, and muzzle indicate an advanced stage of craftsmanship.

rapidly executed designs made while the plaster was still wet. The procession of cup bearers affords an idea of the physique and the dress of the Minoans, while the cat stalking the pheasant and the scenes along the Nile River not only illustrate the excellence of the art, but suggest the intimacy of cultural

[57]

contact between Egypt and Crete. One well-known and striking fresco, which has been ingeniously restored from its fragmentary condition, reveals the technique followed by the Cretans in their favorite sport of bull baiting.

Writing. There is evidence of a knowledge of writing, or printing, in Minoan times. The most significant single object of this nature is the Phæstos Disk (Figure 18), a plaque of clay about six inches in diameter, found at the city of Phæstos

Courtesy of the Metropolitan Museum of Art

FIGURE 16. LID OF A VASE FROM MOCHLOS. Reproduction. Original in Candia. Note the geometric incised pattern and also the naturalistic pose of the dog that forms the handle of the lid.

in Crete, and covered on either side with diminishing circles that were impressed, before the hardening of the clay, with small pictures, including a bird, a rosette, a fork, a fish, a serpent, and so forth. A close study of the disk or of a facsimile will make it clear that the figures when repeated are precisely the same, and hence it is with some justice that the disk is regarded as the earliest known example of printing, though symbols rather than letters have been used for type. The fact that printing did not come into general use until the fifteenth

[58]

century of our own era was due more to the technical difficulty of developing an almost perfectly level matrix for the setting of type than to the failure of earlier peoples to stumble on the idea. No satisfactory interpretation of the inscription on the Phæstos disk has yet been made.

Small, oblong clay tablets have been found, with a series of conventional lines or other geometric marks on them that may represent business transactions or accounts. Some of the pots, too, have been inscribed with letters in ink. That the knowledge of writing was fairly widespread was proved by the discovery of a tantalizingly large number of inscribed, but indecipherable, tablets at Pylos in western Greece shortly before the outbreak of World War II. There is, however, no bilingual key and no document sufficiently long to afford any immediate prospect of deciphering the language, although the resumption of excavations holds out the hope that means of interpretation may some day come

Courtesy of the Metropolitan Museum of Art

FIGURE 17. STEATITE HARVESTER VASE FROM HAGHIA TRIADA. Late Minoan I Period. Reproduction. Original in Candia. The design shows singing harvesters, with long forks over their shoulders, moving in procession.

to light. In the Homeric poems, which deal with the Mycenæan civilization, though they were composed after that period, there is a single reference to writing. It occurs in the passage in which Proteus gives Bellerophon, as he sets out to visit the king of Lycia, a tablet on which are inscribed "baleful signs," to the effect that he is to be put to death. The reference is sufficient to prove a knowledge of writing in Homer's time, but the dating of Homer is, unfortunately, a matter on which there is little agreement. The most recent research has tended to bring his date forward.

Religion. Many religious objects and emblems have been discovered in Crete, of which the most important, or at least the most beautiful, are the little snake goddesses (Figure 19), usually made of ivory and gold. The goddesses are all grace and delicacy in execution, standing little more than twelve inches in height. Attributes of the goddesses, such as the sacred knot, sacred garments, goats, and kids, have also come to light in considerable numbers. Other symbols of religious significance, especially the sign of the double axe and the conventionalized horns of consecration, appear frequently in and about the Palace of Minos. No temples were set apart specifically for the worship of a god, unless the Palace itself be so regarded. For that view there is some justification, since King Minos, according to legend, was of divine origin, and once in nine years went to the Dictæan Cave to receive the laws from Zeus.

Courtesy of the Metropolitan Museum of Art

FIGURE 18. PHAESTOS DISK. Reproduction. Original in Candia. The identity of certain of the repeated incised symbols may be observed on close examination.

The stylized pairs of horns, symbolic features of Minoan architecture, sometimes called the horns of consecration, call to mind the predominant place of the bull in Cretan worship. In fact, there is probably truth in the legend of Theseus, the

[60]

Athenian prince who substituted himself for one of the seven youths who, with seven maidens, were offered each year to the Minotaur, or Bull of Minos, living in the labyrinth in Crete. The labyrinth would be the mazelike Palace of Minos itself, the Minotaur would be a fancied personification of the worship of the bull, if not of the amusement of bull leaping, while the enforced tribute of youths and maidens would represent the subjugation of Athens by Crete, and the exaction of tribute. The slaying of the Minotaur by Theseus tells in allegorical style of the freeing of Athens from bondage to Crete.

There is evidence of a matriarchal religion in Crete, in which the goddess takes precedence over the god. This is indicated both in the important place of the snake goddesses, and in the fact that in gem-engravings and other pictorial scenes in which both god and goddess appear, the latter is given the larger, higher, and more significant position. There are,

Courtesy of the Museum of Fine Arts, Boston

FIGURE 19. CRETAN SNAKE GODDESS. Late Minoan I Period. This delicate ivory statuette with gold adornments is one of a very small number of similar statuettes that have been discovered. Other examples may be found in the Royal Ontario Museum in Toronto and the Fitzwilliam Museum in Cambridge, England.

[61]

in the Cretan religion, similarities with later Greek religion, but there is one striking difference, which implies another racial origin: the gods of Olympus are immortal, but legend tells of the death of the Cretan Zeus and of his burial on Mount Iouktas, where he lies in state, as one can still see, with the aid of a little imagination, from a ship approaching the land.

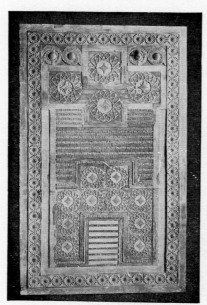

Courtesy of the Metropolitan Museum of Art

FIGURE 20. GAMING BOARD. Late Minoan II Period. Reproduction. Original in Candia. This board is elaborately constructed of ivory, with many inlaid pieces of gold. The color, originally varied and brilliant, has faded with time.

Social Customs. From frescoes, vase paintings, and works in ivory and gold, the story of Minoan society may be reconstructed at length. In dress the men followed the custom of southern countries and wore simply a loin cloth, leaving the upper part of the body uncovered, except in the case of elders and officials, who donned a cloak for the sake of dignity. The snake goddesses are dressed in flounced garments, open at the neck, with high collars at the back and richly embroidered skirts. Both men and women wore their hair long, and hats were not ordinarily used. By a Minoan convention of art, women were represented with white skins, men with red. Men and women alike were narrow-waisted.

The people appear to have enjoyed various forms of enterment. Both men and women are pictured taking part in acrobatic performances over the backs of bulls, while the theatral orea of the palaces, like that built by Dædalus as a dancing-place for the fair-haired Ariadne, was doubtless the scene of dancing, wrestling, boxing, and other sports demanding a limited space. Fortunately, the archæological evidence on such games can be correlated with the descriptions occurring at various places in the Homeric poems; thus, an increasingly clear picture of this phase of Minoan life can be formed. A richly colored gaming board (Figure 20) tells of quiet amusements within the palace.

Offensive armor was comparatively limited, consisting of a long sword and a dagger, the latter carried inside the belt and at the front. A shield of leather and a leather helmet served for protection. Horses were used to draw the chariots, but seemingly they were too small to be ridden.

The place of women in Minoan civilization was from all evidence one of dignity. They are represented in art without veils and in company with men in public. They took part in the exercises and amusements, and the Queen's Megaron in the Palace of Minos is marked by exceptional luxury. Their position was much higher than that enjoyed by the women of Athens a thousand years and more later.

CHAPTER IV

THE MYCENÆAN CULTURE

The Mycenæan Age dates from approximately 1400 B.C. to 1100 B.C. and is thus contemporaneous with the Late Minoan III Period in Crete. The island of Crete continued to be inhabited during this period by the descendants of the same people who had built up the brilliant civilization of the earlier centuries, but they had now fallen into comparative decadence. In contrast, the people of Mycenæ and the neighboring cities of the plain were making great strides forward in the development of a culture that extended its influence into the central and northern parts of Greece, as may be deduced from the characteristic Mycenæan pottery found in those regions.

The remarkable discoveries at Mycenæ and Tiryns resulted at the time in the adoption of terms and the acceptance of divisions of prehistory that subsequent investigations have modified. It is a happy augury for the vitality of the study that the excavations of the Agora, or Market-Place, in Athens, renewed since the close of World War II, have disclosed a splendid Mycenæan, or Helladic tomb, below the classical level of habitation. Thus it becomes clear that a pre-Hellenic culture flourished in Athens also.

The Relation of Mycenæan to Minoan Culture. The relation of Mycenæan society on the Greek mainland to the older Minoan civilization of Crete is a vexed question. The lines of travel across the narrow seas from Crete and up the long bays of southern Greece are so obvious to a sea-faring people and

[64]

the evidence of Minoan influence, especially on the southern communities of the mainland, is so abundant that some scholars have contended that the establishment of Mycenæan culture followed on a Minoan conquest. Others maintain that Minoan elements, though present, are not significant, and that the people of the mainland, who belonged to a different racial group, came originally from the north, bringing with them the

distinctive gray pottery with its soapy feeling, known as Minyan ware, which is not found in Crete. It is by the careful evaluation of a multitude of such minute pieces of evidence that the true story of prehistoric Greece is gradually taking shape.

The Location of Mycenæ. Thus it is clear that a group of powerful cities was established in the Argolid, and there a brilliant civilization flourished for some three cen-

Courtesy of the Metropolitan Museum of Art

FIGURE 21. FRESCO OF THE HUNT FROM TIRYNS. Mycenæan Period. Water-color reproduction. Original in the National Museum, Athens. The fresco illustrates an incident in the boar hunt. Details of clothing and equipment are significant.

turies. The most important of these cities was Mycenæ, located on a site chosen for its adaptability to defense, as well as for its economic advantages. The fortified hill of Mycenæ lies next to higher ground, to which the inhabitants might flee as a final refuge if driven from their city. The fortress was located at some distance from the sea as a defense against piracy, and it commanded the trade routes north to Corinth, west to the interior beyond the mountains, and south to the Argive Plain. From Mycenæ came Agamemnon, leader of the Greek armament that sailed against Troy. Not only in the Homeric story

[65]

of the preeminence of Agamemnon among the independent princes of Greece at that time, but in the writings of the Greek historians of the classical period, is evidence to be found of the superiority of this city over the neighboring settlements. Notable among the latter were Tiryns, a city second in importance to Mycenæ, and Argos, located in the same plain. There are many other sites in continental Greece, including, as has

FIGURE 22. MYCENAEAN STIRRUP VASE. The arrangement of handles and spout are characteristic of such vases from the Mycenæan Period.

been noted above, Athens, in which Mycenæan remains have been found, but the archæological discoveries in the Argive Plain are the richest, and they are typical of the whole. The increasing evidence of a spread of that culture over wider areas does not alter the previous conclusions, supported alike by literature and archæology, as to the major importance of Mycenæ and her immediate neighbors.

Pottery. Though less conspicuous than the palaces and tombs, and less valuable intrinsically than the objects of gold and silver that were found in such abundance, pottery must be accounted the most useful type of evidence for the reconstruction of the culture of Mycenæ, as it was for that of Crete. The potter's wheel was available to craftsmen, and they used it to fashion a variety of graceful vases, which, though probably manufactured at a number of different sites, have a common quality that differentiates them from the ware of the Minoan communities. The vases of Mycenæan style are made with flaring bowls, often wider at the top than the bottom, and the designs draw their inspiration from marine and vegetable life as well as from the more conventional bands and spirals, which are to be seen also on the gold ornamental plaques from the graves. The undulating stalks of the water lily and the twining tentacles of the octopus were both seized upon for their ready adaptability to the curved surface of the vase. The Warrior Vase from Mycenæ, showing six warriors in full armor marching to battle while a woman watches their departure, affords an excellent example of the practical value of vase painting in the study of ancient life.

Engraved Gems. Almost equally characteristic are the gems of the Mycenæan Age, which were cut in intaglio in such stones as agate, jasper, and carnelian. Curiously enough, the designs are in general more animated than the painted decoration of the vases. Animals, frequently appearing in pairs facing one another, are a favorite theme, and among them the lion occupies the most important place. Designs similar to the heraldic lionesses of the Lion Gate at Mycenæ appear on gems that have been found in the city. Domestic animals and human figures, the latter often engaged in pursuits of war or domestic economy, regularly occur on Mycenæan gems. A similar inspiration led to the elaborate cutting of the bezels of gold rings, on one of which a religious scene is portrayed, with the double axe, the sun, the moon, and human figures that may represent the deity and her votaries.

Differences Between Minoan and Mycenæan Cultures. Despite marked similarities in design and workmanship that may be observed in the craftsmanship of the Minoans and the Mycenæans, there are a number of differences between the two civilizations that should be clearly recognized. In the first place, defensive walls are conspicuously absent from Cnossus. Only one conclusion can be drawn from this fact, namely, that the great island empire relied for its protection on a dominant navy, and the legend of the annual payment by Athens of a tribute of seven youths and seven maidens to feed the Minotaur corroborates the interpretation. At Mycenæ and Tiryns, on the other hand, the enormous walls indicate a civilization that relied on fortified cities for protection. The Cyclopean walls of Tiryns, which may even go back to the Neolithic period, are the most arresting examples of defensive wall construction that have survived from prehistoric times. In ruins, they indicate an original thickness of from thirty to forty feet and a height of fifty feet. They take their name from the legend that they were built by a race of giants called Cyclopes. In an age before explosives were known, such walls might well be proof against any form of violence that man could contrive.

Courtesy of the Metropolitan Museum of Art

FIGURE 23. MYCENAEAN STEM CUP.

Types of Wall Construction. There are three types of wall construction, belonging to successive stages of development of the pre-Hellenic civilization (Figure 25). The oldest was the Cyclopean, in which huge rocks were piled on top of one another and the interstices filled with a crude cement-like binding mixture. In unexposed places the filling of the crevices may still be seen in place. Somewhat later, when metal tools for shaping building stones were available, polygonal masonry was developed, in which the natural edges of the stones were cut smooth to fit evenly. In the third type the stones were cut with a saw into even, rectangular blocks, which were laid in courses after the manner of modern brick construction. This is known as ashlar masonry. Polygonal and ashlar construction depended on close fitting of the stones without the use of a binding mixture.

The Lion Gate and the Corbel Arch. The walls facing the

approach to the Lion Gate, the main entrance to the city of Mycenæ (Figure 26), are of ashlar masonry. The gate itself illustrates the principle of the corbel arch. This is not a true arch with a keystone capable of supporting a great weight, but rather is made by each successive course of building stones projecting a trifle beyond the preceding one as the wall mounts until both sides meet at the top. Over the lintel is a triangular space, called the relieving arch, within which a lighter stone is inserted. The absence of a keystone robbed the corbel arch of strength. In the case of the Lion Gate, the stone set within the relieving arch is sculptured to represent two lionesses, with their forepaws raised against a pillar, which, in Minoan-Mycenæan fashion, diminishes in circumference from top to bottom. The heads of the lionesses, which were sculptured and separately attached, have been lost. It is possible that the pillar itself was an inanimate object of worship.

Courtesy of the Metropolitan Museum of Art

FIGURE 24. FRESCO OF WOMAN CARRYING JEWEL-BOX, FROM TIRYNS. Reproduction. Note the rigid processional pose, the schematized hair arrangement, and the elaborate and detailed border.

The Grave Circle. Beyond the Lion Gate, and slightly to the right, as one enters, lies a well-marked double circle of stones. This is the grave circle, which was excavated by Schliemann in 1875, and within which he discovered five undisturbed shaft graves, the tombs of the earliest royal dynasty of Mycenæ. A sixth grave shaft was found shortly afterwards. The graves are rectangular shafts from ten to twenty feet in length and practically square. They are cut into the solid rock of the hillside and faced with stones. Each grave contained the remains of several persons. Some sixteen in all were thus buried, and the funeral offerings escaped the pillage of the intervening centuries. Homer has spoken of this city as "golden Mycenæ," and the treasures of these tombs justify the epithet. Here were

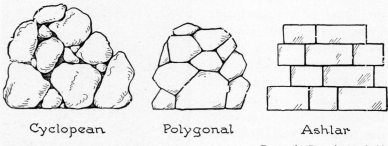

Cyclopean   Polygonal   Ashlar

Drawn by Dorothy I. Chubb

FIGURE 25. CHARACTERISTIC STYLES OF PRE-HELLENIC MASONRY. One or more of the types here illustrated will be found in the walls of many Mycenæan sites.

found golden vessels, golden diadems, bracelets, rings, dress ornaments, and dagger blades inlaid with precious metals and representing Egyptian river scenes or scenes from the hunt. Death masks of gold were found also, and a child's body had been wrapped in thin sheets of gold. Such a wealth of precious metal has been found on no other single site in Greece.

Gold and Silver Smithing. The comparative rarity of sculpture in marble or bronze during the Mycenæan Age indicates no deficiency of artistic skill, for the work of the goldsmith and silversmith, not to mention that of the gem engraver or the ivory cutter, was highly developed. Numerous little circular gold-leaf disks, which were made on a mould, have designs

[70]

derived from plant or animal life, among which the bee and the butterfly may be recognized. Others follow the conventionalized spirals so common in the decorative patterns found in the city of Mycenæ.

Photograph by M. Alison Frantz

FIGURE 26. THE LION GATE AT MYCENAE. The ashlar construction of the masonry and the relieving arch above the gateway are well illustrated. The two top corbel blocks at the right of the lion slab were restored to their original position in 1951.

[71]

A considerable fragment of a silver vase, representing the defense of a besieged city, affords, aside from the inherent interest of so early a portrayal of continuous action in art, the same type of invaluable evidence for the armor and equipment of men that was observed on the Warrior Vase.

Among the most remarkable of the objects found in the shaft graves were the bronze dagger blades, which were ornamented by precious metals inlaid to produce a variety of lively scenes. The artist had by this time learned how to adapt his subject to the available space and to the diminishing width of the dagger blade as it narrows to a point. This was a technique that was to prove quite essential when the Greeks of the classical period decorated with sculpture the triangular pediments, or gables, of their temples. One of the finest dagger blades depicts on one side a scene of the lion hunt. At the wider end toward the handle, five men, equipped with shields, spears, and bows, are fighting with a lion that has turned at bay, while two other lions in full flight retreat toward the point of the blade. The figures are inlaid with gold, both yellow and red, while the armor and the clothing of the men are differentiated by silvery metal. The remaining blades were executed by varying techniques of inlay and relief that indicate the versatility of the artists as well as their knowledge of metallurgy, since the variation of color demanded an understanding of different alloys.

Courtesy of the Metropolitan Museum of Art

FIGURE 27. MYCENAEAN GOLD CUP. The graceful but largely unadorned form of the cup represents one of the best periods of Mycenæan workmanship.

Tholos, or Beehive, Tombs. After the period of the shaft graves, another dynasty came to power in Mycenæ. These people buried their dead in huge *beehive,* or *tholos,* tombs that were built into the hillsides beyond the circle of the city walls.

[72]

A number of them are known, among which the tomb called the Treasury of Atreus at Mycenæ is the largest and most intricately constructed (Figure 28). It was built in the following manner. The hillside was dug open, and a circle about

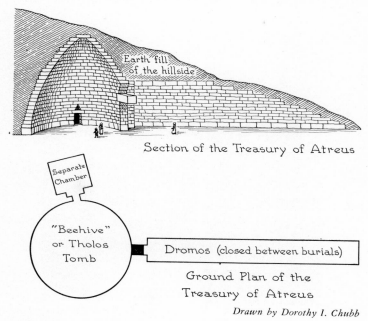

FIGURE 28. SIMPLIFIED SCHEMATIC PLAN OF THE TREASURY OF ATREUS. Details of the ashlar masonry, the lintel, and the corbel arch as developed in the construction of the Treasury may be observed.

forty-eight feet in diameter was laid out. As the walls were built, each successive course of blocks projected slightly inward on the principle of the corbel arch; the walls of the tomb converged like an old-fashioned beehive and met at a point on the top. The height of the tomb was about forty-three feet. The earth of the hillside was filled in over the stones and served to support the structure by its own weight. A door was built into the tomb, with the lintel about on a level with the

[73]

slope of the hill. This enormous lintel is estimated to weigh about one hundred and twenty tons. So great a weight could be put into position by making use of the natural slope of the hill as an inclined plane. A long *dromos,* or passageway, faced with ashlar masonry, led out to the edge of the hill. Bronze

Photograph by Eunice Burr Couch

FIGURE 29. DROMOS OF THE TREASURY OF ATREUS. The details of wall construction should be examined in comparison with the preceding figure.

rosettes once adorned the interior of the tomb, some of which were discovered in the excavations, but they have all since disappeared. In the Treasury of Atreus an additional square chamber was cut into the hillside from one side of the circular tomb, though such a room is not characteristic of all beehive tombs. Apparently, successive royal burials were made in the same tomb, the *dromos* being filled with earth in the intervals. The *tholos* tombs, alike by reason of the discovery within

[74]

them of objects of adornment or ritualistic practice, and through the evidence implicit in their elaborate structure and continued use, tell of a wealthy and stable dynasty in Greece lasting over several centuries.

Helladic Civilization. In other localities of Greece, where a civilization similar to the Mycenæan and known as the Helladic civilization flourished, excavations have yielded vases and other objects, some of which are of major importance. From Vaphio, a comparatively unimportant site, there came two gold

Courtesy of the Metropolitan Museum of Art

FIGURE 30. THE GOLD CUPS FROM VAPHIO. Mycenæan Period. Reproductions. Originals in the National Museum, Athens. The elaborate designs may be contrasted with the simplicity of the cup illustrated in Figure 27.

cups (Figure 30) that are considered by many to be the most beautiful discoveries of pre-Hellenic culture in Greece. They are made of gold in beaten relief, called *repoussé* work, and are lined with a smooth inner cup of gold. The cups were decorated with contrasting scenes, one showing the vigor and energy of bulls caught in nets, the other a quiet picture of cattle standing and grazing beneath the trees. It is a principle of balanced contrasts in appropriate pairs that the Greeks were to seize upon again five or six centuries later for the sculptural adornment of the gables of their temples.

By 1100 B.C., the vigor and power of the pre-Hellenic phase of life in the Greek peninsula had greatly declined. The method of its termination and the state of society during the

[75]

following centuries, preceding the fresh impulse that led to a new period of intellectual and artistic endeavor in Greece, will be explained in a later chapter. Suffice it to say that the current of Mycenæan achievement continued to flow beneath the surface long after the fall of the pre-Hellenic cities and the echoes of a brilliant society of the past were to color the thinking of the poet Hesiod in the centuries ahead.

CHAPTER V

THE HOMERIC POEMS

THE PROBLEM OF THE POEMS

Homer and the Pre-Hellenic Age. Western civilization, which includes our own culture, has produced no finer literary achievement than the poetry of Homer. The two epics, the *Iliad* and the *Odyssey,* deal with the adventures of Mycenæan, Cretan, and Trojan warriors, and with the sites that have become familiar through the excavation of the cities whose names recur so often in the verses of Homer. The island of Crete and the city of Cnossus are first mentioned in the *Iliad;* Idomeneus, the grandson of Minos, was one of the Greek heroes who fought at Troy, and the leader of the Hellenic chieftains was the king of Mycenæ, Agamemnon, son of Atreus. Many of the legends and tales of pre-Hellenic life that abound in later Greek literature have their origin in Homer. And from Homer they have by varied channels found their way through allusions and recollections into the literature of the Western world.

The Translations of Homer. The perennial appeal of Homer has been reflected in a continuous succession of new translations of both the *Iliad* and the *Odyssey,* to which the talents of some of the finest writers of English literature have been turned. In the extracts that follow, in prose and verse, an attempt has been made to illustrate the variety of moods in which the Homeric story has been retold. Their differences are striking, for among them will be found the long and somewhat difficult lines of George Chapman that inspired

Keats to write his lovely sonnet *On First Looking into Chapman's Homer,* the polished verses of the Earl of Derby, the ringing exaltation of Alexander Pope's rhymed couplets, and a number of others.

The Date of Homer. The relation of the Homeric poems to the Mycenæan civilization has led to exhaustive researches into the date of their production. The results of such studies have, however, not been conclusive, for, unfortunately, there is as little unanimity of opinion in the literary as in the archæological field. The period of composition of the Homeric poems has been placed by some scholars as early as the closing years of the Mycenæan Age, that is, at a time when the bard would have had personal knowledge of the society about which he wrote, and by others as late as the seventh, or even the sixth, century before Christ, when Greek letters began to flourish. It is not for want either of meticulous analysis of the poems or bold and vivid imaginative interpretation that the problem remains unsolved. Arguments from probability can never be conclusive, but certain lines of approach that have found their champions may be indicated.

The Nature of the Argument. It is pointed out on the one hand by one group of scholars that archæological excavations at Mycenæ have brought to light details of a civilization that are described by Homer as only an eyewitness could tell of them. Such a passage is that in which Odysseus is represented as pausing in amazement before the bronze threshold of the palace of Alcinous and marveling at the beauty of its adornments.

> And as of sun or silvered moon
> So shone the high-roofed hall
> Of King Alcinous, the great.
> All brazen were the walls
> Through all their length from door-step
> To the furthest room,
> And blue the edging-frieze,

While golden doors enclosed the home
And silver posts upon the brazen threshold stood.

Odyssey 7. 84–89, TRANSLATED BY H. N. COUCH

Similarly, when the young Telemachus, fresh from distant Ithaca, enters the palace of Menelaus at Sparta, he is struck with amazement at its magnificence, and whispers to his companion, Peisistratus:

Dear son of Nestor, mark, I pray,
The gleam of bronze within the ebony hall,
The light of gold, the amber pale,
The sheen of silver and of ivory white!
'Tis like, I say, the hall
Of Father Zeus himself
Upon Olympus' height:
Unnumbered is the store
Of wealth, which stills my heart in awe.

Odyssey 4. 71–75, TRANSLATED BY H. N. COUCH

These descriptions cannot fail to remind one vividly of the rich gold and silver treasures of the bronze age of Mycenæ, and those who believe in an early date for Homer argue that the clarity and accuracy of the word pictures indicate more than a legendary knowledge of the society itself on the part of the author.

On the other hand, anachronistic references to metals and weapons occurring in the epics are cited by other scholars as proof that the poet was writing long years after the Mycenæan Age. Furthermore, it is claimed by some supporters of the late date that the metrical excellence, the attainment of beautiful and sustained similes, and the perfected selection of words in the Homeric poems indicate a long and painstaking apprenticeship in literature, of which the *Iliad* and the *Odyssey* are the culmination rather than the beginning.

The Homeric Question. The problem, however, does not stop with the disagreement about the poet's date, but it em-

[79]

braces also the question of his identity or even his very existence. In the preceding paragraphs Homer has been treated as a historical personage, the author of the *Iliad* and the *Odyssey,* but the identity of Homer is a subject about which argument has raged since Boswell and Johnson first discussed the Homeric Question in the late eighteenth century; or perhaps more definitely, since 1795, when Wolf published his famous *Prolegomena ad Homerum.* At one time scholarly opinion insisted that the Homeric poems were the compilation of many epic lays. Some scholars, on the other hand, prefer to believe that a single author composed the poems or brought them into harmony, in substantially the form in which they are now known. It is not now proposed to settle the date of Homer, or to discuss further the Homeric Question. These topics belong essentially to detailed studies in the epic. Whatever conclusions might be reached through such researches, the inherent literary qualities of the poems would remain quite unchanged, and fortunately the lively freshness of the stories can be appreciated without undue reference to the differences of opinion about dates and authorship.

The Place of the Homeric Poems in Antiquity. There was seemingly no aspect of the life of man in his ancient environment that lay beyond the comprehension of Homer, and as a result, his poems attained an almost oracular authority in antiquity. Human conduct was justified or condemned, lawsuits were decided, and boundaries between states were adjudicated by reason of an appropriate quotation from Homer. The Homeric poems illustrate the principles that are stated in the simple, but profoundly philosophic mottoes: *Know thyself* and *Nothing in excess* that through the subsequent ages of Hellenic vigor constituted the conscious guide of life for the thoughtful Greek. Moreover, in the Homeric poems there will be found evidence of a sense of potential human excellence, which may be described by the Greek word *areté.* A number of translations of this word come readily to mind—*virtue, function, excellence*—but the concept is a subjective one and

[80]

an appreciation of it depends on an understanding of the values that were predominant in Greek thinking at any given time. To an Homeric hero, areté might consist in the pursuit of military glory, which animated Diomedes, or in loyalty to a friend, which led Achilles to accept the gloom of death, or in the defense of one's native land at the cost, not only of life, but of liberty for father and mother and wife, which was the conscious choice of Hector. Although the values of areté might change with the passage of time, the quality itself was always associated with the dignity of human conduct at its best in a particular period.

THE ILIAD

The Theme of the "Iliad." The poems are simple both in content and in language. The *Iliad* tells the story, not of the ten-year struggle before Troy, but of the action during some fifty-one days in the final year of that war. The center of all the argument, through fifteen thousand verses of the world's greatest epic, is the wrath that Achilles cherishes against Agamemnon. The poem starts with a plea of the poet to the Muse to sing of the strife of the two heroes, which brought unmeasured woe on the armies of the Greeks. In Alexander Pope's somewhat artificial but effective couplets the invocation runs thus:

> Achilles' wrath, to Greece the direful spring,
> Of woes unnumber'd, heavenly Goddess, sing!
> That wrath which hurl'd to Pluto's gloomy reign
> The souls of mighty chiefs untimely slain:
> Whose limbs, unburied on the naked shore,
> Devouring dogs and hungry vultures tore:
> Since great Achilles and Atrides strove
> Such was the sovereign doom, and such the will of Jove!
>
> *Iliad 1. 1–7*

A Summary of the Story. The structure of the epic narrative will be found to be simple and continuous. Chryses, an aged priest of Apollo, had come to the camp of the Greeks to ransom his daughter Chryseis, who was the captive prize of Agamemnon, often described as Atreides, or son of Atreus. The old man was contemptuously dismissed, and in his sorrow he prayed to Apollo to send a pestilence on the Greek host. The god hearkened to his servitor, and disaster came upon the Achæan, or Greek, army. At length an assembly was called by Achilles, and there Calchas, the seer of the Greeks, encouraged and supported by Achilles, made bold to tell how the insolence of Agamemnon was the cause of their suffering. Agamemnon was constrained to release Chryseis, but with petulant chagrin he took instead the fair-cheeked Briseis, the captive maid of Achilles, and Achilles in his wrath and sorrow quitted the host of the Greeks, and apart in his tent he prayed to his goddess mother, Thetis, to intercede with Zeus that the god might bring grievous destruction on his own people, until they should acknowledge his worth. This Zeus did, and obdurately Achilles refused all pleas from his hard-pressed comrades to take up arms once more, until at length his own dear companion, Patroclus, donned the armor of Achilles and went out to drive back the Trojans, only to be slain by Hector, Priam's son. Then Achilles, in a passion of sorrow for his slain comrade, put on the beautiful armor which Hephæstus, the god of the forge, made for him at the prayer of his mother, and went forth to meet Hector, the greatest of the Trojan warriors. He slew Hector and dragged his body behind his chariot over the Trojan plain, with his fair gleaming hair trailing in the dust, until at length he was moved by a divine pity and surrendered the body of the dead Trojan to his father, Priam, for burial.

The Effective Simplicity of the Tale. That is the story of the *Iliad*. There are other elements that enter in, plots and battles, councils, raids, and games, but the unifying thread is never complex. In those simple verses are told the tales of courage, love, and pathos of the world's infancy, in language of such sensitive beauty that scholars and statesmen of later times have confessed themselves unable to read the poems without being moved to tears. Alexander the Great, St. Augustine,

Photograph by Alinari

FIGURE 31. AJAX HOLDING THE DYING PATROCLUS. Florence. This group, though from a late period of Greek art, illustrates the well-known scene from the *Iliad*.

[83]

Gœthe, and Gladstone are but a few of the men who have found in Homer the keenest literary delight to which their natures were susceptible. Today students of Homer are turning away from the sterile pursuits of the Homeric Question and are devoting themselves instead to the study of poetic technique and to the beauty of word and phrase and thought in the epics. The poems themselves must be read in their entirety, in Greek if possible, to feel the beauty and the power of the stories. Some of the passages, which follow in brief, have become part of the background of all literature, both ancient and modern.

Helen on the Walls. Although the story of Helen of Troy is introduced only as an interlude in the narrative, it has been treated with consummate skill. Paris, the Trojan prince, had adjudged Aphrodite fairer than her sister-deities Athena and Hera and had received Helen, the fairest among women, as his reward from the goddess of love. To claim his prize he had gone to Sparta and had stolen away Helen, the wife of his host, Menelaus. The Greeks had followed him back to Troy, and for ten long years the city had been beleaguered by them and the finest of the Trojan youth slain for the sake of Helen. Homer has told of her beauty so that it has become an archetype for the loveliness of woman. This he accomplishes through the scene in which Helen makes her appearance before the Trojan elders. In the tenth year of the war the old men of Troy were sitting on the walls, casting their eyes on the armies below, when Helen came toward them.

> Those who were about Priam
> And Panthoös and Thymœtes
> And Lampos and Clytios and Hiketaon,
> Of the seed of Ares,
> Even Ucalegon and Antenor,
> Wise men both and elders of the people,
> Were seated by the Scæan Gates.
> By reason of age they had ceased from war,
> But orators of honied charm they were,

Like unto the cicadas,
That rest within the woods upon a tree
And utter voices lily-clear—
Even such were the elders of the Trojans
Who sat upon the tower.
And as they look'd on Helen
Drawing nigh unto the wall,
Softly one to another they spake
Wingèd words:
"No cause for wonder is it
That Trojans and well-greaved Achæans
For such a woman's sake
Should suffer long and grievous woe;
For like in wondrous wise is she
To the immortal goddesses
In loveliness of countenance."

Iliad 3. 121–158, TRANSLATED BY H. N. COUCH

This tribute to the loveliness of Helen is expressed entirely in terms of her effect on the old men of Troy, who have seen their city ruined for her sake. There is no ecstatic eulogy of Helen's beauty, no tedious catalogue of her charms. Nowhere in Greek literature is the principle of moderation used with more delicate effect than here. From these few verses there has grown the picture of Helen, modified to the fancy of every man and every age, for Homer has said not a word to individualize, and thus to fix by time or place, the beauty of the fairest of Greek women.

The Campfires of the Trojans. Another effective passage, though quite different in its appeal, is found in the description of the campfires of the Trojans as they are seen by the Greeks in the darkness of the night. Hector, son of Priam, king of Troy, has just spoken heartening words to the Trojans, and the warriors have loosed their weary horses from the chariots, kindled the fires, and prepared food for themselves at the end of the day. The translation that follows, though perhaps unduly concerned to elide syllables, is excellent for its expression of precise detail in verse.

[85]

Full of proud hopes, upon the pass of war,
All night they camp'd; and frequent blaz'd their fires,
   As when in Heav'n, around the glitt'ring moon
The stars shine bright amid the breathless air;
And ev'ry crag, and ev'ry jutting peak
Stands boldly forth, and ev'ry forest glade;
Ev'n to the gates of Heav'n is open'd wide
The boundless sky; shines each particular star
Distinct; joy fills the gazing shepherd's heart.
So bright, so thickly scatter'd o'er the plain,
Before the walls of Troy, between the ships
And Xanthus' stream, the Trojan watchfires blaz'd.
   A thousand fires burnt brightly; and round each
Sat fifty warriors in the ruddy glare;
With store of provender before them laid,
Barley and rye, the tethered horses stood
Beside the cars, and waited for the morn.

Iliad 8. 553–65, Translated by The Earl of Derby

It is a beautiful picture of the quiet of man and nature before the storm of battle, but the poet is more interested in the coming action of men than the objective description of nature for its own sake.

The Similes of Homer. The Homeric narrative is everywhere embellished by the introduction of striking similes that heighten the style because they appeal to a basis of comparison known to every listener. There are no miracles in the similes of Homer. A series of three similes, all selected from the second book of the *Iliad* and all designed to convey the idea of vast numbers of men in varying moods, will illustrate the use of this literary device. To afford variety and to indicate that the effectiveness of the simile depends more on content than on form, each one of the three similes has been taken from a different translation. In the first instance Nestor has bidden that the Achæans be summoned to arms.

                 Being abroad, the earth was overlaid
With flockers to them, that came forth, as when of frequent bees
Swarms rise out of a hollow rock, repairing the degrees

[86]

Of their egression endlessly, with ever rising new
From forth their sweet nest; as their store, still as it folded grew,
And never would cease sending forth her clusters to the spring
They still crowd out so; this flock here, that there, belabouring
The loaded flow'rs; so from the ships and tents the army's store
Troop'd to these princes and the court, along the unmeasur'd shore.

Iliad 2. 86–93, TRANSLATED BY GEORGE CHAPMAN

When this great host of the Achæans has been assembled, Agamemnon speaks to them, and, to make trial of their spirit, suggests that they leave Troyland and sail across the sea to their homes. Strange words were these and past hope to common soldiers who had warred about Troy for ten years. A murmur of surprise and a movement of assent swept over the throng.

And the throng swayed like the long waves of the sea, even of the Icarian main, when the east wind and the south stir them, darting down from the clouds of Father Zeus; and even as when the west wind cometh and swayeth the deep grainfield, blowing violently, and the grain bendeth with its ears, so was the whole assemblage of men stirred.

The cumulative force of the comparisons brings to the eyes of the audience the involuntary emotional stirring of a great, tense crowd as they hear unexpected tidings.

But, by the intervention of Hera and Athena, the Greek host is deterred from departure, and thoughts of war are made sweeter to them even than a return to their native land. The Greek army is brought together again for battle.

> Not less their number than th' embodied cranes,
> Or milk-white swans in Asius' watery plains,
> That o'er the windings of Cayster's springs
> Stretch their long necks, and clap their rustling wings,
> Now tower aloft, and course in airy rounds;
> Now light with noise; with noise the field resounds.
> Thus numerous and confus'd, extending wide,
> The legions crowd Scamander's flowery side;

With rushing troops the plains are cover'd o'er,
And thundering footsteps shake the sounding shore;
Along the river's level meads they stand,
Thick as in spring the flowers adorn the land,
Or leaves the trees; or thick as insects play,
The wandering nation of a summer's day,
That, drawn by milky streams, at evening hours,
In gather'd swarms surround the rural bowers;
From pail to pail with busy murmur run
The gilded legions, glittering in the sun;
So throng'd, so close, the Grecian squadrons stood
In radiant arms, and thirst for Trojan blood.

Iliad 2. 459–473, Translated by Alexander Pope

In the last simile, the sustained and recurring nature of the comparison with birds, leaves, flowers, and flies builds up a picture of multiplicity that lends epic proportions to the throng on the plain, a mood that is well rendered in Pope's translation.

The striking and, to modern ears, unusual introduction into a literary theme, of the flies swarming about the milk pails reminds one that no artificial fastidiousness stood between the Greek and an apt illustration. A similar directness of purpose may be seen in the comparison of the Greek warrior Ajax resisting the Trojans to the stubborn tenacity of a lazy ass that will not be driven from his fodder. There is no disparagement in the association; rather the ass is chosen because, from the experience of common life, no other creature will serve quite so well. Ajax gives ground unwillingly before the Trojans, so that he may protect the Achæan ships. The objective and straightforward prose of Samuel Butler conveys the idea effectively.

Or as some lazy ass that has had many a cudgel broken about his back, when he gets into a field begins eating the corn—boys beat him but he is too many for them, and though they lay about with their sticks they cannot hurt him; still, when he has had his fill they at last drive him from the field—even so did the Trojans and their allies pursue great Ajax ever smiting the middle of his shield with their darts. Now and again he would turn and show fight, keeping back the battalions of the Trojans, and then he would again retreat; but he prevented any of them from making his way to the ships.

Iliad 11. 558–569

This passage, too, illustrates not only the aptness of comparison, but also the Homeric literary device of long and sustained similes. The universality of the ideas in the Homeric poems is everywhere evident. Though the heroic tales of gods and men at war are on the most elevated plane of thought, the incidents of common life also receive the pure touch. The felling of a tree, the gasping of the fishes drawn up by the net upon the shore, or the crash of the timbers of a ship that is destroyed by a storm at sea are described with equal vigor.

The Farewell of Hector. The parting of Hector from his wife Andromache and his child Astyanax, when he sets out to battle, introduces a new and gentler theme. Greek literature is usually concerned with interests on an adult level, and it is seldom that a theme of childhood is skilfully handled. The present scene furnishes an exception almost unique in Greek literature as the devotion of the father and the tenderness of the mother mingle for a brief span of time in the simple delight of parents in the natural and spontaneous action of their infant son.

As Hector came to the Scæan Gates and was about to go forth upon the plain, his wife came running to meet him, and a handmaid carried his child. The boy was named Scamandrius, after the river Scamander, but the Trojans called him Astyanax, Lord of the City, for it was the custom to name a child from an attribute of his father, and Hector was in truth the lord and defender of Troy.

> Now Hector smiled
> And gaz'd in silence on his son;
> Andromache stood nigh to him and wept.
> And then she touched him with her hand
> And spake a word and named him:

"Dear Lord, thine own strength
Will be thy doom;
Nor dost thou know what pity is
For thine infant son,
Nor yet for me, unhappy one,
So soon to be thy widow;
For quickly will the banded might
Of Hellas bring thee death.
Better were it then for me,
When thus bereft,
To pass beneath the earth.
No other solace will be mine,
When thou hast met thy fate,
But only woe."

The pleas of Andromache are futile, as futile they must be, for the stern hand of duty beckons to the Trojan prince. Yet there is infinite pity in the words that he utters to his wife.

Then mighty Hector of the glancing helmet
Answered her:
"Truly these things are a care to me,
Dear wife:
But I should feel deep shame
Before the Trojans
And the long-rob'd Trojan women,
If I should shun the battle
Like a coward.
Yea, my own soul forbiddeth me,
For I have learned eternal valor
And ever in the foremost Trojan ranks
To take my stand,
To win great glory for my sire
And for myself.

"Yet well do I know this within my heart and soul;
A day will come when holy Ilios
Shall be destroyed,
And Priam, too, and all the folk of Priam
Of the goodly ashen spear.

"But not so sorely am I troubled
By the woe that will be the Trojan lot in aftertime

And the lot, too,
Of Hecuba and of lord Priam
And of my brothers,
Many and goodly heroes,
Who will perish in the dust,
Subdu'd by foemen's hands;
Nay rather, it is thy grief
For which I weep,
When some one of the bronze-clad Achæans
Will lead thee in tears apart
Bereft of the day of freedom.

"Then, dwelling in Argos,
At the word of another wilt thou ply the loom
And from the founts, Messeïs or Hypereia,
Wilt thou bear water in sore unwillingness,
For harsh need will be upon thee.
And then some man,
Marking thee as thou dost weep, will say:
'This is the wife of Hector,
Who was in battle valiant above all others
Of the horse-taming Trojans
When they warred about Ilios.'
Verily, thus will one speak,
And for thee a new grief it will be
Through want of such a lord
To stay the day of doom.
But may the mounded earth
Cover my dead clay
Ere I hear thy weeping
And mark thy slavery."

As Hector finished his prophecy of doom, which all too soon
was to become a reality, he sought to take his infant son in his
arms before returning to the battle. But the child was frightened at the strange appearance of his warrior father, and
Hector had to put aside the awesome helmet before he could
win the recognition of his son.

Thus speaking, the glorious Hector
Stretch'd forth his arms unto his son:
But the child cried aloud

And shrank to the bosom
Of the fair-zoned nurse.
The sight of his dear father frightened him;
He fear'd the brazen armor
And the horse-hair plume,
For he marked how dreadfully it nodded
From the helmet's top.

Then laughed his dear father
And laughed his lovely mother
And straightway from his head the glorious Hector
Took his helmet
And set it all gleaming
Upon the ground.
Then only did he kiss his son
And hold him in his arms
And speak in prayer to Zeus
And to the other gods.

And then at length he placed his child
In the arms of Andromache;
And she receiv'd him to her fragrant bosom,
With tear-dimmed smiling face.
And her lord had pity as he marked her:
He touched her with his hand
And spake a word and named her:
"Dear wife, grieve not overmuch at heart for me;
No man will hurl me down to death
Beyond my fate;
Yet I declare no mortal man
Hath yet escap'd his lot,
Be he slack or be he brave,
Since first he hath been born.
Do thou now return thee to our home
And to thy tasks
To loom and distaff,
And to the bidding of the servants
In their toil.
War shall be the care of men,
Of all men and chiefliest to me,
Of those who dwell in Ilios."

Thus spake the glorious Hector
And from the ground he took the helmet
With horse-hair plume.
And his dear wife departed toward their home,
With many a backward look,
As the warm tears fell.

Iliad 6. 359–496, TRANSLATED BY H. N. COUCH

Hector appears again in stirring scenes of the *Iliad,* when he slays Patroclus, the comrade of Achilles, and when at length Achilles, to avenge that death, puts aside his wrath and dons his armor to pursue Hector about the walls of Troy, to reject the plea of his foeman that Hector's body in the event of death be restored to his parents, and finally to slay and drag him, bound to his chariot, before the city. It is to ransom the greatest of the Trojans that the aged Priam goes in humility to the hut of Achilles, where the latter, bidden by the gods to show mercy, delivers the dead Hector to the Trojan king and stays the battle until the Trojans may bury him. With the removal of Hector, Achilles' noble antagonist is gone, but with a philosophical acceptance of the continuity of life, the *Iliad* is not closed on that note. The ghost of the dead Patroclus must be placated, and due funeral rites offered, and preparations must be made by the Trojans for the burial of Hector. Thus the few days of action recorded in the poem reach their conclusion.

The Character of Gods and Men in the Homeric Poems. The Homeric poems became in the classical centuries a universal text to which men turned as a source of tradition and guidance. To this extent they assumed the position of the Bible, although they did not embody a code of strictly religious teaching. Composed in an early era, when the poet expressed in verse the contemporary mood of life, the *Iliad* and *Odyssey* reveal much about the religious and ethical beliefs of the time. Nevertheless, it is far from easy to evaluate the relationship between gods and men in Homeric society in terms that will not be misleading.

[93]

Different ages interpret the place and purpose of religion and morality, philosophy and ethics, prayer and worship in different ways. The Homeric gods, though superhuman in their power, were visualized as human in form and conduct. Scenes of the assembly, the banquet, or even of the blacksmith shop, described as occurring on Mount Olympus, are simply divine counterparts of human experience. The gods were stirred by the same emotions as men—by love, hate, ambition, fear—and many a time, as later critics were to point out, the Homeric gods behaved in ways that would be considered disgraceful in terms of human conduct.

Homeric theology was in many respects immature, and it should be recognized at once that the value of the poems lies more in their literary excellence than in their religious significance. Yet the *Iliad* and the *Odyssey* do contain stories of high moral and ethical implications. Courage is rewarded, patience respected, piety wins its measure of honor. Men and women are subjected to stresses and strains, and in the degree to which they are steadfast in duty their names have become in literature symbols of their strength.

THE ODYSSEY

The Theme of the "Odyssey." The *Iliad* dealt with war and the inevitable suffering of reckless and gallant youth; the *Odyssey* combines adventure with valor and recalls from the vantage point of time the mighty efforts and perils of a hero who braved the seas to reach his home after the close of the wars. The tale of the twelve thousand verses of the *Odyssey* may be as briefly told as that of the *Iliad*. For ten years Odysseus was absent from his kingdom of Ithaca fighting at Troy, and for ten more years he was driven over the sea by the god Poseidon or held captive by the nymph Calypso, before he was to reach his home again. His son Telemachus had grown to manhood in that time, and his wife Penelope faithfully wove and unraveled her web within the halls, delaying the impor-

[94]

tunity of her suitors until her husband returned and slew them for their insolence.

The Episodic Nature of the Poem. The action of the *Odyssey* is restricted, for out of all the ten years of wandering only some forty-one days are described. This poem is much more episodic than is the *Iliad*, for, whereas the thread of unity in the *Iliad* was provided through the consequences of the quarrel of Agamemnon and Achilles, the *Odyssey* is a tale of the ingenuity of a man in all the straits in which he becomes involved. By the device of having Odysseus rescued from the sea and brought to the Palace of Alcinous, the hero himself is allowed to tell the tale of his wanderings after the fall of Troy. In the *Odyssey* will be found also many of the stories that are learned in childhood, such as the daily weaving of Penelope's web and its unraveling by night; the story of Proteus, the Old Man of the Sea, who could turn himself at will into a lion, a snake, a leopard, a boar, running water, or a blossoming tree; the lovely tale of Nausicaa, the princess of the Phæacians, and of her adventure with Odysseus; the stories of Polyphemus, of the Læstrygonians, and of Circe, the enchantress who turned the comrades of Odysseus into swine; and finally the tale of the stringing of the bow and the vengeance on the insolent suitors.

The Helen of the "Odyssey." In spite of the easy simplicity of Greek epic narrative, the poet never achieves his results twice in precisely the same manner. Thus Homer has created in the *Iliad* a vision of the beauty of Argive Helen through the tale of her appearance on the walls of Troy. When he wishes to speak again of her charm, as he does in the *Odyssey,* the only similarity to his earlier approach is the indirection by which he accomplishes the result.

Telemachus, the son of Odysseus, having grown desperate as the suitors of Penelope waste his father's substance, set out from Ithaca to visit Pylos and Sparta. There he hoped to learn from Nestor and Menelaus, now returned from Troy, something of the fate of Odysseus. From Pylos he drove, accompanied by Nestor's son, over the wagon road, which has already been mentioned, until he came to Sparta. There he was received by Menelaus, who told him of his wanderings and of the trials of the heroes. Menelaus speaks:

"Yea, though I grieve and mourn
Without ceasing for them all
As I sit within my halls—
And at times I comfort my soul
With lamentation and then again I cease,
For there cometh at length an end
To the power of grieving—
Yet for all I mourn not so much,
Stricken though I am,
As for one, who maketh hateful to me
Sleep and food
When my mind dwelleth upon him.
For no one of the Achæans toil'd so mightily
As Odysseus toil'd and wrought."

Thus he spake and stirr'd in the soul of Telemachus
A desire of lamentation for his sire;
For at the mention of Odysseus' name
A tear he dropp'd
From beneath his eyelids to the ground,
And the robe of purple stain
Before his eyes he held
With both his hands.
Straightway Menelaus marked the youth
And mused within his heart and soul:
Should he allow the boy
To make mention of his sire
Or should he first question
And make trial of him?
And even as he revolv'd these thoughts
Within his mind and soul,
Out from the fragrant high-roof'd chamber
Helen came: like was she
To Artemis, goddess of the golden bow.

And Helen sat upon a couch
And there was a footstool beneath her feet.
Straightway then she address'd her lord

And question'd him in every part:
"God-nurtured Menelaus,
Do we know aught of these our guests
Who have come to our dwelling-place
And who they claim to be?
Shall my word be false or true?
Yea, my soul urgeth me to speak.
Never, I vow, have I beheld
Mortal man or woman
So like in countenance to another—
And as I gaze on him awe layeth hold on me—
As this youth is like unto the son
Of high-soul'd Odysseus,
Even Telemachus,
Whom that hero left a new-born infant in his home
What time ye Achæans for the sake of me,
Unworthy and shameful as I am,
Came unto Troyland,
Breathing fierce warfare in your souls."

The identification of Telemachus is thus accomplished and
the strangers are entertained in the hall with the hospitality of
the heroic age. Presently the hour of the evening meal comes,
and Menelaus calls for the pouring of the lustral water over
the hands of his guests. And the pervading beauty of Argive
Helen is again made manifest.

Fair-haired Menelaus spake a word:
"Let us take thought now
Of the evening meal
And let the servants pour the lustral water
On our hands.
With the coming of the dawn
There will be other tales for us to tell,
Even for Telemachus and myself,
One to the other."

Thus he spake;
And Asphalion, the goodly squire
Of glorious Menelaus,
Pour'd lustral water on their hands.

And then Helen, born of Zeus,
Conceiv'd another thought within her mind:
Straightway into the wine she poured a drug
And of it they drank.
A wondrous drug it was with power
To quiet sorrow, to stay all anger,
To cause forgetfulness of every grief.

Whatsoever man might drink of it,
When mingled with the wine
In the mixing-bowl,
On that day no tear could he let fall
Upon his cheeks,
Not though his mother and his father
Then should die,
Not though foemen with the brazen sword
Should slay his brother or his son
And he should see it with his eyes.

Odyssey 4. 74–266, Translated by H. N. Couch

Helen had entered the great hall and taken her place at the mixing-bowl. And straightway the young Telemachus, travel-weary, sore at heart, consumed with anxiety for his father, found every sorrow driven from his soul. The drug that she casts into the wine is the magic of her beauty. One will search the verses of Homer in vain for a single word to describe her loveliness, yet so compelling has been the creation of the poet that Helen lives anew in every age and in every heart that has known love and the loveliness of woman.

Odysseus and the Cyclops. The story of the adventure with Polyphemus, the cruel and cannibalistic Cyclops, and of how Odysseus outwitted him is one of the world's best horror stories. Odysseus and his comrades had come to the island of the Cyclopes, a rich land, where the one-eyed giants lived with their sheep and their goats and dealt despitefully with all mortals who ventured to the shore. Odysseus with twelve comrades left his ship, bearing food and wine in a huge wine-skin, for he had a foreboding that he should meet a great and

[98]

brutal man. They came to the cave of Polyphemus, but he was away tending his sheep and goats, and Odysseus insisted upon waiting within the cave to meet the giant, and to ask of him gifts due to a visitor.

It was an unhappy plan, for the giant came back and drove his flocks within, and set in the mouth of the cave a huge rock, such a one as two-and-twenty goodly four-wheeled wagons could not bear. Then he saw the comrades of Odysseus, and, scorning their prayers for a host's kindness, pitilessly he seized two of his wretched prisoners and, dashing their heads upon the ground, made his meal of them. Twice again during their imprisonment the giant seized and devoured two of the hapless Greeks. At length the cunning Odysseus devised a plan. He would take the great club of the Cyclops and sharpen it and harden it in the fire, and then, when the Cyclops slept, he would turn the stake in his one eye and blind him. When the Cyclops returned to the cave that night and drove his flocks within, and set the huge door-stone in place, Odysseus tempted him with wine from his wineskin. And when Polyphemus in his folly had thrice drunk of the rich wine to the lees, Odysseus put his cunning plan to the test.

Cyclops, thou askest me my glorious name. I shall tell thee, and do thou give me a stranger's gift, even as thou didst promise. Nobody is my name. My mother and my father and all my comrades call me Nobody.

And the Cyclops replied:

Nobody I shall eat last of all among his comrades, but all the others first. That shall be thy stranger's gift.

Thereupon Polyphemus, being heavy with wine, fell upon his back, subdued by all-conquering sleep, while wine and fragments of human flesh were disgorged from his mouth. Then swiftly Odysseus and his comrades took the great stake and heated it in the fire until it glowed, and they thrust it into his eye, and twisted it with straps, as an auger is spun on a ship's timber, until the roots of the eye were burned away.

Odysseus continues the story:

And the Cyclops groaned mightily and dreadfully, and the rock echoed to his cry, and we started back in terror. From his eye he plucked the stake all spotted with blood, and hurled it from him. And then he called aloud to the Cyclopes, who dwelt about in caves along the windy headlands. And they came at his cry from every quarter, and standing about the cave they asked what troubled him: "Why is it, Polyphemus, that thou hast cried aloud through the ambrosial night, and driven sleep from us? Doth some mortal drive thy flocks away despite thee, or is someone slaying thee by guile or strength?" And then the mighty Polyphemus answered from his cave: "Oh my friends, Nobody is slaying me by guile, nor at all by strength." And the Cyclopes answered him and said: "If nobody is using thee with violence here alone, it is in no wise possible to escape disease, when sent by mighty Zeus. Do thou pray to thy father, Lord Poseidon."

Odysseus concludes:

And when they had spoken thus, they went away, and I laughed within my heart to think how my name and my goodly plan had deceived them.

Yet Odysseus and his comrades had still to escape from their prison, for Polyphemus now removed the great stone from the mouth of the cave and sat by the opening to catch the Greeks as they emerged. But the cunning of Odysseus was equal to the task. Binding together three rams for each of his comrades, he had a man conceal himself beneath the middle one, while he himself clung to the thick wool beneath the belly of the giant's great and favorite ram, and thus Odysseus and his comrades passed out of the cave, as the sightless Polyphemus, fondly thinking to catch them, ran his hands over the backs of his flock.

[100]

The story will repay close study, not only for the spirit of high adventure with which it is written, but also for the evidence of careful planning in structure and content. One will, for instance, not fail to note the dramatic pause at a moment of high tension when the blinded Polyphemus stops the ram, and talks with it at length, before allowing it to pass out of the cave and bear the clinging Odysseus to safety.

The Story of Nausicaa. The story of Odysseus and the Cyclops has a sequel. Polyphemus was the son of Poseidon, the sea-god, and, to avenge his blinding, Poseidon swore to harry the course of Odysseus on his homeward voyage, though he was powerless to prevent his eventual return. Thus it was that in the tenth year of the wanderings of Odysseus when, his comrades all lost, he drew near to the island of the Phæacians, Poseidon, still nursing his passion for revenge, looked on the raft of Odysseus and in great anger roused up a tempest and destroyed it. By the aid of Ino, a goddess of the sea, and through the ever-present help of Athena, Odysseus swam for two days until he came to the island of Phæacia, and there he sank into a deep sleep of exhaustion by the river mouth, beneath the shelter of two olive bushes, one wild and one cultivated, that twined themselves together.

And now Athena, seeking to accomplish an end to the woes of Odysseus, appeared to Nausicaa, the lovely daughter of King Alcinous, in her sleep, and in the likeness of one of her companions she urged upon Nausicaa that she make ready for the day of her marriage.

When Nausicaa awoke, she went to her father under the impulse of the vision, but in modesty she forebore to speak of marriage. Rather she sought permission to go to the river to wash the clothes for him and for her brothers, that they might be well arrayed at the council or the dance. And her understanding father, who saw through her dissemblance, answered:

I do not begrudge thee the mules, nor anything else, my child.

Go, and the servants shall make ready for thee the high well-
wheeled wagon, fitted with the upper rack.

Thus Nausicaa and her fair campanions placed the clothes
in the wagon, and food and wine, and oil to anoint themselves
after the bath, and they drove to the river bank, and busied
themselves with the washing. And when they had bathed
and anointed themselves, they fell to playing ball, and fairest
among all the fair maidens was the princess Nausicaa. Now
at length Athena pursued her plans again, and, availing herself of the universal and ageless inability of a girl to throw a
ball straight, she caused Nausicaa to miss the companion for
whom she intended the ball, and it fell into the eddying stream
of the river near to the sleeping Olysseus. Thereupon the
maidens raised a piercing cry, and Odysseus awoke.

The purposes of Athena were coming to fulfillment. Odysseus emerged from his hiding-place, and the terrified maidens
fled, except Nausicaa. All the tact of Odysseus came to his
ready mind. He sought to know whether the beautiful girl
was mortal princess or goddess like to Artemis in beauty,
form, and stature.

Never have I beheld such a one with mine eyes, neither man nor
woman; and awe cometh upon me as I gaze. Yet once in Delos
beside the altar of Apollo did I mark so fair a thing, a young shoot
of a palm tree growing there.

Thus at length Odysseus sought and gained from Nausicaa
shelter and protection, and she guided him to her father's home.
There Odysseus tarried with the Phæacians for a time, and to
them told the story of his wanderings. And there as he par-
ticipates in the gatherings and the games of the Phæacians,
the most delicate romance of epic literature rises and wanes.

Even as Nausicaa guided the stranger back to the city, she
began to fall in love with him, for when he had bathed and
clothed himself, the ever mindful Athena intervened and with
her divine power made him bold and handsome beyond all

men in the eyes of the princess. And Nausicaa, marveling to behold him, ventures to say to her companions that she would wish to have such a one for her husband, to dwell with her in the island. And so, too, as time goes by, the king, her father, is won over to the stranger, and he says in the hearing of Odysseus that he would be well content to have such a man abide with him and take his daughter Nausicaa as his wife.

It is here that Homer turns away from the idyl of love and romance that he might have woven, to tell instead a tale of love foresworn and the acceptance of duty. The faithful Penelope is still in Ithaca, and the insolence of the suitors still calls for punishment. The day of parting between Odysseus and Nausicaa must come.

When the servants had bathed Odysseus, and anointed him with oil, and about him had cast a fair cloak and a chiton, then he stepped forth from the bath to join the princes as they drank their wine. And Nausicaa, who claimed her beauty from the gods, stood beside a pillar of the close-wrought roof, and marveled as she gazed with her eyes upon Odysseus. And addressing him, she spake these wingèd words: "Farewell, stranger, and when thou hast reached thy native land, do thou think of me upon occasion, for to me dost thou owe the salvation of thy life."

And Odysseus of many wiles answered her and said: "Nausicaa, daughter of great-hearted Alcinous, now may Zeus, the loud-thundering consort of Hera, grant that I reach my home and behold the day of my return. And so there would I offer prayers to thee through all my days, even as to a goddess, for thou, maiden, didst save my life."

Thus ends the tale of Odysseus and Nausicaa, as delicately as it began. Homer was too far removed from romantic sentimentalism to toy with the idea that in a conflict of love and duty it was the nobler part to choose the path of love. There has been no loss of dignity in the case of either character, and, if the poet leaves in the appealing figure of Nausicaa a picture of the restrained acceptance of deep disappointment, he leaves also a conception that impatient and petulant humanity too seldom comprehends in the denial of a great desire. It is the substitution for the actual object of an image of perfection that can be forever cherished without flaw only because it is removed from the proof of reality.

The Rapidity of Homer. Much has been written of the rapidity that Matthew Arnold valued so highly in his criticism of Homer. Whatever the other implications of the quality may be, it embraces at least the sudden, almost abrupt, termination of a story that has been told with the leisurely fullness of the epic. The familiar tale of Circe, the enchantress, turning the comrades of Odysseus into swine will illustrate the startling swiftness with which Homer can move when he wishes. Circe has led the unsuspecting comrades within the palace and seated them.

And she made for them a dish of cheese and barley and pale honey, mixed with Pramnian wine; and in it she placed baleful drugs, so that they might forget their native land. Then she gave to them the cup, and they drank of it, and . . .

The stage has now been set with a wealth of rich detail, but all in a moment Homer leaps to the end of the story, leaving the process of metamorphosis of men into swine to be told after the revelation.

. . . she struck them with her wand, and herded them into the pigsties.

The Humor of Homer. There is a cruel, and bitter mirth that arises among the characters of Homer, not excluding the gods, and which is usually directed against personal misfortune. Such an instance occurs in the *Iliad* when Hephæstus, the lame god, recalls the time that he was hurled by the foot from heaven by Zeus, and how all day long he fell until with the setting of the sun he fell upon Lemnos, and there, with life nearly gone, was cared for by the Sintian folk.

[104]

It is a passage that has been made famous by Milton's adaptation of it to describe the fall of Lucifer:

> And how he fell
> From Heaven they fabled, thrown by angry Jove
> Sheer o'er the crystal battlements; from morn
> To noon he fell, from noon to dewy eve,
> A summer's day; and with the setting sun
> Dropt from the zenith, like a falling star,
> In Lemnos, the Ægean isle.

Hephæstus was lamed by his fall from heaven, and the sight of him hobbling about stirred the gods of Olympus to unquenchable laughter.

In addition, however, to this derisive laughter, there is a gentler humor of meiosis, or understatement, of which an example occurs in the incident of Odysseus and Irus.

Odysseus has at length returned to his own home in Ithaca, but he is still unknown to the suitors. In the great hall, disguised as a beggar himself, he quarrels with Irus, a vagrant, who was wont to beg through the streets of Ithaca, a man well known for his gluttony, his ceaseless eating and drinking. And Irus thought to drive Odysseus, an apparent rival, from the door. "Be off, old man, from the doorway, lest thou be dragged hence by the foot."

As the quarrel goes on, the suitors, delighted to find a chance for amusement, arrange a boxing match between Irus and the unknown old beggar who has come to court.

And as they met in the ring, the goodly, much-enduring Odysseus mused within his heart, whether he should smite Irus mightily, or whether he should hit him gently. And as he reflected thus, it seemed better to him to strike him gently. . . . And so he smote him upon the neck beneath the ear, and crushed in the bones, and straightway the black blood flowed from his mouth, and he fell to the dust with a groan, and drave his teeth together, as he kicked the ground with his feet. And the lordly suitors lifted up their hands, and died with laughter.

One wonders what would have happened had Odysseus been minded to smite his opponent mightily.

The Techniques of Homeric Verse. Perhaps it would be well to repeat, as a modern scholar has advised in the introduction to his book on Homer, that the student who will lay the book of criticism aside and read the poems themselves will choose the wiser part. Yet if he seeks help in recognizing the devices and techniques by which Homer achieves his effect, he may reflect upon such elements as the rapidity of the narrative, the nobility of thought, the avoidance of debasing detail, the array and the repetition of traditional epithets (*ox-eyed, white-armed, loud-resounding, early-born, rosy-fingered, much-enduring, swift of foot*), which recur with the insistence of a *leit-motif*, on the beauty of the similes, and the tenderness with which scenes of suffering and grief are described. The devotion of time to the meticulous analysis of the techniques of Homer is not idle, provided the inquiry is confined by Hellenic restraint and not pursued as an end in itself.

Summary. Something has already been said, not only of the inclusive content of the Homeric poems, but of the universal regard in which they were held in antiquity. They became the backbone of school instruction in classical Greece, filling a place comparable to that occupied by the rules and codes of law in the instruction of children in Chinese and Roman schools. In these poems, without controversy over their origin or their evolution, the Greeks themselves found a norm of literary excellence as well as a moral standard by which to govern their conduct.

THE HYMNS AND THE CYCLIC FRAGMENTS

The Homeric Hymns. The Homeric Hymns, of which some thirty-four have been preserved, were regarded as the work of Homer even as late as Roman Republican times, but more critical scholarship has assigned them to dates varying widely from a period contemporary with the *Iliad* itself to the

Christian era. They are identified as appropriate preludes composed by various Homeric bards to introduce their recitations from the epic.

The Hymns take the form of invocations to the gods, such as Aphrodite, Dionysus, Hermes, or Apollo, and several of them are dedicated to the same deity, suggesting their diverse authorship. They vary in length from five or six verses to more than five hundred. It is not difficult, with a little reflection, to recall passages from the *Iliad* and the *Odyssey* that might suitably be introduced by specific Hymns. Thus the appearance of Apollo in the first book of the *Iliad* might well be prefaced in recitation by the *Hymn to Apollo*. There is the further probability that a particular Hymn might be originally composed for recitation at the city sacred to the deity who was honored in it. Thus the *Hymn to Aphrodite* would be most appropriately sung in Cyprus, sacred to the goddess of love.

The "Hymn to Hermes." The *Hymn to Hermes* tells of the escapades and adventures of the gay, mischievous, and unscrupulous young god Hermes, who invented the lyre from a tortoise shell that he found, stole the cattle of Apollo and confuted that god when he came to protest, and presently charmed Apollo, the god of music, by the skill of his playing. Two extracts are here produced in the light and appropriate translation of Percy Bysshe Shelley. The first tells of the birth of Hermes:

> Now, when the joy of Jove had its fulfilling,
>   And Heaven's tenth moon chronicled her relief,
> She gave to light a babe all babes excelling,
>   A schemer subtle beyond all belief;
> A shepherd of thin dreams, a cow-stealing,
>   A night-watching, and door-waylaying thief,
> Who 'mongst the Gods was soon about to thieve,
> And other glorious actions to achieve.

The astonishing career of the precocious child is told, and the second extract contains in part the reply of the infant, couched in tones of injured innocence, to the angry Apollo, who has accused him, rightly enough, of having stolen his cattle:

> To whom thus Hermes slily answered: "Son
>   Of great Latona, what a speech is this!
> Why come you here to ask me what is done
>   With the wild oxen which it seems you miss?
> I have not seen them, nor from any one
>   Have heard a word of the whole business;
> If you should promise an immense reward,
> I could not tell you more than you now have heard.

> "An ox-stealer should be both tall and strong,
>   And I am but a little new-born thing,
> Who, yet at least, can think of nothing wrong:—
>   My business is to suck, and sleep, and fling
> The cradle-clothes about me all day long,—
>   Or half-asleep, hear my sweet mother sing,
> And to be washed in water clean and warm,
> And hushed and kissed and kept secure from harm."

Homeric Parody. The earliest parody of the Homeric epic, the *Batrachomyomachia,* or the "Battle of the Frogs and Mice," was probably composed in the early fifth century. The poem is still extant, and the humor lies in the transference of the sonorous epic dialogue appropriate to the Homeric heroes to the puny and ridiculous little animals. A few verses from the early part of the *Battle of the Frogs and Mice* in the grandiloquent but facile rendering of Thomas Parnell will serve to illustrate the nature of the poem and the obvious echoes of epic grandeur.

> Once on a time, fatigued, and out of breath,
> And just escaped the clutching claws of death,
> A gentle mouse, whom cats pursued in vain,
> Flies swift of foot across the neighboring plain,
> Hangs o'er a brink, his eager thirst to cool,
> And dips his whiskers in the standing pool;
> When near, a courteous frog advanced his head,

And from the waters, hoarse resounding, said,
"What art thou, stranger? What the line you boast?
What chance hath cast thee panting on our coast?
With strictest truth let all thy words agree,
Nor let me find a faithless mouse in thee."

The lost *Margites,* or "Stupid Man," is a further indication of the early beginnings of comedy.

The Cyclic Fragments. Lastly, a word must be said about the Cyclic Fragments. The epics from which these fragments come were composed in considerable numbers at approximately the same time as the Homeric poems, and, though they have now largely been lost, they exercised marked influence on later Greek literature, especially in supplying the plots of many tragedies. The titles and the content of most of them are known, and it can readily be seen that their purpose was to fill out the cycle of events before, during, and after the Trojan War, for the *Iliad* and the *Odyssey* dealt with only about fifty-one and forty-one days of action respectively.

The *Cypria* was the first in the Cycle, and it covered the action of some thirty years in all, leading up to the point in the tenth year of the Trojan War where the *Iliad* begins. From the point of view of the Cyclic poets, the *Iliad* might then be considered the second poem of the Cycle, and the *Æthiopis* to be the third, in which are told the adventures of Penthesilea, the Queen of the Amazons, who was slain by Achilles, and in the moment of her death looked into his eyes as mutual love was born. The fourth poem was entitled the *Little Iliad.* It, too, belongs within the period of the Trojan War; Odysseus is the hero, and the tale of the Wooden Horse, which Vergil related in the *Æneid,* is told. With the fifth poem of the Cycle, the *Sack of Ilios* by Arctinus, the name of the author is first known. In it is told the story of the capture of Troy, an account that Vergil again has included in the second book of the *Æneid.* The sixth poem, the *Returns,* is ascribed to Agias. It dealt with the hardships of Agamemnon, son of Atreus, and his brother Menelaus on their return from Troy to Greece. It

[109]

will be seen that this poem did for the Atreidæ what the *Odyssey* did for Odysseus. The seventh poem would be the Odyssey, and the eighth and last is the *Telegonia,* written by Eugammon of Cyrene, about the year 556 B.C.

The Decline of the Epic. In the *Telegonia,* Telegonus, the son of Odysseus and the enchantress Circe, is represented as coming home, slaying his father by treachery, and marrying Penelope, while Telemachus, the son of Odysseus by Penelope, marries Circe, and all live happily thereafter. The details of this worthless poem have been briefly sketched because the date is of some importance. In the later divisions of this book it will become clear that 556 B.C., the middle of the sixth century, is far from a period of decadence, but when one compares the feeble romance of the *Telegonia* with the beautiful restraint of Homer in such a description as that of Helen on the walls, it will be seen that in Greece the various branches of intellectual achievement apparently by some compulsion of genius had to run their swift and separate courses to perfection and decline. The *Telegonia,* coming at a time when literature and art in other techniques were just rising in their vigor, is the expiring gasp of a decadent epic that is determined to leave nothing unsaid.

CHAPTER VI

MIGRATIONS; COLONIZATION; EARLY FORMS OF GOVERNMENT

The Transition to Hellenic Society. The year 1100 B.C. has been set down as the approximate time at which the Mycenæan Age came to an end. From this point one must pass in rapid review the four or five centuries that elapsed before the great figures of Greek history began to emerge, whether their activity lay in letters, or government, or art. Before turning to the future, however, a moment's thought should be given to the movement of peoples that was to form the transition between the Mycenæan and the Hellenic cultures. This survey necessarily begins at a point even earlier than 1400 B.C., the date usually assigned to the opening of the Mycenæan Age itself.

The Greek Invasions. However sudden the conclusion of the Mycenæan Age may have been, the process of disintegration assuredly started centuries before. The tribes that filtered down into the Greek peninsula from the north never came in sufficiently large groups to provoke unified resistance or to effect a sudden and marked change in the civilization that they found. They came instead in small bands, and the time of the infiltration extended over many centuries. The most important contribution that they brought with them was their language, which was to become the Greek tongue of the classical period. These northern folk adapted themselves in widely differing ways to the customs of the existing Ægean inhabitants, but the power and effectiveness of their Greek speech presently dis-

[111]

placed the language of the Ægean peoples except for a few geographical and cultural words that survived. The introduction of a new language has in itself confused the picture of racial stocks, for it is very dangerous to argue from the use of a common tongue back to a common racial origin. In our own society it is not rare to find the English language used fully and effectively by people whose parents learned some other mother tongue. In Greece, the existing population accepted the invaders into their society, sharing their own culture with them and in turn adopting the more useful Greek tongue, as well as the more vigorous way of life of the newcomers, until, with the passage of time, they were themselves Hellenized. Nor were the paths of migration confined solely to the Greek peninsula, for at the same time other tribes from the north were crossing the Hellespont from Europe into Asia and making their homes along the coast of Asia Minor.

All through the centuries of the Mycenæan Age, the Greeks continued to make their way into the peninsula in search of homes and farms. The invaders were superior to the Mycenæan peoples in military skill, largely because of their knowledge of the use of iron, which afforded more serviceable weapons than did bronze, and which, as bronze had done, was to introduce a new civilization.

Though the newcomers appear to have lived in comparative harmony with the existing population and to have adopted willingly the Mycenæan culture wherever it offered advantages over their own, it is difficult to discover the precise relationship between the old and new populations. It must surely have differed widely in the various communities, according to the number of invaders and depending on whether they were looked upon as bringing added strength to their adopted homes or as constituting a menace to vested interests. About 1100 B.C., Mycenæ and Tiryns were suddenly destroyed by superior forces, and Argos rose to preeminence. This date, as we have already seen, marks the end of one civilization, though perhaps scarcely in a real sense the rise of another, for many years were to elapse before a society as brilliant and powerful as that of the Mycenæan Age was to appear again.

The Age of Colonization. It must not be supposed, however, that the migrations of wandering tribes ceased with the fall of

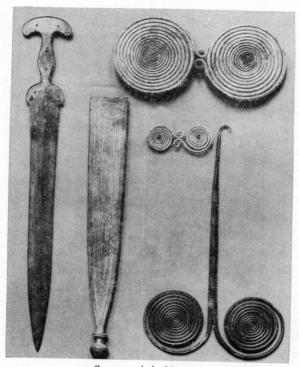

Courtesy of the Museum of Fine Arts, Boston

FIGURE 32. IMPLEMENTS OF THE ARCHAIC AGE. The two fibulæ, hairpin, dagger, and sheath belong in the sixth century B.C.

Mycenæ. The reasons for the migrations southward were those that have always caused the movement of peoples—economic pressure, excessive population, food shortage, love of adventure, political differences, and the inherent restlessness of mankind. Generation after generation, the northern tribes

[113]

continued to filter down into Greece, until similar problems disturbed the new settlements there. Then, for the reasons cited, and also because of the insatiable Greek curiosity to see and learn, men began to move out from the cities of Hellas over the sea. Because of the geographical nature of their environment, they settled either on the islands of the Ægean or on the coast of Asia Minor, where they built new cities and remained to prosper. It was in the course of this movement that such cities as Miletus, Ephesus, and Smyrna were founded. For perhaps three hundred years after the fall of Mycenæ, such sporadic movements continued. By 800 B.C., however, the peoples about the Ægean Sea had become reasonably stabilized, and the period from the eighth to sixth centuries before Christ became a time of formal and organized colonization, during which many of the established cities, both of Greece and of Asia Minor, sent out settlers to find homes for themselves in new lands.

The Organization of a Colony. Colonization was quite different from the earlier unorganized movements of peoples, although similar causes may have prompted it. Colonies were considered and deliberate ventures. Expeditions were organized sometimes at the behest of the city magistrates and sometimes more informally by a group of men who had chosen to seek their fortunes abroad, and in each case certain recognized preliminaries were undertaken. Above all, the oracle at Delphi had to be consulted, and the portents indicating the route to be followed and the site to be selected must be scrupulously observed. The *œcist,* or founder, of the new colony was chosen to be the leader; fire was taken from the sacred altar of the homeland to kindle the first blaze in the new state; the religious rites and festivals of the mother city were fostered in the new home; and enrollment in the body of colonists was limited to a single son from any one family, so that in the event of disaster no family might perish entirely. When a colony grew powerful or overpopulated and wished, in turn, to found another colony, the œcist was chosen from the original

[114]

city. In such provisions as the transference of the sacred fire and the selection of the œcist, some concession to sentiment was made; in all other respects, more practical considerations prevailed.

The members of each new colony were usually, though not invariably, of the same ethnic connection, whether Æolian, Dorian, or Ionian, and, as such, they spoke the same dialect. Common interest dictated the establishment of trade between the mother city and the colony, and an ancient piety rendered war between one and the other improbable. The colonies were, however, a group of separate enterprises, with no thought of imperial union. The colonists shared the universal Greek passion for separate existence, and they strove to maintain for their new community its complete city-state independence.

The Unsettled Times of Colonization. The period of colonization was necessarily one of broken home ties, adventure, political uncertainty, and individual initiative. Those qualities, characteristic of an unsettled society, were reflected also in the individualism of the literature that flourished contemporaneously and in the vigorous experimentation in the art forms that were springing to life in many places in Greece. The colonial movement left its mark on mythology, for the legend of Jason and the Argonauts seeking the Golden Fleece in Colchis commemorates the first penetration of the Greeks into the Black Sea, on the shores of which many colonies were planted, and the wanderings of Heracles were immortalized in the Pillars of Heracles that guarded the Straits of Gibraltar.

The Wide Range of Colonization. As colonization took on a more formal organization and as the limits of the Mediterranean and contiguous areas became better known, the Greeks went farther and farther from the Hellenic mainland in search of new homes at the bidding of Apollo and the Delphic oracle. Many a city that has retained its importance to the present day was founded as a colony during those centuries. Byzantium, which a thousand years later became Constantinople and is today Istanbul, was founded in 660 B.C., and Trebizond, Syracuse, Naples, and Marseilles mark the progress of Greek colonization at that time from the Black Sea to southern France.

THE ESTABLISHMENT OF GOVERNMENT

Experimentation in Government. The restless Greek mind was seldom content to keep one form of government for a long period of time. Some of the unsettled internal conditions within the Greek cities resolved themselves, as has already been seen, in the founding of colonies, and others were revealed in civic strife. All through the eighth to sixth centuries, and, in fact, during the entire archaic age, which for convenience may be understood to include the years after the fall of Mycenæ about 1100 B.C. and prior to 480 B.C., the city-states of Greece were occupied by continual experimentation in government. The numerous English words of Greek derivation referring to types of government, such as *monarchy, democracy, aristocracy,* and *autocracy,* are a testimony to the fact that the Greeks first evolved and tried those forms of administration. In the Homeric poems a government is found consisting of king, council, and assembly. The king served at once as general, judge, and priest; the council acted in an advisory capacity; and the assembly of free citizens gathered to hear the decisions of the first two. These three elements, with modifications in function and importance, seem to have been common to all the early peoples of Western Europe, and with changed names, continue to form the foundation of many European and American governments.

The Institution of Kingship. Though the family, or clan, is perhaps the earliest natural organization of communal life, the kingship was a logical and widespread institution in the first Greek states. The head of the most powerful family would emerge as king, and the people of the community came to look upon him almost as a god, whose function it was to protect them and to maintain justice among the dissident elements. Kingship, for natural reasons, was usually hereditary, but in the last analysis the power of the king was derived from

[116]

the consent of the heads of other families. From this group
of elders a body of aristocrats inevitably grew up, and they,
in turn, were dependent for power on their ability to rally the
free men of the community, who were the citizen soldiers, to
do their will.

Though the organization of king, council, and assembly of
free men, which is known in the Homeric poems, disappeared
in most Greek cities, it may be studied in remarkably pure
form under the kings of Macedon, where it survived all the
vagaries of experimentation until the end of Greek freedom.

Aristocracy. There was from the beginning a constant check
on the power of the king, and with the definite establishment
of the communities in the form of city-states, the acts of the
king came more and more under the critical gaze of those
over whom he ruled. In various ways the old Homeric kingship was superseded, although in Sparta the institution continued, under rigid control, while in Athens the *basileus,* or
king, became an elective magistrate. By the year 700 B.C., the
king had disappeared from most of the states of Greece, both
in name and in function, but the evidence of his former influence continued in many tales and legends.

The Rise and Fall of Tyranny. The natural successors to the
king were the nobles who had constituted his advisory council.
Government by the nobles was, however, not of long duration.
Their rise to power was usually accompanied by strife, and
petty jealousy in addition to rapacious and arbitrary ways
quickly aroused hostility and invited their overthrow. The
result was that for a period of about one hundred and fifty
years, from 650 B.C. to 500 B.C., tyrants seized the power in
many cities. Some energetic man, who might be a noble or a
commoner or a merchant, would make himself the champion
of the oppressed citizenry, and by violence take the power unto
himself. A tyrant in the Greek sense meant such an unconstitutional ruler; there was originally no objectionable connotation to the name, and many tyrants ruled fairly and humanely.

Though tyrannies were known in all parts of the Greek

[117]

world, and though they were a constant threat to any state that experienced internal disorder, three cities of central Greece, Corinth, Sicyon, and Megara, all of which were ruled by tyrants in the seventh century, have a special significance for students of Greek government. In their different ways they illustrate the brilliance and beneficence, as well as the harshness and the suffering, that could accompany tyrannies. It was Periander, the son of Cypselus, and tyrant of Corinth, who started to cut a canal across the isthmus of Corinth. In Corinth, too, there began under the Cypselid tyrants the encouragement of arts and letters that was so often to be the most noteworthy contribution of an unconstitutional ruler to his city. To cite a single utilitarian example, it was at Corinth that the architects, under the patronage of the tyrant, by the invention of roof-tiles made possible the inclination of the roof of the temple, with the resulting pediment, or gable, at either end. The pediment in turn was suited to sculptural decoration, and thus played its part in the development of art.

The essential weakness of tyranny, however, was the absence of any element of responsible government. As years went by and the tyrant was obliged to answer to no person and no advisory body, selfishness and corruption seized upon him, until the very name of tyrant became hateful to the Greeks. By the year 500 B.C., with some exceptions, the phenomenon of tyranny as a form of government had very largely passed from Hellas, overthrown by the rising tide of personal freedom.

Oligarchy and Democracy. With the expulsion of the tyrants, government normally took one of two forms. It became an oligarchy, by which is meant rule by the few and the wealthy, as in Sparta, or it became a democracy, or rule by the many, as in Athens. To the extent that the control of Sparta lay in the hands of the nobles, who comprised not more than one-tenth of the population, its government might be called an aristocracy. The two types of government persisted, and in many of the states oligarchic and democratic elements struggled with one another for power, with alternating periods

[118]

of ascendancy. Oligarchy might flourish in conjunction with kingship, as it did in Sparta, and in a democracy considerations of wealth were not absent. Although it did not happen in Greece, there is nothing inherently inconsistent in a democracy existing under a limited constitutional monarchy.

The Variety of Greek Constitutions. It is difficult to generalize about government in Greece, for the intensity of local prejudices and differences made each community a law unto itself. It is said that when Aristotle undertook to write his *Politics,* he set down as a preliminary survey an account of the separate constitutions of one hundred and fifty-eight different states. To venture far into a discussion of the variations of the constitutions of the separate states of Greece would result only in confusion. It will be sufficient to include a brief statement of conditions in Sparta and in Athens, the two most important cities of classical Greece, and to trace the changes in the latter state, in order to establish the background for the study of art and literature.

Sparta: the Spartiates, Periœci, and Helots. In Sparta, or Lacedæmon, the peoples who had for centuries been filtering in from the north, usually described as the Dorian invaders, subjugated the existing population and established themselves in a union of five villages. In historical times three distinct classes of the population in Laconia, the state of which Sparta was the capital, were known, the *Spartiates,* or Spartan citizens, the *Periœci,* and the *Helots.* The first class were the rulers, and numbered rather less than one-tenth of the total population. Although it is always hazardous to attempt to estimate the numbers in ancient cities, this portion may have amounted to some six or eight thousand citizens. The Periœci, or "Dwellers-about," held a somewhat anomalous position. They occupied and worked lands round about the city, were subject to Spartan discipline, and were excluded from participation in the government, but they were not enslaved and they frequently possessed considerable wealth, sometimes gained through trade. The Helots, who constituted the vast preponderance of the people, were attached to the land as serfs. They had been the original pre-Dorian inhabitants of the country and had been reduced to their degraded position by the Spartans, who had immigrated from the north. The cruelty with which the Helots were everywhere suppressed aroused in them a bitter and lasting hatred of their masters. In war the number of Spartiates engaged was comparatively small, for the great part of the armed forces was made up of Periœci and Helots, who were compelled to serve, the latter in menial capacities. The result of these marked inequalities was a state of enforced equilibrium, and the physical and moral energy of the ruling class in Sparta was expended on the maintenance of an uneasy superiority rather than upon the pursuit of art and letters that flourished in other cities of Greece.

The Constitution of Sparta: the Kings. The type of constitution under which Sparta lived in historical times affords a good example of the retention of the earliest form of Greek government, with the necessary adaptations and limitations. The undue power of kingship was checked in Sparta from the outset by the fact that two kings reigned simultaneously. The dual kingship may have risen from the union of two communities, although the existence of two consuls in Rome suggests that such a device may have been employed deliberately as a safeguard against tyranny. The kings retained the priestly function of their class, and some judicial rights. In war they were the supreme commanders, though the process of limiting royal powers had in historical times taken from them the right of declaring war and vested it with the assembly of the people.

The Gerousia. The Spartan council was called the *Gerousia,* or council of old men. The body was made up of twenty-eight men, over sixty years of age, and the two kings sat with them by virtue of their office, so that the Gerousia consisted properly of thirty persons. The members of the Gerousia were limited to the noble families among the Spartiates, although their election rested with the assembly. When chosen, they served for life, and their primary function was to prepare legislation for submission to the assembly and to act in an advisory capacity to the kings. The power of initiative that lay with them assured great influence to their group.

The Apella. The assembly of the people in Sparta bore the name *Apella*. This was the body of free Spartan citizens, and membership belonged by right to every Spartan over the age of thirty. Theoretically, the Apella had very considerable power. It elected the members of the Gerousia, as well as other magistrates, voted on peace or war, and decided disputes about the royal succession, of which an astonishingly large number have come to light in Spartan history. In reality the seemingly democratic liberalism of the Spartan constitution was severely limited by the removal of all initiative from the Apella. Not only was it refused the right to propose legislation, but it did not even debate the matters that were presented to it by the higher officers. It simply voted to accept or reject, and there were devices by which the magistrates could avoid yielding to the will of a recalcitrant Apella.

The Ephors. In addition to the three essential divisions of government that have just been mentioned, the institution of the *Ephorate* was a Spartan invention to meet her own peculiar needs. Five ephors, whose only qualification was Spartan citizenship, were elected, the number probably being originally determined by the five villages of Lacedæmon. The word *ephor* signifies "overseer," and the function of this group of magistrates was to exercise a proper restraint on the power of the kings. Two ephors accompanied a king to war and reported on his conduct. Mutual oaths were exchanged each month, the ephors pledging themselves to maintain the royal prerogative and the kings promising to govern according to the laws. Thus the ephors seem to have had their origin in the necessity of finding some institution to harmonize the rights of the people with existing authority. The Ephorate may well have been the compromise by which the kingship continued to exist in Sparta when it had disappeared from most other Greek communities.

The Threat of the Helots. Early in the history of Sparta there is evidence of a normal and healthy interest in cultural pursuits. Architecture, ceramics, and sculpture flourished; poets and artists were invited to the court; and the city developed a music peculiarly her own. However, when the rulers of Sparta realized the intensity of the smouldering hatred cherished by the great mass of Helots, all the free play of individual genius in the state came to an abrupt end. Thucydides has pointed out that every question of policy in Sparta was determined in the light of the preservation of Spartan institutions from destruction by the Helots. The *Krypteia,* or secret police, was established for the purpose of mingling among the Helots throughout the land and killing any whose initiative or restlessness seemed likely to cause trouble for the state. The Krypteia represents the type of terrorism that is all too likely to arise in a totalitarian state.

Spartan Society. The result of the constant threat to Spartan institutions was the organization of the state along lines of enforced discipline, so that the name of Sparta has become synonymous with severity and repression. The city became an armed camp; men and women, boys and girls, lived from the cradle to the grave as they were directed by the state, and every natural impulse, every personal ambition, and every individual preference that might possibly interfere with regimentation was crushed.

Sparta undertook to attain a single objective, military efficiency. She achieved it abundantly and overwhelmingly. For two centuries she was well-nigh invincible in battle, and it must be confessed that there is something admirable in the singleness of purpose, the severe simplicity of life, the stability of character, and the self-abnegation with which a Spartan served his state. Literature is replete with anecdotes of Spartan endurance and devotion to duty. The Spartan admiral, Callicratidas, when his helmsman counseled flight at Arginusæ, made reply: "Sparta will be none the worse inhabited for my death; to flee is shameful." Or again when the proud supremacy of Sparta

[122]

came to an end with the defeat at Leuctra in 371 B.C., with an appalling loss of life, Xenophon tells the story of the self-control with which the news was received in the city:

When these things had taken place, the messenger came to Lacedæmon to tell of the disaster. It was the last day of the Gymnopædia, when the chorus of men was dancing in the theater. The ephors, when they heard of the defeat, were grieved, as, I think, was inevitable. However, they did not stop the dance, but permitted it to continue. The names of those who had fallen in battle they reported to their relatives, and they bade the women to make no outcry, but to bear their sorrow in silence. On the next day one might see the kinsfolk of those who had died moving about the city, clad in bright garments and with good cheer on their faces, while the friends of those who had been reported as saved were seen in but small numbers, and they went about with faces cast down in shame and humility.

Athens: the Early Community. An examination of Sparta's more democratic and progressive rival Athens shows that in spite of the preeminent position that Athens attained in classical Greece, it is by no means an easy task to reconstruct the story of her constitutional changes and experiments during the early archaic age. It is clear that in the flux of the migrations, Attica escaped violent upheaval. The Athenians prided themselves on being *autochthonous,* or "sprung from the soil." The persistence of this legend leads to the conclusion that a large proportion of the population, perhaps because the Attic peninsula lies to one side of the paths of migration or because, as Thucydides suggests, the barrenness of the soil held no temptation to an invader, lived from the earliest recollection of man in comparative security. Certainly in historical times Attica, in contrast to Laconia, enjoyed the advantage of a largely homogeneous population, although slavery was an accepted institution. There was no threat of such a menace as a Helot uprising, for every citizen of the Attic countryside found his political life in the democracy of Athens.

The Kings in Athens. Before Attica became a unified state with Athens as the center, many villages had exercised their separate rights. The unification, or *synœcism,* of these different communities belongs to very early times, for its accomplishment was credited to the same King Theseus who slew the Minotaur in Crete. The kings in Athens have receded into the realm of the legendary, although in the tales of Ægeus and his son Theseus, or of the good King Codrus, who gave his life for the city, and with whom the kingship ended because the people despaired of finding a worthy successor, we have evidence of the contributions of the Athenian kings and of the harmonious process of evolution by which they were at length superseded.

The change from the kingship to the rule of the nobles, or *Eupatridæ,* was completed by about 700 B.C., for in historical times one comes upon a type of government in Athens that has succeeded kingship but has by no means obliterated its traces. It was probably by making the kingship an elective office, open to any member of the aristocracy, and then by limiting the term of office to a single year and dividing the kingly functions among a number of successors that the transition to the *Board of Nine Archons,* or magistrates, was accomplished. At this time traces of the early organization of the Athenian state on the basis of families and of four tribes, or clans, persisted. When constitutional changes were later made by Cleisthenes the four tribes were supplanted by a more arbitrary division of the state into ten tribes.

The Board of Nine Archons. The organization of the magistracies, that is, of the Board of Nine Archons, was established at a very early date and maintained with conservative respect for ancient customs. Three members had special titles and functions. There was the *Archon Eponymus,* or "Name Archon," whose duties were for the most part judicial but who is known chiefly because he gave his name to the year. The *Archon Basileus,* or "King Archon," preserved the old name of the king, but his duties were largely limited to priestly offices. The *Polemarch,* or "War Archon," served as commander-in-chief of the army. In addition, there were six *Thesmothetæ,* or lawgivers. There was a strong aristocratic quality to the Board of Archons, for it was elected by the nobles themselves and in every way power was left in its hands.

Athenian history moves rapidly on from this point into the period of names and events that shape the course of Hellenic civilization in its most active centuries.

CHAPTER VII

TOWARD STABILITY IN GOVERNMENT
(632–508 B.C.)

CYLON, DRACON, AND SOLON

Growing Class Strife. Although the essential unity of the Athenian population worked strongly against rigid class distinctions, nevertheless the government of Athens under the kings and later under the nobles, who retained the magistracies for the aristocracy, paid scant attention to the needs of two other classes of the Athenian state, the peasants and the craftsmen. For a time, little effective protest was heard from these two lower groups of the community, but the marked difference between their economic position and that of the nobles afforded precisely the setting of discontent out of which a tyranny might arise.

The Attempted Tyranny of Cylon (632 B.C.). Cylon, a young Athenian aristocrat whose fame had been enhanced by a victory at the Olympian festival and whose interest in tyranny may have been sharpened by his father-in-law, Theagenes, tyrant of Megara, found the occasion one of irresistible appeal. His attempt at seizure of power was planned with the utmost care. The Delphic oracle was consulted, and it was at the bidding of Apollo that he made his attack on the day of "the greatest festival of Zeus," which he naturally, but apparently mistakenly, assumed to be the forthcoming one at Olympia.

Cylon gathered together his own Athenian supporters, to whom were added a force from Megara, and in 632 B.C., he suddenly seized the Acropolis of Athens. He had, however, misjudged the temper of the majority of the Athenian people, who rallied under the leadership of the archon, Megacles, and besieged the band of Cylon on the Acropolis, where the insurgents were quickly reduced to severe straits of hunger and thirst. Cylon succeeded in making his own escape by stealth, and presently the rest of the besieged band, having thrown themselves as suppliants at the altar, surrendered to Megacles, relying on his promise that their lives would be spared. They were, however, treacherously put to death when they left the Acropolis, and thus there was brought upon the family of the Alcmæonidæ, to which Megacles belonged, a pollution that led to their banishment and that still persisted in Greek memory two centuries later, in the time of Pericles, who was a member of the same house. The Alcmæonidæ accomplished their recall to Athens by the liberality with which they provided a marble front for the temple of Apollo at Delphi, for the oracle repaid them by urging upon every visitor of influence the restoration of the Alcmæonidæ to their homeland.

The Continued Suffering of the People. The unsuccessful attempt of Cylon to seize power indicates that he saw in the repression and discontent of the people an opportunity to exploit his own ambitions, but the complete failure of his venture did nothing at all to clarify or improve the unhappy condition of the city. The people continued to suffer under the arbitrary interpretation of law by the nobles. The pre-eminent position of the latter class had at first seemed logical, because they, as the chief possessors of wealth, bore the brunt of taxation for the maintenance of the state and defense of the nation through the equipment of armor and horses, and because they alone understood the application of ancestral custom, which constituted law. The common people, however, began to raise an insistent clamor to know the laws by which they were governed. It was the sort of demand that was satisfied for the Roman plebs by the publication of the Laws of the Twelve Tables, and for the English-speaking people by the granting of the Magna Charta. The spirit of personal liberty was astir in Athens.

Dracon's Law Code (621 B.C.). Eleven years after Cylon's attempt to make himself tyrant, the nobles yielded to the clamor of an awakened people, and in 621 B.C., Dracon, himself one of the thesmothetæ, or lawgivers, was instructed to codify the laws of Athens. Dracon did not attempt to deal with the difficulty by any change in constitutional practice, or by any softening of excessive and unreasonable penalties for crimes, but confined himself to the immediate demand to have the laws publicly displayed and known in advance. When the codes were assembled, it was found that they were cruelly severe. Murder and impiety, theft, forgery, and idleness were alike punishable by death. Dracon did not make new laws; he codified existing practice, though he took an important step in restricting the jurisdiction of noble families in matters of private vengeance. His chief contribution, however, was a classification of degrees of homicide with attendant punishments, and this he was able to accomplish by permitting the courts to sit at different places in the city, so that the overwhelming influence of religious feeling associated with the sacred site of the Areopagus, where the courts regularly sat, might not compel the judges to decree death in every case of homicide. However, even in an early society the proportion of the people who are ever involved in a charge of murder is comparatively small, and the code of Dracon not only did not allay discontent, but actually increased it by bringing into bold relief the harshness of society. "The laws of Dracon are written in blood," the commoners said, or epigrammatically it was put: "These are not the laws of Dracon, but of dracon (dragon)." In the attack on the law codifier they were really, had they but known it, attacking an outmoded pattern of class society. With knowledge came wisdom, and with the indignation of the common people, the assurance of reform. They had still to wait a generation for its fulfilment, but the action of Dracon had set in motion forces that could not be stayed.

Solon as Sole Archon (594 B.C.). For the moment, however, Dracon's codification of the laws did little or nothing to correct the political inequality of the larger part of the Athenian people, or to alleviate the severe economic distress, which had been aggravated by war, crop failures, inordinately high interest rates on mortgages, and incidentally by the invention of coined money with its consequent disruption of a simple economy of barter among the peasants. So alarming did the unrest become that in 594 B.C. the nobles suspended the constitution and appointed one of their own number, Solon, as a single archon for the year, with complete power to rectify the ills of the state. Solon was admirably qualified for the task. A man of sound culture, with literary taste and political judgment nicely balanced, numbered in antiquity among the Seven Wise Men, he demonstrated his comprehension of the task confronting him by proposing a series of laws striking at the root of the national distress. Before being called to the task of constitutional and social reform, Solon had been active in the military life of the city, for it was he who, by his patriotic poems, had roused the Athenians to recover the island of Salamis.

The Economic Reforms. Solon's laws, broadly interpreted, may be divided into two types, dealing, respectively, with economic and political reforms. To relieve the crushing weight of financial hardship, he proposed that men enslaved for debt should be set free, that all current debts secured by a pledge of the land or the liberty of the debtor should be canceled forthwith, and that further loans on like security should be forbidden. Thus by a series of powerful and effective laws Solon removed from Athens the degrading institution of serfdom through debt and ensured liberty to all the people. He was not a visionary and impractical reformer, but had a very sound knowledge of economic principles. Thus, while canceling debts secured by the person of the debtor because justice and political wisdom alike dictated the step, he refused to disrupt the economy of the state by a sweeping revision of obligations or contracts incurred in the ordinary ways of commerce. His knowledge of the intricacies of currency and exchange, even in the early days of coined money, is shown by a significant change that he made in the Athenian currency, removing it from the Æginetan and attaching it to the more adaptable Eubœic standard of money. The technical details of this measure need not detain us, but the careful appraisal of the problems of trade and the adoption of bold remedial measures, when they were indicated, testify to the judgment and ability of the lawgiver. Furthermore, to alleviate the suffering that arose from the mounting cost of food, Solon placed an embargo on the export of all Athenian products, with the exception of olive oil, of which there was an abundant surplus. The Athenians at this time had found it profitable to export their grain, even to the extent of causing a shortage at home. This economic situation was presently to be reversed, and a century later they were obliged to import large quantities of grain from abroad to feed their people.

These laws of Solon, which from the point of view of the wealthier class threatened a radical reduction of their property, were called the *Seisachtheia,* or "Shaking-off-of-burdens." They were drastic and effective, for never again was Athens seriously troubled by an agitation so directly related to the land problem. Coined money was still comparatively new, and Solon moved with caution in the regulation of the interest rates and in other restraining measures. As might have been expected, laws that bore heavily on the wealthy but at the same time stopped short of confiscation or the complete destruction of existing society failed to satisfy the poor and were resented by the rich.

The Political Reforms. Nevertheless, the economic measures of Solon had gone so far toward allaying the danger of an open clash that his fellow citizens pressed upon him the task of making the changes in the constitution that were now recognized as imperative. Within the city, forces were already at work that were to lead in time to political equality among all classes. It was the great contribution of Solon that he directed these forces in such a way that, many years after his own death, the democracy of Athens could arise, though its ultimate form can scarcely have been foreseen by him.

Solon solidified and extended the existing division of the Athenian people on the basis of wealth. Four classes were recognized: the *Pentacosiomedimni*, whose annual income amounted to five hundred medimni of grain; the *Hippeis*, or Knights; the *Zeugitæ*, who could supply a yoke of oxen; and the *Thetes*, who were in general without property. Solon reserved the places on the Board of Nine Archons for members of the highest class. Other public services and privileges were determined by the group to which the citizens belonged. The Thetes, constituting the lowest and poorest level of society, were excluded from all public office. Yet in the face of an apparently strong class distinction, Solon extended the principle of democracy in one important direction, for he opened the *Ecclesia*, or Assembly, to the Thetes, and thus granted to them a voice in the selection of the archons, if not the right to serve in the offices themselves.

The Establishment of the Courts. Another innovation of Solon did even more to extend power and relief to the masses. This was the organization of the courts of justice in such a way that they were constituted from the people as a whole and the humblest citizen of the lowest economic stratum might become a member. Furthermore, the archons, though chosen only from the highest class, might, on retiring from office, be called before the courts of the people to give an account of their stewardship. The establishment of the popular courts led to a gradual diminution in the power of the older court of the aristocrats, the *Areopagus,* and to a steady growth in the influence of the citizens themselves, which eventually culminated in such a democracy as may have existed only in the dreams of Solon.

Estimate of Solon. Solon was in a sense a man of destiny. He was the type of statesman who more than once has risen to leadership in a democratic society at a time of national crisis and who, while imposing the force of his personality on a free people, becomes himself the greatest proof of the freedom and self-discipline of the society that placed him in office. He had accomplished the changes in the constitution the necessity for which had become apparent at the time of the publication of Dracon's law codes, but which the earlier lawgiver had not been able to attempt. Solon now repealed all the laws of Dracon and set up his own statutes on revolving wooden frames, where they might be seen by all. The provisions of Solon's laws are less important than the constitutional program that he set up. Other political innovations lie to his credit, such as the establishment of the Council of Four Hundred and the experiments with a partial election of officers by lot, whereby he sought to invoke the aid of the gods in the decisions of civic administration and at the same time to guard against complete incompetence in office. Yet none of these specific measures is so important as the philosophy of social reform, of mingled courage and caution, that this remarkable man contributed to his sorely distressed city.

PEISISTRATUS

Many stories are told of the last years of Solon, of how he rejected scornfully the suggestion that he assume the tyranny, of the oaths he exacted from the citizens that they would obey his laws without change for ten years, and of the extended travels that he undertook, so that his new constitution might have an opportunity to function of itself and without insistent demands upon its author for change. But the tyranny that Solon refused was to pass to other hands, for, before his reforms could bear fruit in democracy, the city was destined to succumb to the absolutism against which he had striven. If that experience was inevitable, it was at least well that Athens should be ruled by a tyrant so remarkable as Peisistratus.

The Political Emergence of Peisistratus. The future tyrant of Athens had the good fortune to be born at the right time. The genius of Peisistratus found in the Athens of the sixth century precisely the combination of hope and aspiration and undeveloped potentialities to give scope to his energy and vision.

Through the youth and young manhood of Peisistratus, Solon had been busied with his social reforms. The Seisachtheia, bringing relief to the poor, had borne hard on such men of substance as the father of Peisistratus. The normal channels of ambition had been closed to the youth, and presently, seeing the opportunity open to a man of energy, he began to maneuver actively toward the tyranny. The population of Attica fell naturally into three groups, determined by the location of their homes. These were the Men of the Hills, the Men of the Plains, and the Men of the Sea. Factional strife was sharp, and Peisistratus, associating himself with the radical Hillsmen, whose condition had not been alleviated by Solon's reforms, laid his plans for conquest. Solon was old and tired, and ready to lay down the burden. As he left the city for his travels, he warned the Athenians against Peisistratus, and, when the followers of the latter called Solon mad, he replied in an elegiac couplet: "A little time will make clear my madness to the people; yea, it will be clear when truth enters our midst."

In 560 B.C., Peisistratus found his opportunity, and established himself as tyrant, with a bodyguard and all the trappings of the absolute ruler. From 560 B.C. to 528 B.C., he ruled in Athens, with the exception of two considerable periods of exile, from each of which he returned in triumph. The political and administrative capacity of Peisistratus emerges with an examination of his ceaseless activity, whether during his periods of rule or during the years that he spent away from the city.

The Story of Phye. The circumstances surrounding the first restoration of Peisistratus from exile are particularly interesting in the light they shed on the credulity of the Athenian citizens in the sixth century. The supporters of Peisistratus found a woman, named Phye, who was of great beauty and commanding stature, for she stood not less than six feet in height. They clothed Phye in the gleaming armor of Athena, with all the accoutrements of the goddess about her, and they placed her, thus arrayed, in a chariot beside Peisistratus. A procession formed about the chariot, then moved on to the city, preceded by heralds, who proclaimed that Athena was restoring Peisistratus to power, and called upon the people to receive him.

The device was completely successful, and, without striking a blow, Peisistratus found himself again tyrant of the city. Herodotus, in recounting the tale, which he considers the silliest deception of history, waxes indignant at the amazing simplicity of the reputedly wise Athenians. Yet the credulity is far from incomprehensible. Athena, the patron deity, was very real in the eyes of the Athenians, and the sudden spectacle of the physical manifestation of the goddess accorded so well with all the tales of the heroic past from Homer that no murmur of doubt was heard. Herodotus, writing with the sophistication of a later generation, has himself failed to understand the mind of the sixth century.

Courtesy of the Museum of Fine Arts, Boston

FIGURE 33. ATTIC BLACK-FIGURED HYDRIA, OR WATER JAR. Period of Peisistratus. The central design shows a procession of four women carrying water.

The Extension of Peisistratus' Influence. Peisistratus had a capacity for extending his friendship and influence beyond the borders of his community that was rare among the rulers of any ancient city-state. Not only did his contacts reach to Argos,

[134]

where he married the widowed Timonassa, but the ceaseless cultivation of strategic friendships may be observed even during his second period of exile, when he spent some ten busy years on the island of Eubœa and traveling widely through the Greek world. His mind was constantly occupied with his return, and he knew that to that end assistance would one day be necessary. Thus, he extended his aid in various ways to different cities and different men. Thebes profited from his generosity, and Lygdamis of Naxos was assisted by Peisistratus in establishing himself as tyrant of his city. When the time for Peisistratus' restoration came, the friends who had been cultivated in the days of exile either aided him in person or made large contributions with which to hire mercenary soldiers, and Peisistratus, landing at Marathon, entered Athens again, to remain in power until his death.

The zeal and energy with which Peisistratus cultivated foreign friendships did more than advance his personal interest. They promoted through him the power and prestige of the city over which he ruled. Athens was consolidating her position of preeminence among the Greek states in many ways and Peisistratus was unconsciously building better than he knew the foundations for the brilliance of the city under the democracy that was to follow after the Persian Wars.

The Policy of Peisistratus. When Peisistratus first became ruler of Athens, he devoted himself vigorously to the economic advancement of the state. He had available the resources of the silver mines at Laurium at the tip of the Attic peninsula, and seemingly at this time they began to yield larger returns. The Laurium mines throughout antiquity were the chief source of supply for the coinage of Athens, and on more than one occasion they were to turn the strategic balance for or against the city in war.

Peisistratus had watched with intelligent interest the effect of changes that Solon had made in the monetary standard of the city, and he was also clever enough to perceive that, to be a truly successful medium of exchange, not only must a coin conform

[135]

to uniform weight, as Solon had required, but it must also bear the symbol of the state that guaranteed its value. It was in all probability during the reign of Peisistratus that the familiar and widely circulated series of coins was issued, bearing the head of Athena on the obverse, and on the reverse her own wise bird, the little gray owl, and her olive branch, symbols of the city-state of Athens. Everywhere in the ancient Mediterranean area these coins came to be recognized and accepted in trade. Sound trade flourishes only on the basis of national integrity, and the good faith of Athens was proclaimed in the purity of standard of her beautiful silver coins, which she maintained through the vicissitudes of two centuries.

The Encouragement of Enterprise at Home. In agricultural and economic matters at home, the tyranny also contributed much to the prosperity of the peasant class. The cultivation of the olive and the grape was extended. A new water supply was provided for the city. Peisistratus and his sons beautified Athens, summoned poets to the court, and fostered the early manifestations of the drama. Temples to the gods were built and richly adorned through the patronage of the rulers. In the mind of Peisistratus, however, the encouragement of the arts was only a part of the larger plan, a great civic scheme, in the development of which he was as creative as any of the sculptors or architects or poets who surrounded him. Under the protection and to the glory of Athena, the goddess who dwelt on the Acropolis, he established a city that was well governed and that attracted by its advantages a large population from the neighboring countryside of Attica and also from other places in the Hellenic world. By bringing in men of enterprise from outside, Peisistratus gave great impetus to Athenian commerce, while, by promoting the cultivation of peculiarly Athenian products, he increased the wealth of the land.

Impartial Administration. Peisistratus stood for peace in a quarrelsome world. Although he made his city rich and powerful enough in his reign to attack and defeat any Greek state, he gave the goddess on the Acropolis no cause to mourn

[136]

for Athenians killed in war. His reign was so happy, so productive, that even the historians, whose judgment of Peisistratus is influenced by an understandable dislike for the principle of absolutism, are compelled to acknowledge that the people of Athens, who knew his rule by personal experience, in later, less happy days looked back with wistful longing on the fair and impartial government of the tyrant.

The Sons of Peisistratus. When Peisistratus died in 528 B.C., he was succeeded by his two sons, Hippias and Hipparchus, who as joint rulers carried on his foreign and domestic policy. Although they continued to make great material progress, they were men of far different caliber from their brilliant father. They fostered the arts as patrons, instead of giving to them the dynamic understanding that made the encouragement of Peisistratus a creative thing in itself. In 514 B.C., for reasons of a purely personal nature unconnected with politics, two men, Harmodius and Aristogeiton, attempted to assassinate the tyrants during the Panathenaic festival. They succeeded in killing Hipparchus, but his elder brother Hippias escaped. The reaction of the citizens to the assassination was immediate. In a rage they seized Harmodius and killed him at once. Aristogeiton was caught, tortured, and later put to death. There is no evidence of widespread popular animosity at this moment toward the tyrants. However, from that time Hippias, who continued to rule alone, was never at ease. He constantly suspected the formation of plots, and in the repression of imagined sedition grew so harsh that four years later, in 510 B.C., the citizens rose in rebellion, and drove him, with all his kinsmen, into exile. Hippias took refuge at the Persian court, whence, twenty years later, he again entered into the story of Greek history when he traitorously guided a foreign invading army to the familiar beaches of his native land.

Constitutional Forms Retained. Peisistratus and his two sons, called as a family the Peisistratidæ, had ruled in Athens for half a century, from 560 B.C. to 510 B.C. Though it is true that, following the expulsion of Hippias in 510 B.C., the tyrannicides, Harmodius and Aristogeiton, were honored as the liberators of the state and the people came to hate the name of tyrant, the rule of the Peisistratidæ is by no means a black picture in Athenian history. In politics Peisistratus did not overthrow the democratic features of Solon's constitution, but simply allowed the people to play at democratic forms, taking care that his own kinsmen or friends should be elected to all responsible offices. Cynical as the practice sounds, it served a purpose in habituating the Athenians to the forms of democracy, which were to function completely in the fifth century. Within two decades Athens was to face the Persians at Marathon. The power and the concept of liberty that Peisistratus had built into the community were to stand her in good stead at that time.

THE CONSOLIDATION OF DEMOCRACY

The Political Reforms of Cleisthenes. After the exile of the tyrants in 510 B.C., internal dissension broke out in Athens between the democratic party and the oligarchic faction, which was led by Isagoras. The latter, with the aid of Sparta, gained the ascendancy for a time, but the people of the city were outraged at the idea of intervention by another state, and in less than two years the oligarchic faction of Isagoras had disappeared. The apprenticeship in democracy served under Peisistratus had turned men's minds toward self-rule, so that as early as 508 B.C. Cleisthenes, an Athenian noble, succeeded in setting up a democratic government. Cleisthenes recalled that the factional strife among the Hillsmen, the Plainsmen, and the Men of the Sea had paved the way for the tyranny of Peisistratus, and accordingly he took measures to modify the constitution with a view to the elimination of that danger. He set up ten new political tribes in such a way that each tribe should contain a certain proportion of each of the three hostile factions. The somewhat artificial establishment of ten tribes, named after mythological Athenian heroes at the suggestion of the

[138]

Delphic oracle, and designed to serve a specific political purpose, did much to break down the class distinctions that had stood in the way of harmony.

Ostracism. Another political device, the institution of ostracism, is credited to Cleisthenes, although it was not put into practice until the generation after the Battle of Marathon. Under certain conditions an Assembly was convoked, and the people voted for the exile of a man whose policies were con-

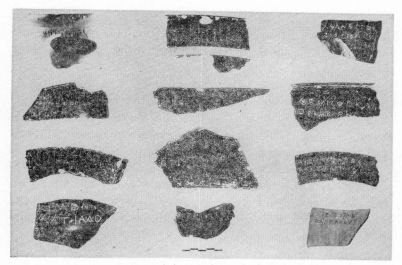

Courtesy of the American School of Classical Studies at Athens

FIGURE 34. OSTRAKA FROM THE ATHENIAN AGORA. Fifth century B.C. The names of various prominent Athenians may readily be deciphered.

sidered harmful to the state. The method of voting was to inscribe on an *ostrakon,* or potsherd, the name of the individual whom one wished to see banished. If as many as six thousand votes were recorded, the man receiving the highest number was obliged to leave Athens and remain away for ten years. In the excavations conducted by the American School of Classical Studies in the Agora, or Market-Place, of Athens before and after World War II, a considerable number of

[139]

ostraka have been found. Such names as Megacles, Xanthippos, Themistocles, Aristeides, Hippocrates, Cimon, and Pericles can be made out even by one with no knowledge of Greek. The form of the letters, mistakes in spelling, care or indifference in spacing, and various other details revealed by close examination indicate the variety of men who case these ballots. They provide a very real and graphic link with Athens of the fifth century.

The Power of the Council. The workings of democracy under Cleisthenes were not radically extended. He contrived to give increased power to the Council, which he now reconstructed as a body of Five Hundred, fifty members being chosen from each of the ten new tribes. Without removing any of the theoretical rights of the Assembly of the people, he succeeded in having its policy and decisions guided by the Council of Five Hundred. Yet the system was far from oligarchic, for the wide and uniform representation of all parts of Attica in the membership of the Council of Five Hundred gave a strong democratic flavor to the institution from the beginning. On the other hand, the great measure of administrative, deliberative, and judicial power that was vested in the Council necessarily restricted the initiative of the numerically larger Ecclesia, or assembly.

Functional Divisions on the Basis of Ten Tribes. To obviate the unwieldiness of so large a deliberative body, Cleisthenes divided the civil year into three hundred and sixty days, and groups of fifty members of the Council, who were called *Prytaneis* during their term of office, served in turn as an administrative committee of the state for a tenth of a year. The existence of the ten tribes afforded a basis for the military organization of the city, and the *Board of Ten Strategoi,* or generals, which played so important a part in the subsequent history of Athens, was elected, one from each tribe, to lead the military forces. In later Athenian history, one will read of a large number of councils and assemblies, designated as the "Council of Five Hundred," or "Five Thousand," or some

[140]

such similar expression. They were constituted in multiples of ten and took their origin from the tribal divisions of Cleisthenes. Some of them were to assume great importance in the history of constitutional development, though others were of comparatively slight significance.

CHAPTER VIII

SCULPTURE IN THE ARCHAIC AGE

The Decline of Art in the Post-Mycenæan Period. During the Mycenæan Period in Greece, artistic endeavor, apart from the architectural masterpieces, manifested itself in frescoes and vase painting, or in the creation of smaller objects such as engraved gems or ivory figurines, as well as in goldsmithing and silversmithing. Only moderate success had been achieved in sculpture, whether in stone or in bronze. The carved lions over the great gateway at Mycenæ will come to mind as one example.

For some centuries after the decline of the Mycenæan civilization the creative urge lay dormant in Greece, and the picture that can be reconstructed during these centuries shows a society that was content, so far as its art went, to mould ordinary vases for utilitarian purposes, or to fashion the simplest sculptured figures.

The Awakening of Genius. The political and constitutional development through the formative years of the archaic age on the other hand was accompanied by growth of the artistic spirit, especially as it is revealed in the work of the sculptors. The same spirit that prompted the Greeks to contend with their physical environment through migration or colonization or to cope with the problems of government was to find another outlet in a dawning awareness of the potential beauty of craftsmanship. Moreover, the eagerness with which the Greeks of the eighth and seventh centuries before Christ turned to creative endeavor was not confined to sculpture alone, nor yet

[142]

to the manual arts, for literature was sharing the same rebirth. Everywhere in Greece men began to experiment in architecture, sculpture, vase painting, die-cutting, literary techniques, and the science of government. When Cylon was attempting to set up a tyranny in Athens in 632 B.C., when Dracon was codifying the laws in 621 B.C., and when Solon was archon in 594 B.C., artists were trying with equal intensity to transfer to marble or bronze the complex anatomy of the kneecap or the natural folds of falling drapery. About all these efforts there was the compelling enthusiasm of men who were embarking on untrodden paths. The lawgiver ignored the fact that King Minos of Crete had undoubtedly confronted similar problems, and the artist knew little of the labors of his Minoan predecessors. Consequently, in spite of the demonstrable indebtedness of the Greeks to their neighbors for many of their ideas, it was essentially a new art that was arising, indigenous to the soil, and discovering for itself the necessary techniques. To assign a date to the beginning of Greek sculpture is difficult, for there was no age when the Greeks were not using their hands in art, but from the middle of the seventh century active and continuous work is known; and, since Greek art falls naturally into the divisions of Greek history, the end of the archaic period of sculpture may be set at the close of the Persian Wars in 480 B.C. The Greeks in the course of time tried their hands on every variety of sculptural art, but it is characteristic of early Greek craftsmanship that they should work almost exclusively with a single theme at a given time. For this reason, certain characteristic types were developed in the archaic age, and they persisted long enough to impart an unmistakable quality to the art of the period.

The Law of Frontality. Among the many art forms that emerged in early Greece, certain techniques met with favor and were widely adopted. One of these, the law of frontality, was observed with scrupulous care at the outset, and even as late as the beginning of the fifth century traces of the style can still be seen. The law of frontality refers to the balanced

[143]

symmetrical pose of archaic statues as viewed from the front. A standing figure is carved with the weight equally distributed on the two feet, though usually with the left foot slightly advanced; the arms rest by the side; the head faces directly forward.

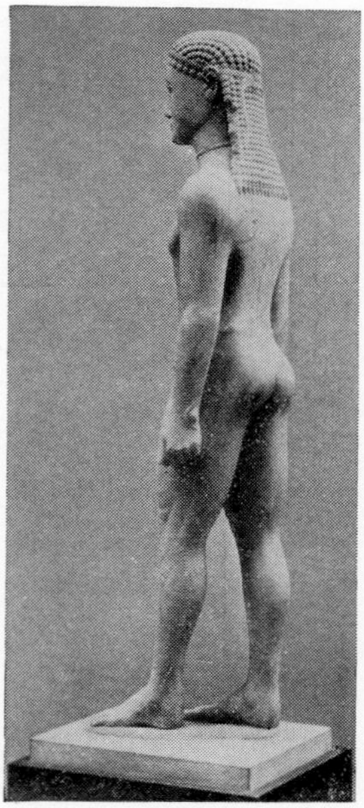

Courtesy of the Metropolitan Museum of Art

FIGURE 35. MARBLE KOUROS, OR YOUTH. Late seventh century B.C. This archaic statue illustrates the schematized hair design and the advanced left foot characteristic of such figures.

The Archaic Smile. Another attribute of early sculpture is the archaic smile. In order to lend expression to the face, the corners of the lips are drawn up, with the result that to modern and untrained observers the statues sometimes seem to take on an appearance of vapid cheerfulness. Moreover, the technique of rendering perspective had not been fully mastered, and the archaic eye, fashioned in full front, is not modified when other positions of the head are portrayed. The problem of representing the soft waves of hair was frequently met by carving a wig-like arrangement of rows of lozenges as in Figure 35. The archaic countenance, however, in general reflects the strength and vigor inherent in archaic art, and there is a vernal freshness about the sincere endeavors of the earliest sculptors that makes their work an unending delight to the beholder.

Types of Archaic Statues. Out of the great number of early archaic statues three distinct types emerged. They were (1) the standing undraped male figure, (2) the standing draped female figure, (3) the seated figure, male or female, usually draped.

The Standing Undraped Male Figure. The first type, the

[144]

standing undraped male figure, which is possibly the most characteristic of all early forms of Greek art, is represented by a considerable number of statues, which have been variously identified as the god Apollo or as young athletes. An excellent example of this type of archaic sculpture may be studied in the *kouros,* or youth, in the Metropolitan Museum of Art (Figure 35). In particular it illustrates the rigidity of the arms placed at the side of the body, the advanced position of the left foot, and the symmetrical schematized treatment of the hair. Other qualities of archaic art, notably the archaic smile, are illustrated in the better known "Apollo" of Tenea. The artist who created this statue had not yet attained any considerable technical freedom, for the point of the nose, the breast, and the abdomen are all on the same plane, indicating

Photograph by Alinari

FIGURE 36. STATUE DEDICATED BY NICANDRA AT DELOS. Late seventh century B.C. National Museum, Athens.

[145]

FIGURE 37. HERA OF SAMOS. Sixth century B.C. Louvre, Paris. The advance in technique over the preceding figure may be observed.

[146]

that the sculptor has simply cut back from the face of the rectangular block with which he started. On the other hand, the effort to show the kneecap presumes a considerable amount of careful study of anatomy among the artists of the school that worked with figures of athletes. The attention to anatomical detail indicates the preoccupation of the early sculptors with athletic forms, and the creation of this type may well be related to the games at the recurring festivals of Greece. The "Apollo" of Tenea should be dated about the middle of the sixth century before Christ, or perhaps a trifle earlier.

The Standing Draped Female Figure. The second type, the standing draped female figure, is illustrated by two well-known statues, the dedication of a certain Nicandra at Delos (Figure 36) and the Hera of Samos (Figure 37), which are identified by accompanying inscriptions. The features of the first statue are too badly marred for any expression to be distinguished, and the second statue is headless. It is

FIGURE 38. STATUE OF CHARES, LORD OF TEICHIUSSA. Sixth century B.C. This massive statue is characteristic of seated archaic figures.

[147]

clear that the two statues, both of which adhere to the law of frontality, belong to an early date in the development of art, the Nicandra dedication perhaps to a time prior to 600 B.C. The treatment of the drapery on the female figure affords an opportunity to follow in one field the developing technique of the artist from the earliest times until mastery was attained. In the Nicandra dedication the drapery lies heavily on the statue, and only in the most primitive manner has the artist been able to indicate the form of the body beneath; he probably depended on paint to give a hint of the texture of the garment. The Hera of Samos reveals the progress which even a few years might accomplish, for this goddess is represented as wearing more than a single garment, while one arm was originally bent at the elbow, indicating some advance in the technique of drapery modeling and in perspective. Both statues show the characteristically large feet of archaic sculpture.

The Seated Draped Figure. The third type, the seated draped figure, is best illustrated by a group of statues that in ancient times stood along the Sacred Way between Miletus and Branchidæ in Asia Minor, although the type was known in many localities of Greece. One of the most distinctive statues of the group (Figure 38) bears an inscription on the side of the chair which reads: "I am Chares, Lord of Teichiussa." In the seated statues, the law of frontality continues to be observed, and there is about them a massive immobility, which had to be overcome before the artists could hope to introduce grace or action. In some of the later seated figures of the archaic period, the progress of the artist in the modeling of the texture of the drapery and in imparting life to the limbs may be seen to have kept pace fully with the application of similar techniques to the standing figures.

At all times the Greek artists felt free to adorn their statues or to delineate details of carving by the use of paint. Time has largely obliterated this evidence and altered the appearance of the statues that are now available for study.

[148]

Modifications and Variations from the Common Types. It must not be supposed that every piece of art from the archaic period can be so neatly classified. Nevertheless, it will prove useful to keep in mind the three principal types, for a reclining figure is but a standing figure laid on its back or side, and a crouching figure is only an adaptation of a seated figure. Moreover, the building of temples was going on simultaneously in every part of Greece, with a consequent demand for sculptural decoration, and the necessity of adapting the pose of sculptured figures to fit the diminishing angles of the temple pediments, or gables, compelled the artists to abandon their early rigid forms and to begin to carve stooping or recumbent bodies. But long after the sculptors had learned to show action in their works, the original archaic principles continued to make their influence felt. A slight modification of the standing male figure will be found in the statue of the Calf-Bearer, dedicated by Rhombos (Figure 39). This is the oldest marble statue, as opposed to statues in softer stone, that has been found on the Acropolis of Athens. The arms of the man are bent up to grasp the feet of the bull calf, and he is wearing a light garment, through which the form of the body can be traced, a technique that was to be greatly developed in the fifth century. On the whole, despite some difficulties of transition from the calf's body to its head, the animal is better portrayed than is the human figure. Although greater freedom of movement is shown in the execution of this statue than of those previously discussed, the artist is still cutting back from the surface as he was with the "Apollo" of Tenea, for the head of the calf, and that of the man, and the man's forearm are all on an identical plane. This statue may be dated about 575 B.C.

The Acropolis Maidens. One of the most remarkable discoveries on the Acropolis was a series of standing draped female figures, many of which were found together in a pit, where they had been buried when the Athenians cleared the debris on their citadel following the Persian invasion in 480 B.C. The figures, which are usually designated as the Acropolis

[149]

FIGURE 39. THE CALF-BEARER. Sixth century B.C. Acropolis Museum, Athens. The problems of perspective, diaphanous drapery, technique of carving hair, the archaic smile, and the provision for the insertion of the iris in the eyes in a different material are well illustrated.

Maidens, conform to the technique of other archaic statues of this style. The law of frontality is observed, and most of them show the characteristic archaic smile, although some have been modeled with a quiet composure of countenance that argues a more advanced technique. A distinctive feature of the Acropolis Maidens is the elaborate detail of the drapery and the delicacy of execution that has been lavished on the modeling of the folded garments, as well as the suggestion of the texture and coloring of cloth that has been effected by both the carving and the application of paint, of which traces remain. To some critics the Acropolis Maidens have seemed over-elaborate. Assuredly they differ from the vigorous and almost harsh outlines of the contemporaneous athletic statues.

One of the Maidens has been assigned to an artist named Antenor on the evidence of an inscribed statue base. Antenor is still better known for a sculptural group of the tyrannicides, Harmodius and Aristogeiton, who slew the tyrant Hipparchus in 514 B.C. The association

Photograph by Alinari

FIGURE 40. ACROPOLIS MAIDEN. Sixth century B.C. Acropolis Museum, Athens. The right arm was made separately and later inserted. Note the evidence of elaborate painting on the folds of the drapery.

[151]

of Antenor with these dissimilar statues presents an interesting problem, which will be discussed under the heading of transitional sculpture in the fifth century (see Figure 82).

Decorative Sculpture. All the statues thus far mentioned have been independent pieces, made without immediate regard

Photograph by Alinari

FIGURE 41. THE GORGON MEDUSA SLAIN BY PERSEUS. Archaic metope from Selinus, 627 B.C. to 409 B.C. Palermo. The artist has not yet solved the problem of portraying the human form partly in profile and partly in full front.

[152]

to the place of their ultimate display. Such sculpture is called *substantive,* as opposed to *decorative* sculpture, which is designed as an ornament for some particular place, such as the pediment of a temple. One series of decorative pieces of particular interest consists of pedimental sculptures from the Acropolis, made of poros stone, a soft and friable local stone, and richly painted. They were intended for the decoration of certain Athenian temples, which were destroyed at the time that the Persians sacked the city in 480 B.C., just prior to the Battle of Salamis. When the Athenians returned to the city, after the Persians had left, they leveled off and buried all the broken fragments on the Acropolis, with the result that for archæological reconstruction and for æsthetic criticism there is available a very distinct and valuable dividing date. Anything found beneath the surface on the Acropolis must date prior to 480 B.C., and the standing temples and statue bases just as assuredly belong to a later date. It is partly for this reason that the date of the last Persian expedition is taken as the end of the archaic period and the beginning of the fifth century. The further significance of the year 480 B.C., which recurs constantly in the story of Greek civilization, will become clear through the discussion of the Persian Wars in a later chapter.

The pedimental sculptures of poros stone are remarkably similar to one another in theme and in composition. The arrangement has been adapted to the triangular space of the pediment, and the subject matter, drawn from mythology, inclines to be more grotesque than does later Greek art. The deeds of Heracles play a considerable part. In one pediment Heracles is shown slaying the many-headed Hydra; in another he is wrestling with the Triton. In these pediments the curling folds of the Hydra and the tail of the Triton respectively lend themselves to the diminishing space of a pediment. The three-headed Typhon is similar in composition, and on it there is evidence of the insertion of metal wings.

The Temple Sculptures of the Western Colonies. It will be recalled that during the period of active colonization many

Greek communities were established in southern Italy and Sicily. In these cities, too, artistic experimentation was actively pursued, producing such examples as the pedimental sculptures on the temple at Corcyra and the series of metopes from the temples of Selinus in Sicily. The metopes, or square sculptured plaques, were made in soft stone, and the subjects for portrayal were chosen from mythological stories. A characteristic group is that which shows Athena watching Perseus cut off the head of the Gorgon (Figure 41), while the winged horse, Pegasus, springs to life from the drops of blood. These metopes illustrate all the difficulties with which the artists in Greece proper contended, and one may observe especially their inability at this time to render in proper perspective a body that should be shown partly in profile and partly in full front. The early Greek instinct to fill all the available space is carefully followed in the archaic metopes and pediments, as it is also in other arts, such as vase painting.

Materials and Techniques. The Greeks in all centers of activity, whether in Athens, the islands, or the colonies, worked in a wide variety of materials to create their sculptural figures, and tools and techniques were quickly adapted to their needs. Wood was doubtless freely employed in early times, but it presently gave place to poros stone, or limestone, of which many of the earliest known pieces are made. This in turn yielded to marble as the artists were able to work in the harder and more beautiful stuff. The marble of Paros and Pentelicus was especially favored, though the coarser-grained stone from Naxos, as well as that from Mount Hymettus and from many local quarries, was also used. Statues were by no means invariably carved in a single piece, but when parts were made separately they were fitted together with great skill.

In later times, bronze came to be even more favored than marble as material for sculpture, but unfortunately as bronze assumed importance for more utilitarian purposes, many bronze statues were melted down because of the intrinsic value of the metal. Bronze casting, which was probably borrowed from

[154]

Egypt, despite the persistent legend of its discovery by two Samians, Rhœcus and Theodorus, demanded considerable technical ability. Statuettes were cast solid, but larger statues were cast in separate pieces that were later riveted together.

The *cire perdue,* or "lost-wax" process, which is still employed in bronze casting, was widely used also in antiquity. The technique may be briefly described thus: To a fireproof core the sculptor added a layer of wax of the thickness which the bronze was ultimately to take, and on the surface of the wax the details were carefully delineated. Next a clay coating was applied to the exterior and the whole was fired, both to harden the clay and to melt out the wax. Molten bronze was then poured into the thin, modeled area formerly occupied by the wax.

In the fifth century some of the more precious statues were of *chryselephantine* work, which signifies the incrustation of wooden or metal frames with gold and ivory plates. Terracotta figures were also made, and some of them, especially the statuettes of the fifth and fourth centuries, have a grace all their own. In estimating the appearance of Greek sculpture, it must be borne in mind that marble and terra-cotta statues were regularly painted in greater or less degree, and in such statues as the Acropolis Maidens the faint traces of color that still remain afford some idea of the vivid and beautiful effect that was attained. Modern convention has habituated art lovers to the gleaming whiteness of marble statuary, but such a statue would doubtless have presented a strange and startling appearance to the great artists of antiquity who were accustomed to the use of color on marble.

Genuine Works and Roman Copies. A distinct advantage that rests with the study of the works of archaic sculpture is the fact that, with all the imperfections of a new art, they are nevertheless the original product of their age. Conversely, in the study of much of the best work of the fifth and fourth centuries, we are dependent on copies that were executed with varying degrees of skill by artists of the first century before

Christ and later to supply the demands of the Roman market.

A Summary of the Qualities of Archaic Art. Wide variations of technique and skill must be expected in the different schools of sculpture in the archaic age, for the separate existence led by the city-states discouraged the ready interchange of ideas and the consequent leveling of styles. Nevertheless, some qualities were developed in common and certain characteristics of art in the archaic period may be summarized. In the first place, the motivation of art in that age was largely religious. The temples themselves, as a form of art, were regarded as the dwelling places of the gods, while in each ancient temple an image of a god had to be placed. The early pieces of substantive sculpture, for example, the "Apollo" of Tenea, the Nicandra dedication from Delos, the Hera of Samos, the seated figures from Branchidæ, the Calf-Bearer, and the poros pediments, were almost without exception either images of gods or dedications to some god. Thus, in addition to the unconscious influence of a religious association with art, there was the very practical consideration that religion assured the artists a continuing market for their products and hence fostered artistic enterprise.

In the second place, the attitude of a Greek toward religion, or art, or any other interest of life made it inevitable that his efforts should be directed toward the portrayal of human forms. Anthropomorphism, or the creation of gods in the form of man, was a primary concept of Greek religion, and it necessarily influenced art, which was fostered by religion.

In the third place, the art of the archaic period was an art of experiment. The artists were finding their way. They met with great difficulty in dealing with such a problem as the representation of the body in profile with the head turned toward the front, while on profile heads the eye continued for many years to be represented in full front. It was a time of specialization, when certain schools of artists chose to work in the athletic tradition of standing male figures, and others confined themselves to the standing draped female figure and

[156]

attained facility within their field. In some cases of transitional art, such as the pedimental sculptures of the temple of Aphæa at Ægina, which were made about 480 B.C., the sculptors had occasion to combine these two techniques with distinctly less successful results in the field to which they were unaccustomed.

CHAPTER IX

THE POETRY OF A TRANSITIONAL SOCIETY

HESIOD AND THE DIDACTIC EPIC

Poetry and Society. The Homeric poems had been composed as stories of a patriarchal society in which the protagonists were demigods or princes, such as Achilles, Hector, and Odysseus, consorting with both men and gods on the field of battle or in the council chamber. Only occasionally is a man of low degree or a peasant singled out for mention in the *Iliad* or the *Odyssey*. Thersites, the ugly and offensive common soldier, and Eumæus, the faithful swineherd, are examples. But when such a one is named, he appears as a necessary adjunct to the tale of one greater than himself. There is little comprehension of the cares and needs of the great body of the people. In the literature of the archaic age, on the other hand, all the problems of class oppression and economic stringency contribute to the stuff of poetry. The contests of tyranny, oligarchy, and democracy, the political uncertainty of newly founded colonies, and the individual struggle for a livelihood in an age of continual instability combined to produce an immediate personal quality in the literature of the eighth to sixth centuries, that is in marked contrast to the epic grandeur of Homer.

The Didactic Epic. The Homeric verse form continued to be used for a time, as might naturally be expected, but the epic that was now written was not a heroic tale of adventure; it was rather a homely teaching to the poor, and as such has earned the name of *didactic epic*. Hesiod, who wrote this type of

[158]

poetry, was a successor to Homer in form if not in content, composing, in the *Works and Days*, a poem of lowlier theme than the *Iliad* and the *Odyssey*. In the poems of Homer, the beauty and nobility of the episodes were inspiring to the readers or hearers, who were too far removed from possible emulation to be conscious of envy. Hesiod, on the contrary, was very closely in touch with the reality of life. The date of Hesiod is uncertain although it falls within the seventh century. He is later than Homer, but the trend of recent classical scholarship has been to place Homer in a period closer to the classical age, and there is recorded a statement of Herodotus that Homer and Hesiod competed for a prize at Chalcis, and that Hesiod was successful. The tradition, however, is more probably a reflection of a brief preference in antiquity for the useful didactic poetry of Hesiod.

In the *Works and Days* Hesiod tells something of his own biography. His father had come from Cyme in Asia Minor to the little town of Ascra at the foot of Mount Helicon in Bœotia. Poverty cursed the family in the old home and the new, and in the bitterness of discontent Hesiod describes Ascra as a hateful place, too cold in winter, too hot in summer, never a home to delight the inhabitant. There the young Hesiod of necessity followed the pursuits of the peasant, but with poetic fancy he chose to believe that the Heliconian Muses one day granted him the fair gift of song, as he tended his lambs below sacred Helicon.

The "Works and Days." As Hesiod eked out the barest and meanest of livings from the infertile land, he knew also, or fancied that he knew, injustice; for the inspiration of his chief poem, the *Works and Days,* is the treachery of his brother Perses, who had deprived him of his fair inheritance. The poem is addressed to this brother, whom he repeatedly attacks as dishonest and worthless. It is divided into four topics, the "Exhortations," which lend a strong didactic tone to it, the "Precepts on Agriculture and Navigation," the "General Precepts," and the "Calendar of Days." The last section is devoted to the common life of the peasant, with admonitions to plant on certain days, to begin weaving on others, to avoid specific tasks at stated times, and so on through a series of superstitions and taboos such as exist in all countries but have in modern society been confined largely to Friday and the thirteenth of the month.

The Precept. Within the poem are included stories and forms that have become a part of the general stock-in-trade of literature. The *precept,* cast in a metrical couplet, has proved at all times an effective way of urging a homely truth or of launching propaganda. Although Hesiod was absorbed in economic misfortune rather than intent upon æsthetic or ethical ends, his development of the technique of gnomic advice in the form of the precept entitles him to a place in literary history. Within the fabric of his poetry such sententious observations as these are found:

> No better lot has providence assign'd
> Than a fair woman with a virtuous mind:
> Nor can a worse befall, than when thy fate
> Allots a worthless, feast-contriving mate;
> She with no torch of mere material flame
> Shall burn to tinder thy care-wasted frame;
> Shall send a fire thy vigorous bones within,
> And age unripe in bloom of years begin.
>
> TRANSLATED BY SIR CHARLES ABRAHAM ELTON

> Lo! the best treasure is a frugal tongue;
> The lips of moderate speech with grace are hung.
>
> TRANSLATED BY SIR CHARLES ABRAHAM ELTON

Pandora's Box. In the *Works and Days* is told the story of Pandora's Box, with its freight of human misery. Pandora had been fashioned by the god Hephæstus as a fair and lovely creature in maiden's form, and with a countenance as beautiful as the immortal goddesses. Athena taught her the goodly handicrafts, while golden Aphrodite poured grace upon her.

And all manner of gifts were given by the gods to Pandora, whose name means "the all-gifted one." She carried a large box, and when she came upon mankind, she opened it, and from it escaped all the plagues and toils and evils that torment the human soul. Only Hope remained locked within, for Hope flies more slowly than her sisters, and the lid was restored before she could escape.

The Conviction of Decadence. The pessimistic conviction that man has sunk to his lowest moral level in the age in which one is living begins with Hesiod in his invention of the Five Ages of Mankind. During the Golden Age, man was exalted and lived at ease; during the Silver Age, sin entered the world and the decline of man began; during the Bronze Age, men became violent, and in death were consigned to Hades. In the Age of Heroes, an interlude not named for a metal, the warriors fought before Thebes and Troy, and in death were translated to the Isles of the Blest, while in the Age of Iron, that in which Hesiod to his sorrow is himself living, man has reached the lowest depths of wickedness and sin. Though it seems to be inherent in human nature to magnify the manifold evils of the present, yet it must be conceded that Hesiod was living close enough to the fall of Mycenæan society, with evidence everywhere to be seen of decline from a higher level, to speak from a definite knowledge of happier and more glorious days in the past.

Other Poems of Hesiod. In addition to the *Works and Days,* Hesiod wrote a genealogy of the gods, called the *Theogony,* and a *Catalogue of Women,* and there is also assigned to him, though mistakenly, an epic entitled the *Shield of Heracles.* The incorrect attribution of this and other poems to Hesiod is indicative of the existence in Bœotia of a whole school of poetry, which seemingly included a considerable number of writers whose names have perished. In style Hesiod not infrequently attains excellence, but his mind is pedestrian and incapable of sustained poetry of a high quality. As a reflection of his times his poems exhibit a bitter resentment of the severity of the peasant's life, but it is a plaint of hopelessness, not a challenge to progress. The germs of social poetry were to mature in the more positive and insistent cries of the iambic poets.

LYRIC, ELEGIAC, AND IAMBIC POETRY

Varieties of poetry. During the archaic period, another type of poetry arose, which in its different forms is described as elegiac, iambic, melic, lyric, or choral poetry, as well as by a variety of other names, depending on the meter and form of composition. Sometimes a poet wrote in more than one style. Useful though these divisions are for a close study of the short poems that flourished in the seventh and sixth centuries, and even continued into the classical period, they may for present purposes be largely disregarded in favor of the general term *lyric*.

The Inspiration of the Poetry of the Archaic Age. In the poems of those who composed in lyric or other strains, there is reflected a type of society quite different from the exalted existence of the kings and heroes of Homer, and also from the dreary peasant life of Hesiod, which, though unhappy, was unlikely to change. The lyric poets were a product of the age of colonization, when tyrannies were being set up and cast down, when economic pressure, political persecution, and the love of adventure were driving men to establish new cities and to plot or fight for control of the government in them. From such a life of unrest there arose an intensely personal poetry. It was the natural literary expression of a frontier and pioneering people. The poets were not interested in the tales of ancient kings, but in the acts of oppression of a definite tyrant, in the scarcity of grain in the village, in the love of a particular maiden, or in the task of earning a precarious livelihood for themselves and their families.

Classification. It is difficult to find a logical classification for these poets. The first attempt to do so was made during the Hellenistic Age, which followed the death of Alexander the

Great in 323 B.C., when scholars at the Library in Alexandria compiled a Canon of Nine Lyric Poets, consisting of Alcman, Alcæus, Sappho, Stesichorus, Ibycus, Anacreon, Simonides of Ceos, Bacchylides, and Pindar. Another group, Archilochus, Semonides of Amorgos, and Hipponax, were treated as iambic poets, while Callinus, Tyrtæus, and Mimnermus were regarded as elegiac poets. The taste and judgment of the Alexandrian scholars were not infallible. It is hard to understand why, except for symmetry, certain names were included in the Canon at all, and why others, such as Theognis and the half-legendary Arion, received no attention. Only a few can now be considered, and the selection will be made from those whose personal careers and writings afford the greatest interest and most definitely illustrate the immediacy of life that is found in this age. They have been grouped according to the nature of their writings and their particular preoccupations, and without regard to any more technical basis of classification.

MARTIAL AND POLITICAL POETRY

Callinus. Some of the earliest poets of the archaic period used the elegiac couplet, a form in which hexameter and pentameter verses alternate, for military poetry. Callinus of Ephesus in Asia Minor, one of the first of this group, composed his martial poetry under the influence of definite historical incidents that fell within his lifetime. The neighboring city of Magnesia had been destroyed by the Cimmerians. Callinus, fearing a like disaster for Ephesus, composed a vigorous martial ode addressed to the Ephesians, chiding them for their apathy, and urging them to repel the invaders before it was too late.

> How long will ye slumber? When will ye take heart
> And fear the reproach of your comrades at hand?
> Fie! Comrades, to think ye have peace for your part,
> Whilst the sword and the arrow are wasting our land.

TRANSLATED BY HENRY NELSON COLERIDGE

Tyrtæus. Very similar in his use of the elegiac couplet for martial poetry is Tyrtæus of Athens and Sparta, who wrote from about 680 B.C. to 660 B.C. Tradition said that the Spartans, who were suffering defeat in their war with the Messenians, consulted the Delphic oracle and were told to seek a leader in Athens. The Athenians, not daring to refuse the demand of Apollo, nevertheless thought to mock and embarrass the Spartans by sending to them a lame schoolmaster, Tyrtæus, instead of the expected general. Tyrtæus composed martial poetry that was so effective in heartening the Spartans that they were successful in the conflict. After the war, Tyrtæus continued to live in Sparta and to cultivate as ardently as any native of the city the qualities of that military state. He wrote a later poem, the *Eunomia,* or *Politeia,* which is a eulogy of the Spartan constitution.

The Exhortation to Battle. A translation of the first few verses of his exhortation to the Spartans follows:

> How glorious fall the valiant, sword in hand,
> In front of battle for their native land!
> But oh! What ills await the wretch that yields,
> A recreant outcast from his country's fields!
> The mother whom he loves shall quit her home,
> An agèd father at his side shall roam;
> His little ones shall weeping with him go,
> And a young wife participate his woe;
> While scorned and scowled upon by every face,
> They pine for food, and beg from place to place.

> TRANSLATED BY THOMAS CAMPBELL

This passage prompts one observation on Greek life. The soldier is not told that death on behalf of one's country is in itself a goodly thing. Horace could say for a Roman public: *Dulce et decorum est pro patria mori,*—"It is a sweet and proper thing to die for one's native land," but a logical and dispassionate Greek, able to face death with courage and resignation if necessary, demanded an explanation of the alternatives. A Greek was too much in love with life to think death a "sweet and proper thing" at any time.

Contrast between Callinus and Tyrtæus. The contrast between the despair of Callinus and the confidence of Tyrtæus may be seen in their martial poems. The Greek cities of Asia Minor had grown soft and weak, so that they were subdued by Crœsus and Cyrus in the sixth century. At the time of Callinus, disaster was already impending, and he wrote as one who was pleading a forlorn cause. On the other hand, Tyrtæus was writing for the Spartans at the turning-point to victory, at a time when they were building up the powerful community that was to remain unconquerable for centuries.

A hint of the comparative brevity of the poems of this whole class of writers is given by the fact that, of the complete examples of the work of Tyrtæus that survive, one runs to thirty-two verses and the other to forty-four, and these are surpassed in length by few others—at least of the earliest poets.

Solon. The elegiac poet Solon is the same Athenian lawgiver whose place in history has already been described. It is possible to attach fairly definite dates to his career. He was archon in Athens in 594 B.C., and he probably lived to see the institution of tyranny under Peisistratus in 560 B.C. Before either of these dates, however, he had composed a poem of propaganda to rouse the Athenians to recover the island of Salamis, which they had abandoned in a way that seemed to Solon a disgrace to the honor of the city. Prose had not yet been developed as a literary form, and consequently Solon was obliged to convey his message in verse, thus using poetry as an instrument of politics. Representing himself as a herald from Salamis, he chanted his poem through the streets of Athens. "I have come as a herald from lovely Salamis, having fashioned my message as song, not argument." And presently, whipping up the sense of national honor, he continued:

I would rather be a citizen of Pholegandrus or Sicinus, changing my fatherland, and no longer be called Athenian; for straightway now will this report go among men: "This man is from Athens, one of the Salamis-yielders."

The attempt was successful, and that the aroused Athenians regained Salamis is a matter of historical record.

When Solon had established his economic and social legislation in Athens he failed to satisfy fully either the nobles or the common people. Nevertheless, he had striven to effect a workable solution and he proudly declared his purpose and his claim to achievement in a poem of which a significant portion is still extant:

> I gave the people freedom clear
> But neither flattery nor fear;
> I told the rich and noble race
> To crown their state with modest grace,
> And placed a shield in either's hand,
> Wherewith in safety both might stand..

> — TRANSLATED BY HENRY NELSON COLERIDGE

Versatility of Solon. The poetry of Solon ranged over a wide field, and not all of it was confined to political themes. The didactic idea, borrowed from Hesiod, colors his admonitions to the Athenians, and many of the extant fragments have about them a reflective ethical quality that would rank him among the philosophers. He composed a poem on the life of man, which, in his orderliness of mind, he divided into ten periods of exactly seven years each. This poetic theme has survived even into modern times, though the division of life has usually become the Seven Ages of Man.

The Seven Sages. Solon is also to be associated with the development of a school of poetry in which axiomatic advice on life was cast in pithy phrases. He was one of the Seven Sages of antiquity, to whom, with many variations in specific attribution, the early Greek maxims were credited. The simplest and most useful method of explaining the nature of this poetry will be to list the Seven Wise Men with an aphorism

[166]

commonly attributed to each: Periander, tyrant of Corinth, *Forethought in everything;* Pittacus, tyrant of Mytilene in Lesbos, *Know thine opportunity;* Bias, of Priene in Asia Minor, *Too many workers mar the work;* Thales, of Miletus, *To be surety brings ruin;* Cleobulus, tyrant of Lindus in Rhodes, *Moderation is the greatest good;* Chilon, of Sparta, *Know thyself;* Solon, of Athens, *Nothing in excess.* The last three mottoes were the basis of practical philosophy on which the thoughtful Greek at all times modeled his life. Some of the others will be recognized in the slightly different phraseology of modern proverbs.

Theognis. Theognis, of Megara, was the type of aristocrat who saw in the shifting of power from the nobles to the common people nothing but inevitable disaster. This estimate of class feeling can be deduced with the greater assurance since the body of poetry that has come down under the name of Theognis is apparently not the work of a single man but a collection of similar verses built around the genuine compositions of Theognis. The poems thus form valuable evidence for the reaction of the aristocrats in the face of the loss of their privileges. Theognis is selfish, monotonous, and personal in his work, much of which is dedicated to Cyrnus, a fellow aristocrat. The inclusion of the name of Cyrnus serves to identify certain verses as the genuine work of Theognis.

The opening lines of Theognis run thus:

Cyrnus, as I utter my words of wisdom, let this seal be set upon them, so that they may never be stolen, and that no one may exchange bad for good. Thus every man shall say: "These are the words of Theognis of Megara; renowned is he among all men."

PERSONAL AND LOVE POETRY

Mimnermus. The mood of individualism revealed in the poems of war and statecraft is even more evident in verses of love and emotion. Mimnermus, probably of Colophon, who was active about 630 B.C., was the first to use the elegiac couplet for mournful and amatory themes, which are now generally associated with that meter. Little is known about his life, although much can be deduced about his temperament and his moods from the extant fragments of his verse. He loved a flute-girl, called Nanno, to whom he addressed many of his plaintive poems. He appears as a seeker after pleasure whose search is never satisfied. It is suggested that either unrequited love or sadness over the declining fortunes of his own and neighboring cities of Asia Minor was responsible for the settled mood of melancholy that characterizes his work.

Mimnermus sang of the transitory nature of all pleasure that earth could offer, and his besetting horror was the inevitable approach of old age, which would rob him of the capacity for physical enjoyment. "What is life, what pleasure remains, deprived of golden Aphrodite? May I die when these joys no longer delight me." In similar vein is his poem contrasting the joys of youth with the melancholy of age.

> Ah! fair and lovely bloom the flowers of youth;
> On men and maids they beautifully smile:
> But soon comes doleful eld, who, void of ruth,
> Indifferently afflicts the fair and vile;
> Then cares wear out the heart: old eyes forlorn
> Scarce seek the very sunshine to behold—
> Unloved by youths, of every word the scorn—
> So hard a lot God lays upon the old.

TRANSLATED BY JOHN ADDINGTON SYMONDS

Mimnermus likewise originated the declaration of a desire for death at the age of sixty, because by that time one's capacity for sensual pleasure would have come to an end.

> Oh that my days, free from disease or woe,
> On placid waters down life's stream may flow;
> And when their course shall reach its sixtieth year,
> Death's friendly sleep may close my sojourn here!

TRANSLATED BY WILLIAM MURE

Solon wrote a reply in poetry on this subject, proposing, in happier vein, that one might choose to live to eighty years rather than to sixty:

> Bear with me, gentle Colophonian friend,
> If I one sentence of thy wish would mend:
> The life of man, on terms like these begun,
> Its prosperous course full eighty years may run.
>
> TRANSLATED BY WILLIAM MURE

The beginning of poetic correspondence rather than the importance of the communication is to be noted.

The style of Mimnermus is graceful and harmonious, and for that reason he was highly regarded in antiquity, but the querulous and sensual personality of the man detracts from the admitted beauty of phrase and meter that is to be found in the verses that survive.

Phocylides and Demodocus. Literary correspondence, introduced by Mimnermus and Solon, continued and in the sixth century was developed into the sarcastic or bitter lampoon by Phocylides of Miletus and Demodocus of Leros, who identified their couplets by the inclusion of their own names in the meter of the lines. Thus Phocylides begins:

This too from Phocylides, the Lerians are scoundrels; it is not that this Lerian is a scoundrel, and that Lerian not; they are all scoundrels, except Procles, and after all Procles is a Lerian. . . .

to which Demodocus replies:

This from Demodocus, the Milesians are not fools, but they do everything that fools do.

Alcæus and his Political Associations. Alcæus and Sappho, both of Lesbos, contemporary writers of the late seventh and early sixth centuries, are the best known of the lyric group. The works of Alcæus might be classified under political poetry almost as appropriately as under personal and love poetry, for he had much to say of the public characters and institutions of his day. Alcæus passed through the vicissitudes incident to factional strife in his native city, Mytilene of Lesbos, and the heat of his political passion has found expression in some of his poems. The tyrant Pittacus, who has already been identified as one of the Seven Sages, Alcæus once described with vituperative eloquence as "low-born, bloated, splay-footed slouch, swaggerer, reveler of the night." His fury is, incidentally, quite unfair, so far as history tells the story, for Pittacus appears to have ruled with wisdom and restraint. The works of Alcæus consist largely of political hymns, love poems, and convivial songs. A number of striking military epigrams are to be credited to his inventive genius: "The device of a soldier's shield wounds no one" and "The best wall of a city is the courage of her men." Alcæus developed the Alcaic strophe, known to all readers of Horace, who adapted it to the Latin language.

The Ship of State. It will suffice to translate part of one political ode of Alcæus, which is not necessarily his most important, but which is of interest because in it he originates the metaphor of the ship of state, that has served poets and politicians of all nations so well and so long.

I know not the direction of the winds; now from this side a wave rolls upon us, now from that, and we in the midst are borne along with the black ship, toiling heavily in the great tempest.

Aside from the interest of the ingenious metaphor, the poem illustrates again the close contact with life that is characteristic of most of the lyric poets. Alcæus lived in a sea-faring town; he was embroiled in political turmoil; and appropriately he has described the distress of the state in terms of a ship tossed in a storm at sea.

Sappho, her Fame in Antiquity. Sappho is the earliest poetess whose work is preserved, and antiquity united to extol her genius. When Solon first heard one of her poems, he is said to have prayed that he might be granted life at least until he had committed it to memory. And much later Plato referred to her as the tenth Muse. Aristotle ranked her equal to Homer and Archilochus. In fact, as Homer was "the poet," so Sappho was in ancient Greece "the poetess."

The Life of Sappho. It is fairly easy to reconstruct a biographical outline of Sappho's life. Her residence in Mytilene and her association with Pittacus, Alcæus, and Solon establish the date of her activity as the early sixth century. In her poems she seems to allude to various members of her family, sometimes in terms of ardent affection, sometimes, as in the apparently historical remonstrance with her brother Charaxus, in sharp reproof. Sappho, living in the free social and intellectual atmosphere of Asia Minor, founded a school of music among the girls of Lesbos, and the poems which she addressed to them and they to her are remarkable for a greater intensity of passion than any of the earlier lyric poets had attained.

The Poems of Sappho. Possibly the finest poem of Sappho is the ode to golden-throned Aphrodite.

> Glittering-throned, undying Aphrodite,
> Wile-weaving daughter of high Zeus, I pray thee,
> Tame not my soul with heavy woe, dread mistress,
>   Nay, nor with anguish!
>
> Come to me now, too, and from tyrannous sorrow
> Free me, and all things that my soul desires to
> Have done, do for me, queen, and let thyself, too,
>   Be my great ally!
>
> TRANSLATED BY JOHN ADDINGTON SYMONDS

In gentler mood is the charming fragment addressed to Cleïs, probably her own daughter. "I have a pretty child, with a form like golden flowers, my beloved Cleïs. And her I would not change for all Lydia, nor for lovely Lesbos."

A tender and intimate poem is the brief greeting to Hesperus,

[171]

the evening star that draws back home all living creatures that have scattered through the day.

> O Hesperus, thou dost draw back
> All things that the dawn has scattered—
> The sheep *thou dost bring, thou dost bring* the goat,
> The child, too, to its mother *thou dost bring*.

TRANSLATED BY H. N. COUCH

If the modern reader is tempted to complain of repetition in this translation, it may be well to recall that Demetrius, an ancient critic, found the charm of the poem in the repetition of the word that has been here rendered "thou dost bring."

The Later Estimate of Sappho. The later classical age was not kind to the memory of Sappho. In an amazingly uncritical manner scandal was attached to her name. But the stories of her love affairs with Archilochus, Anacreon, and Hipponax are chronologically absurd. Archilochus had probably died before she was born, while Anacreon and Hipponax were a generation or more younger than she. It was especially in the conservative city of Athens, where woman's place was one of rigid seclusion, that the freedom of Sappho excited most hostile criticism, and in the plays of Middle Comedy, produced in the fourth century, her life story was presented in variously garbled versions. The literary reputation of Sappho has grown steadily in modern times as careful and discerning study of the comparatively few extant verses has revealed the mingling of her poetic genius with a sensitive and passionate nature. Sappho felt with deep emotion the warmth of friendship with the girls of her school; she was sensitive to imagined slights; and she became distraught with grief at the thought of lost companionship as her pupils left to marry and establish their own homes. The range of her emotions found an outlet in poems of exquisite delicacy of feeling and intensity of expression, that prompted Byron's phrase "burning Sappho." A wiser estimate of the great poetess will be reached by disregarding the temporary wave of adverse criticism in Middle Comedy, and recalling instead the enthusiasm that her work aroused in Solon and Plato and Aristotle.

Anacreon and the "Anacreontics." Anacreon of Teos, whose period of activity centers about 540 B.C., is diverting rather than important. Like Mimnermus he was a devotee of pleasure; but whereas Mimnermus was preoccupied with the vanity of life, Anacreon was merry and abandoned, and believed in seizing the joys of the moment. Songs of love and wine abound in the fragments that have been preserved.

Come, slave, bring me the jar, that I may drink a goodly draught; pour in ten ladles of water and five of wine, for I would ply my Bacchic revel in measured style. Nay, let us renounce this Scythian drinking, with turmoil and shouting over our wine, and drink accompanied by fair songs.

A brief poem by Anacreon on the anguish of love runs thus: "And now Eros, like a blacksmith, has struck me with his hammer, and has plunged me in the wintry torrent."

After the death of Anacreon many poems were written in the style developed by him. They are called *Anacreontics* and are of a nature and quality comparable to the poems of Anacreon himself. The subject matter is normally light, as in the humorous plea to be allowed to drink without remonstrance.

> All her melancholy frowns
> Earth by daily drinking drowns;
> From the earth, too, drink the trees;
> From the breezes drink the seas;
> From the seas in mighty draughts,
> Sol his glitt'ring glory quaffs;
> And from Sol, Lucina bright
> Drinks and silvers o'er the night;
> Friends, why then do you repine?
> I'll regale myself with wine.

TRANSLATED BY THOMAS GIRDLESTONE

PESSIMISTIC POETRY

Archilochus. Another group of poets, whose compositions were also intensely personal, were characterized by a mood of melancholy and bitterness. Archilochus of Paros, who belongs to this group, is one of the earliest of the poets of the archaic period. Nevertheless, because of internal evidence and through ancient references, a considerable body of knowledge about his life may be assembled. The son of a noble father and a slave mother, his active career falls in the early part of the seventh century. At the age of twenty he led a colony from Paros to the island of Thasos, and, if we may judge from his contemptuous farewell to his old home, "Away with Paros and her briny life," and his equally disgruntled greeting to Thasos, "Thrice accursed, the pit of all the ills of Greece," he thoroughly hated whatever place he was obliged to call his home. He fell in love with, and was betrothed to, a girl called Neobule; the engagement was broken by her father, whereupon Archilochus turned his poetic gifts to the composition of lampoons directed against Neobule, her father, and her two sisters, which were so scurrilous that, according to the grim tradition, the whole family sought refuge in suicide.

His Personal Character. Archilochus boasted of cowardice in battle, when he threw away his shield.

> That shield some Saian decks, which 'gainst my grain
> I left—fair, flawless shield!—beside the wood.
> Well, let it go! I and my purse remain:
> To-morrow's bull-skin may be just as good.

> TRANSLATED BY HENRY NELSON COLERIDGE

Though the poem may represent little more than a literary conceit, it shows his delight in offending conventional standards and a curious, perverse pride in boasting of his evasion of duty. Impervious to criticism, he likened himself to the hedgehog, whose defense is to roll up in bristles. Yet there runs through his poetry a homely familiarity of thought that is sometimes

[174]

appealing. Such is the brief summation of the career of the soldier, who finds all the necessities of life in his spear.

> By the spear on bread I'll dine:
> By the spear on benches fine
> My ease I'll take, and there recline,
> And calmly sip Ismaric wine.

TRANSLATED BY H. N. COUCH

The High Regard for Archilochus. Archilochus enjoyed an exceedingly high reputation in antiquity, being held only less in esteem than Homer. It is hard to believe that such honor was merited, although the apostrophe to his own soul, one of the best of his efforts, shows the high, unflinching courage of the pioneering Greeks of the archaic period.

> Tossed on a sea of troubles, Soul, my Soul,
>   Thyself do thou control;
> And to the weapons of advancing foes
>   A stubborn breast oppose;
> Undaunted 'mid the hostile might
>   Of squadrons burning for the fight.
>
> Thine be no boasting when the victor's crown
>   Wins thee deserved renown;
> Thine no dejected sorrow, when defeat
>   Would urge a base retreat:
> Rejoice in joyous things—nor overmuch
>   Let grief thy bosom touch
> 'Midst evil, and still bear in mind,
> How changeful are the ways of humankind.

TRANSLATED BY WILLIAM HAY

Hipponax. Hipponax and Semonides of Amorgos, both of whom belong in the sixth century, carry further the theme of misanthropy and misogyny. Hipponax, embittered by poverty, exile, and personal deformity, is the embodiment of discouragement and disillusion. Indulging in the current literary abuse of women, he wrote his famous limping iambic couplet of bitter satire: "There are two days most blessed in the life of a woman—the day when a man marries her, and the day when he buries her."

Semonides of Amorgos. Semonides of Amorgos is a trifle less bitter, although he, too, directed his diatribes against women. In one poem he compared eight types of women to as many different animals or elements of nature. The first type is of the race of the pig, slovenly about the home; the second, like the fox, is ever prying, peering, and gossiping, "nor is her husband able to stop her, not though he utter threats against her, or knock her teeth out with a rock, or reason mildly with her"; the third, with a nature of clay, is stupid; the fourth, like the sea, is fickle, gay one moment, in a fury the next; the fifth, like an ass, is stubborn; the sixth, like a ferret, is sly; the seventh, like a horse, a rare and valued animal in Greece, is dainty, but impractical and extravagant; while the final type, like the bee, is dutiful and industrious. She is the only one for whom he has a good word. A literary expression of hatred for women is something that is not unlikely to appear in the juvenile writings of a man or a race. A portion of the description of the extravagant woman, who is compared to the horse, is quoted in the translation of William Mure:

> Next in the lot a gallant dame we see,
> Sprung from a mare of noble pedigree,
> No servile work her spirit proud can brook;
> Her hands were never taught to bake or cook;
> The vapour of the oven makes her ill;
> She scorns to empty slops or turn the mill,
> No household washings her fair skin deface,
> Her own ablutions are her chief solace.
> Three baths a day, with balms and perfumes rare,
> Refresh her tender limbs; her long rich hair
> Each time she combs, and decks with blooming flowers,
> No spouse more fit than she the idle hours
> Of wealthy lords or kings to recreate,
> And grace the splendour of their courtly state,
> For men of humbler sort no better guide,
> Heaven in its wrath to ruin can provide.

POETRY OF A TRANSITIONAL SOCIETY

Occasional Poetry

Alcman. There remain a number of poets, as well as a few anonymous poems, to be briefly identified. Alcman of Sardis, who later moved to Sparta, and whose active years lie in the late seventh century, composed *parthenia,* or songs for the choruses of maidens, but he chiefly deserves mention for his unusually beautiful description of nature at rest.

> Asleep lies ev'ry mountain peak
> And vale;
> Each rugged cliff we seek
> And dale;
> The race of beasts and creeping things,
> The brood of teeming earth,
> And all to whom the mountain flings
> A welcome at their birth.
> Asleep the purple ocean's herds,
> The tribes of tiny bees,
> Asleep the flocks of long-winged birds,
> E'en these.

TRANSLATED BY H. N. COUCH

Later Lyric Poets; Pindar. The poetry peculiar to the archaic age continued into the first half of the fifth century, when new influences were changing its purpose and quality. The most prolific writer of this period was Pindar, who is known principally for his verses celebrating the victors in the athletic contests at the national festivals. Two other poets whose work also dealt, in part at least, with athletic victories were Bacchylides and Simonides of Ceos. Poems written to celebrate special occasions have flourished in all ages, but they have seldom been as good as the other creations of the same authors. It is interesting, therefore, to see how Pindar succeeded where others have failed. After brief mention of the victor, he dwelt on the glorious history of the athlete's city, with praise for the institutions of the state and with mythological allusions, and included finally a rather casual reference to the accomplishments of the victor himself, who thus carried on the fine traditions of the city.

The Renown of Pindar. Pindar enjoyed at all times a distinguished reputation throughout Greece. He was a member of an aristocratic family in Thebes and there exercised certain priestly offices. But neither his genius nor his residence was confined to his native city. For a full half-century, from 498 B.C. to 446 B.C., it is possible to trace in some detail his literary career, and to follow his travels as he went about the Greek world attending the festivals and celebrating the victories of the athletes.

Two facts should be kept in mind in estimating the work of Pindar. One is the difficulty of composing poetry on contract, for it seems clear that when he undertook to write an ode in celebration of a victory at the games, later to be sung by a chorus of men and youths, many of the details, such as allusions to the native city and to the feats of various ancestors of the victor, were stipulated for inclusion in advance. The second, and perhaps more important, factor is the embarrassment that he inevitably experienced in adjusting himself to the political climate in Greece following the Persian Wars. Born in 522 B.C., he was thirty-two years of age at the time of Marathon, forty-two at the time of Salamis. In neither encounter did his native city of Thebes play a distinguished or honorable part, and careful analysis of the poems indicates, both by what is said and what is omitted, that Pindar felt keenly the disgraceful defection of his city. Under these circumstances the fact that he should have achieved the highest distinction in the field of lyric poetry is the triumph of genius over great obstacles.

An indication of the respect that Pindar's name commanded long after his death is found in the story that, when Alexander the Great razed the city of Thebes in 335 B.C., he left only the house of Pindar and the temples of the gods standing. More than a century earlier, in 474 B.C., Pindar had won the hearts of the Athenians by his glorious verses in the praise of their city: "Gleaming city, violet-crowned, and famed in song;

[178]

glorious Athens, bulwark of Hellas, sacred citadel." More than all the odes of victory for the national games of Greece which Pindar wrote, these unusual and personal verses of praise lingered with grateful remembrance in the minds of the Athenians.

An Ode to Megacles. The short ode in celebration of a victory in the four-horse chariot race at the Pythian games of 486 B.C. may be translated as an example of the writing of Pindar, because it illustrates admirably in brief compass the pride in city and ancestry and the background of legend that are characteristic of most of the odes. Megacles, of the Athenian house of the Alcmæonidæ, was the winner, and the reference to the marble front, which was erected on the temple of Apollo at Delphi by his forebears, must have been pleasing to him. The great amount of detail in a Pindaric ode is sometimes best seen in a prose translation.

The fairest prelude to song is the name of the glorious city of Athens for the family of the Alcmæonidæ, wide of power, to offer as the foundation for the chants in honor of their victory in the chariot race. What fatherland, what home, mightest thou dwell in, and name as more glorious in honor throughout Greece?

In every land the fame of the citizens of Erechtheus is known, Apollo, of those who at holy Pytho fashioned thy temple a marvel to behold. And now are added for my song five victories, one at the Isthmian games, one glorious conquest at the Olympian festival of Zeus, two at Cirrha, gained, Megacles, by thyself and thine ancestors. At this new and happy victory I rejoice; though I grieve that envy accompanieth fair deeds. Yet 'tis said that rich and abiding prosperity bringeth to a man now this, now that.

An Ode to Psaumis. The following full and considerably expanded verse-rendering by Reginald Heber of the Fourth Olympian Ode is offered by way of contrast to the literal prose translation. The ode deals with the victory of Psaumis of Camarina in Sicily in a mule chariot race. The date of the contest is uncertain. Certain characteristic features of Pindaric odes are found in the opening salutation to Zeus, the direct reference to Psaumis and his victory at Pisa, the site of the Olympian Games, and the mythological allusion to the Lesbian queen Hypsipyle toward the end.

Oh, urging on the tireless speed
Of Thunder's elemental steed,
Lord of the world, Almighty Jove!
Since these thine hours have sent me forth
The witness of thy champion's worth,
And prophet of thine olive grove;
And since the good thy poet hear,
And hold his tuneful message dear;
Saturnian Lord of Etna hill!
Whose storm-cemented rocks encage
The hundred-headed rebel's rage;
Accept with favourable will
The Muses' gift of harmony;
The dance, the song, whose numbers high
Forbid the hero's name to die,
A crown of life abiding still!

Hark, round the car of victory,
Where noble Psaumis sits on high,
    The cheering notes resound;
Who vows to swell with added fame
His Camarina's ancient name;
    With Pisan olive crown'd.
And thou, oh father, hear his prayer!
For much I praise the knightly care
    That trains the warrior steed:
Nor less the hospitable hall
Whose open doors the stranger call;
Yet, praise I Psaumis most of all
    For wise and peaceful rede,
And patriot love of liberty.
What? do we weave the glozing lie?
Then whoso list my truth to try,
    The proof be in the deed!

To Lemnos' laughing dames of yore,
Such was the proof Ernicus bore,

When, matchless in his speed,
All brazen-arm'd the racer hoar,
Victorious on the applauding shore,
  Sprang to the proffer'd meed;
Bow'd to the queen his wreathèd head:
"Thou seest my limbs are light," he said;
  "And, lady, mayst thou know,
That every joint is firmly strung,
And hand and heart alike are young;
Though treacherous time my locks among
  Have strew'd a summer snow!"

TRANSLATED BY REGINALD HEBER

Simonides of Ceos. Simonides of Ceos, who is not to be confused with Semonides of Amorgos, and who wrote in the latter part of the sixth and the first part of the fifth centuries, is best known for his sepulchral epitaphs. Several of them celebrate the heroism of the Greek soldiers in the Persian Wars.

If noble death be valor's finest meed,
For us hath Fortune deign'd her gifts to pour:
With zeal to serve our homeland in her need,
We found in death unaging fame in store.

TRANSLATED BY H. N. COUCH

The famous lines written in commemoration of the three hundred Spartans who died with Leonidas at Thermopylæ are poignant in the simple beauty with which they tell of a deed of unsurpassed bravery and fidelity. "Stranger, go tell the Spartans that we lie here in obedience to their commands." The words may seem at first an inadequate tribute to such an act of faith, but one will agree on reflection that praise is out of place, for it would be an unwarranted detraction from the bravery itself.

Danaë and Perseus in the Chest. Simonides of Ceos has also preserved part of a Greek legend in a brief lament of singular beauty. The story tells how an oracle had conveyed to Acrisius the warning that he would be killed by the son of his daughter

Danaë. Accordingly, when Danaë bore a son, Perseus, her father had them both placed in a chest and cast adrift at sea. The poem of Simonides of Ceos represents Danaë soothing her child in the confines of the chest, as they float upon the waves.

> When, in the carven chest,
> The winds that blew and waves in wild unrest
> Smote her with fear, she, not with cheeks unwet,
>   Her arms of love round Perseus set,
>   And said: "O child, what grief is mine!
> But thou dost slumber, and thy baby breast
>   Is sunk in rest,
> Here in the cheerless brass-bound bark,
> Tossed amid starless night and pitchy dark.
>   Nor dost thou heed the scudding brine
> Of waves that wash above thy curls so deep,
>   Nor the shrill winds that sweep,—
> Lapped in thy purple robe's embrace,
>   Fair little face!
> But if this dread were dreadful too to thee,
> Then wouldst thou lend thy listening ear to me;
> Therefore I cry,—Sleep, babe, and sea, be still,
> And slumber our unmeasured ill!
>   Oh, may some change of fate, sire Zeus, from thee
> Descend, our woes to end!
> But if this prayer, too overbold, offend
>   Thy justice, yet be merciful to me!"

TRANSLATED BY JOHN ADDINGTON SYMONDS

It is unusual in the tenderness and simplicity of the theme of mother and child, for neither in the art nor in the literature of Greece were such topics commonly found at so early a date.

The Scolion. In the archaic age, the *scolion* was developed as a song for the banquet, where intelligent conversation and fine musical performance were prized, and each guest was expected on occasion to contribute to the entertainment by singing a stanza of some known scolion. The chant in honor of the tyrannicides, Harmodius and Aristogeiton, is an illustration of this type of song, and the historical allusion dates this scolion

very definitely after 510 B.C., for in that year the tyrant Hippias
was driven from Athens. One stanza is translated as follows:

Courtesy of the Museum of Fine Arts, Boston

FIGURE 42. THE CHEST OF DANAË AND PERSEUS. Attic red-figured
hydria. Fifth century B.C. The mother and child stand to the right
while a carpenter prepares the chest. The artist has failed to portray the
child's form realistically.

[183]

With a branch of myrtle I'll bear my sword, like Harmodius and Aristogeiton, when they slew the tyrant and set Athens free. Dearest Harmodius, in no wise art thou dead, but 'tis said thou livest in the Isles of the Blest, where swift-footed Achilles and Diomedes, son of Tydeus, dwell.

The Swallow Song. The discussion of the poetry of the archaic age may be brought to a close with the *Swallow Song,* which the children of Rhodes sang in the spring as they went from house to house begging favors.

> She is here, she is here, the swallow!
> Fair seasons bringing, fair years to follow!
>   Her belly is white,
>   Her back black as night!
>   From your rich house
>   Roll forth to us
>   Tarts, wine, and cheese:
>   Or if not these,
>   Oatmeal and barley cake,
>   The swallow deigns to take.
> What shall we have? or must we hence away?
> Thanks, if you give; if not, we'll make you pay!
>   The house-door hence we'll carry;
>   Nor shall the lintel tarry;
>   From hearth and home your wife we'll rob;
>   She is so small,
>   To take her off will be an easy job!
> Whate'er you give, give largesse free!
> Up! Open, open to the swallow's call!
> No grave old men, but merry children we!

TRANSLATED BY JOHN ADDINGTON SYMONDS

The theme and nature of the poem may be compared to the Wassail Song, "Here we come a-caroling among the leaves so green," sung at Christmas, or to the children who go about the neighborhood to ask for "treats" at Hallowe'en.

CHAPTER X

THE BIRTH OF SCIENTIFIC INQUIRY

THE PHYSICAL PHILOSOPHERS

The Beginnings of·Philosophy in the Archaic Age. Still another intellectual movement stirred Greece during the archaic age, flourishing simultaneously with the writing of lyric poetry and the vigorous experimentation in the forms of government. This was the beginning of philosophy. The stimulus to philosophic inquiry was not, however, precisely the same as that which motivated the poets or the statesmen, for the qualities of poetry were personal and intense, while the first scientific inquiry into material substance sought to pursue truth objectively and dispassionately. Nonetheless, philosophy, too, was a natural outgrowth of time and place, for the earliest schools of philosophy grew up, not in the older cities of the Greek mainland, but in the Greek cities and colonies of Asia Minor and Italy. The same adventurous qualities that had induced the colonists to leave their homes and seek a new life abroad animated them with a freer and bolder intellectual outlook than that of their kinsmen who had remained behind on the mainland. Thus the inquiring spirit, which at this time turned one group of men to experiment in sculpture, another to develop new ideas of civil government, and still others to record their emotions or experiences in verse, induced the physical philosophers to question, in a pioneering mood, the origin and nature of the universe in which they found themselves.

The Search for Truth. The great achievement of the early philosophers was their insistence on substituting a material and

[185]

objective explanation of the universe for the older mythical and supernatural stories in Homer and Hesiod that had satisfied their predecessors. Among the early inquirers philosophy and physical science became practically indistinguishable, for it was through a study of physical properties that ultimate truth was sought. One of the earliest and most logical questions, both of children and of a race in its childhood, is that concerning the nature of the familiar material objects that constitute the world. The creation stories common to all early peoples are indicative of this type of inquiry, and it is to the credit of the early Greek philosophers that, with all their mistakes, they substituted a reasoned and logical approach to the problem for the fanciful and uncritical explanations of the poets. The early physical philosophers started from the principle, which seemed to them axiomatic, that some single material substance constituted the basic reality of the universe, and in various ways they sought to discover and define that reality. Even when physical philosophy gave place to humanistic speculation, the search for reality continued.

THE MILESIAN SCHOOL; THALES

Origin of Philosophy at Miletus. It was at Miletus in Asia Minor that the first group of physical philosophers began their speculations early in the sixth century. Miletus was at this time a great and powerful Hellenic city lying on the borders of a barbarian society. There were few, if any, cities in the ancient Greek world to rival her in wealth, might, and intellectual vigor. The school of philosophy that was founded in this Greek city, and from which European philosophy was to emerge, continued its first period of active existence for about one hundred years, until, to the dismay of Greece and with incalculable loss to all civilization, the city was destroyed by the Persians in 494 B.C.

Thales, the Founder of the Milesian School. The principal character in the Milesian school was Thales, one of the Seven

[186]

Sages and a polymath of antiquity. About this extraordinary man many tales grew up in the classical age, of which not a few were apocryphal. The prediction of the eclipse of the sun in 585 B.C. that caused the Lydians and Persians to cease from battle was attributed to Thales. This account belongs in the class of stories that find currency after the event, for, although Thales doubtless had some acquaintance with astronomy on an empirical level, it seems quite impossible that he should actually have been able to foretell a solar eclipse at that time in spite of the fact that many modern scholars have accepted the tale as true. About him also was told one of the first stories of the absent-minded philosopher. While walking, lost in abstraction, he is said to have fallen into a well and excited the laughter of a Thracian slave-girl, the embodiment of illiteracy. The point of the story is presumably that the ignorant slave-girl knew at least enough to keep out of a well, but the Greeks appear to have given too little heed to the reflection that Thales fell into the well because he had his mind on something other than the dust under foot. On the other hand, Thales is said to have demonstrated the practical advantage of science by using his knowledge to acquire a profitable monopoly of the local olive presses. His interest in contemporary political problems is attested by the tales of his association with Crœsus, king of Lydia, in his campaign against the Persians and his advocacy of some measure of protective political unity among the cities of Ionia. This is one of the earliest references to the many, and usually unsuccessful, attempts to effect a federal union among the independent Greek cities whether of the mainland or the colonies.

Water, the Basic Reality. For the history of philosophy, however, Thales assumed real importance by devoting himself to the systematic search for the reality of the universe, which he identified as water. His selection was almost inevitable, for the ready mutability of water into ice, its capacity for vaporization, its presence in the air, on the earth, and beneath the earth, its relation to growth and vegetation, and the apparently ob-

[187]

vious fact that the earth was floating on water, all suggested its universality. Thales happened to be wrong, but it is to his everlasting renown that he was the first man to reject the uncritical explanations of his predecessors and to seek truth in a scientific manner.

Anaximander and Anaximenes. To the Milesian school there also belongs Anaximander, who declared that reality consisted in the boundless—an ill-defined concept—which he seemingly believed to have existed without origin and to be indestructible and inexhaustible. A third member of the school was Anaximenes, who declared that air was the basic reality, pointing out that air included both the boundlessness of Anaximander's concept and the physical definiteness of water, the basic substance suggested by Thales. Thus different philosophers in the same school pursued their studies along similar though separate lines.

The Contradictory Ideas of Change and Permanence. The development of philosophic speculation proceeds, however, from Thales rather than from the similar speculations of either of these two younger contemporaries. The scientific approach to the explanation of the universe, at least as the philosophers sought to reduce all material existence to one basic reality, had one weakness, for it led them to ignore everything that seemed to contradict the theory toward which they were impelled. Thus Thales found in water the universal, omnipresent, and, hence, static and unchanging reality of the world, but conversely he was attracted to water largely because of its changeful nature. Accordingly, the two opposed ideas of change and permanence emerged, and succeeding philosophers undertook to prove the universal truth of one or the other of these ideas, ignoring entirely evidence pointing to the existence of truth in the one that they had discarded. It was not until considerably later that a group of philosophers arose who tried to reconcile the conflicting ideas of various earlier schools of thought. The scientific principle was not yet clearly enough understood for it to point the way to truth wherever it might be found.

[188]

HERACLEITUS

The Doctrine of Flux. Although the concept of permanence was taken up somewhat before its opposite, it is perhaps simpler to consider first the clearly defined philosophy of Heracleitus of Ephesus, who flourished about 500 B.C. and who undertook to demonstrate the universal fact of change, or flux. Heracleitus was a member of a noble family, living, like the lyric poets, at a time when political stability was unknown, and it was natural that in his philosophy he should show the influence of his own inconstant environment. He taught that everything in the universe is in a constant state of flux. There is no enduring reality; everything is coming into being or passing out of being; nothing exists.

The contention is summed up in his often repeated statement: "Everything is flowing." He illustrated his ideas by appealing to facts of nature, pointing out, for instance, that one cannot step twice into the same stream, for each instant the water changes. He taught further that all change takes place in accordance with an immutable law of nature, and on the basis of this law he explained the appearance of permanence, which is to be seen in every stick and stone at hand, as a deception of the senses.

Fire, the Basic Reality. Heracleitus could not entirely abandon the form set up by his predecessor. Instead of accepting, with Thales, water as the basic reality, he suggested fire, which, with an obviously deceptive appearance of permanence, demonstrates the transition out of being of the substance that is being burned and the coming into being of the gases and ash that result. In his emphasis on the unreliability of sense perception, Heracleitus made an important contribution to philosophy.

The Interest of Heracleitus in Society. While Heracleitus, like all his contemporaries, was a physical and not a humanistic philosopher, there are, nevertheless, evidences that his preoccupation with the idea of law in the physical world carried him on to the problems of men living together in orderly society. He declared that citizens should fight in defense of their laws, as they would in defense of the walls of the city. He believed that all law emanated from Zeus, but he was equally emphatic in maintaining the right of an individual to his opinion. There is a certain amount of confusion in the contention of Heracleitus regarding law, for at that time he neither knew nor could evolve a consistent political philosophy by which to guide his thinking. Yet, despite the inadequacy of his political philosophy, the important thing is to observe that in the earliest days of intellectual inquiry such topics were pressing for consideration and solution in the minds of the Greeks. Heracleitus made a major contribution to the advancement of thought by his recognition of the conflict that exists between the senses and reason.

THE ELEATIC SCHOOL; XENOPHANES, PARMENIDES, ZENO

The Doctrine of Permanence. An interpretation of physical science quite opposed to that of Heracleitus was defended by a group of philosophers who taught the doctrine of permanence, or unchanging rest. This new philosophic body has been called the Eleatic school, from its foundation at Elea in southern Italy. Three men in particular, Xenophanes, Parmenides, and Zeno, developed the teachings of the Eleatics.

Xenophanes. Xenophanes of Colophon, the founder of the Eleatic school, lived from about 570 B.C. to about 475 B.C. and is consequently somewhat earlier than Heracleitus. Xenophanes was perhaps more intimately involved in poetry and theology than in scientific philosophy, which was carried forward by his successors. He was himself one of the elegiac poets, and his writings present a poetic and imaginative concept of the philosophy of permanence. There is evident in them not only a passionate anger against moral decadence but considerable sound common sense.

The contribution of Xenophanes to rational theology lies in his declaration of positive belief in a single god, who is, in form and conception, something quite different from man.

"There is a single god," he declares, "the greatest among gods and men, who resembles mortals neither in body nor in mind." This monotheistic idea is a distinct advance, and if Xenophanes continues to refer to gods in the plural, it is only because he cannot shake off a conventional literary usage. Xenophanes found also in the one unchanging god the principle of permanence, which his school maintained to be the basis of reality in the universe.

The Moral Censures of Xenophanes. Xenophanes was led by his fixed conviction to argue in every instance the doctrine of permanence. Nevertheless, his interests ranged also over a wide field, and he showed the zeal of a reformer, directing his writings against ignorance and moral laxity rather than pursuing exclusively the physical speculations of his contemporary philosophers. When the Greek cities of Asia Minor were reduced by the Lydians and Persians, Xenophanes left Colophon and moved to Elea in southern Italy, and it was at that time that he founded his school. Many of the current interests of society irritated Xenophanes. He protested against the undue emphasis on athletics, which paid more attention to the development of a man's body than to his intellect. Nor did he approve of the public recital of Homer and Hesiod, since the unreal adventures of gods and giants were of little importance to men of his own time. Likewise, the religion of the epic poets shocked him, for Homer and Hesiod ascribed to the gods crimes at which man should blush.

The Challenge to Anthropomorphism. Xenophanes urged the nurture of moral responsibility and reasoned judgment, and he is to be associated with the first attack on anthropomorphism in Greek religion, for, he says, it is only the conceit of man that leads him to picture the gods in his own likeness. His refutation of anthropomorphism may best be explained by quoting his few cogent extant aphorisms on the subject.

Mortals believe that the gods are born with their own garb and voice and form.

If oxen and lions had hands with which to paint and produce

statues, as men do, they would fashion their gods after their own form: horses would picture their gods like horses, and lions like lions.

The Ethiopians show their gods as black and flat-nosed, while the Thracians conceive theirs to be red-haired and blue-eyed.

Parmenides and the Doctrine of Rest. With Parmenides, who was a younger successor of Xenophanes in the Eleatic school, we encounter a man who undertook to defend the principle of permanence in more concrete, if slightly cavalier, fashion. He claimed that the only reality in the world was the One, or Being, which is everlasting, motionless, and changeless. Not-being cannot exist, because it is unthinkable, nor can anything else that is unthinkable have being. Motion he states to be unthinkable, and apparent motion, as seen anywhere in the world, must be rejected on the ground that anything that is unthinkable is impossible. If an object is moved from one place to another, it must be moved into an empty space, but since empty space is unthinkable it cannot exist, and therefore motion is impossible.

This type of sophistic nonsense, it must be remembered, was tolerated when all such speculations were new to man, and the physical philosophers were feeling their way toward truth. Furthermore, Parmenides, like Heracleitus, was simply guarding against the deception of the senses, the only difference being that Heracleitus maintained that man was deceived by the false appearance of rest, whereas Parmenides declared that it was the false appearance of motion that confused the senses.

Zeno and his Mathematical Proofs. The last scholar of the Eleatic school to be discussed is Zeno, whose life falls entirely within the fifth century. He undertook to prove by mathematical legerdemain that it was easier to accept Parmenides' strange doctrine of static being than to credit the theory of motion. He advanced four mathematical proofs against the possibility of motion, of which two may be cited by way of

[192]

illustration. He pointed out that, though an arrow in its flight through the air from the bowman to the target appears to move, in reality at any given infinitesimal instant of time it must be located at a certain place, where its motion is zero. Thus its apparent flight is a series of fixed points, or zeros, and no addition of zero plus zero plus zero can produce motion.

Another illustration, which is couched in involved mathematical ratios, has to do with a race between the fleet-footed Achilles and the slow-moving tortoise. The problem, in somewhat simplified form, supposes that Achilles is able to run twice as fast as the tortoise. If the tortoise is given a start of sixteen feet, by the time Achilles has reached the starting-point of the tortoise, the latter will be eight feet farther on, and successively the tortoise will maintain its lead by half the intervening space. Achilles therefore can never catch up with the tortoise, despite any fallacious opinion or deceptive visual appearance that would seem to prove that a man running twice as fast as a tortoise will eventually reach and pass the latter. Logic was thus developed without relation to reality at this point in the history of philosophy.

The Accomplishment of the Eleatic School. The efforts of Xenophanes, Parmenides, and Zeno, and also of Melissus of Samos, who, like Zeno, vigorously refuted every attack on the tenets of the Eleatic school, were essentially negative. Xenophanes stands somewhat apart from the casuistic arguments, though he was emphatic in his own beliefs. Since the later philosophers of the school conceived it to be their duty to defend a position rather than to examine it, they developed a facility in dialectic, which no doubt served a purpose in habituating men's minds to argumentation, thus making possible a later development of more valuable aspects of philosophy. A change of mental attitude was necessary before definite progress could be made, but by their exclusive pursuit of fixed ideas, the philosophers were at least clearing the way for subsequent advance.

[193]

THE PYTHAGOREANS

Pythagoras and his School. The opposing views of the Milesian and Eleatic schools of philosophy and of Heracleitus were vigorously upheld by men who had no disposition to recognize truth in the position of their opponents. These differences were, however, presently to be examined by a body of less biased philosophers, who sought to discover common ground and demonstrable truth in the teachings of their predecessors. Before this effort at philosophic reconciliation is dealt with, another school or group of philosophers who were active at the same period must be briefly described. These are the Pythagoreans, a curious body that embraced the characteristics of a religious order, a political faction, and a school of philosophy. The school was founded at Croton in Italy by Pythagoras, a citizen of Samos, who in the course of his travels moved to Italy. He lived from about 580 B.C. to about 500 B.C. Like all the early philosophers, the Pythagoreans were seeking reality, and they found it in number. Nor is it surprising that to an orderly Greek mind mathematical discoveries should offer a strong appeal. In fact the identification of reality with an abstract concept such as number represents in itself a definite advance in philosophic inquiry.

The Study of Number. The Pythagoreans quickly discovered certain numerical relationships between musical notes, but, in the exaltation of spirit that accompanied the proved accuracy of some natural numerical law that had hitherto lain hidden from human intelligence, they went on to fanciful explanations of the music of the spheres, and to a numerical explanation of the relation of the soul to the body. With reasonable logic they identified the number one with the point, two with the line, three with the surface, and four with the cube. They also evolved various sound mathematical formulæ related to number series. But when they explained five as representing marriage, seven opportunity, and so forth, they quickly lost touch with reality.

[194]

It is significant that in more modern times the control of nature, as exemplified in the development of the various branches of natural science, such as chemistry, physics, and the different studies in electricity, and even more the enormous volume of cooperative research that resulted in the discovery of atomic energy, has depended on learning the mathematical laws that so fascinated the Pythagoreans. The weakness of the Pythagorean position lay in the illogical and fanciful extension that they made of their first stimulating discoveries in musical intervals.

Rules of the Pythagoreans. The Pythagoreans, as an order, enjoined upon themselves, in addition to a pledge of celibacy, contemplation, and worship, a number of curious prohibitions, such as abstention from wool as clothing, beans as food, and iron as an implement with which to stir the fire. In the popular imagination the doctrine of transmigration of souls is also prominently associated with the Pythagorean cult. A similar belief in the transmigration of souls, or the cycles of birth, was shared by other religious bodies. These sensational doctrines, though of some interest, are not of particular importance. The strict prohibitions are probably custom survivals or taboos. These the Pythagoreans seized upon and exaggerated in importance because at this time some men came to realize the insidious effect of a wave of moral laxity that had made the cities of Italy and Sicily, especially Sybaris, notorious for their excessive luxury. In some way, too, the ascetic implications of the prohibitions to which the Pythagoreans subjected themselves were associated with the greater patriotism and civic virtue of an earlier age.

It was during this period that the weakened cities of Asia Minor were falling a prey to Crœsus and the Persian ruler Cyrus, and Pythagoras was aware of the inevitable fate of his former fellow citizens in Samos. He sought, therefore, by the imposition of ascetic rules of life, to check the ravages of moral decline among his followers in their new home in Italy. Similar attitudes can be traced in the diatribes of Xe-

[195]

nophanes, the martial exhortations of Callinus, and even in the whimpering despondency of Mimnermus. They are all symptomatic of the times in which the lyric poets and the physical philosophers lived.

The Importance of the Pythagoreans. In spite of the sometimes inaccurate applications of their knowledge, the Pythagoreans assumed considerable importance in later philosophy for their methods and mathematical discoveries. Plato was often influenced by the Pythagorean theory of numbers in framing his illustrations, and Democritus, who was to make exceedingly important contributions to the theory of the atom, was able to conduct his own research only because of the mathematical discoveries of the Pythagoreans, who had preceded him. The place of the Pythagoreans in the study of geometry is a distinguished one. There was a sense of truth about the strange, and in some respects credulous, school of the Pythagoreans that served the cause of philosophy well.

ATTEMPTS AT RECONCILIATION OF IDEAS

The Movement toward Reconciliation. Naturally, as with the passage of time men gained perspective and were able to evaluate the efforts of those who had initiated the search for reality, they could not remain satisfied with either the explanation of Heracleitus, who denied the existence of all stability and permanence, or that of the Eleatics, who denied the existence of all movement and change. These earlier dogmatic claims had grown out of the attitude that prompted men to pursue one idea to the exclusion of all contradictory evidence, and that method was manifestly not the one by which to arrive at the entire truth.

It therefore became the task of the next group of philosophers, of whom the most important were Empedocles, Anaxagoras, Leucippus, and Democritus, to extract the truth from the biased arguments of their predecessors and to direct philosophic research along more objective and disinterested paths of

[196]

honest inquiry. These mediating philosophers belong to the fifth century rather than to the archaic period, but they were working in the direct tradition of physical philosophy and consequently are more intimately related to their predecessors in their philosophic outlook than to their contemporaries or successors, who turned to humanistic studies.

Empedocles. The first philosopher to be discussed in this connection is Empedocles of Acragas in Sicily, who lived from about 490 B.C. to 430 B.C. He was thus nearly contemporary with the Eleatic Zeno. Empedocles was still searching for reality, as Thales, Heracleitus, and Parmenides had done, but instead of identifying reality with water, fire, or the One, as did the former three, respectively, he said that it was to be found in four elements—earth, air, fire, and water—which might be combined in innumerable ways. Thus permanence would be found in the elements themselves, and change in their shifting positions. If the idea is extended, as he extended it, to account for natural growth by a change in composition, it will be agreed that he contributed a very important idea to scientific inquiry.

Love and Hate, the Motivating Forces. In addition to the four elements, Empedocles predicated two abstract qualities, love and hate, which accounted for motion, the former bringing elements together, the latter driving them apart. The predication of love and hate as forces to control motion is in many respects similar to the modern electrical theory of positive and negative charges, and, if it be objected that love and hate are abstract and unscientific terms, it must be conceded that it is still very difficult to explain with entire satisfaction positive and negative electrical poles. The validity of the idea is not destroyed because the language used to describe it is more poetic than scientific.

The Legendary Empedocles. In a credulous age, the considerable breadth of true scientific knowledge that Empedocles possessed gained for him a reputation for supernatural power. Possibly he welcomed the opinion. Tradition has it that he

[197]

ended his life by a leap into the crater of Mount Ætna, so that he might be thought to have disappeared from earth as a god. Scientific philosophy had brought to the attention of the world some remarkable discoveries, and Empedocles, either sincerely or through vanity, yielded to the temptation to promise for mankind extravagant things. He professed to discover in medicines cures for all ills, including old age, to check the violence of the winds, or to cause them to blow at will, to control the season of rains, and to restore the dead from Hades. Empedocles lived in the same atmosphere that produced an illogical religious zeal among various groups, and by which both the Eleatics and Pythagoreans had been to some extent affected. In this way one may account in part at least for the elements of scientific research and of superstitious belief in his own divinity existing side by side in his mind.

Anaxagoras. With Anaxagoras of Clazomenæ, who lived from about 500 B.C. to 429 B.C., there emerges a philosopher whose career was to bring him in contact with some of the distinguished men and women of Greek history and who was the first man to pursue philosophy as a study in Athens, though he was not a native of that city. He also contributed by his studies to the reconciliation of earlier conflicting ideas, although he worked quite independently of Empedocles. He differed from Empedocles in claiming that reality was to be found not in four elements, but in an infinite number of "seeds" of the elements, as many as are the different objects and qualities known to man. These tiny seeds, he said, were present in varying proportions in all things, and the difference in the appearance of physical objects was to be accounted for by the varying proportions in which they were present in each one.

The Rule of Reason. Anaxagoras made one further important contribution to philosophy by explaining the orderly movement of natural bodies—the sun, moon, and stars—and of natural phenomena, such as the seasons, through the presence of reason, or *Nous,* in the world. Nous was, in his philosophy, an infinitely fine substance, unmixed with any alloy. It was

[198]

very difficult for him to express this idea in a universe of multiple elements, but his attempt to set up reason or intelligence, which he understood by Nous, as a guiding principle of conduct, is in some ways allied to Empedocles' assumption of love and hate as forces controlling motion. With the Nous of Anaxagoras, however, we are coming closer to a philosophy that will take account of the human mind rather than of physical properties as the basis of the understanding of life.

The Rational Explanations of Physical Phenomena. In the middle of the fifth century Anaxagoras moved to Athens. He was the first man to associate himself with philosophy in that city, which within another half-century was to produce Socrates and Plato. Anaxagoras was welcomed to the liberal intellectual circle of Pericles and Aspasia, where he met Euripides and other literary men. When popular feeling turned against Pericles, the Athenians drove Anaxagoras from their city as an atheist, for he insisted, like Empedocles, on an honest scientific approach to intellectual inquiry, and he had suggested natural explanations for some phenomena that had hitherto been interpreted by mythical allusions. Thus he taught that the sun was only a red-hot stone, and not a god. The introduction of new and alarming ideas from the more liberal Ionian cities had already caused some misgivings in Athens, and it was as a result of a law passed in 432 B.C., directed against men who refused to accept the religion of the city and who taught new ideas of astronomy, that Anaxagoras was exiled. Nevertheless, it must not be thought that the Athenians were unduly superstitious, for the exile of Anaxagoras was motivated quite as much by political antagonism toward his friend Pericles as by religious conservatism. Both Pericles and Anaxagoras died in 429 B.C.

Leucippus and Democritus. In the four elements predicated by Empedocles, which move at the instance of love and hate, and in the infinite number of seeds of the elements which constituted reality for Anaxagoras, there were indications of the direction in which physical philosophy was moving. The next

[199]

logical step was the explanation of the physical universe in terms of atoms. It is an arresting thought that the great discoveries of atomic energy in our own day were preceded by the simple, patient, but penetrating inquiries of men who worked more than two thousand years before the fruits of their absorbing search were to be gathered.

The early study of the theory of atoms was pursued in particular by two philosophers, Leucippus, probably of Miletus, and Democritus of Abdera in Thrace. Leucippus is a very shadowy personality, and even those in antiquity who discuss his work are exceedingly vague about the details of his life. If it may be assumed that he came from Miletus, it is noteworthy that, in a sense, physical philosophy began and ended with that brilliant city of Asia Minor, for the problems raised by Thales led logically to the work of the atomists. There is reason to believe that Leucippus first seized upon the idea of the atomic theory, although the continuation of the work by Democritus, whose life touched both the fifth and fourth centuries before Christ, has been more widely recognized. Both in time and in importance, though not in the subject of his study, Democritus belongs with Plato and Aristotle rather than with the early physical philosophers.

Statement of the Atomic Theory. Without seeking to differentiate specifically between the contributions of Leucippus and Democritus, we find that the search for reality has now produced the explanation that all things are made up of an infinite number of atoms, which are too small to be perceived by anything but the mind. They are unchanging and indestructible. The word *atom* means in Greek "that which cannot be cut finer." In conjunction with the ancient study of the atom went the idea of the void, within which motion might take place. The concept of the void, though less spectacular, is almost as important as the atom itself. The smashing of the atom has played havoc with the derivation of certain terms that have long endured, but it is our present responsibility to follow the thought of the Greeks, who were seeking reality, rather than to

[200]

harmonize the search for pure knowledge with the achievements of applied science. In the atoms alone Leucippus and Democritus believed that reality existed. Motion is governed by fixed laws, which arise from the atoms themselves, rather than by the theory of love and hate advanced by Empedocles or the presence of Nous, as advanced by Anaxagoras. The concept of motion was to find its first orderly explanation much later in Newton's Laws of Motion, which, in turn, have been modified by Professor Einstein's studies in Relativity.

The theory of atoms provided in the minds of the Greeks an interpretation of human intelligence itself, for the mind was said to be made up of fire atoms, the most delicate and sensitive of all, which in the correct combination, found in the human body, took on the capacity of perception and thought.

In this way Democritus used the atomic theory to explain the workings of the human mind, with its power of discrimination between truth and error. In the attempt to define the intellect, his claim to distinction lies not so much in the value of the physical explanation that he offered, but rather in the recognition of the existence of the problem. He was also actively concerned with ethics and strove for an honest understanding of moral responsibility. Thus, with Democritus, whose life stretches on into the fourth century, the search for physical reality among the Greeks came to an end. Democritus had found in the atomic theory an explanation of the universe in scientific and nonsupernatural terms which denied neither the existence of permanence nor the existence of change. Philosophy could now move toward a rational explanation of knowledge and thought.

THE ART OF MEDICINE

Hippocrates. Tradition has it that Hippocrates taught the art of medicine to his pupils beneath the shade of a plane tree, which still spreads its branches over the marketplace of the principal town on the island of Cos. The legend may well be true, for that venerable plane is estimated to be more than twenty-five hundred years old. In any case, it was on the island of Cos that Hippocrates, the physician and scientist, was born, about 460 B.C., and it was there that he practiced the art of healing, taught the profession of medicine to his successors, mingled learning with mellow humanism, and carried forward his scientific research until his death in the fourth century.

The numerous Hippocratic treatises on medicine are the product of various hands, but there can be no doubt of the dominant place of Hippocrates himself in the founding of an ancient school of medicine and in the fostering of a high ethical and scientific code for his associates. Although the present value of ancient Greek medical writings lies in the reconstruction of the history of medicine rather than in more utilitarian aspects, the Hippocratic *Corpus* cannot be read without profound admiration for the practical and sane counsel that it contains. Hippocrates was the foremost man of his profession in a great period of Greek achievement, and consequently his writings convey the same impression of mastery that is to be found in the contemporary work of those who attained eminence in other fields, whether Herodotus and Thucydides in history, Sophocles in drama, or Pheidias in sculpture. This statement may be made without disparagement of the important advances in medicine that were made by the physicians of the Alexandrian Age or by Galen in later Roman times.

A collection of the observations of Hippocrates called the *Aphorisms,* is of interest, principally because they are concise statements of medical experience, but also because they contain evidence of the philosophy of life that lay behind the ancient practice of medicine. Thus the first aphorism embodies in itself a high concept of the profession and of the function of the physician.

Life is short, art is long, opportunity keen, experience fallible, judgment hard. It is the duty of the physician not only to perform his own proper task, but also to effect a harmony among the patient, those in attendance upon him, and external circumstances.

[202]

The Oath. The *Hippocratic Oath,* to which those who entered the profession subscribed, may still be regarded in substance as a proper statement of a physician's duty. A translation, in part, runs thus:

I swear by the physician Apollo, and by Asclepius and Hygeia and Panacea, and by all the gods and goddesses, making them witnesses, that I shall fulfill, to the limit of my capacity and judgment, this oath and this covenant: I shall hold the one who instructed me in this art in equal esteem with my parents; I shall share my substance with him; if he be in need of money I shall make him a sharer of mine; I shall cherish his family even as my own brothers; and I shall teach them the art of medicine, if they wish to learn it, without charge or covenant; I shall impart my knowledge, both orally and in every other form of teaching, to my sons, to the sons of my instructor, and to all students who have enrolled and have taken the physician's oath, but to no one else. I shall govern my treatment by the needs of the sufferers to the best of my ability and judgment, and I shall refrain from all injury and wrongdoing. I shall never give a lethal poison to anyone, even if asked to do so, nor shall I ever offer such advice. In a holy and pure manner I shall pursue the course of my life and my profession. Whenever I enter a home, it shall be for the benefit of the sick, and I shall shun all willful misconduct and injury. Regarding anything that I may see or hear in the course of my work, or even apart from my work in contact with the public, if it be such as should not be repeated at large, I shall keep it to myself, considering such things as inviolable secrets. Finally, therefore, if I fulfill this oath, and do not violate it, may I enjoy high repute among all men and at all times for my life and my profession; but if I do violate it and am forsworn, may the opposite be my fate.

In assessing the place of Hippocrates in the history of Greek civilization, it is difficult to know whether he should be treated as a philosopher or a scientist. It is, however, of less importance to assign him to a particular category than to appreciate the high moral purpose, the intellectual honesty, and the scientific attitude of mind that actuated this ancient Greek physician,

[203]

and thus gave to his teaching of the art of medicine a value that has grown rather than declined with the increase of medical knowledge in modern times.

Archimedes. No treatment of Greek scientific thought would be complete without brief mention of Archimedes, the Sicilian, although his dates (about 287–212 B.C.) place him much later than the physical philosophers previously discussed, and his activities are centered about the Syracusan resistance to Rome. Archimedes was one of the most distinguished, and certainly one of the most ingenious, mathematicians of antiquity, his area of interest embracing what in modern terminology would be called Applied Mathematics. He lived at the court of Hieron II of Syracuse, and one of his greatest discoveries, the Law of Specific Gravity, was made while he was in his bath, eliciting from him the delighted exclamation *Eureka—I have found it.* The very practical purpose of his discovery was to test by specific gravity the purity of the gold in his patron's crown.

Plutarch is the source of much of our knowledge of Archimedes, and some allowance must be made for the fondness of that author for pleasing anecdotes. Yet there seems little reason to doubt his invention of "Archimedes' Screw," a mechanical device for pumping water, or his linking of pulleys in such a way as to raise an enormous weight by comparatively slight exertion. Archimedes is said to have demonstrated this last invention before Hieron by lifting a fully-loaded three-masted ship from the harbor. In the pride of his discovery of the principle of mechanical advantage, he cried out: "Give me a place to stand and I will move the world."

During the siege of Syracuse, which to the amazement of the Romans resisted their armies for more than two years, Archimedes devised many of the engines of defense, such as great beams that swung out from the walls and released massive weights to destroy the Roman scaling ladders.

Yet Archimedes would have preferred to be remembered as a pure mathematician. He described his own ingenious con-

[204]

trivances as the amusements of "geometry at play." He regarded as his greatest discovery the ratio of 3:2, which the cylinder bears to the sphere in volume and area, surely a problem in the realm of nonutilitarian scholarship. It was a device of this nature that was inscribed on his tombstone. Cicero, when serving as quæstor in Sicily two centuries later, discovered the monument, overgrown by weeds, and wrote in melancholy reflection on the transiency of fame.

Archimedes met his death at the hands of a common Roman soldier, a member of the force that stormed the city. The soldier was angered when he was rudely bidden by the old man, intent upon a figure drawn on the ground, to stand away from his diagrams. Archimedes, a figure of the declining age of Greek genius, still stands for the objective pursuit of knowledge with its inevitable, unsought projection into the uses of mankind.

CHAPTER XI

TROUBLE IN ASIA: THE PERSIAN WARS

The Threat of Trouble in Asia

Comparative Quiet in Athens. For two decades after the expulsion of the Peisistratidæ, few events of moment took place in Athens, aside from the steady development of the new political institutions that had been established by Cleisthenes. It was well that the Athenians had such a period of quiet in which to practice their democratic government, for, though they little realized it, in 490 B.C., at the Battle of Marathon, Fate had cast Athens for the role of savior of European civilization. But before dealing with the course of the Persian Wars, we must see what nations had arisen in Asia to threaten the security of Greece.

Friction Between Lydia and the Greek Cities. During the centuries of Greek migration and colonization, great empires had risen or fallen in other parts of the ancient world without causing so much as a ripple of anxiety in Greek consciousness. The Hellenic sense of sufficiency within a city-state kept the Greeks from looking upon the rest of the world with either concern or envy. They were now to discover that, whatever their personal preference might be, no people could live in seclusion or entirely unto itself. In the seventh century, when Greek colonies had already been founded all along the coast of Asia Minor, the state of Lydia began to rise to power and to adopt a hostile attitude toward the rich Greek cities of the coastland. Faint echoes of the menace of the Lydian kings were heard by the Greeks. Gyges, the fabulously wealthy

[206]

monarch of Sardis in Lydia, moved against Miletus, and in the elegiac verses of Mimnermus reference is made to the resistance of the Ionian Greeks. The friction between the Lydian kings and the Greek cities of Asia Minor continued for a long period without decisive action.

Crœsus Reduces the Greek Cities. In 560 B.C., the same year in which Peisistratus seized the tyranny in Athens, Crœsus, like Gyges a king of fabled riches, ascended the throne of Lydia and quickly brought the Greek cities, already weakened by excessive wealth, luxury, and lack of unity, under his control. Crœsus was an admirer of Greek culture, and he did little to interfere with the internal life of the Greek communities. Yet the significance of the campaigns of Crœsus lay not so much in the details of his rule as in the fact that free Greek cities were now brought into subjection and compelled to pay tribute to a foreign prince.

The Overthrow of Crœsus. The rapid success of Crœsus in compelling the Greek citizens to acknowledge his overlordship left him in a position of great power and prosperity. The well-organized kingdom of Lydia, lying to the east of the Greek city of Smyrna and bounded by the River Halys, was wealthy and flourishing. Crœsus' relations with his Asiatic and Egyptian neighbors were friendly, and the possibility of disaster seemed remote. Yet the Lydian king was not long to retain his own throne. Deep in the interior of Asia the empires of the Medes and Persians were rising, while the states and cities of Biblical history, Media, Assyria, Babylonia, and Nineveh, were involved in the realignment of power. In 550 B.C. Cyrus the Great, a Persian prince, seized the consolidated empire of Media, which now extended in the west to the River Halys, the boundary beyond which lay Crœsus' kingdom of Lydia.

The Imperialistic Expansion of Persia. Cyrus had imperialistic ambitions, and within a few years, by 546 B.C., he had subdued Lydia, taken over the capital city, Sardis, and made Crœsus his prisoner. The subjugation of Lydia brought the Greek coastal cities under the power of a new and mightier king, who, unlike Crœsus, cherished no respect for Hellenic culture. In 529 B.C., just one year before the death of Peisistratus in Athens, Cyrus died and was succeeded by his son, Cambyses, who extended the Persian empire south and west into Egypt. In 522 B.C. Cambyses died and was succeeded by Darius. These Oriental despots, ruling with autocratic power, had successively built up a great Asiatic empire, which was to threaten the liberty of the free states of Greece. Thirty years, however, elapsed before Darius definitely set out to bring Athens and Sparta within his empire.

Persian Encroachment on Europe; the Ionian Revolt (499 B.C.). During these thirty years, some very significant events took place, which serve as an introduction to the three Persian expeditions against Greece. In 511 B.C., Darius crossed into Europe near Byzantium, and, with the forced assistance of contingents from the Greek cities of Asia Minor, seized all Thrace as far as the River Danube on the north and the River Strymon on the west. This annexation, however, did not directly affect the cities of Athens and Sparta, which, with steadfast indifference to events on their borders, pursued their own ways. In 499 B.C., a more important movement for later European civilization commenced, for in that year Miletus, one of the most powerful cities of Asia Minor, fomented the Ionian Revolt against Persia. The enslavement of the Ionian Greek cities by Crœsus, Cyrus, and the successive kings of Persia had never reduced their spirit, and a struggle for freedom was sooner or later inevitable.

Into this revolt were gathered practically all the Greeks living between the Hellespont and the island of Cyprus. An appeal was dispatched to Athens and Sparta for assistance in throwing off the Oriental despotism. Sparta, because of the domestic threat of the Helots, refused to have anything to do with an expedition against a king whose capital, Susa, was situated an appalling distance away, for it lay fifteen hundred miles, or three months' journey, to the east. Athens, however, and the little city of Eretria on the island of Eubœa, both of

Ionian stock, came to the assistance of their Asia Minor kinsmen with the dispatch of twenty and five ships respectively, an action that Herodotus describes as "the beginning of evils between the Greeks and barbarians."

The Burning of Sardis. In 498 B.C., an Ionian Greek army, in which were included Athenian and Eretrian soldiers, sacked and burned the city of Sardis. When King Darius in Susa heard of the destruction of the Lydian capital, he was consumed with wrath because of the effrontery of the Athenians in taking part in the expedition, and, lest Oriental lethargy should with time dull his just claim for vengeance, he instructed a slave to repeat three times each day in his hearing: "Sire, remember the Athenians!"

The End of the Ionian Revolt. The Ionian Revolt was brought to an end in 494 B.C. with the capture of Miletus by the Persians. The men of the city were put to death, and the women and children sold into slavery. The destruction of that rich center of Hellenism shook the ancient Greek world, and when shortly thereafter the dramatist Phrynichus presented in Athens an historical play entitled the *Sack of Miletus,* the entire audience burst into tears, and the poet was fined a thousand drachmæ for reminding the Athenians of a misfortune that they felt to be their own. It is difficult to overestimate the effect, even upon later civilizations, of the extermination at that time of free Greek thought in so important an area of the ancient world as the Asia Minor seacoast. The future of European civilization hung in the balance. If the tide of Asiatic power had swept on over Greece the growth of free achievement would have been blighted at the outset.

THE THREE PERSIAN EXPEDITIONS AGAINST GREECE (492 B.C., 490 B.C., 480 B.C.)

With the suppression of the Ionian Revolt, the Persians at once set about the task of both punishing and reorganizing the Greek cities that had taken part in the insurrection. Though the records of the period are meager, it seems clear that the Persians accomplished a wiser and more efficient settlement than an Oriental power might have been expected at that time to bring about. The reestablishment of Persian authority over the Greek communities of Asia was, however, only preliminary to a movement against the Greek mainland, which was originally and primarily motivated by the vow of the king to wreak vengeance upon Athens and Eretria for the burning of Sardis, for such an insult to the dignity of Persia was without parallel.

The Expedition of 492 B.C. Two years after the fall of Miletus, Darius was ready to take action against Greece. Mardonius, the son-in-law of Darius, was placed in command of the expedition, which consisted of both land and naval forces. As Mardonius proceeded through northern Asia Minor, he settled the affairs of the Greek cities, and, presently, bringing his army and fleet together at the Hellespont, crossed into Europe. In Thrace and at the island of Thasos he continued without difficulty his mission of reestablishing Persian power, which had been shaken by the Ionian Revolt, for none of the Greek cities was in a position to offer effectual opposition. He came at length to the city of Acanthus at the base of the promontory of Acte. From this city Mardonius marched inland to Macedonia, where the people submitted readily to him. His mission had prospered, and he viewed the future with confidence.

Disaster was, however, close upon him. At Acanthus he was forced to part company with his fleet, which was instructed to round the end of Acte, where Mount Athos rises menacingly from the sea, and to rejoin him in the Thermaic Gulf beyond the three fingers of the Chalcidic peninsula. A storm arose as the fleet stood off Mount Athos, and the ships were helpless in the treacherous waters. The fleet was dashed upon the rocks, and thousands of the crew perished. Meanwhile, Mardonius had begun to suffer loss with his land army, and a retreat to Asia became imperative. So far as Athens and southern Greece were concerned, the first Persian expedition ended with the

[210]

withdrawal of the Persians, following the maritime disaster at Athos, though the expedition doubtless accomplished a definite military purpose for the Persians in bringing Thrace back under control and in securing the submission of Macedonia. Nevertheless, it had done nothing to avenge the insult committed against Persia in the burning of Sardis, and further action was to follow.

The Expedition of 490 B.C. Darius was still firm in his determination to wreak vengeance on the Greek cities. Hippias, the exiled tyrant of Athens, was at the court of Darius, treacherously urging upon him the subjugation of Athens, which he was prepared to rule again as a vassal of the Persian king. In 490 B.C., another Persian expedition set sail for Greece, this time under the leadership of two generals, Datis and Artaphernes, and their instructions were above all to enslave the Athenians and Eretrians and bring them into the presence of the king. Careful preparations were made for the expected conquest. Heralds were sent in advance to demand in the name of the king earth and water from the Greek states as tokens of submission. At Sparta, in defiance of all diplomatic etiquette, the heralds were thrown into a muddy well and told to take from there earth and water to their master.

In order to avoid a recurrence of the shipwreck at Mount Athos, the army this time embarked on a great fleet of six hundred triremes, together with transports carrying troops and horses, and sailed directly from Samos across the Ægean Sea. The island of Naxos was first subdued by the Persian ships, which then moved on to the Cyclades, reducing these islands one by one. Only the sacred island of Delos was spared out of respect to the gods. Late in the summer of 490 B.C., the Persian armada, coming round the south of the island of Eubœa, reduced Carystus and Eretria in turn. After tarrying for a few days at Eretria, the Persians moved on to disembark their troops at the Bay of Marathon, where Hippias recalled that his father Peisistratus had once effected his return from exile. It was no accident that Marathon was chosen for the landing, for on the

[211]

rocky shores of Greece it affords one of the few sandy beaches where such a venture might be tried with any hope of success. The place at which significant battles of antiquity took place was often determined by geographical considerations.

Meanwhile, reports had constantly been reaching Athens as men fled from Eretria, or others who had marked the progress of the Persians came to the city and told what they had seen. The Athenians prepared to defend their land. It was clear that, in spite of appalling numerical inferiority, they must make ready to meet the imminent threat. Accordingly, the Athenians, to the number of nine or ten thousand, marched across the Attic peninsula and took up their position on high ground, looking down on the Bay of Marathon. For some days no action was taken, for the Athenians themselves were divided as to the policy which they ought to pursue. A messenger, Pheidippides by name, was sent to Sparta to appeal for aid before it was too late. The Spartan ephors, hearing of the fate that had already befallen Eretria and recognizing that Athens was faced with almost certain destruction, agreed to lend assistance as soon as religious restraints would permit. They were, however, precluded by ancient custom from marching before the full moon.

Though the reason given by the Spartans seems to have been entirely sincere, the Battle of Marathon was destined to be fought, and the future of European civilization determined before the days elapsed which brought the moon to the full. A body of one thousand Platæans joined the Athenians, and as they waited for the Lacedæmonians to come to their assistance, the Persians began to reëmbark part of their troops, and the Athenians realized that if they remained at Marathon, the Persian fleet could sail around the promontory of Sunium and come upon the unprotected Piræus, while if they hastened back to the city by land, they could be effectively attacked from the rear. The time for decision had come.

The Divided Command. The Athenian command rested with the Board of Ten Generals, with Callimachus as *pole-*

march, or commander-in-chief, but the most vital inspiration emanated from a general named Miltiades. The other generals were said to have yielded their days of command so that he might take charge in the decisive attack. Whatever differences of opinion there had been among the Greek generals were harmonized, and the unselfish polemarch, Callimachus, no less than Miltiades, must have his share of credit for the

Photograph by Alinari

FIGURE 43. THE FUNERAL MOUND AT MARATHON. This mound still holds the remains of the one hundred and ninety-two Athenians who died in the battle, 490 B.C.

victory that was won and for the strategy that made success possible.

The Battle of Marathon. As the Greek army faced the forces of the Persians on the curving bay, it was deployed in such a way that the center, though extended to cover the corresponding division of the Persian army, was left comparatively weak in man power, whereas the right wing, which was led by Callimachus, and the left wing, where the Platæans were massed, were made as strong as possible. As the attack began, the Greek army covered the final intervening space at the

[213]

double, in order to avoid heavy casualties from the Persian bowmen, and in the brief, fierce battle the action developed as the Greeks had planned. The Persian center broke through the weak Greek position, but the wings held and turned on the entrapped Persians, who were driven in confusion to their ships. When the tumult of battle cleared, Herodotus tells that there were found more than six thousand Persians dead and only one hundred and ninety-two Athenians. The very conservatism of the stated numbers in an age of exaggeration lends credence to their reliability.

*Courtesy of the Museum
of Fine Arts, Boston*

Figure 44. Athenian Silver Tetradrachm, 480 b.c. to 430 b.c. The waning moon, symbolic of Spartan delay, is engraved close to the neck of the owl.

The Aftermath of the Battle. Shortly after the battle, the full moon having freed them, the Spartans arrived, gazed upon the dead, praised the valor of the Athenians, and returned home. Praise of others came hard to the Spartans, and perhaps their conduct should be judged more generously than one is at first disposed to do. If the Athenians felt any bitterness toward them, they confined it to the silent reproach of including on their next issue of coins a little waning moon, as a reminder to Hellas of the momentous time when, but for Platæa, they had stood alone at Marathon (Figure 44). The victory at Marathon was an almost unbelievable triumph for the Athenian democracy, and the moral effect on Athens was enormous. It was the proudest moment in her civic life, and it had been achieved by her own citizen soldiers. Themistocles and Aristeides, the generals, Æschylus, the tragic poet, and many another Athenian, had taken their stand on that eventful day and remembered it with pride forever after. Then Æschylus composed the epitaph for his own tomb, he said nothing of

[214]

his immortal plays but recorded only his own name and that of his father and his city and the fact that he had fought against the long-haired Mede at Marathon.

Themistocles and the Growth of Naval Power. More important to the future of Athens than Callimachus or Miltiades, was another general who had fought at Marathon. This was Themistocles, a man who had already envisaged the future of Athens as a naval power. Even before the Battle of Marathon, he had served as archon in Athens and had carried a measure for the fortification of its seaport, the Piræus. The brief naval war between Athens and Ægina, which took place in the ten-year interval after Marathon, indicated again the need for such defense, and Themistocles continued to urge a strong naval policy. In particular, he was able to persuade the Athenians to use the revenue from a new silver vein at Laurium to build up the navy to a strength of some two hundred triremes. All this was accomplished before the Persians struck again. In the campaign of 480 B.C., Athens, thanks to Themistocles, was able to muster an effective navy, while Sparta threw her whole military power into the defense of Greece.

The Expedition of 480 B.C. In 480 B.C. Xerxes, who had succeeded his father Darius as king of Persia, took up the pursuit of vengeance, or of empire, as one chooses to interpret it. The humiliation of Marathon, which was now added to the destruction of Sardis, had sunk deep into the souls of Persia's princes, and Xerxes now prepared an overwhelming armament for the subjugation of Greece. He decided to move on the country by the northern route, keeping his army and navy in touch with one another. The tales of the extent of his preparations and of his army have been grossly exaggerated, and it is often difficult to differentiate between the product of an historian's vivid imagination and fact. But with all possible allowance for error, the army was still immeasurably greater than any that had ever before threatened Greece, and many times as large as that which the Greek states could muster to oppose it.

The account of the assembling, moving, and feeding of the

heterogeneous Persian host constitutes a fascinating tale of ancient war logistics. Herodotus tells awe-inspiring stories of five million men, recruited from forty-six nations, who took seven days and seven nights to cross the Hellespont and who drank rivers dry on the march, but such embellishments seem to have been introduced in order to emphasize the difference between the arrogant pride of the barbarians in their invincible host and the ultimate humiliation to be wrought upon them by the steadfast Greeks. A lesson in the workings of Nemesis was dear to the heart of the historian. On the other hand, one must guard against undue doubt, for the preparation and movement of a host unprecedentedly large brought many strange things to pass. It is probably true that a bridge of boats was constructed across the Hellespont to permit the passage of the army and that a canal was dug across the neck of the peninsula of Athos in order that the ships might not be wrecked at the promontory as they were in 492 B.C. The army may have numbered three hundred thousand men, and the navy perhaps a thousand ships. Even such figures represented forces hitherto unknown to the small city-states of Greece.

The Battle at the Pass of Thermopylæ. After crossing the Hellespont, the Persian forces of Xerxes proceeded through Thrace and Macedonia over part of the route that Mardonius had followed twelve years earlier. For a time the Greeks considered making a stand at the Vale of Tempe in Thessaly, and sent troops north for that purpose. The position was abandoned because there were other passes by which the Persians might have eluded them, and also because they were not able to deal effectively with the Persian fleet at a corresponding point on the coast. Thereupon they took up a position at Thermopylæ, and though this decision necessarily drove the northern Greeks to make peace with the Persians, the selection of the site had two advantages. In the first place, the island of Eubœa approaches the mainland near Thermopylæ, and the Greek fleet, by mustering at Artemisium, the northern promontory of the island, might hope to engage the Persian navy and

[216]

prevent it from entering the narrow straits to land men in the rear of the Greek army. In the second place, the line of the coast in antiquity left only the narrowest defile between the water and the sheer mountain walls about the warm springs of Thermopylæ, and it was possible for a comparatively small body to withstand an enormous invading force at this place.

In late summer Xerxes reached the Pass of Thermopylæ, and some days later his fleet sailed down from the Thermaic Gulf toward Cape Sepias, north of the Island of Eubœa, and anchored off the coast. Then the gods unexpectedly came to the aid of Hellas, for a great storm suddenly descended, and perhaps four hundred Persian ships were wrecked. Although the Persians still retained a numerical superiority over the Greeks, the latter in a subsequent encounter succeeded in destroying additional Persian ships and reducing the discrepancy between the two navies.

The story was told that a certain Scyllias of Scione, who was the greatest diver of his time, leapt into the sea at Aphetæ and swam under water to Artemisium, some ten miles away, in order to bring news to the Greeks of the damage wrought by the storm. Herodotus, who tells the story, judiciously adds that in his opinion the man used a boat.

Meanwhile Leonidas, the Spartan king, who was in charge of the Greek forces, held the Pass, while Xerxes and the Persians allowed four days to go by without action. On the fifth day the attack was made, and the Greek spearmen repelled the Persians. That day and the next the Persian efforts were unavailing. Even the famed Immortals of the Persian army were thrust back, while Xerxes "in an agony of fear for his soldiers, leapt thrice from his throne." The Pass seemed impregnable, but at length a treacherous Greek by the name of Ephialtes undertook to guide the Persians by an obscure mountain path which would lead them to a position behind Leonidas and his soldiers. The mountain road was guarded by a detachment of Phocians, who withdrew to the heights, permitting the Persians to reach their objective.

[217]

When Leonidas realized what had been done, he sent the greater part of the allied troops away, possibly in order that they might find another defensible line farther to the south, but he and three hundred Spartans with him, together with contingents of Thespians and Thebans, scorning a retreat, chose to face the Persians and to die. They did not await the Persian onslaught, but advanced to force the battle in a wider part of the Pass. There was no hope of survival, and they fought with reckless courage so long as spears or arrows or daggers remained to them. Quite recently, deposits of the weapons used in that encounter have been discovered, lending eloquent testimony to a battle in which the Persians had threatened that their arrows would fly so thick that they would darken the sun. When the engagement came to an end, not one Spartan was left alive.

The Results of the Defeat at Thermopylæ. The indubitable fact that the valor of the Spartans is one of the finest examples in the history of mankind of unquestioning devotion to duty must not be allowed to obscure the great strategic victory that the Persians had won at Thermopylæ, for nothing could now prevent them from reaching Athens. Moreover, though the Spartans had been roused to play a noble part in resisting the invaders, their insular policy respecting the other states of Greece quickly reasserted itself, and, abetted by the Corinthians, they urged that the Athenians and all others who dwelt to the north should withdraw to the Peloponnese and join in building a wall across the isthmus of Corinth, behind which they should all take shelter.

The Initiative of Themistocles. It was a stupid and selfish policy, which would surely have spelled disaster for Greece, but for the fact that Athens was fortunate in having as her leader at this time Themistocles, whose naval policy has already come under notice, and who was able to circumvent the narrow plan of the Spartans. Themistocles was one of the ablest, if also one of the most unscrupulous, admirals and statesmen that the city ever produced. He was convinced that the

[218]

safety of Athens lay upon the sea, and so persuasive was he that he induced the Athenians to abandon their city, with the graves and shrines of their forefathers, to be sacked by the impious barbarians, to transport the women and children to the neighboring states and islands, and to trust to the ships as the "wooden walls" in which the Delphic oracle had promised safety.

The Battle of Salamis. To the Spartans and Corinthians, Themistocles pointed out that the wall across the isthmus would be useless if the Persians were left in control of the sea and were able to land anywhere upon the Peloponnese, but even with this argument he had difficulty in preventing the withdrawal of their land and naval forces. After the defeat at Thermopylæ, there was no longer any object in keeping the Greek fleet in that vicinity. Consequently, the Greeks retired to the Bay of Salamis before Athens, and there the Persians followed them, and took up an opposing position. Themistocles realized that the test of a naval encounter must be met, and lest the Peloponnesians should sail away during the night, he devised an ingenious stratagem. Pretending friendship for Xerxes, he sent a message telling him that the Greeks were planning to slip away by night, and urging him to cut off the possibility of escape for the Greek fleet by sending a number of Persian ships to close the strait at the farther side of the island of Salamis. Possibly the reputation of Themistocles for tact and duplicity alike made the suggestion of treachery entirely credible to the Persian king. In any case, Xerxes acted on Themistocles' advice, and in the morning, with all chance of a Greek retreat cut off, a naval encounter was recognized by everyone to be inevitable.

The Accounts of Herodotus and Æschylus. Two detailed accounts of the Battle of Salamis are available, one by the historian Herodotus, who was perhaps four years old and living at the time in Halicarnassus, a city on the coast of Asia Minor, but who undoubtedly heard when he later resided in Athens the reminiscences of many a sailor who had been present at

[219]

the battle. The other account is a poetic description in the *Persians* of Æschylus. The dramatic poet had himself fought at Salamis, as he had at Marathon, and despite the license of poetry, his is the more accurate description. At daybreak the Greeks commenced the attack. Almost at once the confined space of the Bay of Salamis began to work to their advantage, for with fewer and smaller ships they were able to navigate more easily as oars were splintered and vessels shattered one against another. Every effort of the Persians to retreat brought further disaster, though Xerxes, who had stationed himself on Mount Ægaleos, on the mainland, to watch the encounter, had many acts of signal bravery to record. The battle lasted all through the day, and the Persians, who, almost without exception, were unable to swim, lost practically all the men from their wrecked ships. By nightfall the engagement was over, and a great and significant victory had been won for Greece.

The Acclaim of Themistocles. The commanding admiral at Salamis was the Spartan Eurybiadas. The story is told that after the battle all the Greek admirals took a vote as to who had been the ablest. When the ballots were counted, it was found that there were as many different votes for first place as there were admirals, but Themistocles was unanimously awarded the second prize.

Another apocryphal story that grew up around Themistocles in the days of his brilliance concerns a jealous citizen of the tiny island community of Seriphus, who said once to Themistocles:

"It is not yourself but Athens that has made you great. If you had been a citizen of Seriphus, you would not now be thus renowned."

"It is true," Themistocles replied, "that I would not be great in Seriphus, nor would you in Athens."

The Battle of Platæa. The decisive defeat of the Persians at Salamis very quickly altered the plans of the Persian king

[220]

Xerxes. The loss to his fleet had been so great that he feared that the Greek navy might now sail to the Hellespont and destroy the bridge of boats by which the Persian army was to return. Furthermore, the disappointment and chagrin at failure directed the thoughts of Xerxes toward his home, and he was readily persuaded to order the return of the fleet, and himself to withdraw, accompanied by sixty thousand men, to the Hellespont, leaving Mardonius with perhaps three hundred thousand soldiers in Greece to pursue the conquest in the following year. During the winter, Mardonius maintained his army in Thessaly and prepared for the renewal of hostilities. He attempted to bribe the Athenians into withdrawing their support from their Greek allies, but in spite of the inherent Greek difficulty in uniting for corporate effort, the spirit of freedom was invincible and Athens and the Greek states continued their joint resistance to the common enemy. In 479 B.C., the armies of Persia and of Greece came together on the plain about the city of Platæa in Bœotia, where the last encounter was to be fought. The combined Greek forces amounted to as many as one hundred thousand men, the largest joint military enterprise on which the Greeks ever embarked. Their commander was Pausanias, the nephew of Leonidas, and guardian of the child-king of Sparta.

We are fortunate in having in the *History* of Herodotus an account in great detail of the preliminary skirmishes, the location of the different army divisions, and the movements of troops on the field, from which students of military strategy have been able to reconstruct the progress of the battle in relation to the site. These details need not now be told. It is the fact of victory itself that is important, with all that it signified in the triumph of western freedom just when Greece was entering the period of her greatest intellectual activity. When, as the battle raged, Mardonius was slain, the conclusion was certain. Great masses of the Persians were killed; their rich treasures were pillaged; and the scattered remnants of the proud host made their way in sorry plight back to Asia.

[221]

Shortly after the victory at Platæa the Greek navy defeated a Persian fleet decisively at Mycale, near Samos, thus confirming in Asia Minor the moral effect of the success at Platæa. Greece had stemmed the tide of Oriental invasion and opened for a Europe still in a state of barbarism a destiny of free intellectual life, which could tempt a poet of the nineteenth century to exclaim "better fifty years of Europe than a cycle of Cathay."

The Struggle in the West. It is worth noting, in passing, the relations of Greek communities in different parts of the world during the time of the Persian Wars. The Athenians and Eretrians had felt the bond of Ionian kinship strongly enough to become engaged in war for the salvation of the Asia Minor cities on the occasion of the Ionian Revolt in 499 B.C., and at the conclusion of the resulting wars between Persia and Greece, they considered it a primary duty to free the Ionian cities from the Persians. But when both Athens and Sparta were fighting for their lives at Salamis and Thermopylæ and Platæa, no aid from either Dorian or Ionian colonies in southern Italy or Sicily was forthcoming, for these cities were at that very time engaged in repelling another barbarian invasion, which came from Carthage, the Phœnician city on the northern coast of Africa. The western Greeks were also successful in preserving their liberty. The Battle of Himera in northern Sicily, fought between the Sicilian Greeks and the Carthaginians in 480 B.C., the same year as the Battle of Salamis, proved a decisive victory for the cause of Hellenism in the west. It made possible the development of a great civilization there, too, in the fifth century.

The End of the Persian Wars. The third Persian expedition was the last occasion in antiquity when the invasion of Greece by a barbarian army was seriously threatened. The successes of the Greeks continued, and within a few years all the Greek cities of the islands and of Asia Minor that had been reduced by Crœsus and Cyrus during the sixth century were again set free. The Battles of Marathon and Salamis and Platæa have an enormous claim on the world's attention. The question at stake on those fields was not so much the independence of a few small city-states as a conflict between two philosophies of life. Already Greece had mapped her course along the path of free institutions, constitutional government, freedom of the intellect, and the supremacy of law and of reason, while Persia epitomized the arbitrary despotism of an Oriental autocracy over obsequious subjects. The defeat of Persia assured freedom to the western world for twenty-five hundred years. The spirit of Greece in those days of strife and adversity has, however,

Courtesy of the Museum of Fine Arts, Boston

FIGURE 45. SILVER DECADRACHM FROM SYRACUSE. This series of coins, known as Demareteia, were struck from 480 B.C. to 479 B.C. to commemorate the Syracusan victory in the Battle of Himera.

given to the world not the assurance of liberty to be enjoyed without effort, but rather the responsibility to maintain by equal endeavor the opportunity for a free life that was preserved for the world in those days. The history of our own century, with the rise and fall of totalitarian states, the emergence of the democracies, and the continuing fight for freedom, constitutes a reaffirmation of the principles for which Greece stood.

[223]

The Effect on Greece. The victories in the Persian Wars suggest two observations concerning their immediate effect on Greece. The first is a passing comment on the measure of temporary unity which the impending catastrophe forced on the Greek states. If they had been able to work out some form of continuous cooperation in peace, as they had in battle at Salamis and Platæa, the later history of the country might have been happier. The second observation is the fact that the significance of the victories was recognized in Greece at once. No passing centuries were needed to lend perspective. When the Athenians came back to their city after the departure of the Persians, they came with the spirit of men who had been preserved by the gods for a glorious future, and for whom all things were possible. For that reason, the year 480 B.C. forms an excellent dividing line between the hope, effort, and experimentation, not unmixed with apprehension, of the earlier period and the self-confidence and great accomplishment that marked the following years.

CHAPTER XII

HERODOTUS

History and the Historian. It has been said that history teaches nothing, only the historian. In a sense history has always been in the process of becoming, for history is neither more nor less than the sum of men's relationships. Yet history becomes significant as part of man's thinking when some historian takes account of human conduct and records it for the information and instruction of his fellows. The personality, sense of proportion, and philosophy of life of the historian thus assume great importance, for he inevitably becomes a teacher.

The Logographers. History as a consecutive reasoned account of a certain epoch begins in the fifth century. It was natural that it should be so, for in the preceding centuries the Greeks had been too completely engrossed in action, political, artistic, and literary, to pause and evaluate the elements of life that surrounded them. The very circumstances that made the momentary, individualistic lyric poetry a proper outlet for the emotions of the archaic period precluded the rise of serious history at that time. It is true, nonetheless, that the germs of historical record can be observed in the years before the Persian Wars in the writings of the logographers, or record chroniclers. Genealogies were compiled in the sixth century by Cadmus of Miletus and Acusilaus of Bœotia. About 500 B.C., Hecatæus of Miletus, who had personal contact with the Ionian Revolt and who was a widely traveled man, was attempting to set down honestly and objectively some records intended to be more worthy of credence than uncritical legends and traditions.

[225]

He wrote a travelogue called a *Tour of the World,* and illustrated it with a map. Hellanicus of Lesbos lived during the fifth century and is mentioned by Thucydides, but only scattered fragments of his work are known. It is with some justification, however, that history is said to begin with Herodotus, the historian to whom we are indebted for the detailed account of the Persian Wars.

Courtesy of the Metropolitan Museum of Art

FIGURE 46. HERODOTUS. The literary man is symbolized; precise portraiture is not intended at this time.

Life of Herodotus. Herodotus was born in the Carian city of Halicarnassus, perhaps in 484 B.C., that is, six years after the Battle of Marathon and four years before the Battle of Salamis, which were to play so large a part in his great *History.* Partly, it seems, because of political unrest at home, and partly through love of novelty, he started in his young manhood on extensive travels, going first to the island of Samos, where he remained for some years. Toward the middle of the fifth century he went to Athens, which under Pericles had become the literary center of Greece. In 443 B.C., he sailed to Thurii in Italy to take part in the settlement of a colony dispatched by Pericles. He was still living in 428 B.C., three years after the outbreak of the Peloponnesian War. The exact date of his death is unknown.

His Travels. The movements of Herodotus were not limited to Samos, Athens, and Thurii. He traveled extensively in Asia Minor and to the interior of Asia as far as Babylon; he knew

[226]

the region of the Euxine, or Black, Sea and the land of Colchis; in Egypt he pressed up the Nile as far as Assuan; the Greek lands and islands were all familiar to him. Everywhere he moved with the alert intellectual curiosity of the true Greek, and his interest embraced everything that would appeal to an intelligent man. The result was that he found it hard to exclude from his story the fascinating tales that were told to him, whether of gold-mining ants, one-eyed Arimaspians, cattle that backed as they ate, and sheep whose tails were supported on wheeled carts, and as a result he has gained a reputation for both credulity and untruthfulness, which, as we shall presently see, is not entirely deserved.

The Arrangement of His Work. Herodotus was in some respects quite unsystematic in the arrangement and proportion of his work. The account of the Persian Wars, the primary object of his *History,* is found in the last four of the nine books which he wrote. He closed his account appropriately with the taking of Sestus on the Hellespont by the Greeks in 479 B.C., for the capture of that city from the Persians marks the turning of the tide, the recession of Persian aggression, and the beginning of Greek ascendancy through the remainder of the century. Herodotus himself was about five years old when Sestus was taken, but he wrote his history when sufficient time had elapsed not only to make men feel that in the Persian Wars a suitable topic for the first history might be found, but also to give perspective with which to round out and close his theme. The first five books of the *History* of Herodotus are a vast and valued storehouse of facts, social customs, religion, geography, and legend, touching, among others, the little known countries of Lydia, Babylon, Scythia, Colchis, and Egypt.

The Credulity of Herodotus. If not a few preposterous stories found their way into the accounts of strange peoples, one must, in estimating the credibility of Herodotus, bear three things constantly in mind. In the first place, Herodotus has stated more than once that his conception of the duty of the historian is to tell all that he has heard but not necessarily to

[227]

believe it. Such an understanding of his task may rob him of the right to be called critical, but it nevertheless defends the honesty of his purpose. In the second place, many an improbable tale is prefaced by a saving clause to the effect that "it is said" or "the story goes," or even by a frank statement that he himself does not believe the account. In the third place, subsequent anthropological and geographical studies have proved true many of the statements of Herodotus that were once thought to be mere figments of the imagination; and in still other cases, the critical acumen of Herodotus caused him to reject stories that he should have accepted. A single instance will serve. He tells how some Phœnician sailors went south through the Red Sea and about the lower end of Africa, and how, on returning by the Pillars of Heracles, the modern straits of Gibraltar, after two full years, they reported that they had seen the sun on their right hand as they sailed about the continent. "Others may believe the story," says Herodotus, "I cannot." Yet the tale was true, for the Phœnicians had sailed south of the equator, the existence of which the Greeks had no reason even to suspect.

It is evident that the judgment of Herodotus is sometimes colored by the theological concepts of his age. He believed profoundly in Nemesis, which inexorably punished the haughty and the guilty, and it was inevitable that he should see in the central theme of his *History,* the humiliation of the arrogant army of the Persians, the greatest and most significant manifestation of divine retribution visited by the angry gods on those who thought themselves invincible on earth.

The Tales of Herodotus. With an understanding of the mind and interests of Herodotus, and a judicious rather than hostile questioning of parts of the narrative, one may read the early books of the historian with entertainment and also with instruction as the processes of his thinking are revealed by his selective judgment.

Babylonian Marriage Customs. He delighted to record such

[228]

customs as the marriage market which existed among the Babylonians.

The wisest custom that they practiced, in my judgment, is that whereby, once each year, in the various villages the maidens of marriageable age were gathered all together in one place, while the men stood about them in a throng. Thereupon a herald would summon each maiden in turn and offer her for sale, selecting first the most beautiful of all; and when he had sold her for a high price he would summon the next most beautiful girl who remained. Thus they were sold as wives. The wealthiest of the Babylonians would bid against one another for the most beautiful girls, but those of the people who wished to marry but who did not insist on so great beauty would take the plainer maidens, together with a dowry. For when the herald had gone through the group selling the most beautiful girls, he would then summon the ugliest one and dispose of her to the man who was willing to take her with the smallest marriage portion. The dowries were provided from the money received through the sale of the beautiful girls, and in this way the fair maidens provided marriage portions for the ugly.

The frank approval with which Herodotus regards this practice seems out of harmony with the Greek point of view. But the historian is not necessarily advocating the adoption by the Greeks of the practices that he observed; he is simply commenting on the effectiveness of the ideas in the environment where they grew up. He is not the first or the last man who has abandoned an admired institution with a wistful shake of the head.

An Ancient Medical Clinic. Herodotus was also struck by the ingenuity of the Babylonians in the treatment of disease, for he follows the description of the marriage auction with this observation:

The second wisest custom among them is this: since they do not employ physicians, they carry those who are ill out into the market-place, and the passers-by offer advice to the sick, if any one of them has suffered a similar disease or known another who has been afflicted by it. So they come, and offer advice, and praise the remedies by which each of them found a cure for the disease, or knew another to have used successfully. And it is not allowed that anyone should pass a sufferer by in silence, without asking from what disease he is suffering.

It is tempting to think that Herodotus is himself amused by the gratuitous advice that is everywhere offered on illness. *Foreign Views of Birth and Death.* There is a philosophic attitude of reflection on human life behind the practice of one of the Thracian tribes, which Herodotus thus describes:

The Trausi follow the custom of the rest of the Thracians in all other respects, but in the case of birth and death they act in this manner. Whenever a child is born, the relatives sit about and give way to lamentation because of all the hardships which it must undergo, and they recite all human misfortunes. But whenever a man dies, they jest and make merry as they bury him and recall how now, delivered from manifold misfortune, he is in the midst of happiness.

If the Thracians show a certain relentless logic in the practice just described, there is in the Persian attitude toward infant mortality and the avoidance of sorrow a calculating quality that is more than a little repellant.

With them manly valor is demonstrated, next to bravery in war, by the possession of many sons. To the man who can point to the largest number, the king sends gifts each year, for number they regard as strength. They train their sons from the fifth to the twentieth year in three things only—horsemanship, bowmanship, and the practice of truth. Before a boy reaches his fifth year he is never admitted to his father's presence, but is reared among the women. This they do so that, if the child should die young, his death may bring no grief to the father.

A Persian Use of Wine. The strange check on judgment devised by the Persians as an early variety of economical bicameral legislation interested Herodotus:

> They drink wine freely, and it is their custom to take counsel on the most serious matters while they are drunk. On the following day the master of the house in which the deliberations took place proposes to them again, while sober, the decision that they reached the night before, and if it is also agreeable to them when sober, they adopt it; if not, they reject it. Furthermore, the conclusions that they first reach when sober, they consider again while drunk.

The Origin of Language. The strange story that arises from the Egyptians' self-consciousness regarding their antiquity is probably true, so far as the actual experiment is concerned, for there is a record of similar tests having been made in later times by Frederick II of Germany and James IV of Scotland, though their purposes differed. This is the tale:

> The Egyptians used to believe, before Psammetichus became their king, that they were the earliest of human kind. But when Psammetichus became king, he wished to discover what people had been born first, and from his time the Egyptians believed that the Phrygians were earlier than themselves, though they were earlier than all others. Now when Psammetichus was not able to discover, for all his inquiries, what people were the earliest born, he devised this experiment. Taking two new-born children of the ordinary run of citizenry, he handed them over to a goatherd to bring up among the flocks, in such a way that no one should utter a word in their presence, but that they should be secluded in a deserted hut, to which goats should be brought at the proper time, so that they might get their fill of milk, and be cared for otherwise, as might be necessary. Psammetichus did this, and gave these orders, because he wished to learn from these children, as soon as they had passed the stage of meaningless babbling, what word they would utter first. And this actually came to pass. When a period of two years had gone by, the goatherd, carrying out his orders, opened the door one day, and as he entered both children fell upon him, stretching out their arms, and uttered the word "bekos." When the shepherd first

heard this, he did nothing, but when, as he repeatedly came to look after them, the word was constantly used, he indicated the fact to the king, and at his command brought the children before him. When Psammetichus himself heard, he inquired what people called some object "bekos," and learned that the Phrygians used this word for bread. As a result of this experiment, the Egyptians conceded that the Phrygians were older than themselves.

Whatever strictures one may be moved to pronounce on such high-handed treatment of other people's children, he is nevertheless led, through the contemplation of this undoubtedly authentic tale, to reflect on the curiously direct and uncritical interpretation of evidence, which fails to take account of any results other than those that were sought from the beginning. It is the same fault that was observed in the researches of the earliest physical philosophers. Thus it seems never to have occurred to Psammetichus or the scholars of his court, that the word "bekos" that the children uttered was an onomatopoetic imitation of the only sound they had ever been allowed to hear, the bleating of the goats.

Estimate of Herodotus. Such stories as those that have been translated, which might be multiplied greatly, afford the best understanding of the open mind and inclusive interest with which Herodotus went about the ancient world, always eager to see and talk and question men and then to record the things that he thought others, too, might like to learn. At the same time, one should not allow the diverting nature of the anecdotes in the early books of the *History* to obscure the fact that Herodotus had undertaken to render an account of the Persian Wars, and that this part of his *History* is the great achievement that he made. The historical details of the preceding chapter owe their origin almost entirely to Herodotus. A sense of critical selectivity was not part of the mental attainments of Herodotus, but scholars must remain indebted to him both for his history of the great conflict between Greece and Persia and for the discursive interest in man that has preserved such a wealth of fact and legend about the countries that he visited.

[232]

CHAPTER XIII

ATHENS DURING THE EARLY FIFTH CENTURY

The Mood of Elation. It was part of the nature of a small Greek state that emotions of hope or despair were felt quickly by the entire population, following great success or failure. The victorious conclusion of the Persian Wars marked the close of one era and the beginning of another in the civilization of Greece. For purposes of artistic and literary criticism, the years before 480 B.C. belong to the archaic age, while the fifth century may be said to begin with the return of the Athenians to the Acropolis, which the Persians had laid in ruins, and the restoration of the citizens of the other states to their homes, which in varying degrees had suffered the ravages of Persian impiety. Grievous though their sufferings had been, they faced the future not as men whose long efforts had ended in destruction and frustration, but rather as men who had cast off a great load of fear and apprehension, and who might now pursue the several avenues of endeavor, which had been developing throughout the archaic period.

The Pentacontaëtia. The first half-century of the new era, from the end of the Persian Wars in 480 B.C. to the outbreak of the Peloponnesian War in 431 B.C., the Greeks described rather vaguely as the Pentacontaëtia, which means the "Fifty-year-period." For those years there is no detailed historical account in the sense that Herodotus has left a record of the Persian Wars, and Thucydides of the Peloponnesian War. The more important incidents of the period must be reconstructed from

[233]

inscriptions, references in contemporary writers of drama or oratory, and from archæological sources. The total record of knowledge will, however, be found to be great, especially when the cultural achievements in art and architecture are included in the appraisal.

The Significant Achievements of the Pentacontaëtia. From a political and military point of view, the history of the first half of the fifth century is quickly told. The inveterate divisive tendency of the Greek states soon dissolved the hasty alliances that had brought unified action at Platæa, and once more the different cities pursued their separate ways. As a consequence, Greece was never free for any length of time from internal wars. For what seemed to the states involved good and sufficient reasons, Athens or Sparta, Thebes or Argos, Corinth or Ægina conducted their campaigns or sought alliances or concluded truces for five years or thirty years, as the case might be, though seldom were such predetermined efforts to maintain cordial relations completely successful.

Some of the details of military and political affairs require brief description, so that the historical pattern of the period may be understood. But the real story of Greek civilization in the fifth century lies in the chapters that can now be devoted to the drama, to architecture, and to sculpture, for it was the dedication of the Greeks to the achievements of the mind, in spite of the regrettable continuance of armed conflict among themselves, that has made the fifth century forever memorable as the most brilliant age of human genius.

THE REBUILDING OF THE WALLS OF ATHENS

The Stratagem of Themistocles. In all the campaigns of the Persian Wars, Sparta rather than Athens had repeatedly seized and held the initiative of leadership. But it was now the Athenian Themistocles, the clever but unscrupulous admiral who had directed the Athenian fleet at Salamis, who undertook to raise his city to a new position of power in Greece after the withdrawal of the Persians. Themistocles was determined that Athens should in the future be freed from her humiliating position of inferiority to Sparta. To that end it was imperative that the walls of Athens be rebuilt, despite the specious representations of the Spartans, who, with their own city unwalled, urged that all other states in Greece should join with them in throwing down their fortifications, so that the barbarians, if they should again come against Greece, might find no forts from which to direct their own campaigns. It would have been dangerous to reject the Spartan proposals out of hand, but Themistocles was equal to the occasion. Relying on the slowness of communications, he had an embassy of three men, including himself, appointed to treat with the Spartans. Then he went alone to Sparta, and day by day made excuses for the nonappearance of his colleagues and his consequent inability to open negotiations, while the other two remained in Athens and aided the united efforts of men, women, and children to rebuild the walls, which they did in a fever of haste by laying hold of grave monuments, building-stones, architectural fragments, or anything else available.

When news of the Themistoclean stratagem trickled through to Sparta, the wily Athenian protested his innocence and urged that Spartan representatives be sent to Athens to learn the truth. The Spartans acceded to the suggestion, but when their envoys reached Athens, Themistocles contrived to have them kept there until the walls of the city reached a defensible height, and then he boldly declared to the states of Greece, and especially to Sparta, that Athens was prepared to defend her position in the future as the equal of any state.

It is interesting to note that within the present century a purely utilitarian excavation in connection with the roadbed of an electric railroad connecting the Piræus with Athens disclosed part of the Themistoclean Wall and proved by the recovery of sculptured blocks the accuracy of the tale of the hasty rebuilding.

The Defense of the Piræus. It was also at the bidding of

Themistocles that the defenses of the Piræus were built up, and some twenty years later, perceiving the danger that would result if the port were cut off from the city in war, the Athenians united Athens to the Piræus by means of the Long Walls.

THE DELIAN CONFEDERACY

The Organization of the Delian Confederacy. The withdrawal of the barbarians from the mainland of Greece in 479 B.C. left with Athens and Sparta two problems. One was the adoption of adequate safeguards against future aggression, and the other was the liberation from Persian domination of the Greek cities of the islands and of Asia Minor, which, since the sack of Miletus in 494 B.C., had paid a forced allegiance to the Persian king. These purposes were accomplished through the Delian Confederacy, which grew up in the following manner. Pausanias, the Spartan regent who had commanded the united Greek forces at Platæa, continued for a short time after 479 B.C. to direct the Greek armies in the region of the Hellespont. Sparta, however, true to her isolationist diplomacy and always fearful lest a Helot uprising should destroy her institutions at home, was apathetic to so distant an enterprise.

Furthermore, the Spartans, secure in their remote valley, were presently disturbed as rumors began to reach Greece that Pausanias, freed from a lifetime of ascetic Spartan discipline, was making the most of his opportunities in Byzantium by living the extravagant life of an Oriental potentate. The Ionian Greeks resented his conduct and begged Athens to assume the leadership. Pausanias was recalled to Sparta, and Athens accepted the invitation to lead the eastern Greeks. This she did by organizing a League. The cities that joined were principally those situated at vulnerable places in proximity to the sea, the island cities near the coast, as well as those of the Cyclades, and in addition a considerable number of communities in the northern region of Thrace and on the island of Eubœa. More than two hundred states assumed the obligations of membership in the new Confederacy. The avowed purpose of the allied cities was not only to protect themselves against future attacks, but also to press the campaign against the disorganized Persian cities, so that by pillage they might recompense themselves for their earlier losses.

The Basis of Membership. The Confederacy, or League, was organized in the beginning with respect for local autonomy. It was agreed that the union should be voluntary, that the treasury should be located on the sacred and neutral island of Delos under the protection of Apollo, that the council of confederates, or allies, should meet also at Delos, and that the amount contributed by each state to the common treasury should be assessed on the basis of relative wealth by Aristeides the Just, an Athenian, in whose disinterested sense of justice all Greeks felt confidence. There is no doubt as to the honesty and fairness of Aristeides, but a peculiar criticism of the prevailing standard of civic morality among Greek statesmen is implied in his title, for one man is not called "the Just" unless the term distinguishes him from his contemporaries. The entire origin and organization of the Confederacy is a witness to decisions reached under pressure rather than through a reasoned belief in the necessity or value of cooperation. The experiment for these reasons did not turn out to be a major success in political thought, though it did, for a time, fulfill its function.

The Dominant Position of Athens. It was not long before it became clear that Athens would use the Confederacy to promote her own imperialistic ambitions. From the first she provided that the ten Treasurers of Greece, or *Hellenotamiæ*, who collected the tribute, or money paid in by the allies, and administered its expenditure, should be Athenian citizens, and the concession of Aristeides to the smaller states that they might contribute money rather than maintain a separate navy strengthened the hand of Athens when a difference of opinion arose. In spite of the appearance of equality, everything about the League worked to place the executive control in the hands

[237]

of the Athenians. The self-interest of the Athenians in this matter was matched only by the grudging cooperation of the smaller states.

The Right of Withdrawal Refused. For a dozen years the Confederacy fulfilled its purpose in spite of scattered evidence of discontent. Then, in 467 B.C., Cimon, the son of the Miltiades who had led the Athenians at Marathon, defeated the Persians decisively in a battle at the mouth of the Eurymedon River in southern Asia Minor. It now became evident that the Greeks need no longer fear a Persian invasion, and immediately the various states, with their passionate Greek obsession for local freedom, determined to withdraw from the Delian Confederacy. Athens, however, resolutely refused to countenance any secession, maintaining with some justification that Hellas was secure from a renewed Persian attack only so long as the Ægean Sea was adequately patrolled. Several states thereupon attempted to revolt, but they were defeated by the powerful Athenian navy and compelled to continue their contributions to the now hateful union.

The Athenian Empire. In 458 B.C., Athens was engaged in warfare on many fronts, both on the Greek mainland and elsewhere in the Mediterranean area. The year has been called the *annus mirabilis,* or miraculous year, because of the multiplicity of military projects supported by the city. A commemorative inscription records that in a single year soldiers from the tribe of Erechtheïs died in war at Cyprus, in Egypt, in Phœnicia, at Halieis, and at Megara. The Athenians suffered heavily during these years of warfare, but still they retained unimpaired their control of the Delian Confederacy.

At length, in 454 B.C., perhaps because consolidation of resources now appeared imperative if the Empire were to be preserved, the Athenian general Pericles removed the treasury of the Delian Confederacy from the island of Delos to the Acropolis of Athens. The polite pretence of twenty-five years was at an end, and the once voluntary union of Greek states had become an acknowledged Athenian Empire. The sig-

[238]

nificance of the transference of the treasury must be interpreted in the light of an almost fanatical predisposition to independence among the city-states of Hellas. It was a serious defect of the political economy of the Greeks that they were unable to see the advantages of union, but it is nonetheless true that the arbitrary action of Pericles in 454 B.C. must have appeared to the Hellenic states as a gross betrayal of trust on the part of Athens. That date should be kept constantly in mind in studying the rise and fall of Greek civilization. At the moment it signified only another step of Athens toward power, but the new concept of domination was to leave its mark on the young men of the city who were then growing to maturity.

PERICLES AND HIS ATTITUDE TOWARD THE CITY

Pericles Assumes Power. The Delian Confederacy had not been twenty years established before the appearance on the political stage of Pericles, one of the most brilliant men of antiquity. In 461 B.C., this young aristocrat, then some thirty years of age, came into control of the popular, or democratic, party in Athens following the political assassination of the former liberal leader, Ephialtes. Pericles was a member of the powerful family of the Alcmæonidæ, to which also belonged Cylon and Cleisthenes. He was to remain in power, except for a brief period when popular opinion turned against him, until his death thirty-two years later, in 429 B.C. In a sense the biography of Pericles is the history of all Athenian cultural achievement during the most brilliant generation of the city's existence. This intellectual young statesman, who had been carefully trained in arms and in letters, was the associate of the philosopher Anaxagoras. He was a somewhat cold and aloof aristocrat, but nonetheless he controlled the democratic Assembly with his skill. He was, through the years, to draw all the branches of Athenian government unto himself.

The Extension of Democracy. During the fifth century, the government of Athens was moving steadily away from the system established by Cleisthenes and toward a wider basis of democratic control. Under Ephialtes, the power of the Areopagus, the old conservative court of Athens, to which the members were appointed for life, was sharply abridged. The Court was shorn of virtually all powers except jurisdiction in cases of homicide. Perhaps the psychological effect of liberalizing an ancient institution was the most important aspect of this reform. More readily comprehensible as a democratic gesture was the opening of the archonship to the Zeugitæ, the third in degree of wealth of the old Solonian classes. That office had previously been open only to the two wealthier classes, the Pentacosiomedimni and the Knights.

Photograph by the British Museum

FIGURE 47. PERICLES. This portrait, while still idealized, definitely depicts the features of the statesman.

From these reforms it was only a step to a measure of great significance in a growing democracy, namely, the payment of jurors and other officers of the state, for, in this way, responsibility and service were alike extended to a much larger proportion of the population. Furthermore, the system of election by lot was now much more widely used. The archons were selected by lot out of a panel of citizens that had previously been chosen. The Athenians could not, however, risk average honesty and certain mediocrity in the person of the polemarch, if he were to be the commander-in-chief in war, and, consequently, much of the influence of the polemarch passed to the Board of Ten Generals, who continued to be elected. It was as a member of this board that Pericles was to control Athens for so long.

The use of lot for election and of payment for political service indicates the sincerity with which Pericles dedicated himself to the establishment of a thoroughgoing form of democracy. Yet there were restrictive features in the picture that should be recognized: citizenship, for instance, was limited to those persons both of whose parents were Athenians, and the *metics,* or resident aliens, were denied all possibility of becoming enfranchised Athenian citizens. Furthermore, a large group of slaves existed in ancient Athens.

Pericles was an avowed imperialist. He loved Athens and believed in her destiny, and, with single-minded devotion in which scruples over the rights of other states were never allowed to interfere, he set out to make Athens the strongest, the most beautiful, and the most cultured city of the ancient world. He succeeded completely in his mission, and, in doing so, took so largely into his own hands all the details of administration that he became indispensable to the city. Athens, though nominally a democracy, was in reality governed absolutely by her most distinguished son. Yet it would be incorrect to conclude that democracy had yielded to dictatorship, for so long as the Athenian people could, and on one occasion at least did, remove Pericles from power, they maintained their title to self-government.

The Administration of Pericles. For fourteen years Pericles concerned himself with matters of government and the strengthening of the Empire. In 454 B.C., he had been responsible for the removal of the Delian treasury to Athens. In 447 B.C., he commenced an active policy of adornment of the city by rebuilding the temples of the gods, who had preserved it at the time of the Persian Wars. Abundant funds were available from the tribute of the allies to the Delian Confederacy, or more properly the Athenian Empire, and these Pericles diverted in large part to the beautification of Athens. In relation to

[241]

ancient wealth and purchasing power of money, the expenditure on the Parthenon and its embellishment reached almost incredible proportions.

The Political Philosophy of Pericles. An appraisal of the methods and purpose of Pericles presents many difficulties. To some critics he has appeared imperious, if not tyrannical, enlarging the powers of his own state at the expense of the

Photograph by Alinari

FIGURE 48. VIEW OF ATHENS. This photograph, taken from the south, shows the arrangement of the ancient buildings on the Acropolis and on its southern slopes. The Parthenon is unrestored in this view.

development of other members of the Delian Confederacy. The diversion of funds contributed by members of the Confederacy to the uses of the city did not go unchallenged even in antiquity, for Thucydides, the son of Melesias, who is not to be confused with the historian, raised his voice in protest against the practice, only to find himself ostracized by the Athenian people for his pains. Pericles was the guiding spirit in a tide of creative genius that swept over Athens for a generation. Of superior ability and judgment, he directed the democracy without flattery or appeasement. Personal tragedy darkened the latter years of his life. He contracted the plague when it fell on the city and never recovered his strength. Even as Athens entered into the long and exhausting struggle with Sparta, the career of her wisest counselor was coming to a close.

In the fear and misfortune of the early months of the Peloponnesian War, the Athenian people sought a scapegoat and turned against Pericles, convicting him in the courts and depriving him of office. In a short time, however, with uneasy solicitude, they turned again to the old leader, reelected him, and heaped honors upon him. But the end was near, and Plutarch tells of the last hours of the statesman, when, all but unconscious, he roused himself as the bystanders praised his victories and his achievements, to protest that they had failed to mention his greatest accomplishment: "For," he said, "no Athenian ever put on the garb of mourning through me."

Pericles was not a sentimentalist, and he cannot have been unaware, as he uttered these words, of the wars waged throughout his career, but he could reflect on his abstention from personal grudges and political assassination, his policy of caution in tactics and maneuvers, and the pattern of democratic freedom that he fostered in Athens even when his personal influence was strongest. Pericles would have been a skilled officer in the modern field of logistics. He envisioned great objectives, calculated costs and risks, and pursued ends that were civic rather than personal with undeviating persistence. Athens, with all that the city stood for in adornment and intellect in 431 B.C., was very largely his creation. It is merely a question of terminology whether one devotes successive chapters to the achievements of Pericles or describes them instead in terms of the development of the theater, the flowering of art, the extension of commerce, the growth of philosophy, or whatever other descriptive terms may appropriately be adopted to indicate the mental activity of man in one of the truly great, if not the greatest, periods of human history. To the Age of Pericles belong the tragic dramatists Sophocles and Euripides,

the comic poet Aristophanes, the historians Herodotus and
Thucydides, the sophists and their arch enemy Socrates, the
architects Callicrates and Ictinus, the sculptors Myron, Pheidias,
and Polycleitus. Wherever one studies Greek genius in the
middle of the fifth century, he is studying also the character
and purpose of Pericles, for it was in the Athenian democracy
of his creation that genius everywhere came into flower.

CHAPTER XIV

THE ORIGINS OF GREEK TRAGEDY: ARISTOTLE'S APPRAISAL

The writers of Greek tragedy during the fifth century accomplished much more than the entertainment of the throngs that crowded the theaters at the festivals when plays were offered. They were active in an age when religion, philosophy, and sociological inquiry were occupying men's minds as keenly as were the artistic creations of the architects and sculptors. But whereas the latter had found a medium for the expression of their thoughts, one will search in vain for specific treatises on religion or sociology written during the Age of Pericles. Furthermore, although Socrates was teaching during these years, as were the sophists, the great period of philosophic writing is the fourth century. There is, nevertheless, contemporary evidence of moral and social philosophy in the fifth century, for Æschylus, Sophocles, and Euripides afford through their tragedies the clearest guide to the thought of their time. They were living in a period of continuous development and rapid change, when the passage of a decade could greatly alter a people's convictions. For that reason it is important to keep in mind the years that separate the three great writers of tragedy, for the sum of their active lives spanned the entire century.

On the other hand, an understanding of Greek tragedy itself, apart from the background of fifth century life and thought which it reflects, is to be sought, first, through an examination of the early history of this branch of literature in

[245]

the archaic age, and second, by a study of the judgment on tragic values pronounced by Aristotle when in the fourth century he was able to weigh a literary form that had already reached its height and run its course.

THE EARLY FORMS OF TRAGEDY

The Religious Association. Though Greek tragedy reached its maturity in the fifth century, and, in fact, the only complete plays preserved are by fifth-century writers, the origin of tragedy must be sought in the archaic period. From the outset, both tragedy and comedy were associated with religion, for they were sacred to Dionysus, the god of wine, who in his own complex nature was sympathetic with both the depths of sorrow and the ecstasies of joy. In the earliest times, the villagers used to gather at a festival sacred to Dionysus where, dressed in goatskins to represent the satyrs who were his companions, they chanted dithyrambic songs in his honor. The word *tragedy* means literally "goat song," and the origin of tragic drama may be attributed to the primitive *dithyrambs,* or festival songs, sung by men who danced as goats. The choral lyric and the literary dithyramb had thus existed before drama took shape, and it was on the basis of these forms that the action of the early plays was built.

The Three Chief Dramatic Festivals. Three festivals associated with Dionysus assumed importance. The earliest was doubtless the Dionysia of the Fields, or the Lesser Dionysia, which fell in December and marked the completion of the harvest in the various villages of the countryside. It was a spontaneous folk custom, which had arisen in remote antiquity. During the sixth century, another festival, the Lenæa, occurring in January, was more formally instituted in Athens by Peisistratus. In the fifth century, the City Dionysia, or the Greater Dionysia, became the predominant festival of the Athenian state; it fell in March, at a time when sea travel began to be inviting and when the Greeks of other states came to Athens with their merchandise and their tribute. All three festivals continued to be celebrated in historical times. Tragedies were offered in Athens only at the festivals, where they were entered in competition for prizes awarded by the state.

Thespis. In spite of the difficulty of reconstructing the successive steps in the development of the dithyrambic chants of the villagers into the true action of tragedy, it is possible to find in the traditional attribution of certain inventions to Thespis of Icaria, a village in Attica near Marathon, a not improbable account of the earliest innovations. But it is undoubtedly true that the endeavors and experiments of many anonymous predecessors and contemporaries of Thespis united to increase his fame. Thespis traveled about from village to village with a cart, as the troupes of miracle players did in mediæval England. He presented his plays, dramatizing the experiences of the gods, to the delight of the common folk, whose instincts responded to this ingenious method of telling a story, but to the horror of the conservative element, who feared the wrath of Heaven if the gods were represented as uttering sentiments invented for them by the puny mind of man. Thespis persisted, however, and about the year 534 B.C., while Peisistratus was still ruling as tyrant, the first tragedy was officially presented in Athens. Peisistratus had fostered the worship of Dionysus and the development of drama, possibly for political reasons, and the acceptance of Thespis assuredly had the sanction of the tyrant himself.

The Contributions of Thespis. Dramatic performances started, therefore, under the auspices of religion and the state, and thus they continued, exemplifying in fifth-century literature the strong mutual influence of religion and civic consciousness that may be seen also in art. To Thespis was credited the development of the prologue and the recitative element added to the song of the chorus. He also introduced an actor, called the *hypokritēs,* or "answerer," who by his words divided and furthered the story of the chorus. The mask, too, was early introduced, and in classical times it was

[247]

invariably worn by the actors, each of whom took several parts with appropriate changes of masks. Thus the Greek play emerged in its final form as a continuous presentation in which the choral odes alternate with the dramatic episodes, producing an effect quite different from modern plays, which are divided into acts. The introduction of an actor was the most significant step in leading away from the simple dithyrambic chants toward the presentation of thought through action. *Drama* is a Greek word meaning "action."

CHŒRILUS, PRATINAS, AND PHRYNICHUS

Chœrilus. After the drama was definitely sponsored by the state and writers were stimulated by the assurance of a continuing outlet for their productions, three dramatists, Chœrilus, Pratinas, and Phrynichus, rose to some prominence in Greece. Although none of their plays have been preserved, there is evidence available concerning the date of activity and the nature of the work of each. Chœrilus, an Athenian, flourished in the latter days of the rule of the Peisistratids and also in the early years of the Athenian democracy, that is, in the years before and after 510 B.C. A large number of plays are attributed to him, and it may be concluded that many of them resembled brief satyr chants, in which men, dressed as satyrs, sang in honor of Dionysus.

Pratinas. Pratinas of Phlius is said to have entered a contest at one of the dramatic festivals about 498 B.C. in which the other contestants were his older contemporary Chœrilus and the young Æschylus, who was born about 525 B.C. Pratinas was born in the Peloponnese, and we are thus reminded that in the early period contributions to the development of the drama were not confined exclusively to Athens. Pratinas is usually given credit for the formal attachment of the satyr play to the tragic trilogy, or group of three related tragedies customarily offered in competition by each dramatist. By the time of Æschylus it had become the convention for the dramatist to present a tetralogy. The first three plays constituted a trilogy and dealt with a subject of the author's selection, no longer necessarily embracing incidents from the life of Dionysus; the fourth play was a satyr play, in which all the elements of the old satyr, or dithyrambic, songs were preserved in deference to ancient religious associations.

Phrynichus. With Phrynichus of Athens one encounters a dramatist with a more distinct personality, whose works are definitely associated with known historical incidents. He was a pupil of Thespis and won his first prize about 512 B.C. Shortly after the fall of Miletus in 494 B.C., Phrynichus presented in Athens an historical play entitled the *Sack of Miletus,* with the unhappy results that have been elsewhere mentioned. The historical play was rarely presented and seldom successful in Greece, although in 476 B.C. Phrynichus offered, in the *Phœnician Women,* a dramatization of the Battle of Salamis that appears to have met with approval, and Æschylus' later treatment of the same subject in the *Persians* was favorably received. These, however, were exceptions. So far as one may judge from fragmentary evidence, the plays of Phrynichus appear to have had a very large choric element and to have been in the nature of chanted laments rather than dramatic action.

ARISTOTLE'S APPRAISAL OF GREEK TRAGEDY

Aristotle's Definition of Tragedy. The promise of excellence inherent in the efforts and experiments of the early writers of tragedy was amply fulfilled in the fifth century by Æschylus, Sophocles, and Euripides. Not only did they perfect the technique of drama, but they used this vehicle of thought to set forth a mature philosophy of life.

Since they draw their material from universal principles rather than from experiences of isolated and momentary interest, it will be wise before attempting to deal specifically with their lives and works, to have in mind the definition of

tragedy that the fourth-century philosopher, Aristotle, evolved
by a keen analytical study of Greek drama two generations
after the last of the great writers of tragedy had died. Their
works were then available in vastly greater numbers than they
have been at any subsequent time, and it was from a study of
this abundant evidence that Aristotle formulated the following definition, which every student of drama, ancient or
modern, should know by heart:

Tragedy is, therefore, an imitation of an action that is serious
and complete, of a certain magnitude, with the language embellished separately and in accordance with the various parts of the
work, conveying the thought by action and not by narrative,
through pity and terror effecting a *catharsis* of these emotions.

Explanation of the Definition. Some parts of the definition
are quite objective and easy to understand. By "imitation"
Aristotle means something in the nature of vicarious representation. The subject of the tragedy is conceived in the mind of
the poet or drawn from mythological sources and conveyed to
the audience through the movements and speech of actors in
the orchestra. However common such a method of portrayal
may be to modern life, either through the legitimate stage or
through motion pictures, it must be remembered that this had
been a novel experience to the Greeks and to the world when
it was first introduced, and Aristotle felt it imperative to define
his terms. The words "serious" and "complete" are self-
explanatory and serve to differentiate the elevated tone of
tragedy from the mockery of comedy, demanding also that the
thought be carried to its logical conclusion in each play and
not presented simply as a detached incident of life.

When Aristotle requires for tragedy "a certain magnitude,"
he is not referring to the moral tone of the drama, but quite
definitely to the thousand verses or so that must be used to
develop the theme. In other words, a short lament of a dozen
verses, however poignant the thought, would not fulfill Aris-

[250]

totle's definition of tragedy. In speaking of "language em-bellished separately in each part of the work," the reference is to the various meters and figures of speech or rhetoric which may be appropriately introduced in the different divisions of the drama, such as the prologue, the episodes, the choric songs, and so forth. The phrase "by action and not by narrative" is a reminder that drama is a new technique for the portrayal of thought, which must not be confused with such a method as epic narration or history.

Catharsis. It is, however, over the final statement of the definition, "through pity and terror effecting a catharsis, or purification, of these emotions," that infinite disagreement has arisen. An enormous scholarly literature has appeared on the subject. It would, therefore, be an act of intellectual arrogance to set down any dogmatic explanation of the way in which tragedy, by arousing thoughts of pity and terror, succeeds in purifying these emotions in the minds of those who are affected by them. Yet the difference of opinion regarding the precise meaning of catharsis does not alter the fact that everyone with literary appreciation is profoundly moved by the presentation or the reading of tragedy, whether Greek, Shakespearean, or modern, and consequently the problem is partly one of analysis of the emotions. Certainly, it is one that can be felt and ap-preciated as keenly in modern times as in antiquity.

Perhaps the most commonly accepted explanation of Aris-totelian catharsis is that a person in the audience, seeing in the play a representation of some dreadful or awe-inspiring action, has his own pity and terror aroused through the suffer-ing of another, and by that vicarious experience has his nature purged, so that he need not himself undergo the same suffering in order to understand, to sympathize with, and to be benefited by such an experience in life. There is much truth in this explanation, nor is it difficult to grasp, for most readers will know the emotional relief of tears following the observation of the real or dramatized suffering of others. It is akin to the harmonizing of the emotions that is part of the teaching of modern psychology.

A second approach to the problem of catharsis, or purification, of the emotions lies in the philosophic acceptance of suffering through repeated observation or vicarious experience. Thus a medical student or social worker may at first have his emotions harrowed by the suffering of the patients in a hospital, or by living conditions in a slum, but in time he necessarily comes to an intellectual acceptance of the inevitability of pain and the slow progress in the alleviation of poverty and suffering in the world. In such a way the ravages of pity are modified, and men and women are able to pursue their work with emotional composure, knowing that life and thought must continue despite human anguish. Similarly, the audience witnessing the suffering of a tragic hero may first have the emotions of pity and terror stirred, but presently habituation to vicarious grief will purify the breasts of the beholders of these emotions. They will be able to follow the normal pattern of their own lives in a more healthful manner, because of the purification to which they have been subjected. This theory implies to some extent a necessary hardening of the emotions in the face of suffering.

Still another explanation of catharsis depends for its acceptance on an understanding of Aristotle's Doctrine of the Mean, though one must not identify it completely with that doctrine. By the Doctrine of the Mean, Aristotle taught that the highest excellence lay in taking a medium stand between excess and defect. Thus the quality of bravery is a mean, or medium, position between the excess, which is foolhardiness, and the defect, which is cowardice. In somewhat similar manner there is a proper, or mean, amount of pity and terror, which should be felt by all persons. If either an excess or a defect of pity or terror is shown in a tragic situation, then at once all the inexorable forces of nature will strive to restore the mean, whatever the tragic consequences to the offender may be. This explanation throws the catharsis more within the action of the tragedy than upon the audience, although that fact does not necessarily prove it untrue. It will be possible to clarify Aristotle's definition of tragedy as the details are applied to specific plays. The problem is a dual one: first, to analyze as clearly and scientifically as possible Aristotle's meaning, and second, to attempt to understand one's own emotional reaction, for Aristotle had at hand no tools or techniques that are not also available to us. In a matter that is personal and subjective, probably no single explanation can be universally true, though elements of truth will be recognized in many of the reasoned explanations that have been propounded.

TECHNICAL DRAMATIC TERMS AND CONVENTIONS

The Tragic Hero. Aristotle offers some further observations in the *Poetics* about the essential elements of Greek tragedy. In the first place, the tragic hero must be drawn from one of the great mythical families of Greece or from among the gods. Misfortune pursuing the steps of a humble and worthy citizen would not make an acceptable theme for Greek tragedy. Two implications followed this convention. First, the characters were removed by both time and legend from the actual life of the audience and for that reason were not viewed as men in whose experiences the beholders might themselves expect actually to participate. This situation did much to further the understanding of tragedy as an "imitation," or vicarious experience of life, and thereby afforded an emotional relief that was not possible in a more intimate theme. The unsuitability of historical plots has already been observed. Second, the pressure to discover original and unexpected situations was very much less intense in Greek tragedy than in modern drama, and it would be fair to assume that the large democratic audiences of antiquity were generally familiar with the story of the plays, since the plots were drawn from the comparatively limited field that Aristotle has observed. Moreover, the

[253]

dramatists succeeded in using their circumscribed material to express the rapidly changing philosophy of their times.

The Hamartia, or Mistake; Ananke, or Necessity. It would be unwise and, indeed, impossible to force all extant Greek plays into the Aristotelian pattern; it should be recognized further that certain aspects of the discussion which here follows are derived from other than Aristotelian sources. Nevertheless, the judgment of Aristotle on tragedy was based on his familiarity with the great body of fifth-century tragedies, and his essay offers the most cogent single criticism of this field of literature. The development of a Greek tragedy depends on some *hamartia,* or "great mistake," which the hero knowingly or unknowingly makes and which sets in motion the inexorable laws of retribution to punish and correct the error. For instance, Œdipus, in ignorance and under the compulsion of an oracle, killed his father and married his mother. That was his unwitting hamartia, and as a consequence he suffered the terrible cumulative punishment that his mistake demanded. One can more readily understand the Greek feeling for inexorable law, which takes no account of the purity of motive, if he thinks of a person violating a law of nature. Touching a charged electric wire will be followed by the full consequences of the error no matter how innocent of wrong intention the person may have been. That same inevitability the Greeks transferred to moral questions, and the force of inexorable moral law which moves through Greek tragedy with its inescapable train of consequences is called *ananke,* or "necessity."

Hubris and Nemesis. In this same connection, one will think also of *Nemesis* as playing a great part in the mental background of the Greeks, not only in tragedy but in the incidents of life. In Nemesis the Greeks personified the "wrath of Heaven," which would inevitably be visited on a too presumptuous spirit, on too great worldly prosperity, and above all on the insolence of man, whether displayed toward the gods or toward his fellow creatures. For this insolence the Greeks used the term *hubris,* if we may continue to employ the transliter-

[254]

ation that has become accepted in English usage rather than the correct form, *hybris*.

To the Greeks an act of hubris, or insolence, would inevitably call down the punishment of Nemesis. Such a sequence is shown in the picture which Herodotus drew of Persian arrogance, as Xerxes brought his enormous Oriental hosts against Greece only to be defeated by the Greeks at Salamis and Platæa. The proud and magnificent expedition of the Persians was an act of hubris, and their punishment was a visitation of Nemesis. In a sense, in Greek tragedy the hamartia, or mistake, corresponds to hubris, and ananke, or necessity, to Nemesis, but it would not be correct to substitute one of these terms for another. Rather, hamartia and ananke may be viewed as more specific exemplifications of hubris and Nemesis, also present in tragedy.

Anagnorisis and Peripeteia. Two other technical terms, *anagnorisis* and *peripeteia,* should be explained. By anagnorisis is meant the "recognition scene." The methods by which two characters, one or both of whom are unknown to the other at the outset, are brought to a recognition at the proper time reveal the growing technical capacity of the writers from the unconvincing early efforts of Æschylus to the very successful and plausible devices of Euripides. The recognition scene was employed also in comedy, and by the time of New Comedy in the Hellenistic Age a common form of anagnorisis was recognition through material objects or birth-tokens, such as rings, necklaces, or gems, that had been left with a child exposed in infancy. Such devices were held in low esteem by Aristotle.

By peripeteia is meant a change in the action of the play, and peripeteia not infrequently coincides with the anagnorisis, so that both assume considerable importance in the development of a well-knit plot. Peripeteia is sometimes bound up with dramatic irony, where the words of the speaker may be understood in one sense by the audience and in another by himself. This occurs, for instance, in Sophocles' *Œdipus Tyrannus,* where a messenger delivers a speech that, in his eyes, seems to

[255]

solve a difficulty but in reality contains the disclosure that leads on to catastrophe. It will be possible to recognize instances of peripeteia that affect minor parts of the play as well as those that influence the whole course of action in a drama. It should be added that anagnorisis and peripeteia are not present in all plays, although Aristotle observes that they are essential to the best plot structure. In general the peripeteia plays a larger and more striking part in the plays of Euripides than in those of his predecessors.

Summary. The origins and early development of Greek drama have now been examined, and an explanation has been offered of the principal elements of structure, purpose, and emotional appeal of tragedy in the light of the commentary of Aristotle. This has involved a brief discussion of early dramatists, whose plays are no longer extant, and of technical terms, which, of necessity, were dealt with largely apart from their application to particular plays. In the chapters that follow it will be possible to consider a number of tragedies of the fifth century, which will be more readily understood with this information in mind.

CHAPTER XV

ÆSCHYLUS

The dates of the fifth-century writers of tragedy are of considerable significance. Æschylus was born in 525 B.C., Sophocles in 496 B.C., and Euripides in 480 B.C., or, according to some authorities, five years earlier. The relative ages of the three men are brought into relief by an apocryphal story of the return of the victors from the Battle of Salamis, the last great naval encounter of the Persian Wars, in 480 B.C. Æschylus at the age of forty-five had fought in the battle; Sophocles, a boy of good family, now sixteen years old, led the chorus of youths who chanted the song of victory; Euripides watched the procession as an infant in his mother's arms. Æschylus, Sophocles, and Euripides were thus contemporaries but separated by a short generation one from another. Consequently, there is in the work of each dramatist a picture of his own moral and religious attitudes, so that by a comparison of the three the development of the thought of Athens throughout the fifth century may be observed.

Life of Æschylus. Æschylus, the son of an aristocratic house, was born at Eleusis in Attica in 525 B.C. and died in Sicily in 456 B.C., five years after Pericles had assumed power in Athens. The childhood of Æschylus was spent in his native village, where the Eleusinian Mysteries were celebrated in honor of the goddess Demeter. The rites of the Mysteries may have taken a dramatic form and extended their influence to the young Æschylus. It is probably incorrect, however, to regard him as an orthodox proponent of the old religion, for he was once prosecuted on the charge of having revealed the secrets of the Eleusinian Mysteries, and his successful defense before the Court of the Areopagus was that he had never been initiated into the religious cult, in itself a strong indication of unorthodoxy, for the Mysteries were recognized for the inclusiveness of their membership.

Contemporary Events. In the absence of clear evidence, we may assume that the early education of Æschylus was that of a Greek boy whose family was sufficiently prosperous to prepare him for a career in the arts. It is instructive in this connection to recall the experiences that must have been his during the stirring years of his lifetime. Less than a decade before Æschylus was born, Thespis had succeeded in having a tragedy officially accepted by the city of Athens under the patronage of Peisistratus. When the tyrants were expelled from Athens in 510 B.C., Æschylus was a boy of fifteen. Probably in 499 B.C., when he was twenty-six years of age, he first contended in the dramatic festival against Chœrilus and Pratinas, whose names have already been mentioned, but was unsuccessful. In that same year, the Ionian Revolt broke out in Asia Minor and continued until Miletus was destroyed in 494 B.C. In 490 B.C., when Æschylus was thirty-five years old, he took part in the Battle of Marathon, an experience which he prized above all others in his life. This he has made clear in the epitaph, already mentioned, which he composed for his tomb.

This mound hides Æschylus, the son of Euphorion, an Athenian, who died in the land of wheat-bearing Gela. His glorious valor the grove of Marathon might tell, and the long-haired Mede knew of it.

The End of His Life. In 484 B.C., about the year of the birth of the historian Herodotus, Æschylus won his first dramatic victory. In 480 B.C., he fought in the Battle of Salamis and in 479 B.C., in the Battle of Platæa, the final struggles of the Persian Wars. He was then in middle life, forty-five or forty-six years of age. After the Persian Wars, he spent considerable time in Sicily, although he continued to present his plays in the theater at Athens. In 468 B.C., he was defeated in a contest by Sophocles, the first defeat of a Marathonian fighter at the hands of one of the new generation. He died at Gela in Sicily in 456 B.C.

His Extant Plays. Ninety plays were written by Æschylus, of which seven only have been preserved. Fortunately the seven surviving plays include some of his best dramas. The *Suppliants,* which may have been presented as early as 492 B.C., is the oldest extant play of Æschylus and of Greek literature, and the *Persians,* performed in 472 B.C., is the only extant historical tragedy. The *Seven Against Thebes* was brought out in 467 B.C., and the trilogy of the *Oresteia,* or the *Story of Orestes,* including the *Agamemnon,* the *Choephori,* or the *Libation-Bearers,* and the *Eumenides,* or the *Furies,* belongs to the year 458 B.C. The *Prometheus Bound* is of comparatively late date, since a third actor, an innovation attributed to his younger contemporary, Sophocles, was apparently used, but the precise year cannot be determined. It should be added that scholarly opinion on almost every aspect of the *Prometheus Bound,* from authenticity of authorship to the date of composition, varies widely, and views quite contrary to those here expressed will be found.

The Legendary Background of the "Oresteia." The *Oresteia,* with its three constituent tragedies, the *Agamemnon,* the *Choephori,* and the *Eumenides,* presented in 458 B.C., three years after Pericles assumed power in Athens and two years before the death of Æschylus, affords the only opportunity now available to study the development of an ancient theme through a complete trilogy. In the *Oresteia,* Æschylus has built up a story of sin and punishment perpetuating themselves in a family that has from the ancient past been cursed by the gods. Through the veiled references of the Chorus, one b comes aware of ancestral sin dominating the movements of the characters. Blood-guilt had left its mark in the successive outrages

[259]

of Tantalus, who slew his own son, of Pelops who killed his henchman, and of Atreus, who destroyed the sons of his brother.

It is with Agamemnon, the son of Atreus, that the story of the *Oresteia* opens. When Agamemnon had gathered the Greek chieftains together for their expedition against Troy, contrary winds, invoked by Artemis, delayed the naval armament at Aulis. To placate the goddess Artemis, Agamemnon consented to summon from Argos his daughter Iphigeneia, on the pretext that she was to be married to Achilles, and instead to offer her as a living sacrifice. The hamartia, or mistake, of Agamemnon, which occurs prior to the action of the play, was the slaying of Iphigeneia, on the altar of Artemis at Aulis, though the deed was a bitter and grievous one to him. Not until ten years later was Nemesis to bring inevitable punishment on him.

The Action of the "Agamemnon." The opening scene of the *Agamemnon,* the first play of the *Oresteia* trilogy, is laid at Argos on the night that Troy was taken. Clytemnestra, the wife of Agamemnon, during his ten-year absence at Troy has been awaiting the moment of vengeance for the sacrifice of Iphigeneia. She has entered into a plot with Ægisthus, the cousin of Agamemnon, who must himself, under the compulsion of ananke, seek revenge for the crime that Agamemnon's father, Atreus, wrought against his brother Thyestes, the father of Ægisthus, with the brutal slaying of his other children. Thus the inexorable power of Nemesis arising from blood-guilt colors the play from the outset.

As the play opens, the Watchman on the roof of the palace of Agamemnon is musing on the evils within the house, when he is interrupted by the sight of the beacon fire, as from the mountain top it brings the tidings of Troy's capture: "Hail to the blaze of night, that bringeth the light of day, and prepareth many a dance in Argos in gratitude for this glad victory." The Watchman rushes off to convey to Clytemnestra the news "that in very truth Troy hath been taken, as this beacon doth proclaim." Clytemnestra, with cold and unscrupulous poise, feigns joy at the tidings, and to the Chorus of Argive Elders tells in a magnificent passage how the word was brought by successive relays of fire.

Hephæstus, the fire god, sent his bright gleam from Mount Ida, and Ida carried it to the island of Lemnos, whence the great promontory of Athos received it. And the mounting flame bridged the sea, bearing the message to the watch towers of Macistus on Eubœa. Next over the streams of Euripus the beacon came to the sentries of Messapion, and on with rekindled flame sped the messenger fire to Cithæron's mount. Thence across the water to Mount Ægiplanctus passed the fire, until near to the city of Argos on the peak of Mount Arachnæus it was lighted, whence the Watchman from the roof of the palace of the Atreidæ saw it. This is the proof I cite, the message from my lord in Troy.

The song of the Chorus creates an illusion of the passage of time between the news of Troy's capture and the arrival of the victorious Agamemnon in Argos. As they review the years of the struggle, they sing of Ares, the god of war, who exacts his gruesome toll, in words that remind one that Æschylus was writing the play in 458 B.C., the *annus mirabilis* of Athenian military history. At length Agamemnon returns to the city, to be greeted with reverence by the Chorus and by the still dissembling Clytemnestra, who wishes to receive him with more than mortal honors. As he is about to descend from his chariot, Clytemnestra addresses him:

And now do thou step from the chariot, but set not thy foot upon the ground, my lord, thou who hast laid waste Troy. Maidservants, why do ye delay? Straightway spread the purple tapestries, that Justice may guide his steps to a home he little hoped to see.

A foreboding of impending Nemesis troubles Agamemnon, and he hesitates to set foot on the purple tapestries, but he is overborne by the insistent entreaty of his wife and sets foot on the carpet, which he will tread to his death. "Since I am constrained to hearken to thee, I shall go to the halls of the palace, treading on the purple carpet." The fatal step of Agamemnon from the chariot to the purple tapestry has been called the highest dramatic point of tragedy, for this, rather than the moment of actual slaughter, is the point from which the audience senses that there can be no turning back from disaster. As Agamemnon moves toward the palace, Clytemnestra breaks into a wild chant.

There is a sea—and who shall exhaust it?—whence cometh the purple stain, costly as silver, ever renewed, the dye of royal garments. And our house knoweth no want of this.

There follows an interlude while Cassandra, the mad prophetess, daughter of the Trojan King Priam, who has come in the captive train of Agamemnon to Argos, is met with hostility by the outraged Clytemnestra. It was part of the misfortune of Cassandra that she was gifted by Apollo with the power of true prophecy, but with the subsequent frustrating condition that no one would believe what she said. In the long scene in which Clytemnestra, Cassandra, and the Leader of the Chorus converse, Æschylus has made dramatic use of the strange character of Cassandra, who speaks at one moment in the frenzied spirit of prophecy, which lifts her almost beyond human comprehension, and again as a forlorn and pitiable maiden, who has been carried captive from Troy to an undeserved death in Argos. When Cassandra is seized with the power of divination, she speaks, not as one foretelling what is to be, but as one who for the moment projects herself into the future and lives through an act that has not yet transpired. Thus the warning of the death of Agamemnon takes the form of the description of the fatal blows.

Ah, monstrous woman, canst thou do this deed? Having refreshed with the bath thy wedded husband,—how shall I complete my tale? Now quickly will the deed be done. One hand after another stretches forth.

Ah! Ah! look now, look! Protect the bull from his murderous mate. She hath entangled him in the robes and smiteth him with the black horn of evil device. He falleth in the water of the bath. I am telling thee of death wrought in a bath, a guileful murder.

The Murder of Agamemnon. According to Greek convention the murder of Agamemnon was not shown before the audience, but the voice of the king crying out in horror as he is struck down by Clytemnestra in the bath is heard from behind the scene.

AGAMEMNON

Woe, I have been smitten with a mortal blow!

CHORUS

Be silent; who is this who crieth out, smitten with a mortal blow?

AGAMEMNON

Woe, once again have I been struck!

CHORUS

It seems by the moanings of the king that the deed has been done.

A confused and futile discussion follows among the citizens, and then Clytemnestra, throwing aside all pretence, comes forth, avows the deed as her own and acknowledges Ægisthus as her new lord. The play ends on a note of hubris with the speech of Clytemnestra to Ægisthus: "Take no heed of their idle yelpings. Thou and I shall rule over this house, and order things aright."

The Remaining Problems of the Trilogy. On this note the *Agamemnon* ends, but fortunately the remaining two plays of the trilogy are preserved, and in this one instance we can see how Æschylus dealt with the problems that were still to be solved. In the *Agamemnon,* it was made clear how the hamartia of the king, which was the sacrifice of Iphigeneia, an action grievous to himself and evoking even in the *Agamemnon* repeated expressions of sympathy for him, has nevertheless inexorably brought its punishment. And now Agamemnon, in expiation for that crime, has been slain. Clytemnestra has gained vengeance for the death of their child, Iphigeneia, and Ægisthus for the crimes of the previous generation. But the murder of Agamemnon by his wife continues the stain of blood-guilt, and ananke now calls with a voice that will not be denied on Orestes and Electra, the other children of Agamemnon and Clytemnestra, to avenge their father's death.

The "Choephori." The second play of the trilogy, the *Choephori,* or *Libation Bearers,* deals with this problem of necessary vengeance within the family. It is made clear in the *Agamemnon* that Orestes had been sent away from his home in childhood to be reared at the court of the king of Phocis, where he became the bosom companion of the young prince Pylades. Æschylus in the *Choephori* deals with three principal points: first, the return of Orestes to his home and the mutual recognition of Orestes and his sister Electra, who are together to carry out the murder of their mother under the compulsion of ananke; second, the murder of Ægisthus and Clytemnestra; third, the fury of remorse and madness that comes upon Orestes as his punishment after the deed has been done.

The anagnorisis, or recognition scene, is used in this play in one of its earlest forms. It is accomplished by the naïve expedient of having Electra, as she appears with the maidens to pour libations on the tomb of Agamemnon, recognize the lock of Orestes' hair that he has laid there as similar to her own and his footprints as fitting the shape of her feet. The method, however, is not so important as the fact of the recognition. It is simply an example of early art, and it has the virtue of directness and sincerity. When Orestes and Electra become known to one another, they plot the murder of Ægisthus and Clytemnestra, and the intolerable situation in the household caused by the latter two is fully developed. By a false rumor of his own death Orestes gains access to the palace, and quickly the death-cry of Ægisthus is heard from within. A dramatic scene between Orestes and Clytemnestra follows, in which Orestes for a moment falters, appalled at the awful thought of slaying his own mother. Pylades, however, urges upon him his inescapable duty, and Clytemnestra meets death at the hands of her son. The play closes with the gathering madness of Orestes, who is tormented by the avenging Furies of his slain mother. "Oh, Lord Apollo, how they crowd upon me, dripping hateful blood from their eyes. You do not see them as I do. I am driven out; no longer can I stay."

FIGURE 49. ATHENIAN WHITE-FIGURED LEKYTHOS, OR FUNERAL JAR. Early fifth century B.C. The scene shows a youthful warrior cutting off his hair as a sacrifice.

The "Eumenides." In the final play of the trilogy, the *Eumenides,* the story is told of the persecution of Orestes for the curse that he has brought on himself and of how he was purified of his guilt at the Court of the Areopagus in Athens through the good offices of Athena and Apollo. The note of reconciliation on which the trilogy ends is an indication of how Æschylus may have sought in other trilogies to resolve the great moral problems of his dramas.

The Satyr Play. It was the custom in the time of Æschylus to add to a trilogy a satyr play, as a concession to the original form of tragedy, the goat song. The *Proteus,* now lost, was attached to the *Oresteia* of Æschylus in that connection. Pro-

[265]

teus was the Old Man of the Sea, represented in the *Odyssey* as telling Menelaus of the murder of his brother Agamemnon. Æschylus may, in the semiburlesque manner of the satyr play, have introduced some such element into his lost *Proteus*.

Subsequent Treatments of the Same Theme. The plot of the *Choephori,* namely, the murder of Ægisthus and Clytemnestra by her children in vengeance for the death of Agamemnon, was treated also by both Sophocles and Euripides, each of whom wrote a play called the *Electra*. This is the only instance in which the treatment of a similar theme by each of the three great dramatists may still be studied. For that reason it is instructive to observe the varying techniques by which the three dramatists dealt with the same story and to study the skill and purpose with which each of them delineated the characters of Orestes, Electra, and Clytemnestra. In making such a comparative analysis, it must be remembered that, whereas the *Choephori* was the central play of a trilogy, the *Electra* of Sophocles and the *Electra* of Euripides were in each case independent plays, for the practice of writing trilogies and tetralogies was not always continued. Consequently the two later dramatists were obliged to treat within a single play matters that Æschylus was able to deal with both in a preceding and a following one.

The Universality of the Theme. In spite of the mythological setting of the *Oresteia* story, which seems to remove it from contemporary life, it includes, as does all Greek tragedy, themes of universal meaning. Thus it is that a modern American playwright, Eugene O'Neill, has produced in *Mourning Becomes Electra* a trilogy of sin, deceit, and madness in a New England setting, which echoes the mood and moral quality of the plays of the Greek dramatists.

CHAPTER XVI

SOPHOCLES AND THE
PERFECTION OF DRAMATIC STYLE

The Personal Good Fortune of Sophocles. The life of Sophocles spans the greatest years of Athenian history. He was
born at Colonus, a mile from the city of Athens, in 496 B.C.,
six years before the Battle of Marathon, and he died in 406 B.C.
at the age of ninety. In his childhood he was too young to
take part in the battles of the Persian Wars in which Æschylus participated, too young also to have his spirits depressed at
the ravages wrought by the Persians. He was happy likewise
in his death, which occurred two years before the humiliating
fall of his city. Good fortune and an equable temperament
are traditionally associated with Sophocles. His father was a
wealthy manufacturer of arms, a business which flourished in
the troubled years of the fifth century, and hence he never
wanted for material comforts. He was handsome, witty,
talented, welcomed in whatever society he chose to cultivate,
and he was fortunate in the quick appeal that he made to the
audience and the judges of the dramatic profession. In his
lifetime he won twenty first prizes, whereas Æschylus won
fifteen and Euripides but five. These coveted honors, won in
a field of close competition, are the best evidence of the harmony that Sophocles established with his life-long field of
endeavor.

The Development of his Art. Sophocles enjoyed the advantage of an active career prolonged into great old age. For
three score years at least he was able to devote himself unre-

[267]

mittingly to the refinement of art in the production of his tragedies. He is credited in a late source with having appraised his own literary growth in terms of three periods: the

Photograph by Alinari

FIGURE 50. SOPHOCLES. Louvre, Paris. This portrait reveals the composure traditionally associated with the dramatist.

[268]

first, when he was under the influence of Æschylus and his style was heavy and bombastic; the second, when he came to rely on his own genius but produced works that were harsh and artificial to the ear; and the third, with which he and all subsequent critics have been satisfied, when he attained skill and beauty alike in the planning and the execution of his plays. Thus the excellence of the tragedies of Sophocles depends not alone on his genius, but on the assiduous and industrious application of a brilliant mind to the chosen task of his life.

Technical Innovations. Sophocles abandoned the practice of writing trilogies and presented instead at the public festivals three separate plays, each complete in itself. Hence, in order to include within the compass of a single tragedy all the necessary threads of the story, he was compelled to weigh his words with the utmost economy, and as a result, he attained a new and higher level of skill in the structure of his plots. He is credited with a further innovation in the introduction of a third actor. The number of actors never increased beyond this point in classical Greek times.

The Relation of Sophocles to his Age. Lacking the profundity of his older rival, Æschylus, both in language and thought, Sophocles was more nearly on a level with the public. It was inevitable that under a democracy men should begin to question the gods. Broadening experience and philosophical inquiry made it increasingly obvious that not all laws, either political or moral, were imposed on man by the will of Heaven. The doubts thus engendered regarding long-sanctioned traditions began to find a place in the current productions of the theater, and the plots of some of the plays of Sophocles embody the debates on moral problems that were then agitating the minds of thoughtful Athenians. It has sometimes been the custom to regard Æschylus as a reactionary conservative, forgetting that he belongs to a generation earlier than Sophocles and that his cautious queries were developed into open debate by his successors. Sophocles, in weighing such questions as the duty of obedience to law when it conflicts with individual con-

[269]

science, carried the scope of drama forward. At the same time, his urbanity and affability were constantly uppermost, and the problems, social or otherwise, that entered into the plays of Sophocles presented themselves to his mind rather as material for the necessary intellectual and philosophic accompaniment of a work of literary art than as a burning challenge to reform.

The Public Career of Sophocles. Meanwhile the early years of the fifth century were speeding by, obscuring past glories and bringing in new challenges to achievement. In 468 B.C., at the age of twenty-eight, Sophocles won his first victory and that against the veteran Æschylus. It was also the first occasion when a younger man, who had not fought in the Persian Wars, attained the highest place in the dramatic festival, and, with a curious irrelevance, his success aroused a measure of unreasoning bitterness in the city. Yet the reaction is not unnatural, for men who have striven mightily and achieved greatly in one period would be more than human if they viewed their own eclipse at the hands of their juniors without a touch of chagrin. Twenty-five years later, Sophocles was appointed one of the ten Treasurers of the Delian Confederacy, or now more properly the Athenian Empire; in 440 B.C., he was made a general in the Samian War, apparently for his success with the *Antigone,* which had been performed in 442 B.C. Only in a tolerant democracy such as Athens could the people fail to mark the incongruity of rewarding a man with a high state office for presenting a play of which the theme was the propriety of a young girl's defiance of the established authority of the city. In 413 B.C., he was selected as one of the Ten Counsellors after the disastrous Sicilian Expedition. Although Sophocles did not distinguish himself in administrative office, it is instructive to observe in appointments such as these the participation in the life and government of the state that was expected of every citizen, whatever his talents may have been.

The Plays. During sixty years of literary activity, Sophocles produced more than one hundred plays, of which seven have

[270]

been preserved intact. All seven belong to the period of his comparative maturity. The *Antigone,* presented in 442 B.C., is the oldest extant tragedy of Sophocles, and the *Ajax* belongs to about the same time. Of the others it is difficult to determine the precise dates. The *Electra* is apparently quite late. The *Œdipus Tyrannus* seems to have been written after the Athenian plague of 430 B.C., but whether soon or long thereafter is uncertain. The *Trachiniæ* embraces some techniques that argue a late date, while the *Philoctetes,* if it has been correctly assigned to 409 B.C., was written when the poet was eighty-seven years of age. The *Œdipus at Colonus* is the last of his dramas and consequently may be dated not long before 406 B.C. The compelling beauty of the choric passages in this play indicates that Sophocles closed his long career with mental powers unimpaired. There are about this play of old age written by a man approaching the end of his life qualities that suggest the attitude of one who has run the course of human experience, and, as it were, pauses on the further side of the bridge of life to look back with a fineness of perception not granted to younger men.

The "Œdipus Tyrannus." The nature of Sophoclean drama may be illustrated by the examination of a single play, the *Œdipus Tyrannus.* Aristotle ranked this tragedy with the greatest of Greek dramas, and there are few who would dispute his judgment. The *Œdipus Tyrannus* illustrates many of the technical devices of Greek drama that have been discussed in an earlier chapter. The hamartia, or tragic error, the anagnorisis, or recognition scene, the peripeteia, or change of fortune, ananke, or necessity, and above all the consummate skill of the poet in the structure of the plot may here be profitably studied. More important, however, than the technique of writing, is the delineation of character with penetrating vision and the critical appraisal of human conduct under the stress of suffering.

The Greek Audience in Relation to the Plot. Though it is clear that a Greek audience was in general familiar in advance

with the story that was involved in a play, there was one striking difference between the attitude of mind of an ancient spectator and a modern theater-goer who watches the presentation
of a well-known classic. While the modern spectator may be
acquainted with the words and phrases of the play from long
study of the text, the Greek knew only the content of the
legend. Consequently, the principal interest of the Greek
audience lay in an appraisal of the language, the beauty of the
choric songs, and the skill of the plot structure. Greek plays
were not presented again and again on successive days, nor
were they regularly, or even frequently, revived. After their
presentation at one of the festivals, usually the Greater
Dionysia, they were retired into the field of literature. Therefore, only by assuming an ancient audience that was fairly well
versed in the legendary background of a play can one account
for the effective use of the device of dramatic irony in Greek
tragedy. In such a drama as the *Œdipus Tyrannus,* the audience is understood to be aware of a meaning in significant
verses, which escapes the hero who utters them and who is
moving blindly and inexorably toward the fulfillment of his
own fate.

The Incidents Preceding the "Œdipus Tyrannus." Before
the time of the opening scene of the *Œdipus Tyrannus,* a long
and varied series of incidents has taken place, though a careful
analysis of the plot as it is constructed by Sophocles will reveal
the fact that there is no essential detail of information that is
not presently disclosed or predicated as the action develops.
Laius and Iocasta, the king and queen of Thebes, had a son
who, so the oracle had warned them, was destined to slay his
own father and marry his own mother. To avoid so dire a
calamity, the parents of the newborn child had a shepherd
expose him on the mountains with his ankles pierced and
fastened together by metal bonds to ensure his speedy death.
From the mutilation of his feet, the name Œdipus, the Man-
known-by-his-foot, or, according to some, the Man-with-the-
swollen-foot, was later given to him, for, as was inevitable, the

word of the oracle proved stronger than the feeble efforts of
the king and queen to circumvent destiny, and the child survived. The shepherd met on the mountain another herdsman
from distant Corinth, to whom he gave the child rather than
cause its death. The latter took the infant to Corinth, where
he was adopted by Polybus and Merope, the childless king and
queen, and reared as their own son.

Time passed and Œdipus grew to manhood. Then by mis-
chance a comrade in his cups taunted Œdipus, telling him
that he was not the true child of the Corinthian king. Œdipus
went to his parents with the query, and they, loving him as
their own child and in ancient manner accepting adoption as
constituting unquestioned parenthood, assured him that he was
truly their son. Yet the doubts of Œdipus were not wholly
laid to rest, and at length he went in secret to lay his problem
before the priestess of Apollo at Delphi. There he received no
reply to the question that he asked, but he learned that it was
his dire fate to murder his father and to be joined in wedlock
with his mother.

This new and terrible disclosure drove all other thoughts
from the mind of Œdipus. Now believing firmly that he was
the child of Polybus and Merope, and that he must at all costs
avoid the fulfillment of the curse, he resolved never again to
return to Corinth. Consequently he strode out from Delphi
toward the east, and at a place where three roads met he encountered a man of middle age riding in a carriage and attended by a few servants. A dispute arose about the narrow
right of way, blows were exchanged, and Œdipus killed the
stranger, together with all but one of those who accompanied
him.

To the young prince, with a mind brooding on the oracle
of Delphi, the incident meant little enough. But the stranger
in the carriage had been Laius, his own unknown father, and
the first part of the prophecy was now complete. Œdipus continued on his way, until at length he reached Thebes, quite
unconscious that he had returned to his own native city. A

plague was devastating the land through the malicious whim of the Sphinx, who visited pestilence on the people because no one could answer her riddle: "What is it that walks on four legs in the morning, two legs at noon, and three legs in the evening?" Œdipus was able to supply the answer. It is man, who creeps as a baby in the morning of his life, walks in his maturity, and aids his footsteps with a cane in the evening of his days. Thereupon the Sphinx hurled herself from the cliff; Œdipus was hailed as the savior of the city; and presently this strange scion of a royal house was accepted as the new king of Thebes and wedded to the widowed Queen Iocasta, who was his own mother. The second part of the oracle had come to pass.

Meanwhile, the attendant of Laius who had escaped at the time of his master's slaying and who was no other than the shepherd who had been charged with the exposure of Œdipus in infancy, returned to the city with a tale of a band of robbers who had slain the king, an almost inevitable enlargement of the true story of death meted out to Laius and all save one of his guard by a single wayfarer. In Thebes, to his horror, the shepherd now found Œdipus, the slayer of the king, married to Iocasta, and when he later learned that the new ruler purported to be the son of Polybus and Merope of Corinth, he knew everything. The shepherd took the only course open to him and sought a post in the fields far from the circle of the court.

The Plot of the Play. Years went by, and children were born to Œdipus and Iocasta, two sons and two daughters. Then in time Thebes was visited by another pestilence, sent by Apollo. The fruits of the land withered, and the beasts of the field died beneath the scourge. It is at this point that the play of Sophocles opens. The people have turned to Œdipus to save them from such an affliction as he did in times past, and he explains to the suppliant throng that he has already dispatched Creon, his own wife's brother, to Delphi to ask the reason for the anger of the god. At this opportune moment,

[274]

Creon returns from his mission and declares that Apollo is angry because Thebes is harboring an unclean thing, even the one responsible for the death of Laius.

At once Œdipus assumes responsibility for hunting out and condemning to death or exile the guilty man. No more vivid scene of dramatic irony could be imagined than that wherein Œdipus, all unconscious of his own identity, pronounces a curse alike upon the guilty slayer and upon anyone who would shield or protect him, sealing his words by invoking the honor of the legendary founders of Thebes, Labdacus and Polydorus and the elder Cadmus and Agenor, little knowing that he is citing his own lineage.

If ye remain silent, if anyone shall fail to heed this word through fear for a friend or for himself, thus shall I act, and thus must ye hear it from my lips. I charge that no man of this land, whereof I rule and hold the throne, receive the murderer, whoe'er he be, nor speak a word to him, nor make him a sharer in the prayers and sacrifices to the gods, nor admit him to the lustral rites; but I bid all men thrust him from their homes, for this is the unclean thing amongst us, even as the oracle of the Pythian god has revealed it to me. And further I pray that if with my knowledge this defiling presence should be sheltered within my house, I may suffer the same things that I have called down as a curse upon others.

The Recognition Scene. From the tragic irony of the curse which Œdipus innocently invokes upon himself, to the close of the drama, the finely knit plot works itself out through the slow process of disclosure, until the identity, the unwitting crime and the final ineluctable and cumulative punishment of Œdipus are complete. And always it is Œdipus who furthers the inquiry, setting himself unflinchingly to the task that is to bring his own destruction.

Presently a summons is sent to Teiresias, the blind seer, who knows all things through the gift of Apollo. Teiresias, who, except for the shepherd now in the country, alone harbors the truth, is loath to break his long self-imposed silence, but at length the hasty temper of the king provokes a quarrel, and Teiresias repeatedly declares that Œdipus himself is guilty. "I charge thee to abide by thine own proclamation, and from this present day speak no word to the citizens or to me, for thou art the unholy pollution of this city."

In reality the identity of the slayer is now disclosed, but neither Œdipus nor the citizens regard the words of Teiresias as other than the hasty abuse of a man provoked to anger. Œdipus next accuses Creon of complicity in a design to drive him from the throne, and only by the intervention of Iocasta is the quarrel stayed. When the latter discovers that the cause of the altercation has been the charge of Teiresias that Œdipus is responsible for the death of Laius, she seeks to quiet his fears by telling a tale to discredit the truth of the oracles, and thereby she succeeds only in advancing the inescapable process of recognition. To her husband she says:

Dismiss all these doubts, and learn from me that no human creature knows aught of prophecy. An oracle once came to Laius, saying that it was his fate to die by the hands of a child that should be born to him and me. And yet it is a strange band of robbers that has slain him, so goes the tale, at a place where three ways meet. The child, ere three days had passed, my lord caused to be exposed to death on the untracked mountainside. Hence Apollo did not bring it about that the babe should prove the slayer of his sire. Thus did the responses of the oracle falsely tell the future; regard them not.

But the intended words of comfort have produced a strange stirring of memory in the mind of Œdipus. Laius was slain where three ways meet, and he had himself killed a man at such a spot. Among the precarious mountain paths of Greece it was unlikely that two such meeting places should exist. Eagerly Œdipus questions Iocasta about the time of the death of Laius and learns that it occurred but shortly before he himself came to the land. He asks about the appearance of the former king and learns that he was tall, with graying hair, and of a build much like his own. Œdipus now realizes that he has killed Laius and has brought upon himself the curse pronounced against the unclean defiler of the land, for he cries out: "Oh, woe is me! it would seem that but now in ignorance I have called down dread curses upon myself."

Yet it is not the purpose of Sophocles to conclude the recognition thus suddenly, for at first Œdipus believes only that he has slain Laius and laid himself open to his own curse, but he does not recognize the more appalling fact that Laius was his own father. In the second place, the recognition scene, so nearly brought to completion, is now delayed, for Œdipus sees a possible way of escape. He recalls that the sole survivor at the time of Laius' death had brought back word of an attack by a band of robbers. If that tale can be substantiated, he may yet be proved guiltless, for he knows that he was alone when he slew a man upon the highway. Œdipus forthwith has the shepherd summoned from the fields. A choral song marks the close of the episode.

The action is resumed with the approach of a shepherd. It is not, however, the servant from the fields who now enters, but a stranger from Corinth, who proves to be none other than the shepherd who had received the infant on the mountains years before, and who has now come with a message that will produce both joy and grief—that Polybus the king is dead. In the simple mind of the herdsman the logic is clear: now Œdipus will succeed to the throne of Corinth, wherein he may take pride and joy, though he will naturally grieve also at the death of his father. To Iocasta the news promises a happy release from the gnawing fears that have consumed the household, and she dispatches a servant to carry the tidings to her husband.

Maidservant, go with all speed and bear this message to thy lord. Ah, ye prophecies of the gods, where are ye now? Long has Œdipus feared and shunned this man, lest he should kill him. But now he has perished in due course, and not by the hand of Œdipus.

Even Œdipus for the moment would be persuaded, but quickly his mind turns to the second part of the oracle, and he voices the fear that it may yet be his fate to marry his mother, Merope of Corinth. The messenger from Corinth, learning the cause of his concern, gladly tells him that he need entertain no such fear, for he is not in truth the child of Merope. The scene with the Corinthian messenger affords an excellent instance of peripeteia, or change of fortune, in a Greek tragedy, for the man bears a message that should bring gladness and relief, only to find that his successive disclosures encompass the destruction of the king. The process of recognition moves inexorably forward. Iocasta perceives the truth and tries frantically to stay the search of Œdipus into his birth. "Ah, wretched man, mayst thou never learn who thou art," she cries, and a moment later, as she rushes into the palace, we hear her last words: "Woe! woe! unhappy mortal, for this word alone can I utter to thee, and never another hereafter."

In time the herdsman who had been charged with the exposure of the infant Œdipus, who had through an excess of pity spared him, and who had witnessed his slaying of Laius, comes to the palace, where he is confronted by the Corinthian messenger and by Œdipus. It is during this scene that the identity of the king becomes clear even to himself, and the long suspense of the anagnorisis is at an end. Only the cumulative punishment of guilt remains. First we learn of the despairing suicide of Iocasta, then of how Œdipus has blinded his own eyes, that they may nevermore behold the works of his unconscious wickedness. With a sorrowful leave-taking from his unhappy daughters, he turns to the weary life of exile which he had pronounced on himself, and from which he does not shrink.

Estimate of the "Œdipus Tyrannus." In spite of the unrelieved suffering revealed in the story, the tragedy does not produce profound dejection, but rather an Aristotelian catharsis of the emotions, which arises from the contemplation of a strong man, matched with destiny, who clings with unflinching purpose to his concept of right. The hateful implications of the crimes to which Œdipus has been driven by fate recede into the background of one's consciousness, and the mental residue from the tragedy is a sense of the nobility of character with which Œdipus pursues the cause of truth, though it brings his own destruction. The rise and fall of the long-delayed recognition plays about the person of the king, who is never found unworthy of the role for which he has been cast.

Sophoclean Characters. The loss of more than ninety per cent of the plays of Sophocles counsels caution in pronouncing dogmatically on all qualities of his art. Nonetheless, a careful study of the seven extant tragedies will reveal some characteristics that are common to them all, and that have been seen to dominate the *Œdipus Tyrannus.* The singularly beautiful Sophoclean choral odes distinguish every drama. In addition to the refinement of poetic diction, the ingenuity and skill of plot structure, and the prudent sense of selectivity which reduces the rambling legends to a significant dramatic theme, one will be impressed by Sophocles' delineation of his principal characters and by the identification of particular moral qualities with each of them. Œdipus lingers in the memory not only as a Theban prince whose life has carried him through harrowing vicissitudes to disaster, but also as the embodiment of single-minded devotion to duty, even though it be accompanied by unwisdom and lead on to catastrophe. In the *Antigone* the young girl, Antigone, disobeys the ordinance of the new king, Creon, and, guided alike by her sense of divine will and by sisterly devotion, offers ceremonial burial to her brother. The dissuasion of her loving but timorous sister, Ismene, serves only to accentuate the qualities of firmness and piety that cling about the name of Antigone. In the same play Sophocles has created another distinctive character, that of the

[279]

arrogant and unyielding bureaucrat, Creon, who nurtures his own self-importance until Nemesis and ananke unite to bring him low.

The association of a moral quality with an individual character is made so intimate by Sophocles that the two become in the end little less than synonymous. The Greek hero Ajax, in the tragedy of the same name, grieving because the arms of Achilles have been awarded to Odysseus rather than to himself, is driven to madness and suicide by the obdurate intensity of pride and hatred. In the *Philoctetes,* three characters are recognizable from the beginning to the end for their distinctive traits: the crafty Odysseus is the embodiment of guile and cunning; the young Neoptolemus is ingenuous and noble by nature; and Philoctetes reflects the spirit of suffering and unforgiving resentment. It will readily be seen from these examples how the tragic mask might be used in the theater to depict the moral qualities of the several characters, especially when it is recalled that the action of a Greek play is confined to a single day and that as the characters are introduced, so do they remain until the end.

The Universality of Types. It need occasion no surprise that Sophocles should have undertaken to create specific types in his plays, or that he should have succeeded so completely in doing so, for he was simply accomplishing in drama what his contemporaries were doing in art. It was in the fifth century, as will presently be shown, that the sculptors were achieving the abiding forms of gods and heroes. The Zeus of Pheidias was to portray the Greek conception of the father of gods and men; the Discobolus of Myron and the Doryphorus of Polycleitus were to idealize the athletic figures of the time; the Ionic frieze of the Parthenon was to symbolize the worship of Athena in the city. The creation of types was the mark of the fifth century, and they are to be observed alike in art and literature.

CHAPTER XVII

EURIPIDES AND THE REJECTION OF TRADITION

Æschylus and Sophocles had found in the form of tragedy, which they inherited and enlarged, a fitting vehicle for their art and philosophy. Perhaps they exhausted its potential limits: at any rate, in the career of the next and last great dramatist of the fifth century we find an absence of harmony in the pursuit of his literary work that is in marked contrast with his older associates.

Life of Euripides. Euripides was born on the island of Salamis, probably in the year 480 B.C., though it is not necessary to treat too seriously the tradition that the day of his birth coincided with the Battle of Salamis. Some authorities put the year of his birth as early as 485 B.C. In any case, he belongs to a generation distinctly later than that of Æschylus or Sophocles. The youth of Euripides was spent at the home of his parents in the village of Phlya, near Athens, where, despite the meagerness of evidence relating to his boyhood and the acerbity of Aristophanes' jibes at the poverty and squalor of his early surroundings, there is every reason to believe that he passed the childhood of one to whom many privileges of education and culture were available. He was too young to have known anything of the Persian Wars, and by the time that he reached years of understanding, Athens had already entered upon the promise of the fifth century. When Pericles assumed power in 461 B.C., Euripides was but nineteen years of age and had already been engaged for a year or more in the composition of tragedies, although it was not until 455 B.C., when he was twenty-five years old, that he was first able to compete in a dramatic festival. In the following year, 454 B.C., when Athens betrayed the states of the Delian Confederacy by the transfer of the Treasury, Euripides was in late youth, with his habits of thought already formed by a society that was forgetting the stern traditions of equity that characterized the generation of Marathon. The first of the few victories won by Euripides belongs to the year 441 B.C.

Tradition makes Euripides a pupil of Anaxagoras, the philosopher, and Protagoras, the sophist, the former of whom was driven out of Athens on the charge of religious unorthodoxy in 429 B.C. From such persons as these, as well as from Socrates and the sophist Prodicus, with whom he must surely have associated, Euripides absorbed the questioning and doubting philosophy of the city, which was reflected in the intensity of his attacks on current and accepted beliefs. Though Euripides was apparently but little liked by his contemporaries, his popularity grew in his later years, and there is a pleasing story that many an Athenian soldier taken captive at Syracuse during the military expedition that met defeat in 413 B.C., gained his freedom in return for delighting his Syracusan captors by reciting verses from the plays of Euripides. The poet died in Macedonia in 406 B.C., a few months before the death of his older rival, Sophocles.

Euripides' Relation to his Time. Tastes and styles changed rapidly in the fifth century. Æschylus had written his sonorous verses about themes that lay closer to the lives of the gods than to the daily experience of man; Sophocles had examined some of the moral and ethical problems of his time, but without passionate intensity; Euripides, on the contrary, imparted his own burning conviction on social problems to his plays, but in so doing he attacked the conservative elements in Athens with a ferocity that defeated his own purpose by alienating sympathy. He was touched by philosophic speculation, so that he became more and more uncompromising in his denunciation of injustice.

[282]

In further contrast to the peaceful career that was traditionally the lot of Sophocles, Euripides was unhappy in his home life, unfortunate in his marriage, and during his earlier years intensely unpopular with the citizens of Athens, whose sufferings he had at heart more than any other writer of the age. He won but five first prizes in all, one after his death.

The Plays. Ninety-two plays, presented in the half-century between 455 B.C. and 405 B.C., are attributed to Euripides. Of these, nineteen have been preserved, if the *Rhesus,* of doubtful authenticity, be included in the list. The entire group belongs to the later years of his life, for none can be dated earlier than 438 B.C. The extant plays, with dates, when they are known, are listed: *Alcestis* (438 B.C.), *Medea* (431 B.C.), *Andromache* (430–424 B.C.), *Heracleidæ* (429 B.C.), *Hippolytus* (428 B.C.), *Hecuba* (423 B.C.), *Mad Heracles* (423–420 B.C.), *Suppliant Women* (421 B.C.), *Trojan Women* (415 B.C.), *Iphigeneia among the Taurians* (414–412 B.C.), *Electra* (413 B.C.), *Phœnician Women* (413–407 B.C.), *Helen* (412 B.C.), *Orestes* (408 B.C.), *Bacchæ* (uncertain date), *Cyclops* (uncertain date), *Ion* (late date), *Rhesus* (late date, uncertain authenticity), *Iphigeneia at Aulis* (405 B.C., produced posthumously).

The plays are not of equal merit. Among those that have been most highly regarded by modern critics are the *Bacchæ,* a strange tale of orgiastic religious rites centered about the female votaries of Bacchus, the *Medea,* with its theme of jealousy and revenge, the *Hippolytus,* a story of unrequited love and deception, the *Trojan Women,* a powerful drama of the suffering of the innocent in war, the *Iphigeneia among the Taurians,* a play of adventure and escape verging on melodrama; the *Alcestis,* a tragicomedy, and the *Electra,* with its treatment of matricide. Of these, a fuller discussion of the *Medea* has been included in this chapter, and a brief development of the plot of one or two of the others will also be found.

Contemporary Events in Relation to the Plays. Although Euripides was too much the detached philosopher to allow external events to color very markedly the mythological theme of his plots, it is nonetheless interesting in looking over the dates of the plays to reflect on the political circumstances of the years in which they were produced. The *Alcestis* was presented in 438 B.C., the same year that Pheidias' statue of Athena Parthenos was dedicated; the *Medea,* offered in 431 B.C., coincided with the opening of the Peloponnesian War; the *Heracleidæ* belongs to 429 B.C., the year of Pericles' death; the *Suppliant Women* to 421 B.C., the year of the Peace of Nicias; the *Trojan Women* was offered in 415 B.C., the year that the Athenian expedition sailed to Syracuse; and the *Electra* in 413 B.C., the year of the destruction of that armament. Though it would be profitless to seek specific historical themes in the plays of Euripides, he was writing as a citizen of Athens, and it is clear that the influences of the contemporary scene left their impress on him, for both political change and literary productivity pursued their ways in the crowded years of the fifth century.

The "Medea"; the Background of the Story. It is difficult to find a play of Euripides that would be generally accepted as characteristic of his work, for his range of interest and technique is wide. Nevertheless, if one must be selected to illustrate his achievement, the *Medea* may serve the purpose, for no play from the Euripidean collection is more skilfully written or more powerful in its emotional effect. As with the *Œdipus Tyrannus* of Sophocles, the essential incidents that lie behind the segment of the story that has been chosen for the drama are embodied in the plot itself, though the audience may also be presumed to have had some knowledge of the circumstances that brought Jason and Medea together. Jason, the son of Æson, and rightful heir to the throne of Iolcus in Thessaly, had been dispatched by his usurping uncle, Pelias, to bring back the Golden Fleece from Colchis as a labor necessary to the recovery of his birthright. With fifty chosen heroes of Greece, Jason had sailed on the Argo, and at Colchis the king, Æëtes, had promised to surrender the Golden Fleece if Jason would slay the sleepless dragon that guarded it and sow its teeth. This and other tasks impossible of human accomplishment Jason was able to perform with the aid of Medea, the sorceress daughter of Æëtes, who used her magic art to help the Greek hero, for she had fallen passionately in love with him. Together they fled from Colchis, and Medea sealed her perpetual estrangement from her childhood home by slaying her own brother. When they reached Iolcus, Medea again put her baleful powers at the service of her lord, and wreaked vengeance on Pelias by persuading his daughters that she could restore him to youth by boiling him in a cauldron with magic herbs. In the act, however, she omitted the herbs, and Pelias was killed. Jason and Medea now fled to Corinth, where they lived in company with their children. At length Creon, the king of Corinth, proposed to have Jason wed his daughter, first putting aside Medea, the barbarian wife from Colchis. It is at this point that the play of Euripides opens.

The Plot of the "Medea." In the play of Euripides a prologue was frequently used to acquaint the audience with the setting. In the present instance the old Nurse of Medea appears at the outset and sorrowfully soliloquizes on the evil pass to which they have come:

Would that the Argo had never sailed to the land of the Colchians through the dark Symplegades, and would that never in the glades of Pelion had the tall pine been felled to furnish oars for the hands of the Argonauts, who brought back with them the Golden Fleece to Pelias; for then never would my mistress Medea have sailed to the citadels of Iolcus, smitten at heart with the love of Jason.

The further soliloquy of the Nurse, her dialogue with the attendant, and the anguished voice of Medea heard from within the palace disclose not only the imminent betrayal that Jason has resolved to commit, but also reveal the frenzy of grief and reproach into which Medea has fallen, and the wild untamed spirit of the woman, whose passion for vengeance is to form the theme of the tragedy.

[285]

As Medea enters into the action of the play, two elements in her character and situation emerge into clear relief. One is the overmastering passion for revenge against those who have brought her to dishonor and disgrace, in which the righteous wrath of a woman mingles with the more than human frenzy of the Colchian sorceress. The second is the sense of isolation and hopelessness in which the unhappy Medea finds herself, with all sanctuary denied her, whether in her ancient home of Colchis, in Jason's former home at Iolcus, or even in humble obscurity in Corinth, for Creon, the king, requires her instant banishment. Thus we hear from the lips of Medea such words as these addressed to the Chorus of Corinthian women:

> They say that we women live a life untroubled in our homes, while men must strive with the spear. How fond is their thought! I would rather take my stand three times behind the shield in war than bear one child. But these words mean less to thee than to me, for thou hast still a city, a father's home, the joy of life, and the comradeship of friends, while I, alone and cityless, am reviled of my husband, seized captive from a foreign land. Neither mother nor brother nor kinsman have I with whom to take shelter in my misfortune. Therefore I crave one thing only from thee, that thou keep silence if any way or device be found for me to take vengeance on my husband and requite him for these ills.
>
> For a woman may be weak in all else and filled with fear to look upon the clash of steel, but when she finds herself wronged within her home, there is no mind more frenzied with hate than hers.

Medea is now resolved to act, and she pursues her purpose with the guile of a Clytemnestra and the persistence of an Œdipus. From the credulous Creon, who has ordered her banishment, she obtains a day's respite, ostensibly to prepare for her departure but in reality to make ready the fearful vengeance that shall embrace Jason, Creon, and the princess whom Jason is to marry, and which shall even encompass the death of her own sons in her obsession for revenge.

Two principal scenes take place between Jason and Medea, prior to the last exultant moment when she vaunts over him in the success of her baleful plan. The first involves a fierce quarrel, in which the caviling, sophistic justification that Jason offers for his conduct is met with the withering fury of Medea's rage and scorn. Recalling the services that she has rendered to him at so great cost to herself, she hurls her reproaches at him.

Thus hast thou profited at my hands, basest of all men, and now thou hast betrayed me. And thou hast taken a new bride though children were already born to thee. If thou wert a childless man, there might be pardon in seeking a new marriage. Hath all faith in oaths departed? Must I think the gods no longer rule, and that new laws are now ordained? For of thyself, thou dost know thine own falseness.

The second meeting occurs when Medea has been able to carry her plans further, and in particular after she has gained from Ægeus, the king of Athens, a sworn pledge of sanctuary in his land, for it is a necessary part of her vengeance that she should live to gloat on the suffering that she has wrought, and that she should not perish in the holocaust. Hence Medea greets Jason with the pretence of reconciliation. She craves pardon for her violent words and commends the wisdom of his conduct. She would have her children remain in Corinth and live in harmony with the king. And she, too, will aid the entreaty that banishment may not be pronounced against them, for she will send by their hands gifts to the princess, Jason's new wife, a fair robe and an embossed gold chaplet. This must be the children's task:

When ye have come nigh to the palace, beseech your father's new bride, who is my mistress now, and beg that ye be not exiled from this land, and give to her this adornment. But this above all is needful, that she receive these gifts into her own hands. Go now with all speed; may success attend you and may you carry back to your mother the good news she longs to hear.

The dramatic irony of the moment brings tension, for only the sorceress knows the baneful power of her gifts, and peripeteia is imminent when an attendant tells how the princess has received the offerings with gladness and granted the prayer for the children's safety. Another part of Medea's vengeance lies yet ahead for her, and for a moment the human heart of a mother falters as she embraces her children and talks to them in words that fall on uncomprehending ears.

Presently a messenger rushes in with the fearful news of the agonized death of the princess and her father, who have been consumed by the magic burning power of the gifts that Medea had sent. And now with cold, unnatural calm, Medea turns to the last task that confronts her, the slaughter of her own children, that Jason, too, may suffer and also that the vengeance of the Corinthians may not descend on them.

I am resolved upon this deed, to slay at once my sons and quit this land, nor shall I delay that they may meet death at another and less kindly hand. For it is inevitable that they should die.

In keeping with Greek convention, the death of the children is accomplished behind the scenes, and the play closes with the arrival of Jason just in time to see his wife borne off in a chariot drawn by winged dragons, taking with her the bodies of his sons, which, with a last refinement of torture, she refuses to give up for burial. The supernatural means adopted for the conclusion of the plot illustrates the *deus ex machina,* or "the god from a machine," which was adopted with increasing frequency in the later days of Greek drama.

Estimates of the "Medea." The *Medea* is a play of powerful emotion, with bold and striking delineation of character and with a well-conceived and well-executed plot. The introduction of the *deus ex machina,* which ordinarily means the substi-

[288]

tution of an inartistic convention for skilful resolution of the plot is more acceptable in this instance because the method of its incorporation harmonizes with the magical powers of Medea herself. If the play is assessed with Aristotle's definition of tragedy in mind, it will be apparent that the element of terror rather than pity predominates in the major characters, and the catharsis of the emotions will be sought in the spent fury of the hatred and vengeance of a woman who has been drawn as a barbarian sorceress beyond the pale of Hellenic conduct and who therefore reveals the emotions of jealousy and revenge writ large. Where pity can be identified in the drama it will be seen in connection with the king of Corinth, his daughter, and the slain children of Jason and Medea. Nor should one fail to note the sympathy that is aroused for Medea herself as a homeless outcast even in the minds of those who must condemn the enormity of her conduct.

The long and brilliant success of this tragedy, revived in America in recent years, with the character of Medea portrayed by the actress Judith Anderson, testifies to the universal principles involved, for even audiences quite untrained in Greek dramatic techniques have fallen under the spell of the tale.

The Breadth of Euripides' Interests. The analysis of a single play of Euripides affords a less satisfactory understanding of the quality of his art than does a similar brief treatment of the work of Æschylus or Sophocles. This is due not only to the fact that more than twice as many tragedies of Euripides have survived as of either of the two older dramatists, but also to the wider range of interest that engaged his attention. The atmosphere of the middle of the fifth century, which led Sophocles, in common with Pheidias and Polycleitus, to create eternal and static types, was already yielding to the more personal and individualistic attitude that is to be observed in the achievements of the fourth century, and Euripides was enough younger than Sophocles to come more directly under the influence of this change of emphasis.

Hence one will not seek consistency of treatment in the

various plays of Euripides, but rather he will observe the variety of emotional themes. Thus, the strained and harsh qualities of hate and vengeance that are part of the strength of the *Medea* are balanced by the softer and more tender moods of some of his other tragedies. For example, the unusually beautiful *Alcestis* tells of the love and devotion of the young queen of Thessaly, Alcestis, who gave her own life to save her husband, Admetus, when he was doomed to die if he could not find a willing substitute. The strange conduct of the boisterous, hard-drinking, but good-hearted Heracles, who enters the house of mourning unawares and presently rescues Alcestis from Death, indicates the degree to which Euripides was prepared to depart from the usual conventions of Greek tragedy.

Problems of human suffering were treated with great sympathy by Euripides. The *Trojan Women* deals, in a spirit of unrelieved sadness, with the pitiable plight of the aged queen Hecuba and the daughters of Priam after the fall of Troy and with the fate of the young Astyanax, Hector's son, who was thrown from the battlements. The verses of this tragedy carry one back to the scenes of sorrow in the *Iliad,* when Hector, parting from Andromache, foretells her lot of slavery, and when the unhappy Priam laments the sad fate of the city which must come to pass with the death of Hector.

The tense and complicated plot was masterfully handled by Euripides, and he frequently resorted to the *deus ex machina* for its solution. Such a play is the *Iphigeneia in Tauris,* which he based on a variation of the tale of the sacrifice of Iphigeneia. In the alternate legend, Artemis rescued the maid from the altar and made her priestess at a temple among the barbarous Taurians, where it was her duty to prepare for sacrifice all strangers who came to those inhospitable shores. The action of the play deals with the arrival of Orestes and Pylades, their capture, and the preparation for the sacrifice of Orestes by his sister, who knows not his identity. It thus affords admirable opportunities for Euripides to develop dramatic suspense and at length to effect with consummate skill an anagnorisis, or

[290]

recognition scene, which resolves the story in romantic success rather than in tragedy. The happy ending of this play, as with the *Alcestis,* indicates the departure of Euripides from the more formal canons of tragic composition.

The *Cyclops,* in which the Homeric story of Odysseus and Polyphemus is dramatized, is the only complete extant satyr play, and, with the exception of the fragmentary *Ichneutæ,* or "Trackers," of Sophocles, affords the best opportunity to study that type of literature. The play is brief and adheres to the regular structure of tragedy. It should be recalled that the *Alcestis,* to which reference has been twice made above, stood as the fourth play in a trilogy and embodied some elements of the satyr play.

The Modernity of Euripides. The kinship of Euripides with modern society has been the subject of frequent comment. It will be realized on reflection that his modernity, like the freshness of all Greek thought, lies not in any superficial resemblance to a transitory experience of present-day life, but in the universality of his themes. Thus such a theme as the devotion of Alcestis to her husband is reenacted in every instance of supreme love and sacrifice. The tenseness of the recognition in the *Iphigeneia in Tauris* depends on the same agonizing suspense that has vivified many subsequent plays; and the depths of anguish in which the wanderers from captive Troy are enveloped in the *Trojan Women* has its modern counterpart in every tale of poignant human suffering that has accompanied the devastation and exile occasioned by war in our own day.

CHAPTER XVIII

THE GREEK TEMPLE: ITS STRUCTURE AND THE ARCHITECTURAL ORDERS

The drama was one of the most brilliant and mature manifestations of the Greek mind in the fifth century. There were, however, other avenues of cultural activity that were also being explored, and an examination of Greek architecture, especially as it is known from the temples, reveals both the early stages of its growth and its splendid fulfilment in the adornment of the Acropolis in the Age of Pericles. As in the case of the drama, the development of architecture was closely connected with the religious and public life of the people.

The Simplicity of Greek Architecture. In the style of their building, as in other forms of art and in literature, the Greeks followed a conservative path. They voluntarily restricted themselves to a few established principles, within which their genius found ample scope for the refinements and variations that gave individual beauty to each creation. In the Minoan and Mycenæan Ages, there were no separate temples to the gods, but in the archaic age and in subsequent periods almost every community erected one or more buildings in honor of a deity. The simplest form of the temple suggests the early wooden enclosures that were built as shrines to protect the image of a god or to mark a place of sacred significance, and the principle of "post and lintel" or uprights and crosspieces, introduced at the outset, continued to be the basis of virtually all construction throughout the classical period in Greece. For this reason there is a massiveness about the early temples,

[292]

designed to support the great weight of marble. Lacking the ingenuity of the Romans, and without their passion for the construction of utilitarian projects, the Greeks did little with the arch or the vault or the dome. Instead, their powers of invention were devoted to the creation and adornment of structures suitable for the deities whom they chose to honor.

GROUND PLANS OF TEMPLES

Technical Terms. A temple, unless for specific local reasons, was always oriented from east to west, with the entrance to the

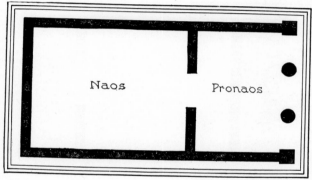

Drawn by Dorothy I. Chubb

FIGURE 51. SINGLE TEMPLE "IN ANTIS."

east. When the three distinct chambers of the temple were present, the vestibule to the east was called the *pronaos,* or fore-room; behind this was the *naos,* or sacred chamber, in which the cult statue of the god was placed; and the room to the rear, which took the form of an open porch, usually without a door connecting it to the naos, was called the *opisthodomos,* or rear-room.

The Temple in Antis. When the walls of a temple ended in a square column or pilaster, that column was called an *anta,* and such a temple is described by the Latin phrase as a temple *in antis* (Figure 51). The accompanying ground plans will

[293]

prove almost self-explanatory. When a temple is *in antis,* columns stand between and not in front of the *antæ,* or square columns attached to the ends of the wall. There are both single and double temples *in antis.* The double temple *in antis,* as will be observed in the plan, has the opisthodomos (Figure 52).

The Prostyle Temple. When the columns stand in front of the end walls of the temple, the descriptive term is *prostyle* (*stylos* = column), and the number of columns is indicated by a further word, such as *tetrastyle, hexastyle,* or *octostyle,* to

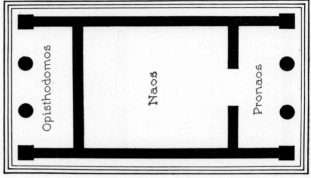

Drawn by Dorothy I. Chubb

FIGURE 52. DOUBLE TEMPLE "IN ANTIS."

indicate four, six, or eight columns respectively (Figure 53). A prostyle temple will always have an even number of freestanding columns at the ends. No more disturbing violation of the symmetry of Greek architectural principles can be found than the three columns that are occasionally seen in structures of the Greek revival period in America.

The Amphiprostyle Temple. A logical extension of the prostyle arrangement led to the construction of free-standing columns at either end, in which case the temple is called *amphiprostyle* (Figure 54). There, too, an even number of columns will invariably be found at either end. In the typical

[294]

plans that are shown, it will be observed that considerable variation occurs regarding the inclusion of the pronaos and the opisthodomos together with the naos. Only in the larger temples were all three rooms present.

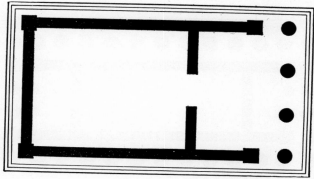

Drawn by Dorothy I. Chubb

FIGURE 53. PROSTYLE TEMPLE TETRASTYLE.

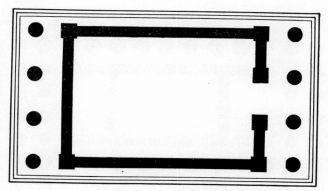

Drawn by Dorothy I. Chubb

FIGURE 54. AMPHIPROSTYLE TEMPLE TETRASTYLE.

The Peripteral Temple. When a free-standing row of columns runs all about the temple, it is described as *peripteral*. A peripteral temple may be also either a temple *in antis* (Figure 55) or a prostyle temple (Figure 56). The former

[295]

type is somewhat more common. The peripteral temple afforded a covered passage all the way around the temple. It was a popular style in Greece and was used during the entire classical period. It is not necessary to have an even number of columns on the sides of a peripteral temple.

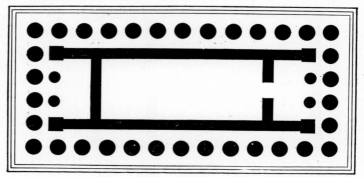

Drawn by Dorothy I. Chubb

FIGURE 55. PERIPTERAL TEMPLE "IN ANTIS."

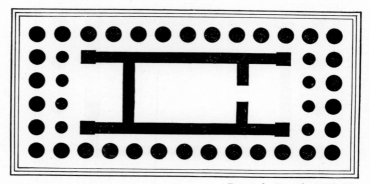

Drawn by Dorothy I. Chubb

FIGURE 56. PERIPTERAL TEMPLE AMPHIPROSTYLE TETRASTYLE.

The Dipteral Temple. The great weight of marble beams required supporting columns quite close to one another. As a consequence, any increase in the space between the temple wall and the columns of a peripteral temple required additional

[296]

structural support, which was provided by two rows of free-standing columns surrounding the temple. Such a temple is called *dipteral* (Figure 57). Two rows of columns, however, will be found only rarely and in very large temples.

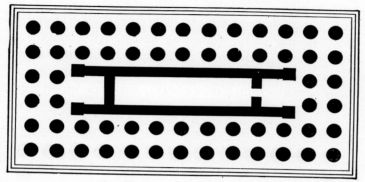

Drawn by Dorothy I. Chubb

FIGURE 57. DIPTERAL TEMPLE.

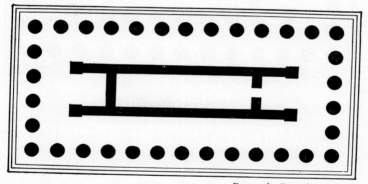

Drawn by Dorothy I. Chubb

FIGURE 58. PSEUDO-DIPTERAL TEMPLE.

The Pseudo-Dipteral Temple. Occasionally, only a single row of columns is found, but it stands so far from the temple wall that space is left for another row. Such a temple is called *pseudo-dipteral,* or "false dipteral" (Figure 58). The wide spaces in the pseudo-dipteral temple required a lighter roof

[297]

construction, and it was therefore not used with great frequency. Unfortunately, the archæological evidence for roof construction is less abundant than for walls or columns, and reconstructions of roofs are therefore capable of less exact documentation.

The pseudo-dipteral temple may take another form, in all respects similar to the foregoing except that engaged, or attached, columns, with only half the shaft of the column exposed, are built into the walls of the temple (Figure 59). This form of construction did not serve any very useful purpose, either structural or ornamental, and was not widely used.

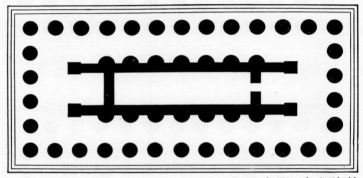

Drawn by Dorothy I. Chubb

FIGURE 59. PSEUDO-DIPTERAL TEMPLE.

Variations of the Ground Plans. The ground plans given above have been simplified, and there are many variations of these types. An examination of the ground plan of the Parthenon, or the Erechtheum, or the temple at Bassæ will indicate how markedly the architects modified their plans to accommodate them to the available space or to the particular needs of each temple. Other ground plans will also be found, such as the round temple, and the *hypæthral* temple, the latter differing from the dipteral temple only by the inclusion of an entrance from either end and a court open to the sky in the center. Nevertheless, an understanding of the more common

[298]

ground plans will facilitate a study of the intricacies and adaptations that are encountered, for the inherent conservatism of the Greek artist was always present to check flights of fancy. The ground plans that have been described and illustrated are not confined to any one of the three orders of architecture.

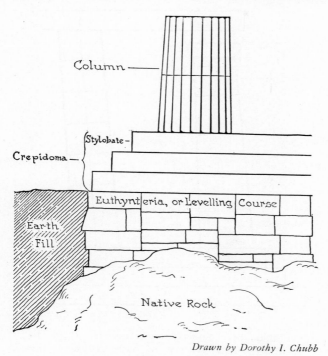

Drawn by Dorothy I. Chubb

FIGURE 60. SIMPLIFIED SCHEMATIC PLAN OF THE FOUNDATION OF A GREEK TEMPLE. This plan illustrates the erection of a Greek temple from the bedrock up to and including the lower drums of the columns.

ARCHITECTURAL ORDERS

There are three orders of Greek architecture, the Doric, the Ionic, and the Corinthian, the last being a modification of the Ionic. Although all three were used contemporaneously, the Doric was probably developed first and the Corinthian

[299]

last. The Ionic order was known during the archaic period, but the more important extant temples of that order belong to the fifth century and later when the austere lines characteristic of archaic art in general were yielding to a taste for greater adornment.

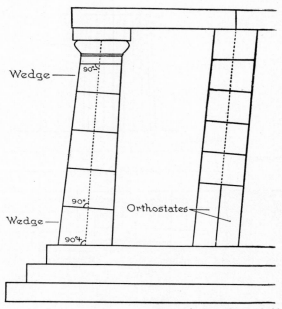

Drawn by Dorothy I. Chubb

FIGURE 61. SIMPLIFIED SCHEMATIC PLAN TO ILLUSTRATE THE BATTER OF THE COLUMNS AND WALLS OF A TEMPLE.

The Doric Order: the Substructure. With the principal ground plans in mind, the essential features of the Doric order may be illustrated by a series of sketches, indicating the various parts of the temple from the bedrock to the acroterion, or decorative sculptured figure which was placed at the peak of the roof and sometimes also at the base of the sloping sides (see Figure 65). In preparing to erect a temple (Figure 60), the Greeks cleared away the earth to the bedrock The founda-

[300]

tion of the temple, from bedrock to the ground level, was then built up with successive layers of marble, or other stone, in which attention was given to the solidity of the substructure but not at all to its appearance. Thus, old blocks, marred from previous usage, were acceptable material. The last layer, which was even with the ground, was laid with particular attention to the level upper surface, for on it the superstructure had to stand without the aid of mortar, though not, be it remembered, without iron dowels set in the marble blocks and embedded in lead. This leveling course was called the *euthynteria,* a name which in Greek conveys the idea of evenness.

The Crepidoma and the Stylobate. On top of the euthynteria were built the three steps characteristic of most Greek temples; the Hephæsteum, or so-called Theseum at Athens, with two steps, is a distinct exception. The three steps, properly called the *crepidoma,* are often referred to as the *stylobate,* but, strictly speaking, the stylobate, which means "that on which the column stands," should refer to the top step alone. The entire foundation includes the crepidoma, the euthynteria, and the stone foundation down to bedrock.

The Columns and the Walls. On the stylobate, that is, on the topmost of the three foundation steps, the Doric column rests directly, without a base. On the same level, or floor, the temple wall also rests, and the foundation, as it is understood in connection with the wall, is called the *teichobate* (wall stand), rather than the stylobate (column stand). The lowest course of stones of the wall, which are called the *orthostates,* stand on edge and are twice as high and half as thick as succeeding courses above them. In the accompanying drawing it will be seen that both the column and the wall incline slightly inward. The inward inclination is known as the *batter* of the walls or the *batter* of the columns (Figure 61). The degree of slant away from the perpendicular has been greatly exaggerated in the drawing. It amounted to about three inches in a total height of twenty feet or more, and consequently was almost imperceptible.

Since the central axis of the column rises at an angle of less than ninety degrees on the inward side, a correction of a similar amount must be made on the topmost drum of the column, so that the architrave, which rests upon the columns, may lie horizontally. The delicate curves and inclinations of Greek architecture, which were planned with the greatest care, lend grace and vitality to the buildings even when they are so slight as to defy casual detection. Mortar was not used in temple construction, but the horizontal and vertical courses were bound together with metal clamps, or cramps, and dowels.

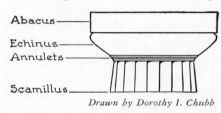

Drawn by Dorothy I. Chubb

FIGURE 62. DETAILS OF THE DORIC CAPITAL. This part of the column was made as a single piece.

The Capital. The capital of a Doric column was made in a single piece (Figure 62), including the *abacus, echinus, annulets,* and the *scamillus,* although the scamillus refers properly to the line of juncture between the bottom of the capital and the top of the next column drum. Great variations in the curves and angles of this architectural feature existed in different periods, and the beauty of the structure as a whole depended on the taste and skill of the architect in these respects.

The Entasis of the Column. A further refinement of the column is the *entasis,* or slight swelling between the base and the top. This occurs about one-third of the way up from the the bottom and it never exceeds in diameter that of the base of the column itself. Any exaggeration of the entasis mars the beauty of the column instead of adding to it.

The Column Drums. Each column was fluted after the drums, or sections, were set in place. The flutings are continuous and are usually twenty in number, though they sometimes occur in other multiples of four. The sharp ridge separating two flutings on a Doric column is called the *arris.* The surface of contact between two column drums was ground

[302]

with great precision at the outer rim, and the drum was slightly hollowed in the center, to insure very accurate fitting, as no mortar was used. This process was called *anathyrosis,* or "contact-tooling" (Figure 63). To aid in setting and placing columns a block of oak was sometimes set in a carved space in the center of the drums. Some of these wooden blocks, hermetically sealed through the centuries, have been saved from overturned columns of the Parthenon to capture the imagination of the observer by the preservation through more than two thousand years of a substance that might have been destroyed by a half-hour's exposure to fire on any one of the days since a contemporary of Pericles set them in place.

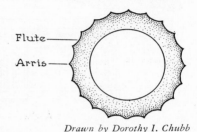

Flute—

Arris—

Drawn by Dorothy I. Chubb

FIGURE 63. CROSS SECTION OF A DORIC COLUMN.

The Entablature. On top of the columns and centered from one column to another, except at the corners, where an adjustment is made, rest the *architrave blocks* (Figure 64). At the top of the architrave there is a small band called the *tænia,* extending the full length of the architrave. Beneath the tænia and over each column and each intercolumniation there is a little cleat called the *regula,* and beneath each regula are six small drops of marble, called *guttæ.* It will be observed that the tænia forms a continuous division between the architrave and the frieze.

Above the architrave lies the Doric *frieze,* made up of alternating *triglyphs* and *metopes.* Each triglyph stands above a regula. The metopes are wider than the triglyphs, being nearly square, and are sometimes decorated with sculpture, though such decoration is not essential to the order. The triglyph, or three-grooved tablet as the name indicates, was probably a schematized representation of the end of a wooden beam; by the same token the metope signifies the space between beam-ends (*opæ*).

[303]

Above the Doric frieze the cornice rests, extending out over it to form a protection against the rain. The underside of the cornice slants upward and is ornamented over each triglyph and each metope with a thin flat slab, called the *mutule,* which

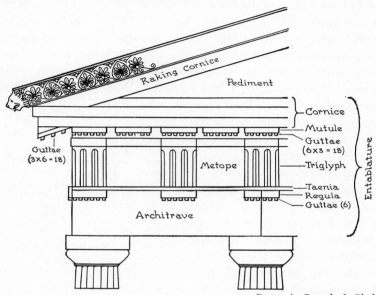

Drawn by Dorothy I. Chubb

FIGURE 64. PLAN OF THE ENTABLATURE OF THE DORIC ORDER. This plan studied in conjunction with Figure 60 will illustrate virtually all the exterior details of a Doric temple.

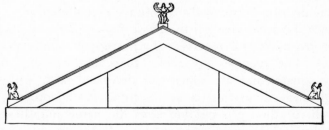

Drawn by Dorothy I. Chubb

FIGURE 65. PLAN OF THE PEDIMENT SHOWING THE ACROTERIA.

in turn is decorated with eighteen guttæ. From the front only six guttæ can be seen on the mutules, corresponding to the six guttæ which hang below the regulæ. A careful and continuous study of the several plans will help to make this explanation clear; the student who is fortunate enough to find a building of the Greek revival or tradition on his campus will be rewarded by scrutiny of the architectural features in three dimensions with a plan in hand.

The Pediment. At either end of the temple the cornice slopes up to form the pediment (Figure 65) and is called the "raking cornice." The pediment may or may not be sculptured. At the top of the pediment, and also at either end, a decorative figure called the *acroterion* rested, while along the cornice at the sides of the temple provision was made for carrying off the water from the roof through lion's head waterspouts.

Criteria for Dating. Among the minor, but important, criteria for dating Doric temples are the curves of the echinus on the capital, which became more pronounced in later times, and the craftsmanship of the lion's head waterspouts, which follow the development of Greek art from the stiffness of the archaic period to the more naturalistic representation of the fifth century and later. The archæologist and historian of art will also take careful account of such secondary evidence as the shape and manufacture of the iron clamps and dowels, the dedicatory offerings, and the technical development of decorative sculpture in determining the period of a particular temple. Surprisingly accurate estimates can often be made by assembling and assessing all available indications.

Original Wooden Structures. There are some indications that the Greek temples, which in extant examples date no earlier than the seventh century before Christ, were originally constructed of wood. Among these are the evidences of very heavy timbers, that continued even in later times to be laid to support the enormous weight of the marble roof of a temple. A further indication of the original wooden structure of Greek

[305]

temples is the presence of the triglyphs in the Doric frieze. The assumption is that the beams to support the ceiling were laid with their ends coming flush with the edge of the architrave. The triglyph may therefore be regarded as an ornamental conventionalized sheathing for the end of a wooden beam, as has been suggested above.

Photograph by Alinari

FIGURE 66. TEMPLE OF CONCORD AT AGRIGENTO IN SICILY. Details of construction may be correlated with the plans given in Figures 60 and 64.

Examples of Doric Temples. There are many standing temples of the Doric order in Greece that have their peculiar points of interest. The Hephæsteum, or so-called Theseum of Athens (See Frontispiece), is the best preserved temple that now remains. Two important groups of Doric temples were built at Acragas, the modern Agrigento, in Sicily and at Pæstum in Italy (Figure 66).

The Heræum at Olympia. The oldest known Doric temple

in Greece is the Heræum, or Temple of Hera, at Olympia, which is to be dated in the seventh century (Figure 67). The ground plan of the present Heræum, which is clearly the

Photograph by Alinari

FIGURE 67. HERAEUM AT OLYMPIA. Seventh century B.C. The different sizes of the drums of the columns and variations in the capitals are illustrated.

latest of a series on the same site, shows a peripteral temple *in antis,* with pronaos, naos, and opisthodomos present, the opis-

[307]

thodomos being the oldest known example of this feature. The orthostates of the walls are still standing, and probably the upper wall courses were once made of sun-dried brick, which has disintegrated with the weather. The unusually great distance between the columns, added to the fact that no stone or marble blocks from the architrave have come to light, suggests

Photograph by Philip Gendreau, New York

FIGURE 68. THE PARTHENON, 447 B.C. TO 432 B.C. This photograph illustrates the restoration of the central columns of the Parthenon in modern times.

that the entire entablature may have been of wood, for the weight of marble demands limited spaces between supporting columns or other architectural members. The columns differ from one another both in the number of flutings and in the number of drums. In fact, the style and technique of the existing columns indicate that they were erected at different periods

[308]

from the seventh to the third centuries before Christ. It is probable that as the original wooden columns decayed, they were replaced one by one with marble columns. Pausanias, who visited Olympia in the second century after Christ and who has left a detailed record of the temple, mentions an oak column that was standing in his day. The extant remains of the temple thus illustrate the transition of architecture from wood to stone.

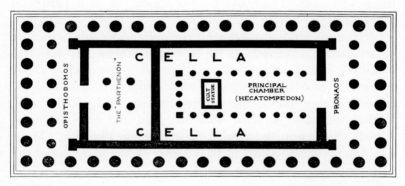

Drawn by Donald W. Burl'ngame

FIGURE 69. SIMPLIFIED GROUND PLAN OF THE PARTHENON. The Parthenon is essentially a peripteral temple, amphiprostyle, hexastyle (compare Figure 56). However, some variations appear. The pronaos to the east and the opisthodomos to the west are similar in arrangement. The third division, the cella, or naos, was divided into two chambers, a large eastern room, the hecatompedon, in which the cult statue was placed, and a smaller room to the west originally called the "Parthenon" before that name was assigned to the whole building.

The Parthenon. The most famous of all Doric temples is the Parthenon. It stands today, denuded in large part of its magnificent pedimental sculpture and of its two great friezes, the Doric and the Ionic, dominating the ruins of the Acropolis, expressing the greatest values of Greek architecture, simplicity of design and the æsthetic quality and purpose that distinguished form, proportion, and execution. The elements have washed away all traces of the paint that must once have

[309]

brought out its many artistic details with startling clarity, but kindly time has, over the centuries, oxidized the iron in the Pentelic marble of which it is built, turning the originally light stone to a tawny yellow that glows against the brilliant blue Athenian sky with an arresting effect that compensates the modern observer for the loss of ancient color.

The Form of the Parthenon. The Parthenon was commenced in 447 B.C. and was substantially completed by 432 B.C., three years before the death of Pericles. It is a peripteral amphiprostyle temple, with eight columns at the eastern and western ends, and seventeen on the sides, built upon the site of an earlier sanctuary to the goddess Athena. It was embellished with a sculptured pediment at either end, a Doric frieze of which all the metopes were sculptured, and an Ionic frieze running about the upper courses of the cella wall. Within the naos, or cella, stood the gold and ivory statue of Athena Parthenos, the work of the sculptor Pheidias. These adornments are discussed in the chapter on the sculpture of the fifth century.

The Architectural Refinements. The architectural refinements of the Parthenon, if described in detail, would involve very many technicalities. Yet the beauty of some of the refinements of the Doric order, especially as they appear in the Hephæsteum, or so-called Theseum, a temple of 465 B.C. and the Parthenon itself, may be briefly recapitulated. The columns of the early Doric temples, which, for example, at Pæstum in Italy, were in height only four times their diameter, are in the best fifth-century temples lightened and lengthened to five times their diameter or even a trifle more, the heavy overhang of the capitals is reduced, the inward inclination, or batter, adds vitality to the structure, and the entasis is superbly proportioned. Optical illusions are compensated for by making the corner columns thicker than the others lest they should actually appear thinner as they stand free against the light, and the stylobate of the Parthenon has an upward curve along the ends and the sides, the latter curve being calculated as of four and three-eighths inches. To cite a time-honored experiment, a man's hat placed at one end of the stylobate cannot be seen from the same level at the other end because of the upward curve of the center. The intention was doubtless to overcome an illusion of sinking, which would have resulted from a completely level stylobate; the result of this and many other careful and precisely planned details of building is to lend to the great and massive temple an intangible air of grace and life.

Photograph by Boissonnas

FIGURE 70. INTERIOR OF THE PARTHENON. This photograph was made after the restoration of the columns, lighter in color, to the left.

The Propylæa. The Propylæa, or monumental gateway to the Acropolis, consisted of a complex structure, chiefly Doric though with some Ionic features, designed by the architect Mnesicles, and in part constructed between 437 and 432 B.C., during the time of the ascendency of Pericles. As originally planned, a great central building was to have been flanked by four wings. Certain curtailments, however, proved necessary as the completed structure would otherwise have encroached

[311]

on the sanctuary of Artemis Brauronia and on the site of the little temple of Athena Nike, or the Wingless Victory, to the south.

The Proplyæa served as a ceremonial entrance to the Acropolis. It contained in one of the wings the Pinacotheke, or Picture-Gallery. The paintings exhibited there, which were seen and described by the traveler Pausanias in the second cen-

Photograph by Alinari

FIGURE 71. THE PROPYLAEA AND THE TEMPLE OF WINGLESS VICTORY. Fifth century B.C. The large rectangular structure in the center foreground belongs to Roman times. The Propylæa formed the ceremonial entrance gate to the Acropolis.

tury A.D., have long since perished. Certain of the unfinished southern parts of the Propylæa are of interest because of the evidence that they afford on ancient methods of building.

The Ionic Order: the Columns. The Ionic order of architecture was freely used contemporaneously with the Doric, although the two orders were not equally popular in the same localities. Geographically, the Doric order predominates in western Greece, whereas the early Ionic temples are almost without exception found in the east, for the order originated

[312]

in Asia Minor and extended first to the islands along the coast. While the Ionic order thus moved in some degree from the east to the west, the Doric order, with its more severe forms, never moved from the west to the east. There is, however, much that is common to the Doric and Ionic orders; the Corinthian also has many similarities with the other two. The foundations, both below and above ground, are the same in all three orders, and it is not until the column is reached that a difference appears. The Doric column rises directly from the stylobate without a base, but the Ionic column has a base, consisting of any one of a variety of combinations of the *trochilus, torus,* and *astragalus.* The trochilus is a large concave curve, the torus a large convex curve, and the astragalus a very small convex curve. Three types of Ionic column bases are illustrated in the diagram (Figure 72).

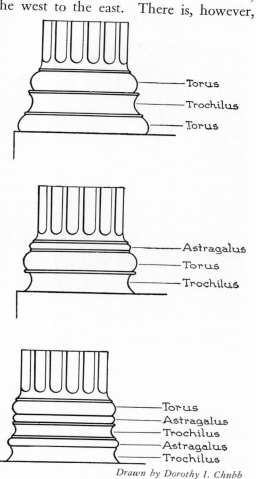

Drawn by Dorothy I. Chubb

FIGURE 72. DESIGNS OF TYPICAL IONIC COLUMN BASES. Other variations in arrangement of the parts here named will be found.

[313]

The channels of the Ionic columns differ from the Doric flutings, for, unlike the latter, they do not meet in a sharp line. Instead, a narrow ribbon-like band, called the *fillet,* takes the place of the arris of the Doric column and separates the flutings, of which in the best period there are normally twenty-four on each column. The capital of the Ionic column offers still another point of difference. It consists normally of a volute, which varies somewhat in detail, though the effect is always more elaborate and ornate than that of the Doric capital.

FIGURE 73. IONIC COLUMN RESTORATION. This figure illustrates the form of the capital, the flutings, and the base.

The Entablature. The transition from the volute capital to the architrave is effected by an egg-and-dart moulding or cushion, and the architrave, which rests on this cushion at the top of the columns, has three *fasciæ,* or "bands," on its surface (Figure 74). The frieze, if present at all, rests directly on the architrave. If the Ionic frieze is ornamented, the sculpturing is continuous. The Doric frieze, it will be recalled, consists of alternate triglyphs and metopes. The cornice of the Ionic order rests on the frieze or architrave as the case may be. *Dentils* may or may not be present. The Ionic columns are usually taller and more slender than Doric columns in proportion to the diameter of the lowest drum, thus making a more graceful but less sturdy building.

[314]

The Erechtheum. The Erechtheum on the Acropolis at Athens is an Ionic temple of highly complicated and original design, comprising within a small area both variety of structure and wealth of ornamentation (Figure 75). This temple

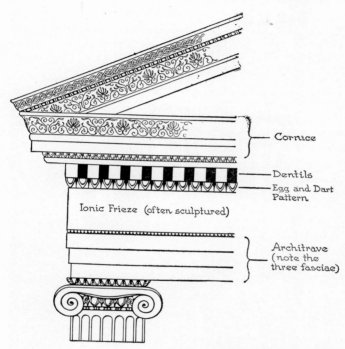

Drawn by Dorothy I. Chubb

FIGURE 74. PLAN OF THE ENTABLATURE OF THE IONIC ORDER. This figure should be compared and contrasted with the plan of the Doric order, Figure 64.

was erected on a sacred site, where previous sanctuaries had been built even as early as Homeric times. The present temple, however, was constructed in the latter years of the fifth century, during the critical period of the Peloponnesian War. Though the delicate beauty of the refinements of this temple reflects the highest architectural capacities of the artists who

[315]

were nurtured under the patronage of Pericles, it must be recalled that its actual date falls after his death.

Religious conservatism led the Greeks to reverence sacred associations, and consequently the ground plan of the Erechtheum was adapted to the existing memorials of divinity as

Photograph by Eunice Burr Couch

FIGURE 75. PORCH OF THE MAIDENS (SOUTH PORCH OF THE ERECHTHEUM). Fifth century B.C.

well as to the uneven configuration of the land. The result is that the porches were built on markedly different ground levels, and the high columns of the north porch present a very different appearance from the small but exquisite Caryatids, or Maiden-columns, of the south porch. As a consequence, the

[316]

skill of execution and the resulting beauty of the Erechtheum may be appreciated
more adequately through a
successive and detailed study
of its various parts than by an
attempt to assess the temple
as a whole.

The effect of sacred association is further illustrated by
the construction of the north
porch, which was built over
some indentations in the rock
that were taken to be the
marks of Poseidon's trident
from which a salt spring had
flowed. In order to avoid the
sacrilege of covering the hal-
lowed scars, one opening was
left in the floor of the porch,
while an aperture in the roof
may be thought to have allowed access to the divinity of
Heaven. Needless to say, so
subjective an interpretation
has not been universally accepted, but there can be no
doubt that local circumstances
everywhere modified the plans
of the architects.

The south porch, or Porch
of the Maidens, illustrates the
inclusion of human figures as
supporting columns in the
finest form that device ever attained in Greece. The Cary-

Photograph by the British Museum

FIGURE 76. CARYATID, OR MAIDEN
COLUMN, FROM THE ERECHTHEUM.
Fifth century B.C.

[317]

atids (Figure 76), for such the figures are called, are not identical. They were sculptured in such a way that, by the slight bend of the knee over which the drapery falls, the group gained coherence, and the Caryatids support the entablature lightly and gracefully and without the illusion of effort which is almost invariably present in similar figures.

The Temple of Athena Nike, or Wingless Victory. A very small temple of the Ionic order was built on a bastion of the

Drawn by Dorothy I. Chubb

FIGURE 77. TYPICAL CORINTHIAN CAPITAL. For the relative degrees of elaboration, compare the Doric capital, Figure 62, and the Ionic capital, Figure 73.

Acropolis just south of the Propylæa (See Figure 71). This was the Temple of Athena Nike, or the Wingless Victory. The architect was the same Callicrates who worked on the Parthenon. The little temple, which was originally built about 426 B.C. and has suffered many vicissitudes of rebuilding even in the nineteenth and twentieth centuries, is of interest as a purely Ionic temple built in Athens toward the end of the fifth century, but its chief claim to fame has always rested on the Ionic frieze of its balustrade, which depicts in high relief

[318]

a series of wingless Nikæ, or Victories, of which the best known is the Victory, or Nike, binding her sandal (See Figure 97).

The Corinthian Order. The Corinthian order is scarcely distinct from the Ionic, its chief difference lying in the form of the capital, which is circular, and decorated with conventionalized designs of the acanthus leaf (Figure 77). The Corinthian order was effectively used on the Choregic Monument of Lysicrates in Athens and there were Corinthian elements in the fifth-century temple at Bassæ, which was built by Ictinus, one of the architects of the Parthenon.

The various architectural members of the Corinthian order were freely decorated with paint in ancient times, and in fact all the architectural orders relied on the use of bright colors, especially red and blue, to make the different parts stand out clearly in the brilliant Greek sunlight. The Corinthian order was definitely later in its development than either the Doric or Ionic, reaching its highest peak in the Hellenistic Age and later. It is thus contemporaneous with the personal and sometimes casual themes that were then appearing in sculpture and other forms of art.

Architecture of the Fifth Century. The brief survey of the development of the temple has dealt with architectural achievements both earlier and later than the Age of Pericles. It was, however, in the fifth century that the great temples were erected to the gods, the Propylæa, or Periclean Entrance Court to the Acropolis built, and the city otherwise adorned. The architectural monuments are themselves works of fifth-century art, and the necessity of producing sculptural adornments for the temples gave to the artists the assurance of a continuing field of endeavor, without which comprehensive art projects could not be undertaken. The Parthenon, to cite the most conspicuous example, was built during the rule of Pericles between 447 B.C. and 432 B.C. Fortunately, the patronage of Pericles and of the city never interfered with the free play of

[319]

the artist's own conception of his task. The art of the fifth century may be described as civic, religious, and impersonal in quality. It covers a span of seventy-six years, from 480 B.C. to 404 B.C., only the equivalent of one long lifetime, but into that period are crowded the finest achievements of Greece.

CHAPTER XIX

THE GREEK THEATER

In the most significant years of Greek civilization the individual citizen found his pleasure and his emotional outlet in the common enterprises of the community rather than in his private affairs. Thus it is that in architecture the principal structures were everywhere those of public concern.

The Nature of the Evidence. The theater was almost as important an institution of the Greek city as was the temple, for it afforded the necessary background for the development of Greek drama. The evidence regarding the form of the ancient theater is of two distinct types. In the first place, there are the extant dramas of the fifth century, from the action of which some conclusions may be drawn as to the structure of the theaters in which they were presented. In the second place, the ruins of theaters have been uncovered in practically every ancient Greek city. It is, however, by no means a simple task to correlate the literary and archæological evidence and arrive at consistent conclusions, for the internal evidence of the fifth-century plays may usually be interpreted in more than one way, while the theaters have in most cases suffered from the reworking of the Romans or from the vandalism of the dwellers in Greece during the Middle Ages.

Moreover, perishable properties of the theater are no longer available for study with the result that more than one appealing theory advanced by a modern student of ancient drama rests largely on an ingenious interpretation of cuttings in a

[321]

marble floor or block. The most perfectly preserved Greek theater is the one at Epidaurus, a town lying sufficiently apart from traveled ways to have escaped both rebuilding and wanton destruction. The architect who built this theater was Polycleitus the Younger, who brought it to completion in the latter half of the fourth century. Consequently it contains some features that were not known in the days of Æschylus, Sophocles, or Euripides. In fact, most of the permanently constructed theaters outside Athens belong to periods later than the fifth century.

Photograph by Alinari

FIGURE 78. THE GREEK THEATER AT SYRACUSE IN SICILY. The incomplete circle of the orchestra indicates rebuilding in Roman times.

The Form of the Theater: a Composite Plan. Though there is virtually no problem in connection with the archæological interpretation of the Greek theater that is not controversial, a workable reconstruction can be made in somewhat the same manner as the growth of Greek tragedy itself was traced (Figure 79). The early dithyrambic chants were sung by the dancing satyrs, or goat-men, probably on the circular threshing-

[322]

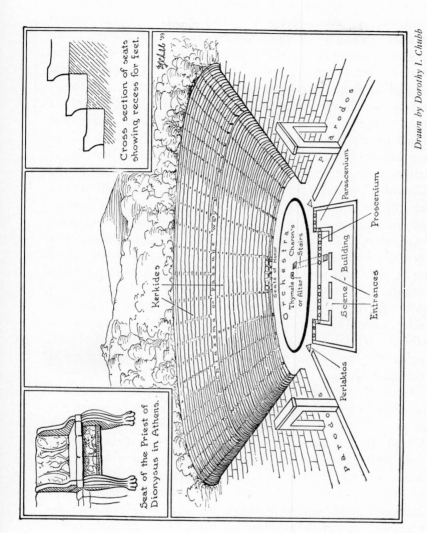

Cross section of seats showing recess for feet.

Seat of the Priest of Dionysus in Athens.

Parodos

Parascenium

Proscenium

Scene-Building

Entrances

Periaktos

Parodos

Orchestra

Thymele
Charon's
or Altar
Stairs

Seats of Honor

Diazoma or Passage way

Kerkides

Drawn by Dorothy I. Chubb

FIGURE 79. COMPOSITE PLAN OF THE GREEK THEATER. Features from many Greek theaters are included. Note the relationship of the theater to the terrain at the rear.

floors of the Greek hillsides. Such a circular area became an integral part of the later theater, where it was called the *orchestra,* or "dancing place." The action of Greek drama regularly took place in the orchestra, and not on a stage. The religious association of the drama led almost at once to the location of a *thymele,* or altar, in the center of the orchestra.

Originally the spectators grouped themselves on a hillside, and as the drama became more formalized, it was natural to select a site where a circular indentation in the hill might afford to the largest number an unobstructed view of the action below. Thus the seats of the Theater of Dionysus at Athens were admirably situated against the south slope of the Acropolis. When a permanent stone theater was built against the hillside, the seats were divided by aisles, and the wedge-like sections were called *kerkides,* or "wedges." Somewhat more than halfway up, a *diazoma,* or passageway, was normally introduced to facilitate the entry and departure of the crowds, and above the diazoma there were twice as many kerkides as below. The seats of honor in the Greek theater were on the ground level at the center; they may still be seen with identifying inscriptions in the Theater of Dionysus at Athens. This fact in itself is one of the strongest arguments against the theory that any type of raised stage was used in the classical centuries.

At the back of the circular orchestra, on the side opposite to the seats, a *scene-building,* or tent, was erected in which the actors, each of whom played several parts, might quickly change their masks and costumes. The entrances into the scene-building might be interpreted as the doors leading to houses, or temples, or palaces, as demanded by the action of the play. At either end of the scene-building, *parascenia,* or extensions beside the scene-building, were connected with the latter and projected somewhat in front of it. Directly before the scene-building and the parascenia ran the *proscenium,* or part before the scene-building. This took the form of a row of columns standing on a stylobate about eight feet in front of the

wall of the scene-building and connected to it by an entablature. The proscenium roof may have afforded a place from
which the actors spoke on occasion, when it was desirable to
represent them as appearing on a higher level, or when gods
were portrayed. If the scene-building rose to two stories, as it
sometimes did, the second story was called the *episcenium,* and
it was visible above the proscenium, which ordinarily was only
one story in height.

Between the parascenia and the end walls of the auditorium
were the *parodoi,* or entrances for the Chorus, which were
sometimes furnished with doors. Scenery was used to some
extent, for there are literary references to the painting of
scenery, and the evolution of the meaning of the word *scene,*
which signifies "tent" in Greek, and was used in connection
with the theater to designate what has in this description been
called the scene-building, indicates one use of this theatrical
device. In addition there were two *periaktoi,* which probably
took the form of tall prisms, painted with different scenes on
each of their three sides and pivoted in such a way that they
could be quickly turned to indicate a change of setting. The
exact location of the periaktoi is a matter of considerable doubt,
but they may have been placed on either side of the scene-
building close to the parodoi.

Some Theatrical Devices. In the theater at Eretria and in
some other localities, an underground passage led from the
region of the proscenium to the center of the orchestra. This
was called *Charon's Stairs,* and through it ghosts or other characters who were presumed to come from the underworld might
emerge from below. One such striking instance occurs in an
early play, the *Persians* of Æschylus, in which the ghost of the
dead Persian king Darius returns to chide his son Xerxes for
his folly in attacking Greece. A useful piece of dramatic
equipment was the *eccyclema,* which took the form of a
wheeled and movable platform. By this device, some actions
within a house or palace, such as violent death, which was
never displayed before a Greek audience, could be dramatically

[325]

shown after the fact, by wheeling forth the eccyclema, on which the corpse lay. The *deus ex machina,* to give it the Latin name by which it is usually called, signified the introduction of a god from on high by means of some mechanical device in order to unravel by his supernatural powers a plot that had grown too intricate for human solution.

It should be clearly understood that, both in the description of the Greek theater that has been attempted and in the accompanying plan, details have been introduced from various theaters and from the literary evidence of the entire classical period of Greece. In no single theater of antiquity were all used together. In most Greek theaters, including the Theater of Dionysus, at Athens, the orchestra will now be found in the form of a half-circle rather than a complete circle. This change was made by the Romans, who introduced a wide low stage, encroaching on the circle of the orchestra.

Refinements of the Theater. In addition to the Theater of Dionysus at Athens, which, in spite of the changes made in Roman times, is invested with particular interest because of its association with Attic drama, and the theater at Epidaurus, which is the most perfectly preserved extant example, other important theaters may be seen at Eretria, Delos, Priene, Ephesus, and Syracuse, to mention only a few cities. They were built with careful and exceedingly successful attention to acoustic properties, and with many refinements of technique that can be appreciated only by a detailed study of the separate buildings. The theater at Epidaurus, for instance, was planned with the seats above the diazoma on a slightly steeper pitch, and with the rows of seats following a fixed radius only over the central two thirds of the circle. Either edge was thrown further out on the arc of a circle of greater radius, so that the spectators sitting at the ends might have a more adequate view of the play. A similar result was sometimes attained by extending either end of the auditorium on a tangent with the circle rather than continuing the arc. The seats of the theater were normally quite low, suggesting that the audi-

[326]

ence provided themselves with robes or cushions. Since the plays continued throughout the day, some such concession to comfort would have been necessary in any case. The seats were undercut, so that a spectator might have room for his

Photograph by Alinari

FIGURE 80. CHOREGIC MONUMENT OF LYSICRATES. About 335 B.C. This monument is the sole survivor of a series that once lined the street. Note the walls of the Acropolis at the back, and the modern buildings in the foreground.

[327]

feet without unduly disturbing the person sitting in front of him. Some of these details have been indicated in Figure 79.

One cannot fail to mark in the location of the theaters of Greece the extraordinary beauty of the sites that seem everywhere to have been available, for the seats on the hillside almost invariably faced a magnificent view of mountains and the sea. The theater was in every respect, intellectual, emotional, and physical, a part of the life of the ancient citizen.

Courtesy of the American School of Classical Studies at Athens

FIGURE 81. RESTORATION OF THE BUILDINGS IN THE ATHENIAN AGORA. Note the Hephæsteum, upper left, the circular Tholos, and the many-columned Stoa.

Other Types of Architecture. Though the temple and the theater are the most significant types of architecture in Greece, other buildings also served the civic needs, and excavations have disclosed them for interpretation both as works of art and as evidence on the Greek way of life. The comparative simplicity of the private dwellings of the Greeks during the period when the magnificent public buildings were erected reflects the preoccupation of the people with the institutions of the city; the *stadium* and *gymnasium* testify to their love of athletics; the *stoa,* or roofed colonnade, and the *lesche,* or portico ordinarily enclosed on three sides, both admirably suited as gathering places for those who wished to converse with their fellows
[328]

in centers of activity, recall their gregarious instincts. Memorial monuments, both funeral and choregic, lined the appropriate ways, and the long history of internecine war in Greece has produced an imposing series of military walls and fortifications throughout the land.

CHAPTER XX

THE ART OF THE FIFTH CENTURY: SCULPTURE

The Period of Highest Artistic Achievement. It was during the fifth century, or, more specifically, during the years that separated the Battle of Salamis in 480 B.C. from the downfall of Athens in 404 B.C., that Greek art fulfilled the promise of the vigorous years of experimentation that had gone before. The triumph of Athenian democracy in the conflict with Persia not only afforded a moral stimulus to free endeavor, but also, in the years that followed, a definite outlet for artistic creation, especially in sculpture, was assured under the enlightened government of Pericles. As a consequence, the abundance of material from the fifth century that is available for study, both in the form of original statues and of copies that were executed in Roman times, presents its own problem of classification. While the temples erected at this time were being decorated with sculptural reliefs, there were in addition various schools of artists working prolifically to produce substantive statues. The three most important sculptors of the fifth century were Myron, Pheidias, and Polycleitus, and in the distinctive qualities that attach to the work of each the development of sculptural technique may be followed.

TRANSITIONAL SCULPTURE

The Tyrannicides. The transition from the sculpture of the archaic age to the perfection of the middle and late fifth

[330]

century must, however, first be traced through a number of examples that precede the works of the three outstanding sculptors of the period. The group representing Harmodius and Aristogeiton, the Tyrannicides, or tyrant-slayers, who had killed the tyrant Hipparchus, son of Peisistratus, in 514 B.C., affords an excellent starting point, for it has the advantage of association with known historical characters, and consequently with definite historical dates, which lie both in the archaic period and in the fifth century. The tyrant Hipparchus, son of Peisistratus, was slain in 514 B.C., and immediately thereafter Harmodius and Aristogeiton, the assassins, were put to death by the angry throng of citizens, who appear to have been completely loyal to the tyrants. It was not until Hippias, the brother of Hipparchus, who continued to rule alone, was driven from the city in 510 B.C., that the people began to exalt Harmodius and Aristogeiton as their saviors. Shortly after 510 B.C., the sculptor Antenor made a bronze group of the Tyrannicides and placed it in the city, where it stood until 480 B.C., when it was carried off to Persia by Xerxes.

When the Athenians returned to the city soon after 480 B.C., they set up a second group of the Tyrannicides to replace the one that had been lost, this time the work of Critius and Nesiotes. The original group by Antenor was removed from Persia many years later and restored to Athens by Alexander the Great or one of the generals who succeeded him. Thereafter the two groups, that of Antenor, which was made shortly after 510 B.C., and that of Critius and Nesiotes, which was set up a generation later, stood side by side in the city.

Both groups perished in antiquity, and there are left, as with so many other ancient works, only copies from which to judge the originals. The best of these is to be found in the life-size marble figures from Naples (Figure 82), though the incorrect substitution in modern times of a fourth-century head on the body of Aristogeiton produces a somewhat incongruous effect. Whether the Roman copy goes back to the earlier or the later Greek work has been the subject of extended debate. There

[331]

Photograph by Alinari

FIGURE 82. THE TYRANNICIDES, OR TYRANT SLAYERS. Roman copy of a Greek original of the early fifth century B.C. National Museum, Naples. Note the archaic hair arrangement on the figure to the right, and the incorrect substitution of a fourth-century head on the figure to the left.

[332]

can, however, be little doubt that it was derived from the group of Critius and Nesiotes.

A certain weakness of composition is present in this group,

Photograph by Boissonnas

FIGURE 83. BRONZE ARCHAIC ZEUS. Early fifth century B.C. National Museum, Athens. This figure was discovered in a wrecked vessel near Artemisium, north of the island of Euboea.

for the tyrant-slayers are represented as advancing to destroy their foes, and thus one becomes aware of a center of interest lying outside the group, namely, the tyrants themselves, who

[333]

FIGURE 84. THE CHARIOTEER OF DELPHI.
Early fifth century B.C. Delphi. The law of
frontality is largely maintained in this transitional figure.

are to be attacked. It is a fault of early arrangement, which was to be realized and corrected by the Greek artists soon thereafter. As an example of transitional sculpture, belonging in the early years of the fifth century, the group of the Tyrannicides continues to illustrate many of the rigid and exact qualities of the archaic period. There has been some departure from the law of frontality, and the archaic smile is no longer present on the face of Harmodius, but the connection with the standing male figures of the earlier century is still plain.

The Zeus from Artemisium and the Charioteer of Delphi. Two beautiful bronze statues of the early fifth century afford an opportunity to study the technique of sculpture at a little later date. One is the statue of Zeus, which was recovered from the sea near Cape Artemisium within recent years (Figure 83). The bearded god stands poised to hurl his thunderbolt. There is fine feeling in the power of the figure, and if, like the group of the Tyrannicides, it still lacks the object of attack to complete the theme, the omission is less noticeable, because of the impersonal majesty of the deity. The second bronze statue of the period that challenges attention is the Charioteer of Delphi (Figure 84), a life-size figure that once formed part of a group of four horses and a chariot. An adequate motivation for the position in which the charioteer stands is thus afforded. Much of archaic technique survives in this statue. The youth stands quietly erect, modifying the law of frontality only by an extended arm, but it is clear that the artist has chosen the posture to suit his purpose and not because of an inability to deal otherwise with it. The departure from archaic forms may be noted further in the fact that the standing male figure is now entirely draped. Moreover, the substitution of a serene dignity of countenance for the archaic smile proclaims the increasing technical capacity of the sculptor. Furthermore, a detailed examination of the statue reveals great skill in such matters as the grace and power of the hand that grasps the reins and in the folds of the chiton above the high girdle. In such works as these the growing mastery of the artist over his material can be traced. The identity of the artist and his city is disputed, although an inscription indicates that the group of which the charioteer is a part was dedicated by Polyzalus of Syracuse. The work is to be dated shortly after 480 B.C.

The Ægina Pediments. On the island of Ægina, which lies a few miles off the harbor of Piræus, the Temple of Aphæa was built, apparently just about the year 480 B.C. The pediments of the temple were adorned with scenes from the Trojan War, and if it is true that they were planned and executed after the Persian Wars, they may well have been intended as an allegorical representation of the recent struggle between the Greeks and Persians. The technical execution of the eastern pediment is distinctly superior to that of the western one, possibly because a more advanced school of artists worked on it. The sculptures, with their obvious debt to different hands, make an interesting study of the artistic attainments of the Greeks at the transitional period, for, whatever may have been the actual date of execution, the artists had assuredly been trained during the latter years of the archaic period.

The Fallen Warrior from the eastern pediment (Figure 85) illustrates the manner in which the archaic artist was able to represent the agony of death. It should be borne in mind for comparison with the Dying Gaul, which was made during the Hellenistic Age (see Figure 141). Another excellent figure from the eastern pediment represents an archer, crouching with drawn bow. In this case the pose of the archer is adapted to the sloping cornice of the pediment, and the battle scene, of which he makes a part, affords the needed motivation for the bow shot. The Ægina pediments were extensively restored by the modern sculptor Thorwaldsen in the nineteenth century, and for that reason must be studied with caution if one is to gain a true picture of the original work.

The Temple of Zeus at Olympia. The first great temple to be built in Greece during the fifth century was that of Zeus at Olympia. It was commenced in 470 B.C., just ten years after the Battle of Salamis, and completed in 457 B.C., or shortly thereafter, that is, four years after Pericles came into power in Athens and ten years before the Parthenon was begun. Pheidias executed the cult statues of both temples and, according to Plutarch, exercised a general supervision over their decoration. Though the sculptures of the Parthenon are more competent in workmanship, there is in the decoration of the Temple of Zeus a tremendous strength, which arises from the struggle for at-

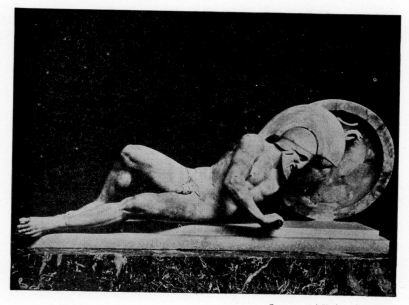

Courtesy of University Prints

FIGURE 85. THE FALLEN WARRIOR. Early fifth century B.C. Glyptothek, Munich. This figure formed part of the pedimental sculptures of the Temple of Aphæa at Aegina.

tainment rather than from perfection.

The Olympia Metopes. Only twelve metopes of the Doric frieze on the Temple of Zeus at Olympia were sculptured, eight across the front and the two adjoining on either side. On them were carved the Twelve Labors of Heracles, and the execution of the figures, with competent transition from profile

[337]

to full-front aspects of the body, testifies to the rapid development of art that had already taken place in the fifth century. Although the metopes have suffered the ravages of time, several

Photograph by Alinari

FIGURE 86. HERACLES AND ATLAS. Fifth century B.C. Olympia. This group is one of a series of twelve metopes from the Temple of Zeus at Olympia, representing the Labors of Heracles.

of them have escaped complete destruction. The finest, both in execution and in composition, is that which represents the

[338]

myth of the Golden Apples of the Hesperides (Figure 86). One of the Twelve Labors of Heracles required him to secure the golden apples, and this he accomplished by the roundabout method of persuading the giant Atlas, who supported the heavens, to go for the apples while Heracles temporarily bore the skies on his shoulders. The whole composition is conceived with a gentle humor that makes no sacrifice of dignity. Atlas, having returned with the apples, proffers them to Heracles, who is already more than occupied in supporting the Heavens. A folded cushion rests on his aching shoulders, while one of the daughters of Hesperus raises a willing, but scarcely effectual, hand to help bear the weight of the sky.

The Olympia Pediments. The decoration of the two pediments illustrates a conception of balance which has already been noted in pre-Hellenic times in the contrasting, but balanced, scenes on the pair of gold cups from Vaphio. On the eastern pediment of the temple the preparations for the chariot race between Pelops and Œnomaus are shown. The scene is one of quiet just before the race begins. The two chariots face each other with the horses at rest, while a squire crouches before each. The balance is almost painfully exact, with Zeus standing in the center, and a standing male figure on one side balanced against a similar figure on the other, a crouching figure against a crouching figure, a reclining figure against a reclining figure. The western pediment, in contrast to the scene of calm on the east, shows the battle of the Centaurs and Lapiths at the marriage of Pirithous, where all is frenzy and confusion. Only the quiet and imposing figure of Apollo, who stands in the center with head turned to the right and arm extended, is at ease. In the balance of figures within a pedimental group and through the contrasting moods of the two pediments, the sculptors who worked on the Temple of Zeus gave to Greece an idea of artistic planning that was to be used with increasing effectiveness by their successors.

The Sculptors of the Olympia Pediments. Pausanias, a late traveler and writer who visited Olympia in the second century

[339]

after Christ, more than five hundred years after the building of the temple, is the authority for attributing the eastern pediment to Pæonius of Mende in Thrace, and the western pediment to Alcamenes, a pupil of Pheidias. Pæonius is known as the sculptor who made a winged Nike, or Victory, which also stood at Olympia, and which will be discussed a little later.

Mature Art of the Fifth Century

Myron

Myron of Athens is the first of the group of three outstanding sculptors of the fifth century. His career may be placed in the early half of that century, for tradition relates that his son Lycius worked on the statues that were erected at the entrance to the Acropolis in 446 B.C., a year after the Parthenon was commenced. Probably Myron was then already dead. By the time of Myron, athletic sculpture had progressed far beyond the rigid symmetry of the archaic "Apollos," for considerable capacity in the execution of athletic subjects is already shown in such figures as the warriors of the Ægina pediments, the Tyrannicides, the Zeus from Artemisium, and the Charioteer of Delphi. In each of these figures, the hand of the artist had been trained in the archaic technique, even though his mind and eyes were on the future.

The Discobolus. Myron, working in the tradition of athletic sculpture, achieved his greatest success in the Discobolus, or discus-thrower (Figure 87). In this statue, of which a correct copy shows the head looking back toward the discus and not, as in most copies, away toward the goal, Myron has completely mastered the problem of representing the human body in any position and when viewed from any angle or any direction. The young discus-thrower is shown with body poised, just at the instant before he hurls the discus. The details of anatomy, the taut muscles, the toes dragging backward on the ground, and the firm but easy flow of the musculature illustrate some of the techniques of sculpture that have been mastered. The

[340]

Photograph by Alinari

FIGURE 87. THE DISCOBOLUS OF MYRON. Roman copy of a Greek
original of the fifth century B.C. Museo Nazionale delle Terme, Rome.
The action of the figure is self-contained.

[341]

question of grouping, which marred the Tyrannicides because of the projection of interest beyond the substantive statue itself, is likewise satisfactorily handled in the Discobolus, for the lines of the body lead the eye inward and there is no thought of the target, but only of the athlete. The face alone shows less strain than one might expect from the intensity of the posture, but the reason probably lies in the fact that Myron is still far from the age of individualism or portraiture. He has represented the idealized athlete rather than any particular model.

Perhaps one hundred and fifty years separate the "Apollo" of Tenea and the New York *Kouros* from the Discobolus, and in that time the artists have left behind them all the restrictions that are implicit in the law of frontality and have achieved the freedom that comes with the capacity to show the human form in action as well as at rest. Never after the time of Myron did these technical problems offer a hindrance to creative art.

Roman Copies and Literary Testimony. No ancient original works of Myron have been preserved, and consequently an evaluation of his art must be made from Roman copies, and also from the fairly abundant references in ancient critics. Pausanias tells of a group of Athena and Marsyas by Myron, in which Athena is represented just as she has thrown down the flutes that she could not play without distorting her features, while Marsyas stands back in astonishment. There are many references to the intensely real emotion that Myron was able to instill into his work. The Roman writer Petronius says of him that he could "almost mould in bronze the souls of men and beasts." One need not take too seriously the tale of the bronze heifer from his workshop that was so lifelike that it deceived living cattle, but the story is not without its significance as evidence of his creation of realistic effects.

The contribution of Myron in the early fifth century to the development of art is the mastery of technique for the faithful portrayal of the body of man or animal in any position. All his known statues were in bronze, and the delicate perfection of detail that he was able to achieve is explained in part by his reputed skill as an engraver of bronze plate. He did little or nothing to show variations of emotion on the face. The portrayal of facial emotion was not fully developed until the fourth century.

Pheidias

The intimate association of Pheidias with the Temple of Zeus at Olympia and the Parthenon in Athens, his execution of the gold and ivory cult statues for each of these temples, and the warm praise accorded to him by later authors, notably Plutarch and Lucian, have combined to give him a reputation of the highest order. It is, unfortunately, difficult to document his work by specific identification of ancient statues. Of the independent substantive pieces of sculpture made by Pheidias, it is possible to judge only through ancient literary descriptions, or contemporary copies, which appear sometimes on smaller objects, such as coins and gems, and also through late Roman copies, which were made for the commercial market. The Lemnian Athena has been claimed to be a Roman copy of a statue that Pheidias made for the people of the island of Lemnos about 450 B.C. It affords an excellent illustration of the technique of a fifth-century work in the style and tradition of Pheidias. The pose is quiet and dignified; the drapery falls in simple folds over the left knee; the face is calm and dispassionate.

The Athena Promachos. Three colossal statues by Pheidias merit particular attention. It should be borne in mind that the term *colossal,* as applied to sculpture, simply indicates that the figure is more than life size. One such early statue was the bronze figure of Athena Promachos, or Athena, the Defender of the City, which, according to tradition, was made from a tithe of the spoils of Marathon and consequently is to be dated somewhat after 490 B.C. The goddess stood in the open at the western end of the Acropolis of Athens, and the Greeks liked to believe that the helmet and the point of the

[343]

FIGURE 88. THE VARVAKEION STATUETTE OF ATHENA PARTHENOS. Fifth century B.C. National Museum, Athens. This statuette affords the best evidence of the original form of the chryselephantine statue of the goddess by Pheidias.

[344]

spear caught the eye of the returning Athenian sailor as he rounded the promontory of Cape Sunium. The statue has long since perished, and its appearance can be conjectured only from descriptive passages and ancient copies.

The Athena Parthenos. In the case of two other colossal statues of Pheidias there is a little more evidence, though both of them have likewise perished. They are the Athena Parthenos, a standing colossal *chryselephantine,* or gold and ivory, cult statue of the goddess, which stood in the Parthenon of Athens, and a seated colossal figure of Zeus, which occupied the naos of the Temple of Zeus at Olympia. The Athena Parthenos was dedicated in 438 B.C. A description of the statue by Pausanias, supplemented by a number of more or less satisfactory copies (Figure 88), affords some idea of the nature of the beautiful and impressive goddess. She stood with a winged figure of Victory poised on her right hand. With her left hand she held a spear and supported her shield, within which was coiled the serpent that was her attribute. The shield was elaborately decorated, and every part of the statue was adorned with the most beautiful and delicate workmanship of which the greatest of Greek artists was capable. When Pericles fell into disfavor in Athens, an indirect attack was made on him through a charge that his friend Pheidias had embezzled gold intended for the statue of Athena. Pheidias proved his innocence by having the gold adornments removed and weighed. This anecdote indicates the method in which chryselephantine statues were made by attaching thin and removable sheets of modeled gold to a wooden frame.

The Olympian Zeus. The cult statue of Zeus at Olympia was made after the temple was completed in 457 B.C., and is probably earlier than the Athena Parthenos. Though Pheidias was provided with a workshop of the same size as the naos of the temple, so that he might construct the figure in relation to its eventual location, the harmony of the statue with its surroundings was apparently less perfect than in the case of the Athena Parthenos, for the seated figure of Zeus was so large

[345]

that the god could not have arisen without thrusting his head and shoulders through the roof of the temple. This incon-

FIGURE 89. HEAD OF ZEUS. Fourth century B.C. This head was probably influenced by the statue of the god made by Pheidias for the Temple of Zeus at Olympia.

[346]

gruity of size did not, however, impair the impression of dignity and majesty that emanated from the statue, and it established the artistic type for the father of gods and men in antiquity. Pheidias himself declared that he took as his model for the god the verses of Homer in which the poet says: "The son of Cronus nodded his dark brow, and the ambrosial locks tossed on the god's undying head; and he caused great Olympus to shake."

Literary Evidence on Ancient Statues. To illustrate the importance of ancient written evidence in evaluating a lost work of art, two or three literary references to the statue of Zeus may be translated. The Roman Quintilian said of it: "Its beauty seems to have added something to the received religion, so adequate to the deity is the majesty of the work." Lucian tells of the emotion with which visitors looked on the god.

Those who approach the temple do not think that they see ivory from the Indies or gold from the mines of Thrace, but the very son of Cronus and Rhea, brought by Pheidias to earth and established as the guardian of a Hellas come to peace and unity with herself; at once mild and dread in his serene expression, the giver of life and all good gifts, the common father, savior, and protector of mankind. For Zeus alone of gods is named both father and king.

The Sculpture of the Parthenon. In spite of the vicissitudes of time and the uncertainties of attribution, the extant sculptures of the Parthenon afford a magnificent body of evidence for the art of the sculptors of the fifth century. The limiting dates are known (447–432 B.C.), and the surviving material has the great advantage of being genuine Greek work. Pheidias is said to have exercised a general direction of the task, but it has commonly been argued that so great a mass of work must have been produced by a whole school of talented artists working according to a common plan, and that the actual contribution of Pheidias himself may have been comparatively small. Such an argument is, however, subjective, and it may well be

[347]

that Pheidias, presumably a man of great physical vigor and an artist of sure and quick touch, working assiduously and continuously day after day over many years, produced a very much larger part of the sculptural decoration of the Parthenon than has usually been supposed. There have been other men whose output, both in literature and in art, has been so great that the ability of one person to produce so much in a lifetime might have been doubted if the facts were not well known. The names of Plato, Michelangelo, Sir Walter Scott, and Charles Dickens come to mind as examples.

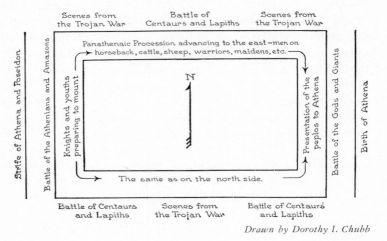

Scenes from   Battle of   Scenes from
the Trojan War   Centaurs and Lapiths   the Trojan War

Strife of Athena and Poseidon

Battle of the Athenians and Amazons

Panathenaic Procession advancing to the east—men on horseback, cattle, sheep, warriors, maidens, etc.

Knights and youths preparing to mount

N

Presentation of the peplos to Athena

Battle of the Gods and Giants

Birth of Athena

The same as on the north side.

Battle of Centaurs   Scenes from   Battle of Centaurs
and Lapiths   the Trojan War   and Lapiths

Drawn by Dorothy I. Chubb

FIGURE 90. SCHEMATIC PLAN OF THE ARRANGEMENT OF THE PARTHENON SCULPTURES. This plan should be studied in relation to Figures 68, 69, 70, and 91.

There were ninety-two sculptured metopes of the Doric frieze, some fifty colossal figures in the pediments, and more than five hundred and twenty feet of continuous Ionic frieze. These pieces of decorative sculpture are the most valuable evidence available for a study of the technique of Pheidias and his associates.

The Meaning of the Sculptures. The Parthenon was built as the home of Athena Parthenos, the virgin goddess of the

[348]

city, and the decorative sculptures on every part of the temple, for all their apparent diversity of subject, unite in portraying

Drawn by Dorothy I. Chubb

FIGURE 91. PLAN OF THE ARCHITECTURAL AND SCULPTURAL FEATURES OF THE PARTHENON. This drawing illustrates the relative location of the pediments, the Doric frieze, the Ionic frieze, the cella wall, the columns, the roof, and the stylobate of the Parthenon. The drawings of sculptured figures are not intended to convey precise information regarding the restoration.

scenes that are associated with the birth, the life, and the worship of the goddess, or mythological scenes from the early tradition of Athena's city, such as the battles of Gods and Giants or of the Athenians and Amazons. The sculptures can be adequately studied only with the aid of the large and detailed publications devoted to the Parthenon. However, a schematic design (Figure 90) and a drawing indicating the architectural parts of the Parthenon that were decorated with sculpture (Figure 91) will serve to show the location of the sculptures on the temple and the topics illustrated by them.

Photograph by the British Museum

FIGURE 92. THE "THREE FATES." Fifth century B.C. These figures from the east pediment of the Parthenon have been variously interpreted. Note the adaptation of shape to the form of the pediment, and the skillful portrayal of diaphanous drapery.

The Pediments. It has been pointed out that in the pedimental groups of the Temple of Zeus at Olympia, for which Pheidias made the cult statue, a rigid symmetry was maintained in the balance of figures on either side of the central deity. A generation later, in the Parthenon and in contemporary art elsewhere, a balance was still maintained in the pediments, but the stiffness of absolute identity of types had been overcome. On the eastern pediment of the Parthenon the birth of Athena, the patron goddess of the city, was shown, while

[350]

the subject of the western pediment was the Battle of Athena and Poseidon for possession of Attica. The pedimental figures have been badly damaged. However, the group of the Three Fates (Figure 92), if such they be, from the eastern pediment, is an extraordinarily fine example of one of the most important

Photograph by the British Museum

FIGURE 93. CENTAUR AND LAPITH. Fifth century B.C. This metope is taken from the Doric frieze of the Parthenon.

sculptural techniques of the fifth century. This is the development of "wet" or "diaphanous" drapery, in which the form of the body is shown through the texture of the garments.

The Doric Frieze. The metopes of the Doric frieze were sculptured on all four sides of the temple, and thus constituted

[351]

Photograph by the British Museum

FIGURE 94. THE PANATHENAIC PROCESSION. Fifth century B.C. This figure represents a slab from the Ionic frieze of the

the most extensive Doric decorative sculpture of antiquity. The subject matter was balanced to produce an effective and consistent arrangement of the decorative sculpture in the various parts of the Parthenon. At the eastern end the metopes were carved with scenes from the Battle of Gods and Giants, while the western end was given over to the legendary incidents of the Battle of the Athenians and Amazons. The north and south sides were decorated with two themes, representing incidents from the Trojan War and from the Battle of Centaurs and Lapiths, set in a double chiastic arrangement. Along the north side, the scenes from the Trojan War occupied the spaces toward either end, while the Battle of the Centaurs and Lapiths filled the central position. On the south side, the arrangement was reversed, and a group of metopes showing the struggle against Troy was located in the center, separating scenes from the Battle of the Centaurs and Lapiths at either end.

The best preserved metopes are those showing the Centaurs and Lapiths, and despite the sameness of theme, the artists have contrived to introduce infinite variety into the different scenes of conflict between a Centaur and a Lapith. A study of a number of metopes of like subject makes clear the diverse workmanship, although they all bear unmistakable signs of a common inspiration. The figures are well and freely adapted to the space available for decoration.

The Ionic Frieze. There is in the long Panathenaic Procession which forms the subject of the Ionic frieze of the Parthenon, a proper mingling of the conventional and the novel, so that, while no two figures are identical, the whole is nevertheless bound together as a single composition. The procession is represented as starting at the western end, where the horses are being lined up in position and youths and knights are preparing to mount. In spite of the frequent repetition of similar themes, the idea of continuous action is skillfully carried out, and the apparent interest shown by the participants in the procession, as they marshal the spirited animals, carries the eye naturally and easily from point to point. Along the north and

[353]

FIGURE 95. SEATED DEITIES. Fifth century B.C. This slab is taken from the Ionic frieze over the east end of the Parthenon.

south sides of the temple, the procession is shown as it advances toward the east. Men are riding on horseback (Figure 94); maidens bear offerings; and beasts are driven to the sacrifice. A survey of the slabs of the Ionic frieze will reveal the effectiveness with which the overlapping of horses and riders has been shown in low relief. At the eastern end the procession is pictured as turning the corner from both directions and advancing to the center, which lies over the entrance to the temple. Priests and maidens are shown at either side; in front of each group stand five male figures representing together the ten eponymous heroes of the Attic tribes, while next on either side are six seated figures representing as a whole the twelve great deities of Olympus (Figure 95). In the middle, directly over the entrance, the scene of the presentation of the *peplos,* or sacred robe, to Athena is shown. This ceremony took place during the Panathenaic Procession and was thus familiar to every Athenian.

The Elgin Marbles. The decorative sculptures of the Parthenon have been widely scattered. Some are still in place on the temple, where they have suffered severely from the weather during the years that they have stood without cover. Other pieces are located in the Acropolis Museum in Athens and in the Louvre in Paris, but the most numerous and best preserved of the Parthenon sculptures are now housed in the British Museum, where they were taken by Lord Elgin early in the nineteenth century, and happily are preserved from the ravages of time and neglect. They form the most important part of the collection known as the Elgin Marbles.

Polycleitus

The Doryphorus. The last great sculptor of the fifth century was Polycleitus, whose birth and career in the Peloponnese is a reminder that not all art centered in Athens. Polycleitus, like Myron, worked very largely in bronze and devoted himself principally to the creation of athletic statues. In the Doryphorus, or spear-bearer (Figure 96), of which a number of Roman copies have survived, he created a canon of form,

[355]

indicating by that statue the principles of proportion which he believed should be followed in sculpture and which he described in greater detail in a treatise, likewise called the *Canon,* now lost. In a sense the athletic figures of Polycleitus are the

Photograph by Alinari

FIGURE 96. DORYPHORUS OF POLYCLEITUS. Roman copy of a Greek original of the fifth century B.C. National Museum, Naples. Note the heavy square-cut athletic figure characteristic of Polycleitus.

culmination of the early archaic "Apollos," but the Polycleitan statues were created at a time when anatomy, movement, and perspective no longer presented any difficulties to the artists.

Polycleitus illustrates also the comparatively limited field in which Greek artists, like the Renaissance painters, were content to strive for perfection. All his works bear distinctive similarities, as can be observed in both male and female figures. Thus the Roman copies of the Diadumenus, a statue of a young man attaching a fillet to his hair, and the statue of the Amazon reveal the characteristic pose of Polycleitus. The figures are heavy set, muscular, and athletic, with heads that appear to have been blocked out to conform roughly to an original square of marble, with the weight of the body resting on one foot, while the other is about to leave the ground for the next step. The pose, which shows an athlete at rest yet on the verge of motion, is typical of Polycleitus.

The home of Polycleitus was apparently in Argos, and we must not forget, in recalling his works, to mention a colossal chryselephantine cult statue of Hera, which he made for the temple that was built to replace one destroyed by fire about 422 B.C. The work belongs to the latter years of his life, but the date is useful in the same way as is the association of Pheidias with the known dates of the Parthenon in fixing the successive activities of the three principal artists of the fifth century, Myron, Pheidias, and Polycleitus.

The Close of the Fifth Century

Relief Sculpture. Aside from the place of relief sculpture in the decoration of the Doric and Ionic friezes of the Parthenon, this branch of art was widely used in the fifth century in connection with ornamental facings, with tombstones, and with votive tablets. The charming relief from the Temple of Athena Nike, or Wingless Victory, on the Acropolis, representing a figure of Nike adjusting her sandal (Figure 97), was executed in the same style of diaphanous drapery as the Three Fates of the eastern pediment of the Parthenon. The artist remains unknown, but there can be no doubt that the work belongs to the latter half of the fifth century. A votive relief, dedicated appropriately at Eleusis, where the legend of Demeter and Persephone became the basis of the Eleusinian Mysteries, shows the two goddesses in company with the youthful Triptolemus, to whom they taught the arts of agriculture and the taming of the horse. The long, straight folds of drapery and the slightly bent knee are characteristic of fifth century art, though there are suggestions, especially in the conventional waves of the hair, of archaic tradition. Another votive relief of exceptional simplicity and beauty is the Mourning Athena (Figure 98), which represents the goddess gazing down with restrained grief upon a pillar that may be imagined to bear the names of Athenian soldiers who have fallen in war. The *annus mirabilis,* with its tale of dead, furnishes such an occasion. The year 458 B.C., however, is possibly a little early for the artistic qualities of the work.

Photograph by Boissonnas

FIGURE 97. NIKE, OR VICTORY, ADJUSTING HER SANDAL. Fifth century B.C. Acropolis Museum, Athens. This slab is taken from the frieze along the balustrade of the Temple of Athena Nike, or Wingless Victory, on the Acropolis.

The Nike of Pæonius. One other statue, the work of an artist already mentioned, should be included because of its interesting historical implications. This is the Nike, or Victory, of Pæonius (Figure 99), which was set upon a high triangular

[358]

FIGURE 98. THE MOURNING ATHENA. The goddess looks sadly on a column that may bear the names of Athenians who have died in war.

[359]

FIGURE 99. THE NIKE, OR VICTORY, OF PAEONIUS. Fifth century B.C. Olympia. Note the flying pose and the use of diaphanous drapery. A small modern reproduction may be seen at the lower right.

[360]

base at Olympia by the Messenians, probably to commemorate their share in the victory of Cleon over their ancient enemies, the Spartans, at Pylos and Sphacteria in 425 B.C., when two hundred and ninety-two Spartans were made prisoners. The base of the statue bears a cautious but proud inscription, indicating that it was dedicated by the Messenians "from the spoils of the enemy." Apparently, regarding discretion as the better part of valor, they forbore to identify a still powerful neighbor by name.

A difficulty in the identification of the artist arises in the fact that Pausanias attributed the eastern pediment of the Temple of Zeus at Olympia to Pæonius. The figures on this pediment were made between 470 B.C. and 457 B.C., and show a strong archaic influence, while the Nike of Pæonius, a statue of decidedly more advanced technique, was necessarily made after 425 B.C. The dates do not preclude the possibility that one man may have done both pieces of work, but they do raise an interesting point of criticism, for if Pæonius is in reality the artist in each case, it is clear that his style underwent a very marked change between the periods of his youth and his old age.

Qualities of Fifth-Century Art. In summary, it will be observed that the essential attributes of fifth-century sculpture, as of architecture, are religious and civic. Moreover, these qualities are frequently present in the same work. Thus the Ionic frieze of the Parthenon represents in the Panathenaic Procession a tradition of the city, which was likewise a ritual sacred to Athena, the goddess of the land. The ideals of fifth-century art were lofty, and the themes were developed in various fields at a time when technical perfection had been attained. Fortunately, the combination of mechanical ability and æsthetic purpose coincided at a period when the Greek artist was intent upon using his craft to express truthfully the nobility of thought that was also being proclaimed by the philosophers and dramatists of Greece. For this reason, the sculptural creations of the fifth century have an appeal that is universal, for they were executed when the Greeks had not yet become preoccupied with the personal and momentary problems that necessarily limit the scope of art.

CHAPTER XXI

DOMESTIC AND COMMERCIAL CRAFTS

The people of ancient Greece, just as their modern fellows, pursued the more prosaic ways of private life, working as artisans, sailors, or peasants, tilling their fields, reaping their harvests, and searching the market stalls of the Piræus for bargains in kitchen utensils and provisions as well as the book shops of the city for rolls containing the works of the poets or philosophers. Children played with trinkets and toys, attended schools or studied with private tutors. Youths fulfilled their military duties to the state, married and established their homes, reared their families, and buried their dead as has been done in every other society before and since.

Something of this quiet side of ancient life appears with an examination of the minor arts of Greece, the work of the potter and the vase painter, the gem-engraver, and the coin designer. There need be neither disparagement nor apology in grouping these arts and crafts together. The greatest values of Greek civilization are unquestionably to be found in the literature and in the national or religious works of art, such as the temples and the statues of the gods. Vases, small metal objects, coins, and gems were, it is true, fashioned with unusual skill and often with exquisite taste, but the men who worked in these fields were clever rather than profound. They were adept in a craft that demanded no great vision or high purpose.

The Greeks themselves described as *banausic,* or menial, crafts that depended on skill rather than on the development of the spirit and personality of man as an integrated whole.

[362]

Nevertheless, the domestic and commercial crafts of Greece were practiced by a people endowed with rare feeling for beauty of line, proportion, and composition, with the result that the objects used in everyday life are often of artistic as well as of sociological interest.

VASE PAINTING

The Value of Ceramic Evidence. The very significant place occupied by pottery in the interpretation of an ancient site was explained in connection with the Minoan culture. The same qualities in pottery of classical times continue to commend vases to the excavator and the scholar. Their indestructibility enables them to preserve their story through every vicissitude that ever beset an ancient town. The modification of structure, shape, and design illustrates the growth of artistic consciousness. The familiar uses to which vases were put, ranging through funeral offerings, storage jars for grain, honey, or oil, wine coolers, and utensils for cooking or other household uses are evidence of the daily routine of Greek life. But vase painting occupies an even larger place in the story of classical Greek civilization, for two reasons. The first is the æsthetic pleasure to be derived from the beauty of the shapes and decoration. The second lies in the historical and mythological interest of the vase scenes, which usually were selected to illustrate an ancient myth, an Homeric incident, an athletic scene from the games, or an occurrence in social or military life.

The Varieties of Greek Vases. In making a brief and readily comprehensible classification of Greek vase making and vase painting, there are peculiar difficulties that do not occur in connection with the study of such a field as sculpture. Confusion arises from the fact that local communities originated specialized types to a greater extent than was the case with sculpture, where, for instance, it was natural to place Myron and Pheidias, the Athenians, in sequence with Polycleitus, the Argive. In the case of vases, however, the types that flourished

[363]

at Cyprus, Rhodes, or Melos, or even so close to Athens as
Corinth, differed so markedly from Attic, or Athenian, ware
that they must be treated separately and not as a consecutive
whole. In order to avoid too complicated a division, some of
the distinctive types of vases from a number of Hellenic communities will be considered first, and thereafter the development of Attic vase painting will be briefly traced.

Non-Attic Vases

The Sites of Manufacture. Although the terms that are applied to varieties of vases are frequently related to the place of
their manufacture, some types strayed beyond those limits. Thus
Corinthian ware was unquestionably associated with Corinth,
but vases of the peculiar shape and decoration so designated
were also manufactured elsewhere in Greece. Proto-Corinthian
and Corinthian pottery involve questions of chronology, for
Corinthian pottery seems to lie midway between the earlier
and later stages of the type that is known as Proto-Corinthian.
Geometric pottery flourished in its most distinctive form in
the Dipylon cemetery outside the walls of Athens, but so
natural an early design, depending as it did for decorative
effect on the symmetry of straight and intersecting lines, was
followed as a matter of course at many other centers. So too
the Rhodian, Melian, Camiran, and Cæretan vases each have
their peculiar characteristics, with their problems of dating,
artistic development, and meaning.

Proto-Corinthian Ware. Because of the problems inherent
in differentiating Proto-Corinthian from Corinthian ware, it is
less confusing to treat the two consecutively than to attempt
a completely separate classification. Two characteristic shapes
of the Proto-Corinthian style are the *lekythos* and the *alabastron,* the former a small cylindrical vase with high narrow
neck and flat circular top joined to the body by a single vertical
handle, and the latter a little perfume vase with rounded
bottom, incapable of standing alone. Both types were used

for toilet purposes, and a third form, the *pyxis,* a little cylindrical box with a lid, which was also designed to contain cosmetics or other articles, is frequently found. Though Proto-Corinthian ware is not confined exclusively to these shapes, they are sufficiently typical to merit special attention.

Certain types of decoration mark the Proto-Corinthian style. First, Mycenæan and geometric motifs are found and, later, narrow bands of animals, with the ray pattern on the foot, the guilloche on the handle, and the intricate lotus and palmette on the shoulder. The vases belonging to the later stages of this technique frequently had a scene from mythology making a frieze around the center of the body of the vase. A small and characteristic Proto-Corinthian vase (Figure 100) shows the attack of Bellerophon from his winged horse, Pegasus, against the triform Chimæra, a monstrous combination of lion, goat, and serpent. The remainder of this little vase is exquisitely decorated with a scene from the hunt—showing hare and hounds—with a pattern of rays at the base, and with intricate conventionalized floral motifs on the shoulder and elsewhere. A technical study

*Courtesy of the Museum of
Fine Arts, Boston*

FIGURE 100. PROTO-CORINTHIAN LEKYTHOS. Seventh century B.C. Drawing. This figure may be advantageously studied for the form of the vase, the detail of design, and the arrangement of the handle.

[365]

of the manufacture indicates that this ware was made from a yellowish clay, with brown and red paint used for the decoration. The technique of fine miniature art is very highly developed in these charming little vases.

Corinthian Ware. The vases of the Corinthian style, though somewhat later than the earliest Proto-Corinthian ware, are less exquisitely made and designed than the companion type.

Courtesy of the Metropolitan Museum of Art

FIGURE 101. TYPICAL CORINTHIAN VASES. Seventh century B.C. The designs are archaic and somewhat grotesque.

The earliest Corinthian vases, which may be dated in the seventh century, are small in size. Certain of the shapes of the Proto-Corinthian style, such as the pyxis and the alabastron, persist. The cup-shaped *scyphus* and the *œnochoe,* or wine-pourer, as well as the exceedingly common *aryballos*—a small spherical bottle—are also typical of this period.

In design, some of the Proto-Corinthian features, such as the frieze of animals, continue to be used. These now include the lion, the boar, the antelope, and also a wide variety of birds

[366]

and mythical creatures. The available space for ornamentation on Corinthian vases is usually crowded, with the areas about the animals, even between the legs and in the loop of the tail, filled with rosettes or other conventional motifs. Human figures begin to appear, and in the earlier forms the qualities of archaic art which were observed in sculpture can also be seen. In later Corinthian vases, the animal friezes give place much more often to human designs, and the excessive crowding of the field is likewise modified. With the introduction of mythological scenes, the characters are identified by painted inscriptions, which record their names in the letters of the Corinthian alphabet, thus affording excellent evidence for the epigraphist.

Rhodian Ware. In the archaic period, which includes the eighth to sixth centuries before Christ, vase painting flourished on a number of islands of the Ægean, as well as in the Greek communities of Asia, North Africa, and Italy. As a result, there are definite styles of vases, known from their place of origin as Rhodian, Melian, Naucratite, Cyrenaic, Cæretan, and so forth. It is not feasible to set down peculiarities common to the work of these communities, but some qualities obtain among all. The vases are, in general, much larger than the miniature perfume receptacles that occurred so frequently in Proto-Corinthian ware. Furthermore, in preparing the surface for decoration, especially in the earlier period, a light-colored wash of clay, called a slip, was applied first to the surface of the vase, and the designs in black glaze were thereafter added.

The patterns show considerable Oriental influence, arguing commercial contacts with the East. Plant designs were regularly used, and animals were introduced, usually in continuous procession around one or more friezes on the vase. The tendency to fill all available space with some form of decoration is still present, and, as can be seen in the characteristic Rhodian œnochœ (Figure 102), a considerable amount of ingenuity has gone into devising concentric circles, dotted patterns, swastikas, and other conventional motifs to fill the spaces about the antelopes, the birds, and the griffins which form the principal subject of the friezes.

Rhodian and other eastern styles show the normal progression away from animal and plant designs toward the introduction of human figures engaged in various activities.

Courtesy of the Museum of Fine Arts, Boston

FIGURE 102. RHODIAN OENOCHOE, OR WINE-POURER. Note the combination of mythical animals, running deer, and conventional designs.

Attic Vases

The Distinctive Styles. Attic vases are not without their own problems of classification, but at least the chronological order may be established fairly safely for the successive development of three distinctive styles, represented respectively by geometric, black-figured, and red-figured ware.

Geometric Ware. The use of geometric lines to create attractive vase patterns is not confined to Athens. It is a technique that would inevitably appeal to an early potter, who would very quickly learn to combine his strokes, zigzags, squares, and triangles into a symmetrical and pleasing design. This par-

Courtesy of the Metropolitan Museum of Art

FIGURE 103. ARCHAIC ATTIC GEOMETRIC VASE. Eighth century B.C. This vase of a funerary type combines rigid geometric design with pictorial human figures.

ticular type of pottery in Attica is usually called Dipylon ware because the largest and finest specimens have been found in the vicinity of the Dipylon Gate of the city. At a very early time, the lines and crosses of geometric ware gave place to accompanying friezes on which human figures were shown. Such scenes as that of a warship drawn to the beach, with a

[369]

band of warriors bearing shields and spears and marching in procession from it (Figure 103), or a funeral procession showing the mourners, the horses, and the chariots, are characteristic of Attic geometric pottery. Though Dipylon ware is inferior in the technique of manufacture and decoration to the vases of the Mycenæan Age, there is in the great funeral *amphoræ,* or two-handled jars, a vigorous sense of design and proportion, which marks the beginning of a new art destined to enjoy a long career in Athens.

Black-Figured Ware. Passing by Proto-Attic ware, which followed the geometric period, we come to the black-figured style, which was flourishing in Athens in the early part of the sixth century, contemporaneously with the sculpture of the archaic period. The technique of the black-figured style allowed the artist first to sketch his design on the reddish surface of the vase, and next to paint in the figures with solid black lustrous varnish. The heavy silhouette was then relieved and details of muscles or garments were indicated by cutting through the black varnish with an incising instrument. Sometimes color was added. The Greeks were able to produce on their vases a black glaze of peculiar beauty and of such permanent luster that it is difficult to avoid highlights in photographing them.

A great number of shapes occurred in both the black-figured and the red-figured styles. Among these the amphora and the *cylix,* or goblet, are distinctive, though by no means exclusive, for such quaint varieties as the aryballos, or perfume bottle, formed from a cluster of cockleshells, are also found. The use of inscriptions observed in connection with Corinthian ware continued, and vases of the black-figured technique are frequently signed by the potter and the painter. Among them Amasis developed the series of human figures to serve in lieu of a conventional design. Execias was very successful with the cylix, and Nicosthenes specialized in a type of amphora with wide, flat handles that suggest conscious imitation of metalcraft. These men are but three of a large number of artists who used this style and whose names and works are known to a greater or less degree. By this time the subject matter of the vases was frequently, if not regularly, drawn from known legendary sources.

The precise dates of the black-figured Attic technique defy delimitation. In origin it is a product of the archaic age, and by the middle of the fifth century the red-figured technique had largely succeeded it. On the other hand the older black-figured style continued to be used even into the Hellenistic Period, especially in the conservative Panathenaic vases, which were given as prizes at the Panathenaic festival. In spite of some deficiencies of artistic skill, there is in the Attic black-figured technique an originality and vigor that has an appeal not felt in the more refined and graceful vase figures that follow, for in the red-figured style the Hellenic restraint of the finest periods too quickly gives way to decline.

Courtesy of the Metropolitan Museum of Art

FIGURE 104. ATHENIAN ARYBALLOS, OR PERFUME BOTTLE. Late sixth century B.C. The design takes the form of a group of cockle shells.

Red-Figured Ware. The technique of decoration found in red-figured vases was substantially the reverse of the black-figured method. The designs, whether inanimate or animate, were represented by the natural red color of the clay, while the background was filled with the lustrous black varnish that was known from the earlier ware. Around each figure ran a preliminary relief line of paint, exceedingly difficult to reproduce in modern forgeries, but which can be readily detected on ancient vases by holding them at an angle to catch the proper gleam of light. The details of the figures, the face, hair, and garments, were drawn on the red silhouette before the vase was hardened by fire.

[371]

A large number of painters who worked with the red-figured technique are known, and such names as Epictetus, Euphronius, Hieron, and Brygus, to mention but a few, become increasingly familiar as the history of fifth-century vase painting is studied in detail.

Courtesy of the Metropolitan Museum of Art

FIGURE 105. ATTIC RED-FIGURED LEKYTHOS. Early fifth century B.C. Qualities of archaic technique are still apparent.

The Growth and Decline of Red-Figured Technique. Although Attic red-figured vase painting follows the black-figured style and becomes the most distinctive ceramic art of the fifth century, it must not be supposed that the sequence of styles is strictly maintained; for even in the late sixth century, the red-figured technique was occasionally adopted, and there are many vases of a transitional nature that display a combination of both styles. The red-figured technique follows the course of sculpture through a rigid style, a mature and natural stage, and finally into a grandiose and self-conscious manner. In the case of red-figured vases, the first two stages may be designated as the severe style and the fine style, respectively; in the later period the sense of exact lines and painstaking effort is quickly lost in the florid and the garish. Several characteristic examples of the red-figured style follow. In a red-figured Athenian lekythos (Figure 105), which is to be dated about 480 B.C., the goddess Athena is shown holding a helmet in her left hand. There is much power and artistic sense in the figure, although some deficiencies of technique remain. The full-front body, the head in profile and turned

[372]

to the right, the foot in profile and turned to the left, and the rigid folds of the drapery reveal the qualities of an art that is making the transition from the archaic age to the fifth century.

A red-figured Attic volute *crater,* or mixing-bowl, which was made some thirty years later, about 450 B.C. (Figure 106), shows definite development in artistic capacity. The decora-

Courtesy of the Metropolitan Museum of Art

FIGURE 106. ATTIC RED-FIGURED VOLUTE CRATER, OR MIXING BOWL. Middle of the fifth century B.C. Note the elaboration of design and the effort to indicate perspective.

tive schemes represent mythological stories and domestic incidents. The Battle of the Greeks and Amazons is shown on the body of the vase, and the narrower panel on the neck depicts a youth and maiden, with attendants. The symmetrical palmette pattern is executed with the highest taste. Though

[373]

*Courtesy of the Museum
of Fine Arts, Boston*

FIGURE 107. ATTIC RED-FIGURED LEKYTHOS. Attributed to the Pan Painter. Early fifth century B.C. The naturalistic design of the hunter and his dog is characteristic of the best work of this painter.

the artist is still sufficiently conscious of reality as against illusion to feel it necessary to show all sixteen legs of the four horses, nevertheless there is vigor and freedom in the representation of the battle scene. The design compares favorably with the sculptural capacity of Myron and his contemporaries of the middle of the fifth century.

A pleasing vase painted by an anonymous artist who has, in modern times, been called the Pan Painter (Figure 107) is decorated with a hunting scene. The hunter, equipped with bow and arrow, has paused for a moment to look at some quarry that has attracted the dog's attention. It is a momentary pose, skillfully rendered by an accomplished craftsman, who was troubled by no problems of perspective in his art.

Distinctive Styles and Shapes. From the many varieties of vases, a few types and shapes may be passed in rapid review. The *rhyton* was a vase with an opening at the bottom, which consequently had to be emptied at once, whether for the pouring of a libation, or for any other purpose. It is very frequently in the form of an animal's head, though the conventional decoration of borders and the insertion of a handle are not omitted for that reason. The lekythos, a tall, cylindrical vase with a thin neck and vertical handle, has a long history and appears

Courtesy of the Museum of Fine Arts, Boston

FIGURE 108. ATTIC RED-FIGURED WARE. Two rhytons and a lekythos.

in both the black-figured and red-figured techniques, and also with a white background, not to mention its introduction in marble as a grave monument. The white-ground lekythoi were regularly used as funeral offerings, and on them scenes appropriate to death were frequently drawn. The white background is not, however, confined to funeral lekythoi, but it found a place also in the cylix and pyxis (Figure (109), where it flourished even in the early part of the fifth century. Another class of vases, very largely confined to Ionic ware, but occurring also in the early Attic period, regularly introduces large conventionalized eyes as a design. Among the shapes

[375]

that have been selected for their bizarre appearance is a drinking cup in the form of a cow's hoof (Figure 111). The design, which is in good red-figured style of the middle or early part of the fifth century, appropriately shows a herdsman watching a cow. Another distinctive mode of decoration is found in a series of broad, shallow cylices of the black-figured technique that are described as "little master" cups because the design and the inscriptions are made in small size (Figure 112). There is a pleasing absence of crowding in these vases, and more often than not a single delicately drawn little animal is the sole decoration visible on a panel. Two other designs, both late and both from Italy, should be mentioned.

Courtesy of the Metropolitan Museum of Art

FIGURE 109. ATTIC PYXIS, OR TOILET VASE. Early fifth century B.C. The technique shows red-figured work on a white background.

One is the plate, which is regularly decorated with two or three fish. These plates usually show the hasty and inexact drawing of south Italian ware. Finally there is Arretine ware, which differs from vase painting in that the designs are made in a mould in which the vases are cast, though variations of the technique are also found. The Arretine ware, which begins to be made about the middle of the first century before Christ and continues for a hundred years thereafter, is probably influenced by the high relief of metalwork.

This rapid survey of Greek vases has covered a span of more than six hundred years. There are few fields of artistic effect

[376]

in which so long a span of growth and decline can be studied in a single medium.

PAINTING

The Archæological Evidence. The largest body of evidence on Greek painting must always remain the vases, which, by their fortunately enduring quality, have preserved intact the work of the most skillful of Greek draughtsmen. There are, however, other extant examples of the painter's art that reveal both the planning of design and the skill of execution, and

Courtesy of the Metropolitan Museum of Art

FIGURE 110. LADLE WITH CONVEN-
TIONALIZED EYE DESIGN.

also afford the basis for study of the pigments that were used and the technical processes that were followed. In this connection, the frescoes of the Minoan-Mycenæan Period must be studied, as well as the tomb paintings of the Etruscans, the wall decorations of Pompeii, and the portrait plaques that have been preserved in the dry sands of Egypt or discovered in the excavations further to the east in Asia, for they are all influenced by Greek art or afford evidence regarding the activity of the Greek painters. Fur-

Courtesy of the Metropolitan Museum of Art

FIGURE 111. DRINKING CUP. Early fifth century B.C. The shape in the form of a cow's hoof is indicative of some of the oddities of this type of work.

[377]

thermore, the Greeks used paint freely, as has been mentioned at various times, in adorning their statues, coloring the details of architecture, and painting the funeral stelæ or the sculptured sarcophagi. The traces of color that still remain on the Acropolis Maidens, the terra-cotta figurines from Tanagra, the Volo funeral stelæ, and the Alexander Sarcophagus will recall the readiness with which the Greeks turned to paint as an accessory.

Courtesy of the Metropolitan Museum of Art

FIGURE 112. CYLIX, OR DRINKING CUP. Late sixth century B.C. Vessels of this type are called kleinmeister or "little master" work because of the small and delicate designs.

The Literary Evidence. Nevertheless, it must be conceded that, aside from vases, the examples that have been mentioned fall far short of an exposition of classical painting in Greece, for in either date, or place, or purpose, they are ancillary to other interests. The truth is that the great paintings of the fifth and fourth centuries have without exception perished because of the unenduring medium. We are left, therefore, with only the intangible evidence of literature to reconstruct the art of the painters who lived in Greece contemporaneously with the builders of the Parthenon and the Erechtheum and with the sculptors who made the Doryphorus and the Cnidian Aphrodite. Fortunately, the literary evidence is abundant, and

[378]

it may with some confidence be correlated with the existing technique of vase painting. Thus we know with certainty the

FIGURE 113. MARBLE GRAVE STELE. Water-color reproduction. Original at Volo. Third or second century B.C. This stele, elaborately painted in antiquity, is from Pagasæ in Thessaly.

[379]

names of various painters, such as Polygnotus, Apelles, Micon, and Panænus, and something of their style and technique. There are also descriptions, sometimes in exhaustive detail, of specific pictures, such as the Sack of Troy, the Visit of Odysseus to Hades, the Meeting of Odysseus and Nausicaa, or the Slaying of the Suitors, themes taken from the *Odyssey*.

METALCRAFT

Materials and Objects. The attempt to classify the crafts of a people will indubitably lead to some inconsistencies, for a selection of objects of metal smithing or casting will bring together articles as diverse as bronze statuettes, armor, jewelry, gold and silver vessels, and mirrors, all of which might with consistency be discussed from the viewpoint of their purpose. Furthermore, a classification, either by material or function, will inevitably transcend chronological periods. However, if each object is separately examined, it will be possible to detect the qualities that determine its date. For the present it will be sufficient to illustrate by a number of pictures the facility attained by the Greek artists in working with gold, silver, and bronze through the centuries.

The Corinthian Libation Bowl. A gold libation bowl of the seventh century shows the exquisite simplicity and strength of design of the archaic period (Figure 114). It is fashioned in nine lobes, with a delicate bead pattern embossed at the bottom of each lobe within the bowl. So handsome and costly an object would be recognized without further evidence as the product of princely patronage, but it is gratifying to be able to read on the outside, in the archaic characters of the Corinthian alphabet, an inscription that identifies the bowl; it was a dedication made from the spoils of a conquered town by the sons of Cypselus, who was tyrant of Corinth from 657 B.C. to 627 B.C. Thus the purpose and the date of the bowl are established beyond question.

Bronze Armor, Fibulæ, and Mirrors. Bronze was used from

pre-Hellenic times for at least two distinct and widely separate purposes—the making of arms for battle and the making of *fibulæ* for fastening garments or for adornment. Many examples of each type have been found. Bronze swords, daggers, arrowheads, helmets, breastplates, and greaves, the essential

Courtesy of the Museum of Fine Arts, Boston

FIGURE 114. GOLD LIBATION BOWL. Seventh century B.C. The form is simple, with a minimum of decoration.

equipment of the warriors, as well as metal appurtenances for the horses used by the cavalry, may be examined in the classical collection of almost any museum. A common type of bronze safety pin is the sail fibula, in which the point of the pin is sheathed behind a flat sail of bronze, while the spring is provided by a single loop of metal. These fibulæ are frequently decorated in the geometric style. Mirrors also were made from polished bronze disks (Figure 115), in which the face would be reflected, though less distinctly than in a silvered glass. The Biblical verse: "For now we see through a glass, darkly; but then face to face," affords a commentary on the obscurity of ancient mirrors. Nevertheless, they provided an excellent field for the art of the bronze worker, especially in the elaborate decoration of the accompanying stands and mirror covers.

Jewelry. From Mycenæan times until the end of the Greek period jewelry of great delicacy and beauty was constantly produced. Brooches, necklaces, rings, and plaques testify to the skillful hands that were at work. One of the finest examples of miniature goldsmithing is to be found in an exquisite gold earring of the fifth century fashioned in the form of a chariot with a pair of rearing horses, driven by a winged Nike, or Victory (Figure 116). Everything about the tiny object bespeaks the art of the fifth century; the modeling of the horses recalls the Ionic frieze of the Parthenon, as do the folds of drapery. So delicate is the work that the wheels actually

Courtesy of the Metropolitan Museum of Art

FIGURE 115. DECORATED BRONZE MIRROR AND STAND. Late fifth century B.C. The elaborate design with numerous small figures may be contrasted with the simplicity of the previous illustration.

[382]

turn on the axles. Possibly the earring was destined for the adornment of a statue rather than for actual use; there is, however, no lack of earrings intended for practical purposes, such as those prettily modeled in the shape of a resting dove, or of Ganymede being carried off by the eagle, or in innumerable other styles.

The Shield of Achilles. The most illuminating evidence for ancient craftsmanship in metal, however, lies neither in actual objects, exquisite though they are, from the Vaphio cups to the Boscoreale treasure, a collection of silver vessels and plates from Boscoreale near Pompeii, nor in the vase paintings, which are a rich source of information about the ancient metal shop, but in the Homeric description of the shield of Achilles. It is true that the poet is not hampered by the in-

Courtesy of the Museum of Fine Arts, Boston

Figure 116. Gold Earring. This miniature object illustrates both refinement and skill in craftsmanship.

tractability of material, yet it is scarcely possible that he can have constructed entirely from his imagination the tale of the shield that Hephæstus made for Achilles at the request of Thetis. In minute detail, yet without loss of poetic imagery, Homer tells of the intricate pattern of the shield, of the heavenly bodies embossed upon it, of the scenes of peace and war, of the ambuscade of cattle, and the dancing of youths and maidens. So vivid is the description that one almost forgets that it is a work of art with which the story deals, and follows instead the

[383]

fortunes of the characters that adorned it in the poet's imagination. When, in the narrative of the *Iliad,* the shield is finished, Thetis takes it from Hephæstus with the helmet and greaves,

Courtesy of the Museum of Fine Arts, Boston

FIGURE 117. HEPHAESTUS MAKING THE ARMOR OF ACHILLES. This Attic red-figured amphora from Nola illustrates the well-known incident from the *Iliad.*

and, seeking out her son Achilles, lays the armor before him. And if any additional note is needed to indicate the magnificence of the wrought metal, it is found in the reaction of the soldiers present.

The goddess cast the arms before Achilles, and they echoed there all in their beauty. And trembling laid hold on the Myrmidons, nor did any man dare to look upon them, for they were affrighted.

HOUSEHOLD UTENSILS AND TERRA COTTAS

The Onos and the Bobbin. The Greek instinct for beauty led to the decoration of many of the utensils that were intended for ordinary domestic tasks. The implements of weaving were

Courtesy of the Metropolitan Museum of Art

FIGURE 118. ONOS, OR "DONKEY." Sixth century B.C. This protection for the knee in spinning combines utility with art.

decorated with the same scenes as vases. The women used a cylindrical, thimble-shaped protection for the knee when preparing wool. It was made of terra cotta by the same process as vases, and was called an *onos,* or "donkey" (Figure 118). The example that has been illustrated is beautifully decorated with two four-horse chariots, in the black-figured technique; the artistic style, especially as it is observed in the pose and expres-

[385]

sion of the charioteers, reveals the archaic character of the work. It is to be dated in the second half of the sixth century. Bobbins, or reels, were similarly made.

Courtesy of the Museum of Fine Arts, Boston

FIGURE 119. OIL LAMP. Græco-Roman Period. Innumerable terra-cotta lamps, usually with simple designs of this nature, have been found.

Lamps. In the earliest times the Greeks seem to have relied for their light on the open fire, or, if necessary, on torches, which could be moved from place to place, and which at a later time were employed to add zest to the relay race on horseback. In the classical period, olive oil was regularly used in a wide variety of lamps, which were made of terra cotta or bronze. A vast number of the lamps that have been found belong to the late Greek or Græco-Roman Period, and inasmuch as they were cheap and common utensils and subject to soiling by the grease and soot inherent in their use, the decoration was usually executed in indifferent manner, frequently with the figure of a hare (Figure 119), a bird, or a dolphin. On the other hand, more elaborate lamps fashioned in the form of boats or other objects attained to novelty, if not always to beauty, of design. The holes in the lamps were intended for pouring in the oil, and for the insertion of one or more wicks. In spite of the inadequate light and the disagreeable odor, the Greeks managed to illuminate their homes sufficiently to make possible some reading by night. At the same time, living in a southern land of brilliant sunshine, they rose early and contrived to make greater use of the daylight hours than is usual in modern society.

Terra-Cotta Statuettes. There is no particular period to which the manufacture of terra-cotta statuettes can be assigned. The instinct to mould animate objects is evident in the crude animal or human shapes of some of the early vases of the archaic period. Contemporaneously, the terra-cotta idols were made and decorated with geometric designs, appropriate to the early period of their manufacture. Tanagra, a town in Bœotia, was an important center for the manufacture of figurines, and a great many with definite characteristics are to be attributed to the Tanagra artists. They were made in many cases from moulds, and for the most part were cast hollow. One group of Tanagra figurines regularly represents draped female figures, who may be standing, or walking, or seated at ease, or engaged in any of a variety of household tasks. They were painted in bright colors, and the brilliance and delicacy of the ornamentation can still be conjectured from the traces

[387]

of pigment that remain. Such figurines were usually cast as single statuettes, though groups, such as two girls playing at knuckle-bones, were not uncommon.

Curiously enough, in this form the Greek artists seem to have relaxed, and even in the fifth century they made scenes of a trivial or domestic nature which can rarely be paralleled in marble or bronze sculpture earlier than the Hellenistic Period. A group of the barber and his customer, or a figure of a man

Photograph by Alinari

FIGURE 120. GROUP OF TANAGRA FIGURINES. Louvre. These small figures, usually elaborately painted, show such characteristic poses as a woman playing the lyre, dancing maidens, travelers, and similar scenes.

seated on the ground attending to the pot in which he prepares his meal over the fire, offer studies in realism for which works of idealized style in the fifth century make little preparation.

COINS AND GEMS

The Significance of Coins. The study of Greek coins involves problems of economics and human inventiveness that almost outweigh in interest the artistic qualities that inhere in the finest numismatic work. Behind coined money lies a long

[388]

history of trade by barter, of the use of metal as a measure of comparative value, and finally the emergence of a unit of metal of established weight and with a value guaranteed by the official stamp of a city, which would be recognized and accepted over the ancient world. When once the coinage of money was established, it proved so great a stimulus to trade

Courtesy of the Metropolitan Museum of Art

FIGURE 121. BRONZE MONETARY INGOT. The ingot is cast in the form of an ox-hide.

and so great a convenience in every transaction that the civilized world has never since chosen to dispense with it.

It was inevitable that the earliest basis of valuation or barter should be in terms of flocks, and when metal began to supplant the cumbersome ox as a basic unit of exchange, some of the accompaniments of the earlier association persisted. The talent of gold in the Homeric Age seems to have been taken as the value of an ox or a cow. Consequently, when heavy ingots of copper, or bronze, were struck to serve as currency, they were first fashioned in the shape of ox-hides that had been

[389]

pegged out, and they further suggested their origin by having one side show the rough hairy surface of the hide, and the other the cured inner surface with the edges turning up (Figure 121). If this seems absurd, it may be well to remind ourselves that some of the early automobiles made in this country continued to boast a whipsocket.

The Invention of Coinage. Tradition ascribes the invention of coinage to the Lydians in the late eighth or early seventh century before Christ, though the name of Pheidon of Argos, who reigned in the seventh century, is also associated with it. When Pheidon introduced into Argos small silver coins of the Æginetan standard, he marked the departure from the older economy by dedicating in the Temple of Hera the bundles of spits, or iron rods, that had previously served as currency. Such bundles of spits have been found in the excavations of the Argive Heræum, and they may well be the original dedications of Pheidon himself.

The Artistic Qualities. Important though the details of the invention and the striking of coins are for the numismatist, and far reaching though the repercussions of coinage were on the social and economic life of the ancient world, it is only the artistic quality of the coins that can now briefly engage us. The engraving of dies for Greek coins involves the most delicate craftsmanship, and, with few exceptions, the type of art conforms to the qualities of the age. Some of the finest coins were signed by the artists who made them. Where the design seems to lag behind contemporary development in other fields, as, for instance, by the retention of the archaic features of Athena on the Athenian coins of the fifth century, the reason is to be sought in the conservatism of economics. The older form had become known and acceptable, and the magistrates hesitated to introduce any modifications in style that might lead to the questioning of Athenian exchange in the busy ports of the Mediterranean.

The different cities adhered with considerable consistency to a single device on their coins. This gave rise to colloquial names. Thus, from their characteristic types, the coins of Ægina were called "tortoises," those of Athens "owls," those of Corinth "colts." The punning type was common, and Rhodes decorated her coins with a rose, Phocæa with a seal, and Selinus with a celery leaf, because the respective names of the cities were thus suggested.

In a study of Greek art, which all too often is dependent on the reflection of Hellenic achievement through Roman copies, coins have the great advantage of being original creations of the artists of Greece. Consequently, they afford a consecutive history of artistic achievement, from the earliest electrum coins marked with geometric striations, through the later pieces stamped with incuse squares, and on through the fifth century, when definite types were used for the various cities. In the Hellenistic Period, portraiture of a high order appeared on the coins of many cities.

The Greek coin engravers solved the problem of adapting their composition to a small circular area in low relief. Such a subject as the lion attacking the bull, which was described by Homer in the design of the shield of Achilles and which occurred on the poros pediments of the Acropolis, was

FIGURE 122. COIN OF ACANTHUS. Fifth century B.C. Note the adaptation of the scene to the circular area of the coin.

executed with equal taste and effectiveness on the fifth-century coins of Acanthus (Figure 122). The materials of Greek coins were chiefly electrum, gold, silver, and bronze, with the finest examples struck in silver.

Gems. The art of gem engraving varies from the coin engraver's in one important respect: whereas the coin engraver made his figures on dies, which were then used to strike the coins in various metals, the gem was itself the work of art,

[391]

to be worn for adornment, and, if necessary or desirable, to be used as a seal. Yet both have the qualities of miniature art, in which a sense of form and delicacy of execution were essential to the creation of the beautiful examples that are known.

Gem carving has a longer history than die cutting, though it is less closely knit into the economic and political life of the cities. In the Mycenæan Age the carving of gems was a recognized art, and the examples that have been discovered reveal the vigor and skill that were characteristic of the period. In

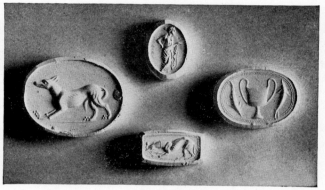

Courtesy of the Metropolitan Museum of Art

FIGURE 123. MINIATURE ENGRAVINGS. Three gems and a gold ring. Fifth and fourth centuries B.C. The photograph was made from casts, which reproduce more clearly than the originals.

the intervening centuries, when civilization lay dormant, gem engraving likewise declined, but in the archaic period and in the fifth century the gems reveal the qualities of contemporary sculpture.

There was no limit to the subjects that attracted the interest of the gem-cutters. As in other branches of Greek art, the human form predominated and men and women were shown in all the pursuits of ancient life. At the same time, animals, birds, fishes, and inanimate objects such as vases, chariots, or musical instruments were effectively used in the designs.

Gem engraving attained sufficient dignity to induce the gem-cutters in some instances to sign their work. Possibly the most famous of the artists was Dexamenus, who was active in the fifth century, and we are fortunate in having enough of his signed gems to form some estimate of the development of his craft. It is usually possible to date the gems by their style, but accompanying inscriptions afford welcome corroborative evidence.

A more detailed scrutiny of Greek gems will afford an opportunity to identify the different stones that were used, such as chalcedony, garnet, topaz, sardonyx, and carnelian, as well as the characteristic shapes that were developed at different times. It will lead also to a study of the allied arts of cameo cutting and the carving of cups and plates out of sardonyx or other stones. But a limit must be set to the discussion of the field of Greek arts and crafts, which offers endless fascination.

THE LATE FIFTH CENTURY:
THE PELOPONNESIAN WAR (431–404 B.C.)

Athens After the Death of Pericles. The brilliant achievements of the middle years of the fifth century owe an imponderable debt to the inspiration of the great democratic leader of Athens, Pericles. For nearly a third of a century, from 461 to 429 B.C., he ruled over the state, guiding its policy and its thought by the force of his own personality. It is fruitless to question whether the course of Greek art and letters would have followed other paths had Pericles lived for a decade or more beyond 429 B.C., for the impact of war and the growth of philosophic inquiry were bringing new forces to bear on Greek life. Yet the men who had been trained in the Periclean tradition continued to work for another twenty-five years before disaster overtook the Athenian state and definitely altered the course of its fortunes. The history of the closing years of the fifth century must, therefore, be understood both in relation to contemporary thought and as a background to the sharply modified national psychology of the fourth century.

The Peloponnesian War (431–404 B.C.). Shortly before the death of Pericles, which occurred in 429 B.C., Greece had already embarked on the long struggle of the Peloponnesian War, in which Athens and Sparta were the chief protagonists, although most of the other states of Greece allied themselves with one side or the other before the contest drew to a close.

[394]

The loss of man power during the twenty-seven years of the war was so great that the quality of Greek genius declined for lack of men who might have carried forward the promise of art and literature nurtured in the days of Pericles.

The Causes of the War. Three immediate causes for the war are usually cited. In the first place, Potidæa, on the Chalcidic peninsula, was a colony of the Dorian city of Corinth and at the same time a member of the Athenian Empire, though an unwilling one. The Athenians insisted that the appointment of Corinthian magistrates in Potidæa should cease, and they undertook to enforce their demands in the face of the refusal of both Corinth and Potidæa to concede the justice of the claim. These demands of Athens on Potidæa infringed sharply on the sovereignty of the latter city, and they were prophetic of the later policy of Athenian imperialism. In the second place, Corinth had founded the colony of Corcyra, on an island of the same name west of Greece, and Corcyra had in turn founded the colony of Epidamnus on the mainland and further to the north. When difficulties between Corinth and Corcyra arose in connection with the administration of Epidamnus, Athens interested herself on behalf of Corcyra and lent naval assistance against Corinth. In the third place, the Athenians issued certain Megarian Decrees affecting—in fact ruining—the prosperous carrying trade of the Dorian community of Megara with the cities of the Athenian Empire.

It will be observed that none of these controversies seriously affected Sparta, the real antagonist of Athens in the struggle. The true cause of the war, though simple enough, was much more deep-rooted than any single overt act of Athens. Racial antipathy between Dorians and Ionians, commercial rivalry, and imperialistic ambitions played their part. But above all was the continuous and consuming resentment against Athens for holding free Greek states in the Empire against their will, and the fear lest others, still independent, should finally be drawn into the net. That was the real, though unavowed, cause of the war, as judged by the historian Thucydides.

[395]

The Opening Strategy. Athens had an unrivaled naval armament, but she was on the whole inferior to the Spartan troops on land. Pericles therefore urged on the Athenians a war policy by which they should concentrate their energies on maintaining control of the sea, so that necessary supplies might freely enter the Piraeus, while the people of Attica came within the walls of the city and resolutely refused to meet the Spartan armies in the field. He also advised that no attempt be made to extend the Empire during hostilities. The war commenced in 431 B.C. with an expedition of the Spartans into Attic territory, where they ravaged the land, cutting down the slow-growing olive trees and thereby destroying for several years the chief agricultural productivity of the state. It was a severe test of the strength of Pericles to restrain the infuriated Athenians within the walls, while they impotently watched the destruction of their homesteads. The Spartan pillaging expeditions into Attica were repeated during the summers of 430 B.C., 428 B.C., 427 B.C., and 425 B.C., five campaigns in all.

The Plague. Meanwhile extraneous and unpredictable events modified the fortunes of war. In 430 B.C., a terrible plague fell upon Athens and ravaged the city, which was crowded with refugees from the countryside living under abominable conditions of sanitation. The plague appears to have destroyed as many as one fourth of the population, and its effect on the morale of a people just setting out on a long, exhausting war was incalculable. Public fury turned on Pericles, and he was cast out of office; but he had held in his own hands all the departments of government—army, navy, treasury, and public works—for so long a time that the city could not dispense with his services, and he was quickly restored to power. But his career was nearing its end. He contracted the plague himself and died in 429 B.C. The plague reappeared in slightly less malignant form in 427 B.C., and it is probable that the decision of the Spartans not to invade Attica in the years 429 B.C. and 426 B.C. was due in each case to the presence of the plague in the city in the previous year.

The Emergence of Cleon. After the death of Pericles, the power passed to the hands of a vulgar demagogue by the name of Cleon, a tanner by trade. The war, as it dragged on, was marked by ferocious cruelty. At the outset the Platæans had put to death without trial one hundred and eighty Thebans, whom they captured in their city, and when, in turn, Platæa was reduced by siege in 427 B.C., the Spartans executed an even larger number of the Platæans, after putting to them a single question, impossible to be answered affirmatively: "Have you done anything to aid the Lacedæmonians in this war?" When Mytilene, on the island of Lesbos, revolted from the Athenian Empire, Cleon succeeded in having a measure passed in the Assembly providing that the men of the revolting city should be put to death and the women and children sold into slavery. The measure was revoked when the Assembly took calmer counsel on the following day, but the incident is indicative of the declining morality and the proportionately rising barbarity of the Greeks during the war.

Cleon's Triumph at Sphacteria. In 425 B.C., Cleon, taking the place of Nicias, the general who ought logically to have taken the command, to the amazement of the Hellenic world, friend, foe, and neutral, succeeded in capturing two hundred and ninety-two Lacedæmonian prisoners on the island of Sphacteria, which lay off the promontory of Pylos in the land of the Messenians on the west coast of the Peloponnesus. It was to celebrate this victory that the Messenians set up the statue of Nike by Pæonius. The possession of the prisoners gave Athens a great advantage. It prevented further Spartan incursions into her territory, and, had the headstrong Cleon been willing to listen to reasonable terms, an advantageous peace might then have been concluded. The war, however, continued, though the scene was shifted to Thrace and the Chalcidice, where an exceedingly competent Spartan commander, Brasidas, by his tact, an unusual quality in a Spartan, was winning allied cities of the Athenian Empire to the side of Sparta. The failure of the Athenian admiral and historian Thucydides, to save Amphipolis, one of the Chalcidic cities that went over to Brasidas, at this time, led to Thucydides' twenty-year exile, which, to the immeasurable gain of literature, gave him the opportunity to write his scholarly history of the Peloponnesian War.

The Peace of Nicias. In 422 B.C., a battle was fought in the Chalcidic campaign in which both Cleon and Brasidas were killed. They had been the principal obstacles to peace on either side, and consequently it was possible in the following year, 421 B.C., to conclude the Peace of Nicias, so named for the Athenian general. It was to have lasted for fifty years, but it endured in reality for less than one.

The heavy losses of the first decade of the war, especially as they had been aggravated by pestilence in the opening years, now brought about a period of moderate quiet, which was, however, disturbed by raids, minor engagements, and a mutual disinclination to observe the terms of the treaty. There were no heavy military campaigns. Had the peace concerned Athens and Sparta alone, it might have endured, but the allies, particularly those of Sparta, felt that their interests had been sacrificed, and they were far from cooperative in their observation of the terms. In 416 B.C., during the years of comparative peace, Athens forced the island state of Melos into her Empire and wreaked an unworthy vengeance on the Melians, who had sought to preserve their privilege of neutrality. When next hostilities became severe, the quarrel lay between Athens and a remote Dorian city, Syracuse.

The Sicilian Expedition (415–413 B.C.). By 415 B.C., the Athenians had sufficiently recovered from the war and the plague to launch another great imperialistic project. This time they undertook to destroy Syracuse in Sicily, the greatest city, next to Athens itself, of the ancient Hellenic world. The incidents leading up to the actual encounter were somewhat as follows. The Dorian cities of Syracuse and Selinus had been pressing the communities of Leontini and Segesta, which were Ionian in origin and had previously been allied with Athens. The Segestans sent an embassy to Athens, seeking aid from her and promising to finance the war against the common Dorian foe in Sicily. Money was of the essence, and Athens sent an embassy to investigate the financial standing of Segesta. The Athenians were entertained lavishly each night in the home of a different Segestan, and each time they saw evidence of boundless wealth in the profusion of gold and silver plate. What they did not observe was that the plate had been collected from the whole city and was being transferred to each successive banquet for their benefit, and they returned home completely duped.

The Mutilation of the Hermæ. The Athenian Assembly, after hearing the enthusiastic report of the ambassadors on their return from Sicily, disregarded the sane counsel of Nicias against giving it credit and listened instead to the youthful folly of Alcibiades, the nephew and ward of Pericles, who supported it. Intense enthusiasm swept over the people, and almost without a dissenting voice they voted to equip a great fleet for the expedition against Syracuse. Thirty thousand men sailed to Sicily under the command of three generals, Lamachus, Nicias, and Alcibiades. Lamachus was a competent if uninspired general; Nicias was a pious and timid conservative who had openly opposed the project; and Alcibiades was a brilliant and dissolute young aristocrat, strongly in favor of the venture but with a reputation already gained for impiety and irresponsibility. On the morning that the expedition was to weigh anchor, the Athenians were horrified to discover that during the previous night the Hermæ, guardian statues of the god standing before each home, had been mutilated. It was a most unpropitious act, smacking of treason, and gloom overcast the city as the fleet set sail.

The Charges against Alcibiades. The enemies of Alcibiades waited until he had departed, and then, charging him with the mutilation of the Hermæ, demanded his recall and trial. Although the religious scruples of Alcibiades probably would not have deterred him from the act, there is little reason to believe that he was responsible, for he, above all others, was

[399]

anxious to have the expedition sail under good auspices. However, his political foes succeeded in securing an order for his recall to stand trial, and the state galley came to Syracuse to summon him. Alcibiades left Sicily, but he had no intention of returning to Athens. Instead, he went to Sparta, where he gave the enemy valuable advice against his own state. It was at his suggestion that they sent out a Spartan commander, Gylippus, to aid the Syracusans in the field. He also induced the Spartans to seize and fortify Decelea, a strategic point in Attica itself, and thus to shut off the Athenians from the silver mines of Laurium.

The Progress of the Syracusan Campaign. Meanwhile, fortune had not favored the Athenians in Sicily. The commanders failed to agree on a policy of campaign. Had they done so, they might have been successful, for Syracuse was quite unprepared to withstand an attack. Instead, valuable time was lost; the morale of their army was weakened; and the Syracusans became aware of the divided counsels of the Athenians. Lamachus was killed and replaced by the general Demosthenes, and the Assembly unfortunately refused to recall Nicias, though he himself requested it on the grounds of illness. Always pious, Nicias was deterred by an inopportune eclipse of the moon when withdrawal from a position, fast becoming untenable, was still possible. As a result, the Athenians were defeated in a seafight in the harbor, and when, finally, without supplies, they attempted to march through hostile country to a place of safety, they were slaughtered like sheep by the Syracusans as, thirst-crazed, they threw themselves down at the River Assinarus to drink. This tragic defeat of the Athenians was commemorated by the triumphant Syracusans in some of the most beautiful coins issued in Sicily.

Nicias and Demosthenes were executed with torture, and most of the surviving soldiers were thrown into the stone quarries of Syracuse, where they suffered from the terrible heat of the day and the cold of the night. Curious in the tale of bloody vengeance is the anecdote about the Athenian prisoners

[400]

who won their freedom as a reward for reciting the verses of
Euripides to their captors.

The End of the Peloponnesian War (413–404 B.C.). The
heavy loss of manpower in Sicily, following only a half generation after the depletion of the population wrought by the
plague, was a blow from which Athens could not recover. For
nine years the war with Sparta continued with varying success,
but the old power and prestige of Athens were gone. Sparta
with Persian aid ventured to send a fleet into the Ægean Sea;
disaffected subject states of the Athenian Empire seized the
opportunity to revolt; and in 412 B.C., the Persian king began
to reassert his authority over the Greek cities of Asia Minor.
Sparta, to her shame, acquiesced in the encroachment of the
barbarians on the Greek cities, as the price of Persian financial
assistance. The proud days of Marathon and Salamis were
sadly tarnished as the century drew to a close.

The Closing Exploits of Alcibiades. Meanwhile, Alcibiades
had made himself unacceptable to the Spartan court and had
gone over to the Persian satrap, Tissaphernes, a wily man as
unscrupulous as Alcibiades himself. Alcibiades was pursuing
a deliberate, if devious, path leading to his restoration to
Athens, and by playing one force against another, using his
influence with Tissaphernes and promising to secure Persian
aid for Athens if he were restored to favor, he succeeded in
411 B.C. in having himself recalled to the city and elected one
of the Board of Ten Generals. In 408 B.C., Tissaphernes was
replaced as Persian satrap by a more honest and competent
man, Cyrus, the son of the Persian king, and in the same year
the Spartans sent out an exceedingly able naval commander,
Lysander, who immediately entered into a cooperative pact
with Cyrus, thus voiding the agreement between the latter's
predecessor, Tissaphernes, and Alcibiades. In 407 B.C., the
Athenians suffered a trifling naval defeat at Notium, and, although Alcibiades was not present at the battle, he lost his
influence with the Athenians and was succeeded as commander
of the fleet by Conon. Alcibiades withdrew to a palace on the

[401]

Hellespont, and he was destined to play little further part in Greek history.

The Battle of Arginusæ (*406* B.C.). Two battles of consequence were yet to be fought, the first a success for Athens, the second for Sparta. In 406 B.C., the Athenians were successful in a naval encounter at the small islands of Arginusæ near Lesbos. The political and social repercussions of the battle were much more significant than the victory itself. A strong wind arose after the engagement, and the crews of some twenty-five Athenian ships were lost. The question of responsibility was raised in the Athenian Assembly, and there was much shifting of blame back and forth between the generals and the trierarchs, or commanders of the ships. The eight generals involved were recalled to Athens to stand common trial in the Assembly, rather than individual trial in the courts. This is one of two occasions when Socrates refused to obey improper orders, for, as president of the tribe charged with the responsibility of the court on the day of the trial, he declined to put the illegal motion calling for a single judgment.

The Execution of the Generals. The generals were, nevertheless, condemned to death, and six of them, including the son of Pericles, were executed. The other two had the good judgment not to return to Athens at the time. It has not been the custom of civilized nations to execute their own unsuccessful generals. The action of the Athenian Assembly was an instance of the political instability that was the Achilles' heel of a gifted people. Shortly after the incident, with a revulsion of feeling, the Assembly brought to trial the instigators of the motion to execute the generals and wreaked a petulant vengeance on them. Such rash, impulsive acts are part of the price that a country must pay for direct democracy, untrammeled by the restraints of slow-moving judicial bodies.

The Battle of Ægospotami (*405* B.C.). In 405 B.C., the year following the Battle of Arginusæ, the Athenian fleet under the command of Conon took up a disadvantageous position on the open beach of Ægospotami in the Hellespont. Alcibiades,

[402]

from his near-by fortress, warned the Athenians of their imminent danger, but he was dismissed with scant ceremony. Although Spartan law limited the command of an admiral to a single year, the Spartan fleet arrived, with the able Lysander serving in the capacity of secretary. In a battle which was really a surprise attack, the Spartans captured the entire Athenian fleet with the exception of twenty ships. Possibly there was treachery. Conon escaped with the twenty ships, and, remembering the fate of the generals after the Battle of Arginusæ, discreetly sailed for Cyprus rather than for Athens. Some years later he returned to Athens and rebuilt the Long Walls that were destroyed at the close of the war.

The News Reaches Athens. The end had come for Athens. Her manpower was exhausted; her ships were gone; and the morale of her people, after a quarter century of war, was at its lowest ebb. The historian Xenophon tells in a dramatic paragraph of the arrival in the Piræus of the messenger ship, the *Paralus,* with news of the defeat.

In Athens, when the *Paralus* arrived during the night, the disaster was reported, and the sound of wailing passed up from the Piræus through the Long Walls to the city, one man telling the news to another. On that night no man slept, but all mourned not only for those who had perished, but much more for themselves, for they thought that they would now suffer the same excesses that they had wrought against the Melians and many others of the Greeks. On the following day they summoned the Assembly, and there they resolved to block up the harbors with the exception of one, to make the walls ready, station guards, and to do everything else necessary for the city to stand a siege. They were busied about these matters. And immediately after the seafight the rest of Greece, with the exception of the Samians, revolted from the Athenians.

The breakup of the Athenian Empire was at hand.

The Strategy of the Spartans. Lysander and the Spartans did not at once make the attack on the Piræus that the

Athenians awaited. The self-sufficiency of Athens depended entirely on her ability to import foodstuffs, and Lysander, well aware of that economic dependence, was content to shut off the grain ships at the Hellespont and starve Athens into submission. One man at least in Athens realized the situation. This was Theramenes, a moderate oligarch, who had been active in Athens at the time of Alcibiades' restoration in 411 B.C. Theramenes believed sincerely in a form of government in which elements of oligarchy and democracy should be judiciously mixed, but for his moderation he earned in the end the hatred and distrust of the extremists of both parties. At this time, he proposed in the Assembly that he be sent as an ambassador to Lysander to discover the terms on which peace might be made. The Assembly elected him, and he spent three months and more with Lysander, waiting simply until economic stringency should bring the Athenians to a realization of their utterly hopeless position.

The Terms of Peace. In 404 B.C., peace was finally made with four principal conditions: (1) the Long Walls from Athens to the seaport and the fortifications of the Piræus should be demolished, (2) Athens should relinquish all territory outside Attica except the island of Salamis, (3) Athens should retain a navy of only twelve ships, (4) Athens should follow the leadership of Sparta in peace and war. When the terms were accepted, the walls of Athens were razed by the citizens to the music of flute-girls, for it was fondly believed that the day of freedom had dawned for Hellas. Such a combination of exhilaration and ill-judgment has probably accompanied the close of every long and trying war, not excluding those of our own experience. It is only as the months pass that men are sobered by the realization that the problems of hate and disruption engendered by war continue to stalk the ways of peace.

Humiliating as the terms of the peace that ended the Peloponnesian War were to an imperial city, they might, by the conventions of the time, have been much more severe. Corinth and Thebes urged the annihilation of Athens, but Sparta, re-

[404]

membering the services of the Athenians to Greece at Marathon and Salamis and also fearing the power of Corinth and Thebes if Athens were too much weakened, checked the barbaric severity of the other cities.

The Thirty Tyrants. The defeat of Athens brought a brief overthrow of the democratic form of government, which, with modifications and interruptions, including the long tyranny of Peisistratus and his sons, had flourished in the city since the archonship of Solon in 594 B.C. In its place, and with the support of Lysander, a small oligarchical group of thirty men was selected, ostensibly to draw up a new constitution for submission to the Assembly. This group, which came to be called the Thirty Tyrants, delayed their real function, and instead exercised an arbitrary power themselves. They started by purging the city of the *sycophants,* or private informers, who had long been a curse to decent citizens, but quickly they added to the proscription lists the names of personal enemies and of wealthy *metics,* or resident aliens, whose property they might confiscate.

Wishing to incriminate as many as possible in the reign of terror, they instructed reputable citizens to participate in the arrests. On one such occasion, Socrates set himself against injustice at the risk of his life, when he refused to join with four colleagues in arresting Leon of Salamis, a just man. Perhaps as many as fifteen hundred Athenians were put to death during the orgy of the Thirty Tyrants. Thousands of others fled from the city. The exiles, in turn, banded together under a certain Thrasybulus and presently seized the Piræus. In a battle that followed, the forces of the Thirty Tyrants were worsted, and the most bloodthirsty of the oligarchic leaders, Critias, was killed. Even those who had previously entertained oligarchic sympathies had been sobered by the excesses of the Thirty Tyrants. In 403 B.C., the democracy was restored, but it, too, was a chastened and saddened democracy, as we shall see when we study the change in interest that came over the artists and writers of Athens during the fourth century.

[405]

CHAPTER XXIII

THUCYDIDES, XENOPHON, AND ARISTOPHANES

The historian of the Persian Wars had been Herodotus, who was born some four years before the end of that struggle. The details of the Peloponnesian War were recorded by two historians, Thucydides and Xenophon, whose years of maturity were contemporary with it. In addition to Thucydides and Xenophon, the comic poet Aristophanes has left in his political comedies a vivid picture of the condition of Greece during the war. Moreover, a large number of political and civic inscriptions constitute further valuable sources of our knowledge of the fifth century.

THUCYDIDES

Life of Thucydides. Details regarding the life of Thucydides are meager, for he attained to such a completely impartial critical analysis of history that his own story seldom entered into it. It is known that he was the son of Olorus, that his family had estates in the region of Thrace, and it may be conjectured from the period of his activity that he was born in the decade between 470 B.C. and 460 B.C. His contact with Herodotus is suggested by the story that he burst into tears of appreciation on hearing the older historian read part of his work, whereupon Herodotus congratulated the father of Thucydides on the excellent literary taste of his son. Thucydides was a general in the Peloponnesian War, and on his failure

[406]

to save Amphipolis from the Spartan general Brasidas in 424 B.C., he was exiled from the city of Athens. That punishment, continuing for twenty years, gave him the opportunity to travel about Greece during two decades, visiting both camps, observing and assessing intentions and motives, and incorporating them into his magnificent history. Thucydides apparently lived until about 396 B.C., but in his *History* he covered the story of the Peloponnesian War only as far as 411 B.C.

The Contents of His "History." In the *History,* which is divided into eight books, one will find a brief introductory account of prehistoric Greece, a rapid sketch of the *Pentacontaëtia,* or "Fifty-year-period" between the Persian and Peloponnesian Wars, a treatment of the proximate causes and the real cause of the Peloponnesian War, and a detailed description of the struggle, arranged by summer and winter campaigns. Here one will look for an evaluation of the policy of Pericles, for the story of the Athenian plague, the rise of Cleon, the campaigns of Brasidas, and the Sicilian Expedition. Thucydides has interspersed into the *History* from time to time speeches which he places in the mouths of contemporary characters, political or military, and which are intended to serve as a commentary on the pretensions or the purposes of the different states.

His Conception of the Historian's Task. Herodotus stated his view of history to be the inclusion of all known tales. Thucydides, on the contrary, declared that only after the most painstaking search had he admitted anything to his story. He was conscious of the excellence of his effort and declared with prophetic vision that his work was to be a possession for all time, not a plaything of the moment. Both in language and in economic and political reasoning, the *History* of Thucydides makes exceedingly difficult reading. Only with repeated study and after gaining some wisdom in the ways of government and diplomacy as well as in historical methods, can one hope to comprehend the magnitude of his intellect and of the critical task that he has accomplished.

[407]

His Objectivity. Throughout the long and accurate treatment of that life and death struggle between Athens and Sparta, of which Thucydides realized the significance as fully as any statesman or general of the time, he maintained the same logical and critical attitude that he was able to impart to the tale of his own personal fortunes. Nowhere does the objectivity of Thucydides become so clear as in his neutral and dispassionate account of the strategical misadventure to which he owed twenty years of exile under penalty of death, and to which the world owes the composition of his incomparable history. The circumstances leading to his exile were as follows. The Spartan general Brasidas had been active in Thrace, and Thucydides was in command of an Athenian fleet in those waters. Thucydides himself describes the situation thus:

> In this way they surrendered the city of Amphipolis, and Thucydides with his ships sailed into Eion late at night. Brasidas had just occupied Amphipolis, and only one night prevented him from seizing Eion: for if the ships had not come speedily, he would have taken the city at dawn.

That is the incident for which Thucydides was banished, and with superb Hellenic reserve, that is all that he chooses to say about it, though he later adds, by way of explanation of his historical methods, another sentence or two:

> I lived through the entire war; I was at an age to comprehend its action; and I gave unremitting attention to it, so that I might acquire accurate information. It was also my experience to be banished from my country for twenty years after my command at Amphipolis, with the result that I was able to follow more accurately the course of events on both sides.

The Siege of Platæa. The very austerity of language and economy of phrase that Thucydides uses adds to the vividness of his narrative. An illustration of his descriptive style may be found in the story of the opening incidents of the siege of Platæa. It will be noted that the effectiveness of the account is due to the introduction of obscure and unidentified characters, rather than to wealth of detail. The city of Platæa lay in Bœotia near the border of Attica. In the first year of the Peloponnesian War three hundred Thebans organized a surprise attack, entered Platæa, and seized the government. When the citizens realized the comparatively small number of their captors, they began to plan a counterattack, assembling together in secrecy by digging through the mud-brick walls of their contiguous houses, so that they need not appear openly in the streets. Then, at the dead of night, they launched their furious attack on the bewildered Thebans. Anyone who has wandered in the dark through the mazelike streets of even a modern Greek village of the countryside or the islands will realize the helpless panic of the strangers in Platæa.

The scene of fury and hate and fear is punctuated by the trivial acts of unidentified characters.

With a great uproar the Platæans charged the enemy, while at the same time the women and slaves stood on the rooftops, screaming and yelling and hurling down stones and tiles on the Thebans.

A heavy rain added to the confusion, and at length the terrified Thebans fled through the moonless night, hampered by the maze of streets and the mud.

Moreover, a certain one of the Platæans had closed the gate by which they entered, the only gate that had been opened, and he had fastened the bar with the point of a javelin rather than the bolt.

This act of an unidentified Platæan, which Thucydides emphasizes by adding the homely detail of the improvised bolt, was the direct cause of keeping within the city the greater number of the Thebans, whose execution was later to bring bloody retribution on Platæa.

The panic-stricken flight of the Thebans took them up and

down the streets of the city, causing some of them to climb the city wall and throw themselves over, though most perished in the attempt. A few managed to escape through an unguarded gate, cutting the bar "with an axe that a certain woman gave to them." It was a curiously human act of mercy, or perfidy, which saved the lives of a few Thebans while there was yet time for escape. The reader of the description of the incident is himself seized with the terror and confusion of that night in Platæa, in which only two individual characters emerge, the Platæan who closed the gate with a javelin, and the woman who handed an axe to the desperate Thebans, and both are nameless and obscure.

The "Funeral Speech of Pericles." The modern practice of honoring the unknown soldier originated with the Athenians, and is described in Thucydides' account of the ceremony commemorating those slain in war, which serves as the setting for the most memorable speech of his *History,* the *Funeral Speech of Pericles.* At the close of the first year of the Peloponnesian War, the Athenians, following the custom of their forefathers, buried with a public service those who had fallen in battle, interring their bones in the fairest suburb of the city. For three days the bodies lay in state, and they then were borne on wagons in coffins of cypress wood, the bones of each man being placed in the common coffin of his tribe. "And one empty bier, covered with a shroud, was borne in the procession in memory of those whom they were unable to find when the bodies were gathered for burial."

The speech of Pericles is preserved only in the version that Thucydides has composed for him, and which proves to be not so much a eulogy of the dead as a statement and justification of the Athenian way of life. Yet there can be little doubt that the historian heard and recorded some of the rich phrases that fell from the lips of Pericles on that day. ·

The speech opens thus:

Most of those who have already spoken here praise the man who added this speech to our custom, thinking it a goodly thing that it should be spoken over those who have fallen in war. But to me it would have seemed enough that only in action should honor be paid to those who proved themselves brave in action; and that the valor of many men should not rest, for belief or doubt, with a single man, according to whether he speak eloquently or not.

After paying tribute to the ancestors who have bequeathed a free state to the men of Athens, Pericles says a word about the democratic form of government under which they live, and the opportunities that it affords to the citizens.

We have adopted a polity that does not imitate the customs of our neighbors, but rather we afford an example to them. And our society is called a democracy because we live under the control not of the few but the many. Yet, whereas men are all on an equality in private matters, the esteem which a man enjoys depends on his own excellence and not on the class to which he belongs. Furthermore, if a man has any benefit which he can confer on the city, he is not prevented by poverty and the obscurity of his position from doing so.

Pericles is proud also of the spirit of relaxation with which the Athenians have been able to temper the discipline of life. Festivals and games are celebrated to the joy of all; homes are adorned with the refinements of civilization; and, with an eye on the Athenian mastery of the sea, he can add:

Because of the power of our city all things from all the earth find their way to her, and it is our privilege to enjoy the fruits of our own land with no more complete sense of security than we do the products of other men.

Pericles likewise finds satisfaction in the Athenian system of education with its freedom for individual taste in opposition to the rigid code imposed upon the Spartan youth, for in the moment of danger the Athenians prove themselves equal to the demands of courage and endurance as thoroughly and as

[411]

promptly as do those who have been subjected to continuous regimentation. The moral philosophy of his fellow citizens he summarizes thus: "We are lovers of beauty with moderation, and we are lovers of wisdom without weakness. Wealth we regard as an opportunity for service, not as an occasion for boasting."

The praise of the dead has taken the form of an exaltation of the city, so that those who listen to Pericles may realize how great a heritage has been preserved for them by those who have given their lives in its defense.

For this reason I have spoken at length about our city, for I have wanted to make clear that the contest for us involves a greater hazard and a greater reward than it does for those who enjoy no similar privileges.

Thus these men who have died proved themselves worthy of the city. Those of us who are left may pray for a happier lot, but we must show a spirit no less bold against the enemy. I would have you day by day gaze upon the power of the city until you become enamored of her, and when she has attained to great majesty in your eyes, then reflect that it was by courage and a conception of duty and a sense of obligation in danger, that these men secured your heritage. They gave their lives for the common good, and for themselves they gained honor that is ageless, and the noblest of tombs, not that in which they lie, but that in which their valor remains forever recorded on every occasion for praise or action. For the whole world is the tomb of famous men, and it is not alone the epitaph on the funeral stelæ of their native lands that records their worth, but it is an unwritten memorial of the spirit rather than of matter that endures in the hearts of men even in lands not their own.

Only at the end of his speech does Pericles return to the local scene of mourning, with a word, not of commiseration but of comfort for the relatives who remain, and with an admonition to those whose privilege it will yet be to serve the state: "And now when you have mourned, each for your own, go your way."

Estimate of Thucydides. Enough has been said to indicate the method of Thucydides, with his exacting standards of accuracy, and the concise and objective style of composition that was a necessary complement to his purpose. In addition, however, to his literary and historical capacities, the most arresting fact about Thucydides is his exceptional mentality. He lived in the proudest years of Athenian achievement, contemporary with the dramatists, artists, and philosophers who shed luster on the Age of Pericles, and for the profundity of his thinking there is none with whom he will not bear comparison. He records the reactions of man in the stress of siege and battle, when the contest was for the freedom of the individual and of the city-state, dearer than life itself.

XENOPHON

Life of Xenophon. In some respects, Xenophon belongs more properly to the fourth century, for the greater part of his work was composed in that period. However, he wrote a conclusion to Thucydides' history of the Peloponnesian War, and consequently he must be considered with the other Greek historians of the fifth century, especially since he is one of the writers on whom we are dependent for the account of the great war between Athens and Sparta.

Xenophon was born in Attica about 430 B.C., the year of the Athenian plague and one year before the death of Pericles. He was the son of a rich father and grew up in Athens during the unsettled years of the war, with the opportunity to cultivate sport, hunting, philosophy, adventure, or scholarship at will. He was never a serious student, but he did have a taste for both philosophic speculation and personal adventure. He came strongly under the influence of Socrates. In 401 B.C., in the confused period following the downfall of Athens, he sought diversion by joining a mercenary expedition which the Persian prince Cyrus was leading against his kingly brother Artaxerxes.

Xenophon's account of that expedition, the "March of the Ten Thousand," is presented in his *Anabasis*.

In 399 B.C., he returned to Athens, but the execution of his old master, Socrates, made the city intensely distasteful to him. He joined a second mercenary expedition in 396 B.C., this time with King Agesilaus of Sparta, who was fighting in Asia. In 394 B.C., at Coronea in Greece, he found himself fighting with Sparta against his native city of Athens. He was given an estate in the Peloponnese by the Spartans, and there he lived the pleasant life of a country gentleman, writing his versatile books, pursuing the sports of the field, and training his sons, with some recollection of his old loyalty, to fight on the side of the Athenians at Mantinea in 362 B.C. He died about 354 B.C., possibly at Athens.

The "Hellenica." The *Hellenica* or *Greek History,* of Xenophon, though not his most important work, is the one that justifies grouping him with Thucydides, for in that treatise he began his story with the year 411 B.C., at the point where Thucydides broke off. The *Hellenica* continues to record the events of the Peloponnesian War and of the fourth century down to the Battle of Mantinea in 362 B.C. It is the source of our knowledge of the oligarchic revolution in Athens, of the Battles of Arginusæ and Ægospotami, of the exploits of Conon, and of the demolition of the Long Walls, which marked the end of the Athenian Empire. The early chapters of the history are strongly colored by a Thucydidean style, which is, however, not long maintained. The pro-Spartan bias of Xenophon is everywhere evident, and the Spartan King Agesilaus is obviously his ideal hero.

The "Anabasis." The *Anabasis,* as has already been mentioned, is the tale of the "March of the Ten Thousand." When Cyrus was killed and the Greek generals were treacherously put to death in the interior of Asia, Xenophon became one of the leaders of the mercenary army who brought it successfully back to the Black Sea. The stories of war, travel, and intrigue not only make of the book an excellent adventure tale, but embrace exceedingly important information on the geographical conditions of a little-known region and about the social customs of many peoples. The organization of the Greek army from within its own ranks and the maintenance of successful discipline through the hardships of the long march to safety also afford a striking proof of the power with which the democratic ideals had seized upon the people. Most readers will recall the dramatic point in the book in which the soldiers, after their long months of hard and often hopeless marching through the inhospitable interior of Asia, reach the mountain crest from which they look down upon the sea, which means to them a long-despaired-of highway to their homes, and raise the cry: "Thalassa! Thalassa!"—"The sea! The sea!"

The Socratic Writings. Four treatises, the *Memorabilia,* or *Recollections, Apology,* or *Defense, Symposium,* or *Banquet,* and *Œconomicus,* or *Householder,* tell of the association of Xenophon with his master Socrates. They are not of profound philosophic importance, although their value in forming an accurate estimate of the character and personal peculiarities of Socrates is not to be disregarded.

The Lesser Works. The variety of Xenophon's interest is further attested by his remaining books. The *Cyropædia,* or *Education of Cyrus,* is an idealized account of Xenophon's conception of the proper education of a prince, and it includes much of his own political philosophy. In the *Constitution of Sparta* he shows again his strong prejudice in favor of that state. The *Hiero,* which takes its title from the name of the tyrant of Syracuse, deals with the advantages and disadvantages of tyranny from the point of view of the tyrant himself. Xenophon also wrote interesting amateur essays on hunting, horsemanship, and cavalry maneuvers.

Estimate of Xenophon. Xenophon lived in stirring times and was intimately associated with the greatest characters of his day. Furthermore, he had the necessary literary training to write of adventures and experiences that so frequently fall to the lot of men who, through lack of education, are either indifferent to the significance of history in the making or powerless to record it. For these reasons the writings of Xenophon are invested with no mean historical importance. It was, however, his misfortune that he should always challenge comparison, both in historical and philosophic composition, with Thucydides and Plato who dealt with similar themes and who were unquestionably his intellectual superiors.

ARISTOPHANES

Aristophanes' Relation to His Times. Reasons might be offered for discussing the work of Aristophanes and the other writers of comedy in connection with the dramatists rather than with the historians, for the comic poets never allowed historical accuracy to stand in the way of a good joke, and the nature of comedy almost inevitably invites the distortion of truth. Yet the qualities of Athenian comedy during the fifth century were so vitally conditioned by contemporary political circumstances, the characters and allusions were so intensely personal, and the plays so often related to the progress of the Peloponnesian War itself, that the purpose of Aristophanes and his associates will be more clearly grasped if comedy is treated in connection with history.

The Origin of Comedy. With the death of Sophocles and Euripides in 406 B.C., the creative phase of Athenian tragedy had come to an end. Another type of drama, comedy, had been flourishing contemporaneously with tragedy for some two decades, and by reason of literary style and historical allusion, had grown quite as important as tragedy. The latter had been first officially sponsored in Athens about 534 B.C. Comedy in time was also adopted by the state, coming in, as did tragedy, with the religious sanction of Dionysus, but it did not flower until about a century later. It originated with the revel songs of the villagers, somewhat as tragedy began with the dithyrambic chants of the country folk at the times of festival. Comedy, however, because of its later development and because it built on the existing dramatic structure, was always more artificial than tragedy.

The history of Greek comedy is divided into Old, Middle, and New Comedy, of which the latter two, Middle and New Comedy, will be described in connection with the literature of the fourth century and the Alexandrian Age respectively. Though something is known of the life and work of a considerable number of fifth-century comic writers, fortune has preserved the plays of only the greatest of them, Aristophanes. A fairly satisfactory account of the nature and significance of Old Comedy can be built about this one man.

Nature of Old Comedy. Old Comedy, as portrayed by Aristophanes in the fifth century, was essentially political, social, personal, and local. For no branch of ancient literature is a close knowledge of Athenian life more necessary, if one would understand it fully, than for Old Comedy. The plays depend for their success on a travesty and mockery of dishonesty or insincerity in public affairs. The statesmen, soldiers, sophists, and dramatists of the city, even the gods of Olympus, are mentioned by name or paraded in the theater as targets for the wit of the writer and the amusement of the audience. No person, alive or dead, and no institution was immune from the intensely clever, very pointed, often scurrilous and frankly indecent barbs of the comic poets.

Appraisal of Old Comedy. In the plays of Aristophanes there are many passages of vigorous humor and riotous coarseness that were calculated to fulfill the first function of a comic poet, which was to cause the exclusively masculine Athenian audience to split their sides with laughter. It would, however, be a mistake to think of Aristophanes as trivial or insincere or essentially vulgar. It was an age of uncensored frankness, and the poet was not troubled about niceties of language. Yet Aristophanes was a consummate artist, and his choral passages are to be numbered among the most beautiful in Greek poetry. Furthermore, the purpose of the comic poets, or at least of Aristophanes, was to restore the city to the stern and sound

[417]

morality of the early days of Athenian freedom as it existed at the time of the Persian Wars, and from which he saw it slipping all too rapidly. The passionate sincerity of his reforming zeal is attested by Saint John Chrysostom, who is said to have found in the plays such high-minded motives that he was induced to keep them constantly by him, even to use them as his pillow by night, for he knew no writer more pure and austere.

The license of Old Comedy was checked once or twice by the state, but when that occurred it was itself a sign of the decadence of the times. So long as the Athenians remained confident of the inherent security of their free institutions, they could afford to laugh at the foibles of their statesmen and themselves, and they did laugh, loudly and uproariously. When the city of Athens was destroyed in 404 B.C., Old Comedy was doomed, for laughter comes hard to those whose fortunes have been shattered.

The Plays of Aristophanes. Aristophanes was born about 445 B.C., and died about 385 B.C. Of his forty comedies, the eleven that have been preserved are listed with the dates of their production: *Acharnians* (425 B.C.), *Knights* (424 B.C.), *Clouds* (423 B.C.), *Wasps* (422 B.C.), *Peace* (421 B.C.), *Birds* (414 B.C.), *Lysistrata* (411 B.C.), *Thesmophoriazusæ* (411 B.C.), *Frogs* (405 B.C.), *Ecclesiazusæ* (392 B.C.), *Plutus* (388 B.C.). The dates of the plays are much more significant than they were with tragedy, for contemporary political life is the stuff of his creations. Aristophanes was born half a generation after Pericles assumed power in Athens and some nine years after the Athenians in their arrogance had set up the Empire on the basis of force. He grew up very much out of sympathy with the current democracy, protesting against the outrage to the old morality. Many of his plays are filled with attacks, both open and covert, on what he considered the sophistic philosophy of the tragic poet Euripides, though the precise allusions are sometimes difficult to interpret.

The Pacifistic Comedies: "Acharnians," "Peace," "Lysistrata."

It is difficult to divide the extant plays of Aristophanes arbitrarily into categories, and yet it may be more illuminating to consider together those which seem to lead to common ends, than to catalogue them one after another. Thus there is one group, consisting of the *Acharnians,* the *Peace,* and the *Lysistrata,* which contain definite propaganda against war. They were all produced during the Peloponnesian War and were prompted by the sufferings of Greece during that struggle. The *Archanians,* which is the earliest play of Aristophanes still extant and which was produced in 425 B.C., when he was about twenty years of age, has preserved elements that suggest the form of the old village revel song. The real point of the play, however, is the vigorous attack on the war party, that had for six years compelled the Athenians to endure the distress of confinement within the crowded city. Four years after the presentation of the *Acharnians,* in 421 B.C., the year of the Peace of Nicias, which put a temporary stop to the war, Aristophanes offered the *Peace.* This play, too, is in the nature of propaganda for the peace party, and deals with the suffering endured by both sides during the struggle. Despite all its mockery, the comedy carries with it an earnest hope and plea for continuing peace under the Treaty of Nicias. Finally, in 411 B.C., when Athens was still staggering from the appalling loss of the Sicilian Expedition two years earlier and the war was entering its final stage, which was to end in the destruction of the city, Aristophanes launched in the *Lysistrata* one more powerful protest against the folly of the war. In this play, the women, despairing of any common-sense attitude on the part of the men, themselves proceed, under the leadership of a strong-minded woman, Lysistrata, or "Disbander-of-the-army," to exert the pressure necessary to procure peace.

The Political Comedies: "Knights," "Birds." A second group of comedies, the *Knights* and the *Birds,* is chiefly distinguished for political satire, although the latter play is so largely dependent for its development on the contemporary expedition of Athens against Syracuse, that it might as reasonably be classed among the pacifistic plays. The *Knights* was produced in 424 B.C., six months after Cleon's successful exploit at Pylos and Sphacteria, when he made good his boast by capturing the Spartans to the number of two hundred and ninety-two. The play is a virulent political attack on Cleon, the vulgar demagogue, and incidentally on the Athenian people for supporting such a man in office. The *Birds,* which was performed in 414 B.C., the second year of the ill-fated Sicilian Expedition, is a fantastic satire on the wild folly of that project, which was regarded as imperialistic by the peace party in Athens.

The Comedies of Literary Satire: "Thesmophoriazusæ," "Frogs." Two comedies, the *Thesmophoriazusæ* and the *Frogs,* are built about a parody and satire on the tragic dramatists. The *Thesmophoriazusæ,* or "Women celebrating the Festival of the Thesmophoria," presented in 411 B.C., was directed against Euripides, who had frequently been the object of Aristophanes' wrath for his alleged corruption of the city, as well as for his declining tragic style. More important than the development of the rather weak plot is the extended parody of the meters, rhythms, and metaphors of the new tragic poetry, which was so distasteful to Aristophanes. The *Frogs,* presented in 405 B.C., is a much better literary satire than the *Thesmophoriazusæ.* It is, in fact, the finest comedy of Aristophanes.

The "Frogs." An analysis of the action of the *Frogs* affords at once an insight into the nature of Old Comedy and an illustration of the rapidity with which current events were translated into the verses of the comic theater. The *Frogs* was presented at the Lenæa early in 405 B.C. and was awarded the first prize in the competition sponsored by the state. There are in the play two distinct historical threads. The first, or basic, theme is a dramatic appraisal of the tragic dramas of Æschylus, Sophocles, and Euripides, especially of Æschylus and Euripides; the less obvious theme is the political fate of Athens as the Peloponnesian War draws to a close. The Athenian audience was alert to the historical implications.

The Qualities of the Tragic Writers as Reflected in the "Frogs." To make clear Aristophanes' criticism of the writers of tragedy, it will be necessary to recall the times and characteristics of the three men about whom he wrote. Æschylus had been born under the Peisistratids; he had witnessed the coming of democracy to Athens and had fought to preserve it at Marathon and Salamis. His philosophy of life and poetry is aloof and conservative. He is convinced that no better education can be found than that which preserved the city through the trial of the Persian Wars. Sophocles was enough younger to be influenced by the intellectual inquiries of the philosophic circles of the city, but his own unvarying good fortune robbed his plays of social intensity. Consequently, he is represented in the *Frogs* as retaining in Hades the characteristic good humor of his earthly existence, and for that reason declining to enter the contest between the dramatists. Euripides, on the other hand, though he wrote in the language of tragedy, had the heart of an iconoclastic philosopher. The established order of society, and even the gods themselves, were repeatedly attacked in his plays in what seemed to Aristophanes outrageous and sophistic language.

The Significant Dates. Æschylus had died in 456 B.C., and a half century later, in 406 B.C., both Sophocles and Euripides followed him to the grave. The setting was ideal for a man of Aristophanes' talents, and the *Frogs,* presented about four months after the death of Euripides and two months after the death of Sophocles, could not have been more opportunely timed.

The Political Scene in 405 B.C. There also lies in the background of the play a strong consciousness of the political and military situation in the city. The Peloponnesian War had broken out in 431 B.C.; the plague of 430–427 B.C. had destroyed one fourth of the population; Pericles had died in 429 B.C.; the disastrous Sicilian Expedition of 415 B.C. to 413 B.C.

had cost Athens thirty thousand lives; Alcibiades, the brilliant but corrupt general, was in exile. And now, some six months before the presentation of the *Frogs,* the Athenians, by Herculean efforts, which included the unprecedented step of offering freedom and enfranchisement to the slaves, had won a notable naval victory at Arginusæ, and for the moment the spirits of the people were elated. In that political atmosphere the comedy was offered.

The Action of the "Frogs." Dionysus, the god of tragedy, despairing of finding any longer a good poet on earth, has decided to go down to Hades in order to bring back Euripides. He is represented as an effeminate and foppish god, clad in a saffron robe and women's slippers, but over that garb he has cast a lion's skin, with the intention of passing for Heracles on his trip to Hades. He enters the orchestra, accompanied by his slave Xanthias, who, heavily laden with bundles, rides on an ass. Dionysus cries out indignantly against his grumbling slave:

DIONYSUS

Well, is this not the height of insolence and complete self-indulgence! Here am I, Dionysus, son of Beerbottle, walking and toiling myself, and allowing this fellow to ride, so that he may not be distressed or carry a burden.

XANTHIAS

What's that? Am I not carrying anything?

DIONYSUS

How can *you* be carrying anything, when you're carried yourself?

XANTHIAS

Why I'm carrying these bundles.

DIONYSUS

How?

XANTHIAS

Much against my will.

[422]

DIONYSUS

> Isn't the ass carrying what you are carrying?

XANTHIAS

> Well, I don't know how it is, but my shoulder hurts.

In this trivial dispute as to whether Xanthias or the ass is really carrying the bundles, one has at the outset a satire on the sophistry of Euripides.

Dionysus and Xanthias proceed to the door of Heracles' house and call forth that hero in order to learn from him the route to Hades, for he had once gone there to bring back the three-headed dog Cerberus. Heracles, greatly amused at the disguise of Dionysus, asks his purpose in going to Hades. Dionysus explains that he wants to find a creative poet capable of composing a noble, bold expression, such as, "the airy chamber of Zeus," or, "the foot of time," or, "a person's soul not being perjured through the falsehood of the tongue." He is citing characteristic examples, though intentionally confused in recollection, from tragedies extant at the time and well known to the audience.

Heracles affably suggests several ways by which Dionysus may reach Hades—by hanging, by poison, or by jumping from a high tower—all of which are rejected with horror. Finally Heracles consents to describe the terrifying journey across the River Styx in Charon's skiff. At this point the attention of the audience is directed to the Ferryman of the Dead and his boat by a Dead Man, who, as he is borne across the orchestra, has a few words to say. Charon receives Dionysus into his boat but refuses to take aboard any slave who had not volunteered for naval service at Arginusæ. Xanthias offers the customary excuse that he has sore eyes, but his plea is rejected, and he is compelled to walk around the shore of the lake, while Charon and Dionysus make use of the skiff. Charon requires the unfortunate god to earn his passage by rowing the boat, which causes him great discomfort.

CHARON

Here, sit by the oar. [*Dionysus misunderstands and awkwardly sits on the oar.*] If there is anyone else to sail, let him hurry. [*To Dionysus.*] You stupid dolt, what are you doing?

DIONYSUS

What am I doing? Why, I'm sitting on the oar, as you told me to yourself.

CHARON

No, Fatbelly, not there; sit here.

DIONYSUS

All right.

CHARON

Now stretch your arms out.

DIONYSUS

All right.

CHARON

Oh, don't keep talking nonsense. Brace your feet and row as though you meant it.

DIONYSUS

Well, how can I row? I've had no experience. I know nothing of the sea, and I'm not a Salaminian.

CHARON

You can do it easily enough, for you will hear the most delightful melodies, when once you start.

DIONYSUS

Melodies from whom?

CHARON

From frogs that sing like swans—marvelously.

DIONYSUS

Say the word!

As they row across the lake, Dionysus becomes involved in

[424]

a verbal controversy with a Chorus of frogs in the marsh, who punctuate their song with the refrain *Brekekekex koax koax.* Arrived at the further side of the Stygian Lake, Dionysus and Xanthias are reunited, and Charon, after receiving his pay, withdraws with his skiff. A Chorus composed of Initiates into the Mysteries now appears. This second Chorus is not characteristic of all Greek comedies.

At length Dionysus, hopeful that his disguise may prove effective, knocks at the door of Pluto, the god of Hades, and announces himself as "the mighty Heracles." He is unexpectedly successful, for Æacus, the servant of Pluto, who remembers the misdeeds of Heracles when he tried to steal the dog Cerberus, bursts forth from the door and abuses him so soundly that Dionysus loses his taste for the role and hastily persuades Xanthias to assume the lion's skin and play the part of Heracles, while he takes up the bundles and acts the slave.

No sooner has this change been made than Persephone's maid emerges and invites Xanthias, supposing him to be Heracles, to a banquet. Dionysus promptly compels his servant to change costumes again, and once more he appears as Heracles. Thereupon two women innkeepers, who had been robbed by Heracles on his previous trip, appear and abuse Dionysus with the bawdy vigor of Billingsgate fishwives.

FIRST INNKEEPER

    Oh, Plathane, Plathane, that scoundrel is back again,
    the one that came to our inn and ate up sixteen loaves.

SECOND INNKEEPER

    Yes, by Zeus, the very one.

FIRST INNKEEPER

    And he ate twenty pieces of meat, at a half obol a
    piece.

SECOND INNKEEPER

    And there was a lot of garlic.

FIRST INNKEEPER

> [*To Dionysus.*] You didn't think I'd know you with
> your buskins on. Ah yes! And I haven't mentioned
> all that pickled fish, by Zeus, nor the fresh cheese, you
> wretch, which you gobbled down, baskets and all.—
> And then when I asked for pay, he glared at me and
> roared.—You and your dirty gullet, I'd like to take a
> stone and smash the teeth you used to eat up my goods.

Dionysus is frightened and once more effects a change of
costume with his slave, and Xanthias is again Heracles.
Thereupon Æacus returns to the scene with a warrant for the
arrest of the supposed Heracles, who is now Xanthias, and the
confusion of identity by this time has grown so great that
they strike upon the plan of flogging the pair one after another, in order to determine who is the slave and who is the
god. The former might be expected to scream with pain
while the latter should not feel the lash. But both Dionysus
and Xanthias sustain the blows in stoic silence, or when they
are compelled to cry out in anguish, they disguise their ejacula-
tions by filling out a verse of poetry, which they pretend to be
reciting, "Apollo!—thou who dost rule over Delos and Pytho,"
or by pretending that a thorn in the foot or the smell of onions
has occasioned the involuntary tears. Unable to reach a conclusion by this method, Æacus escorts both Dionysus and
Xanthias off to submit to the judgment of Pluto and Persephone, to the rueful reflection of Dionysus that such a plan
would have been welcome before the beating.

The Parabasis. Only the second Chorus is left in the
orchestra, and at this point occurs a characteristic feature of
Greek comedy, the *parabasis,* in which the Chorus advances
to the front of the orchestra and addresses the audience in the
person of the author on matters usually unrelated to the play.
In the *Frogs,* the parabasis deals, among other things, with the
political turmoil of Athens, the stringency of war measures,
the debasement of the currency, and the proposed recall of
Alcibiades.

[426]

The Agon. When the action is resumed, Xanthias and
Æacus reappear and Æacus explains how Æschylus has for
fifty years held undisputed the chair for tragic excellence in
Hades, until the upstart Euripides now challenges him. Thus
the way is prepared for another characteristic feature of Greek
comedy, the *agon,* or "contest." In the agon of the *Frogs,*
Dionysus, who, as the Greek god of tragedy, has some knowledge of tragic drama, has been selected to judge between Æschylus and Euripides. The literary contest between the two poets
runs to considerable length, and in various ways their comparative merits and defects are evaluated—the prologues, the
meters, especially of the choric passages, and the weight of the
iambic verses. Much of the argument is severely technical,
but there is no mistaking the type of contest which Aristophanes humorously reconstructs. Thus one will appreciate
the jibes of Euripides at the bombastic and incomprehensible
phrases of Æschylus—"Scamanders, battlements, griffins,
bronze-inlaid upon the shields," or "hippogriffs and gorgons"
—as contrasted with the lowly and homely style in which
Euripides himself takes pride. Or, again, one may read the
criticism of the ponderous prologues of Æschylus, filled with
"woe and lamentation," in contrast with the contemptuous
parody of a Euripidean monody on the robbery of his hen-
roost which Æschylus composes and delivers in mock heroic
manner.

Most important and amusing of all is the scene in which
Dionysus brings out a great pair of scales and invites Æschylus
and Euripides to pour into the scale pans each a verse of his
own poetry.

"Would that the barque Argo had never flitted on her way,"
is the first contribution of Euripides, who selects the well-
known opening verse of his *Medea.* "O river Spercheius and
grazing land of cattle," is the reply of Æschylus, who chooses
a verse from his lost *Philoctetes.* When the scale pans are
released, the verse of Æschylus is found to weigh more heavily,
for, says Dionysus, he has thrown in a river, like the wool-

merchants, who wet their fleeces before selling them so that they may weigh more heavily, while Euripides has employed a light, winged verse.

Thus the contest continues, but never do the insubstantial verses of Euripides equal in weight the massive phrases of his opponent. At length Pluto, the god of the underworld, urges Dionysus to reach a decision, promising that he may take back to earth with him the dramatist of his choice. Dionysus, contrary to his original intention, selects Æschylus, and when Euripides reproaches him for breaking his oath and leaving him to death, Dionysus is able to paraphrase to Euripides his own caviling words from the *Hippolytus,* "It was my tongue that swore, not my mind," and to argue with sophistic Euripidean logic that death is life and life is death, and that shame is nothing more than an ephemeral convention.

Estimate of the "Frogs." Comic parody appears in the *Frogs* as one recognizes verses from many of the extant tragedies woven into the fabric of the comedy. Even more striking is the mood of high courage in the closing song of the Chorus, as the chosen bard returns to his second birth in the city, which, fatigued with a generation of war and revolution, may now hope for a counsel of wisdom and a cessation from the shocks of war. But this was the earnest prayer of a sincere man for a happy issue that was not to be. Tragedy never revived in Athens, and within another year the naval victory of the Spartan Lysander at Ægospotami was to spell the doom of the Athenian Empire.

The Domestic Comedies: "Clouds," "Wasps," "Ecclesiazusæ," "Plutus." Finally, four plays, the *Clouds, Wasps, Ecclesiazusæ,* and *Plutus,* deal with social problems within the state, and may be designated as the domestic comedies. Of these the most celebrated is the *Clouds,* presented in 423 B.C. It is an attack on the sophists, who, with their new learning and their disregard for truth, have weakened the morale of the young men of the city. Aristophanes, more intent on caricature than truth, has made Socrates the archsophist, doubtless because

[428]

Socrates, who was at that time a man of about forty-six years of age, of eccentric habits and still more eccentric appearance, was well known in the city and would be readily recognized by the audience.

The *Wasps,* presented in 422 B.C., is a satire on the unmeasured passion of the Athenians for litigation. A few years before the presentation of this play, Cleon had raised the daily pay of a juryman to three obols, and as a consequence the Athenian rabble could indulge its taste for vicarious litigation by sitting in the courts all day long, and in addition be paid for the privilege.

In 404 B.C., the Athenian democracy fell, and the two extant plays of Aristophanes that were presented after that date reflect the new qualities of fourth-century literature. The *Ecclesiazusæ,* or "Women in the Assembly," was offered in 392 B.C. It carried the theme of a feminine revolt even further than the *Lysistrata* had done, although the occasion was not war, but social legislation. The women of the city are represented as getting control of the Assembly and bringing the men into subjection. The *Plutus,* which belongs to 388 B.C., is the last play of Aristophanes that has been preserved. It takes its name from the god of wealth and is a satire on a society that has been disrupted by a redistribution of property. Plutus, who had been deprived of his sight by a jealous Zeus, regains the use of his eyes and is thus enabled to assign his riches with judgment. The unworthy are reduced to poverty, and the upright exalted, although the contentment of the new society is not all that might be expected. This social comedy is a prelude to the abandonment of political themes and the adoption of a comedy of manners, characteristic of Middle and New Comedy, which were to flourish in the fourth century and later.

CHAPTER XXIV

TRANSITIONAL PHILOSOPHY:
THE SOPHISTS AND SOCRATES

Religion. The moral and ethical ideas of the Greeks as they existed in the fifth and fourth centuries had been in the process of formation long before they were written down. Accordingly, a knowledge of Greek religion, at least in the earlier centuries, must be gained from the poets, philosophers, and historians, rather than from specific religious documents. The first religious ideas are found in the tales of the gods in Homer and in the genealogies of Hesiod. In the attack on anthropomorphism by Xenophanes a new note enters, while in the different settings in which Æschylus, Sophocles, Euripides, and Aristophanes represent the deities, changing ideas about the relations between men and gods can be traced. In addition, the accounts of various cults—such as the Orphic religion, the Eleusinian Mysteries, or the healing shrine of Epidaurus— and of rituals—such as the Panathenaic Procession, which is represented in sculpture on the Ionic frieze of the Parthenon— are of major importance as sources for the study of Greek religion. Many ethical and moral problems, however, were thought to belong more properly to philosophy than to religion, and as a guide in the conduct of his life the Greek knew nothing better than the old mottoes "Know thyself," and "Nothing in excess."

Humanistic Philosophy. Philosophy is in a somewhat different situation, for while there are few specific philosophic writings of the fifth century to engage our attention, the study

[430]

of philosophy was feverishly pursued during those years by the sophists and by Socrates. The interest in physical and material studies that had occupied the philosophers of the archaic age now waned and men began to be occupied with humanistic inquiries. The reason for that modification lies ultimately in the basic preoccupation of the Greeks with man, which may be traced through art and literature no less clearly than through philosophic speculation.

Thus scientific philosophy had engaged the attention of the Greeks for a century or so, until they concluded that they had exhausted the promise in that field. In the absence of the laboratory method, further research in physical philosophy was unlikely to yield valuable results, and they began to feel also that it did not contribute anything with which to feed the spirit and the soul of a sensitive people. Therefore, it was inevitable that they should turn to a study of man in his relations to the state, his fellow citizens, and the gods. Some of the early results of this type of philosophy are to be seen in such plays as Sophocles' *Antigone,* with its examination of the problem of individual conscience in conflict with civic authority.

THE SOPHISTS

The Rise of the Sophists. Unfortunately, other influences entered in almost at once to corrupt the purity of thought. The growth of the Athenian democracy and the development of the Empire opened up a new career for young men of good family in Athens through participation in public affairs. In fact, that was almost the only field in which they could exercise their talents, and, for success either in the law courts or the Assembly, an ability to argue readily and effectively was absolutely necessary. In order to provide such training, there came to Athens a host of teachers, or *sophists,* the names of a number of whom are well known—Protagoras of Abdera, Hippias of Elis, Prodicus of Ceos, Gorgias of Leontini. It should, however, be very definitely understood that the pres-

[431]

ence of the sophists in Athens was a symptom rather than a cause of the moral decline of the state. The sophists came to fill an existing demand, but they did not originally create it.

Prejudice Against the Sophists. One of the striking things about the sophists is the foreign origin of practically all of them. In an age when the idea of self-sufficiency in the city-state was very strong, there was something inherently suspect to the public mind about a body of men who flocked in from many parts of the ancient world and quickly attached to themselves eager groups of youths who avidly pursued their studies under foreign direction. There can be little doubt but that many of the sophists were able, sincere, and learned men. They usually commenced their training with a course in rhetoric, but a broader curriculum, embracing literature, history, geography, language, grammar, ethics, and social studies, was quickly added.

A further circumstance aroused public antagonism against the sophists. This was the fact that they accepted fees and consequently made their services available only to rich young men who were willing to pay lavishly for the privilege of associating with them. It is probable that the average man of cultural interests in the middle of the fifth century gave little enough heed to the ethical implications of the payment and receipt of remuneration for instruction, and he was ready enough to include the Athenian Socrates with the other teachers as a wise man, or sophist. However, it was Socrates himself, and later Plato speaking for him, who insisted that the acceptance of payment for teaching destroyed all possibility of honest and disinterested instruction. There were vital differences between the ethical and moral teachings of Socrates and those of the sophists, as will presently be made clear, but it may be doubted whether payment for teaching constituted the inevitable barrier to intellectual honesty that Socrates, and more particularly his aristocratic pupil Plato, attributed to it.

Errors of the Sophists. The course of training offered by the sophists appears on the face of it both innocent and desir-

[432]

able, but, partly because of the unscrupulousness of the Athenian youths themselves and partly because of the dangerous skill of the sophists, the latter soon began to teach subversive doctrines calculated to undermine the integrity of youth. The attitude of the sophists was cynical. Not only did they claim that man had never reached the truth of any inquiry, but they denied the very existence of truth. Success in debate was considered more important than objective truth of exposition, and very quickly the teachings of the sophists took on the quality of opportunism, which gave to the word *sophistry* the connotation that it still bears.

Even before the influx of foreign teachers there was a great deal of critical questioning already to be found in Athens. The institutions of the state, religious traditions, government, and society in general were being subjected to searching scrutiny. To this atmosphere the sophists readily adapted themselves, teaching that laws are but the regulations of an older generation which in a democracy should be modified with the times. From that point they proceeded to argue that conventional morality, honesty, and justice need not restrain one when his advantage lies in other directions. Up to a certain point it is possible to agree with the sophists, for there can be little criticism of a teaching that seeks to free men's minds from the unreasoning acceptance of inherited prejudice and superstition. The error of the sophists, however, lay in their failure to substitute any sound basis of eternal truth for the faith they rejected.

In estimating the place of the sophists, it must be repeated that they did not so much create a situation as minister to one which they found in existence. They were not genuine philosophers, for they did not pursue truth as embodied in the reasoned beliefs of a school, but rather they were economic rivals one with another, who profited by the conversion of men to their own particular courses of study. All through the middle years of the fifth century the moral fiber of Athens was breaking. Her decay had begun in 454 B.C., when she betrayed her allies by the transfer of the Delian treasury to Athens, and in the stress of the Peloponnesian War, with the best of her citizens lost in battle or through the plague, she was being driven on to a policy of individualism and ruthless self-interest. It may be laid to the charge of the sophists that they profited from the moral decadence of Athenian society and that they made no effort to arrest the insidious progress of the dissolution.

SOCRATES

The Position of Socrates. While the sophists tried to free men's minds from dogmatism and, as a consequence, introduced the pernicious idea that the voice of folly must be passively heard simply because each man has a right to his opinion, another and a greater force was being exerted in the cause of intellectual honesty. This was the querulous and inquiring voice of the stonecutter Socrates. Socrates was born in Athens about 469 B.C. His parents were of humble stock, although not destitute. He received the ordinary training of a Greek boy and was taught the trade of his father, which was sculpture. He took part in the activities of Athens as the other citizens did, holding office in the Assembly and fighting in the Peloponnesian War at Potidæa, Amphipolis, and Delium. From the writings of Plato and Xenophon and from incidental passages of Aristophanes' *Clouds,* parody though it is, some sort of picture of Socrates can be reconstructed. He was of heavy, massive appearance, short of stature, and with features so coarse as to be almost grotesque. He walked barefooted about the city of Athens, clad in sorry raiment and with a peculiar rolling gait that made him an easily recognizable figure. From beneath his shaggy eyebrows his piercing eyes were turned on an interlocutor in debate with a fierce intensity that must have disconcerted many a venturer into the field of dialectic.

Socrates' Conception of His Own Mission. The consuming interest of his life was philosophy. He laid no claim to knowl-

Photograph by the British Museum

FIGURE 124. SOCRATES. The individualized style of
the portrait suggests a fourth-century date.

edge. In fact, he reiterated again and again his own ignorance, a pretence that has come to be called "Socratic irony." He had learned that the Delphic oracle once replied to one of his friends that no man lived who was wiser than Socrates. Thereafter, apparently with complete sincerity, he devoted his life to seeking to discover what the god could have meant. In time he came to the conclusion that he was wiser than others only because he was conscious of his ignorance, whereas they lived in the foolish conviction of their wisdom.

Akin to his acceptance of the oracle of Delphi was his belief that he had an inner voice, which he called his *dæmon,* that guided his conduct and dissuaded him from unwise decisions. Possibly the dæmon, which he evidently believed to be something peculiar to himself, was the supernaturally keen voice of conscience speaking to one of the greatest of the world's moral teachers. In any case, Socrates was a man of such extraordinary intellectual and ethical gifts that a thorough comprehension of his life and character lies beyond the grasp of average minds. Some things must be taken on faith in the realm of philosophy as well as of religion.

The Dialectic Method. Socrates believed that truth existed somewhere in the world, even though man might never hope to find it completely. He taught that even partial truth could be attained only if each successive step in an argument gained the assent of both parties to the debate. Socrates conducted no school and no formal classes, but everywhere throughout the city, in the market places and the public gathering places, spent his days in talk and argument with those who delighted to join his circle. About him assembled groups of young men, who brought to him ideas which he proceeded to discuss, though he steadfastly refused to accept payment, insisting that he had nothing to teach. Through question and answer, rather than by consecutive discourse in which error might easily go undetected, he developed an important philosophical technique—the dialectic method.

The Science of Definitions and Inductive Reasoning. Two

other contributions to the progress of philosophy must also be credited to Socrates. They are the science of definitions and inductive reasoning, and in these Aristotle said that the whole constructive method of Socrates lay. Socrates believed that before one could argue intelligently about any object or any doctrine, it was necessary to know exactly what differentiated it from all other things. From this conviction and this method arose the science of definitions. Inductive reasoning grew in part from Socrates' belief that philosophy should contribute a guide to life. He taught that in any situation demanding a decision, one should be able to call upon a general moral law for guidance. That law may be discovered by extracting the common denominator from all pertinent analogous situations. Thus, if one is seeking to discover the law of justice, he will imagine a number of incidents, each involving the application of justice—such as the restoration of borrowed property, the fair representation of one's neighbor, the intellectual honesty with which a drama is composed— and by finding a common element in these and other specific examples of justice, he will arrive at the ultimate law of justice. This is inductive reasoning. When once the law has been established, deductive reasoning, which is much more common and which implies the recognition of a specific conclusion from the established general law, may be called into play to carry the study further.

Differences Between the Sophists and Socrates. This brief statement of the method of Socrates will make clear a fundamental difference between Socrates and the sophists, with whom from antiquity to the present he has so often been associated. The sophists adapted themselves to the circumstances of the moment, yielding to the immediate demand and readily sacrificing any true convictions which they might personally have had. They claimed that there was no absolute truth, whereas Socrates maintained that truth did exist, however difficult of attainment it might be, and that the search for it was worth any effort. Socrates was totally indifferent to the opinion

[437]

of the city. So long as his duties to man did not conflict with his conscience he served in the various capacities in which any citizen was expected to play his part in a democratic community, but he never allowed conventional standards to deflect him from his clear concept of just conduct. The familiar, and substantially correct, reconstruction of Socrates as a strange-appearing and eccentric old man, who moved about the streets of Athens engaging all and sundry in debate, and ever protesting his own ignorance, must not lead to the conclusion that his pursuit of truth was aimless. On the contrary, he had fundamental and positive social ends in mind, and through all his activities, the development of the dialectic method, the science of definitions, and inductive reasoning, he was working toward a natural, honest, and proper basis for human conduct.

Sources of Our Knowledge of Socrates. Like more than one great moral teacher, Socrates himself wrote nothing. His thought and philosophy are known to us only in the writings of his disciples, especially Plato and Xenophon, and also, if the comic distortion is corrected, through the caricature of Aristophanes' play. Moreover, it must always be kept in mind that Plato has identified his writing so completely with the mind and personality of Socrates that it is often difficult to isolate and attribute a particular philosophic principle either to him or to his master. In all these sources Socrates emerges as one who cherished wisdom and sought to arouse all those about him to pursue it because he believed that wisdom was the prerequisite of virtue, and that only by the attainment of knowledge could the moral character of man be improved.

Certain weaknesses appear in his method. He is too much the classifier of moral ideas and too thoroughly convinced of the effectiveness of dialectic as a means of revealing the truth. In fact, his greatest error arose from his own single-minded devotion to truth and honesty. It produced in him a too ready belief that when men know the right course, they will follow it. A more cynical and realistic appraisal of human morality observes that men fall so far short of the philosophic ideal of

[438]

virtue that they all too often see and approve the better course, and choose the worse. Nor did the dialectic method afford the complete protection against false conclusions that Socrates thought, for the process of question and answer, if conducted by a clever and forceful thinker, is likely to lead a conscientious witness away from the truth, while constructive discourse or personal study will bring to light many facts lost in clever conversation.

The Death and Subsequent Influence of Socrates. In 399 B.C., when a war-weary and bruised democracy still bore the scars of the savagery of the Thirty Tyrants, Socrates, now seventy years of age, was brought to trial for his life on the double charge of scorning the national gods and introducing new concepts about divinity, and of corrupting the youth of the city. The defense offered by Socrates is recorded in the *Apology* of Plato. How far the Platonic speech preserved the actual occurrences of the court is open to question, but the defense takes the form, not so much of a refutation of the charges as a vindication of Socrates' own way of life and his ceaseless instigation of his fellow Athenians to follow the path of virtue with a greater intensity than they pursue the less important problems of government or money-making.

A reluctant and far from unanimous jury condemned Socrates to death. His obstinate refusal to compromise or accommodate himself to the jurors constituted contempt of court and left them with no recourse but condemnation. But Socrates deliberately chose this method as a justification of his life-long principle, and his closing days, during which he refused all opportunity for escape, were spent in philosophic conversations with his friends and disciples. The incalculable influence that he has exercised on all subsequent western thought constitutes his true memorial. For his denial of the subjective standard of the sophist Protagoras that "Man is the measure of all things," which would allow each man to be the judge of his own moral honesty, and for his insistence that truth must be sought in an abiding standard, he has deserved the grateful allegiance of all lovers of truth.

[439]

CHAPTER XXV

CITY–STATE RIVALRIES:
THE EMERGENCE OF MACEDON
ALEXANDER THE GREAT

THE LEADERSHIP OF SPARTA AND THEBES

The Significance of the Dates of the Fourth Century (404–323 B.C.). In the history, the art, and the literature of the fifth century, it is everywhere evident that the successful conclusion of the Persian Wars in 480 B.C. marked the dividing line between experiment and fulfillment. Prior to that year the Greeks had worked under the constraint of fear, but in the decades that followed victory there was no longer any external threat to thwart the flowering of the Hellenic genius.

The year 404 B.C., that is, the year of the defeat of Athens in the Peloponnesian War, is an equally significant date in dividing the distinct types of endeavor that belong to the fifth and to the fourth centuries, but the change that then took place was a very different one. Before 404 B.C., the spirit of the Athenians was that of a free, proud, and powerful people; after 404 B.C., it was that of a humbled and introverted one. The year of the death of Alexander the Great, 323 B.C., marks the close of the period known as the fourth century. Alexander's widespread conquests had led to the diffusion of Greek culture over vast areas of the ancient world, and the consequent extension of Hellenism so modified the nature of Greek thought expressed in art and letters as to initiate still another era, called the Hellenistic Period.

Events of the Transitional Years. One or two events belonging in reality to the fourth century have already forced their way into the discussion of the fifth century. The reign of terror under the Thirty Tyrants in 403 B.C. has been noted, as has the March of the Ten Thousand in 401 B.C., in which Xenophon participated, and of which he wrote in the *Anabasis*. The successful movement of that body of Greek troops through the unknown heart of Asia is of very considerable significance in a long survey of the relations between Europe and Asia. Eighty or ninety years earlier, in 490 B.C. and 480 B.C., the Greeks were rallying in a desperate struggle at Marathon and Salamis to drive back the armies of Persia; seventy-five years after the march, by 323 B.C., Alexander the Great was to bring that same Oriental nation under the sway of Hellas. The March of the Ten Thousand, therefore, lies midway between the Persian threat to Greek liberty and the subjugation of Persia by a Macedonian king. The death of Socrates in 399 B.C. has also been mentioned as a date in the fourth century that closes a long fifth-century career.

The Trend of Fourth-Century History. The historical details of the fourth century are so confused and in many cases of so little significance in comparison with fifth-century events that a recital of them would do little to clarify an historical background for a study of art and literature during the period. Nevertheless, it is possible to reach an understanding of the basic principle of interstate relationships and to point out one or two important battles, as well as to indicate the significant contributions of Philip II of Macedon and his son, Alexander the Great.

The guiding policy of the Greek states was the rapid formation of alliances to break down the too great power of any one city. This policy had already become operative in the fifth century, when Athens had built up her Empire, and Sparta, Corinth, and Thebes, the three most powerful independent states, had united to destroy her and succeeded in doing so in 404 B.C., when by the conditions of peace they caused the walls

[441]

connecting Athens and her port, the Piræus, to be razed and the Athenian fleet to be largely dismantled.

Spartan Hegemony. It was inevitable that the instinct for independence should have led the Greek city-states within the Athenian Empire to ally themselves with the Spartans, who promised to restore their liberty. But when the hegemony, or leadership, of Greece passed from Athens to Sparta in 404 B.C. and an opportunity was afforded to destroy the Athenian Empire, the Spartans, too, quickly forgot the cause of city-state liberty for all Hellas, for which they had fought in the Peloponnesian War. Even during the struggle, Sparta had sent out *harmosts,* or "governors," to organize the cities as they were set free from the dominance of Athens. By the end of the war, the rule of the resident harmost, with a local committee sympathetic to his aims, had been set up by Lysander in virtually all the cities that had once been members of the Athenian Empire. This pattern of government through a foreign leader supported by a cooperating group in a conquered state is familiar from the practice of conquest and government in many areas in our own day.

The harmosts imposed on the cities an oligarchic form of government and ruled with the stupidity and lack of sympathy to be expected from a state that was without experience in the government of others. The cities found to their dismay that what they had tolerated as a temporary and necessary expedient in war was to become a permanent foreign administration. The result was a general disillusionment among the outlying communities of Greece. But more significant was the formation of a new alliance in Greece itself, for Athens, Corinth, and Thebes now united to free themselves from the hateful dictation of Sparta.

The Rebuilding of the Walls of Athens. Late in the Peloponnesian War, Sparta and Persia had worked in harmony against Athens, but early in the fourth century they quarreled, and Agesilaus of Sparta led a mercenary force against the Persians in Asia Minor. Persia, in turn, exerted herself to promote the alliance of Athens, Corinth, and Thebes against Sparta, and she placed in charge of her own navy Conon, the Athenian admiral who had judiciously remained away from Athens after his defeat at Ægospotami in 405 B.C. In 394 B.C., Conon, commanding a Persian fleet, decisively defeated the Spartans at Cnidus, and in the following year, 393 B.C., he sailed boldly into the Piræus and superintended the rebuilding of the fortifications of that port and of the Long Walls connecting it with Athens. The walls that can still be seen in ruins about the Piræus are therefore the walls of Conon and not those of Themistocles. The erection of Conon's walls reversed in some measure the effect of that dramatic day in 404 B.C. when the walls between Athens and the Piræus had been razed to the music of flute-girls.

The Political Strategy of Sparta. During the early years of the fourth century, it was the policy of Sparta to break up any growing alliance that might threaten her supremacy, even though this meant an unjustifiable interference in the internal affairs of other states. She presently became aware of the rising threat from the powerful city of Thebes, with whom the other Greek cities, who hated and feared Sparta's power, were associating themselves. Consequently, in 382 B.C., a Spartan army made a successful attack on Thebes and set up in power a small oligarchical pro-Spartan group. The arbitrary establishment in Thebes of a government favorable to Sparta was simply a continuation of the policy that had been initiated through the system of Spartan harmosts ruling with the help of obsequious councils of citizens.

The Theban loyalists sought refuge in Athens, where they were organized under an able commander, by the name of Pelopidas, who in 379 B.C. led his band secretly back to Thebes, slew the Spartans who were in charge, and established a democratic form of government in the city. This was accomplished with the unofficial assistance of private Athenian citizens, for peace formally existed at that time between Athens and Sparta. A year later, however, Athens was to ally herself openly with

Thebes and to enter into a state of war with Sparta. Associated with Pelopidas was a philosopher, named Epaminondas, who appeared harmless enough to the Lacedæmonians, but who, as Tyrtæus had done in Sparta three centuries before, was to inspire the youth in Thebes with ideals of freedom and patriotism.

The Battle of Leuctra (371 B.C.); Theban Hegemony. For a time the democratic government continued to exist in Thebes, but nothing further had occurred to dislodge Sparta from her preeminent position in Greece. However, eight years after the successful raid of Pelopidas, in 371 B.C., the Spartans marched into Bœotia to crush the Theban power. The two armies met in the Battle of Leuctra, and the Thebans were victorious. Both the date and the battle are important. It was the first time in history that the Spartans had been defeated by inferior numbers; the old tradition of Spartan invincibility was shattered, and the hegemony of Greece passed to Thebes.

The Battle of Leuctra also marked the introduction by the former philosopher, Epaminondas, of a new military maneuver, for, instead of advancing with a long line of battle of equal depth, he massed a wedge of Thebans fifty spears deep on the left wing, and while his weaker lines held the attention of the Spartans elsewhere, he penetrated at that one point. This ingenious method was long employed in military strategy, until the invention of gunpowder destroyed its effectiveness.

In the following year, 370 B.C., Epaminondas took his Theban soldiers into Laconia, a new experience for Sparta. Success in battle had bred insolence in the Thebans, and had given currency to the expression "Leuctric pride." The initiative, both in war and in diplomacy, rested for the moment with Thebes, and the lesser communities began to look to her rather than to the Spartans, who had for so many centuries dominated the life of the Peloponnese. The former allies of Sparta were encouraged to revolt, and a new city, Megalopolis, or Great City, was founded as the capital of an Arcadian confederacy. Twice again Epaminondas led his forces against Sparta, freeing the Messenians and Sparta's serfs, the Helots, but breeding anarchy rather than order in the Peloponnese; and then the basic policy of the Greek states manifested itself once more, drawing Sparta and Athens together to destroy the power of Thebes, which had grown too great. The Athenians responded to the first Spartan appeals with an army sufficient to save the Lacedæmonians from destruction. From the outset there was no doubt that Athens would find her traditional enmity toward Sparta less intense than her fear of an unrestricted Theban ascendancy over Greece.

The Battle of Mantinea (362 B.C.). In 362 B.C., Epaminondas, with the aid of some other states, undertook to break down the new-formed alliance, and the Battle of Mantinea was fought against Sparta, Athens, and their associates. The actual battle was a victory for the Thebans, but it ended their power, for Epaminondas was killed. Since Pelopidas had been slain during the previous year, Thebes was now leaderless. Theban success had been built too much on the personality of these two men, and there was no one left to carry on the work of the state or to consolidate Greece. The Battle of Mantinea in 362 B.C., like the Battle of Leuctra in 371 B.C., is of distinct importance in the confused history of the alliances and counteralliances, raids, and battles that mark the first four decades of the fourth century.

The End of Theban Hegemony. At Mantinea the leadership of Greece passed from Thebes, but it descended to no other state. Quiet reigned, not the quiet of good will or constructive statesmanship, but the quiet of exhaustion and impotence. Since the beginning of the Peloponnesian War in 431 B.C., the Greeks had ruthlessly slaughtered the flower of their manhood, and now the end had come. Xenophon closes his *Hellenica* with an account of the Battle of Mantinea, and there is no better way to picture conditions in Greece in 362 B.C. than to translate the final paragraph of his history:

When the battle had been fought, the very opposite of what all

[445]

men expected came to pass. For when practically the whole of Greece, ranged on different sides, had met, there was no one who did not believe that if a battle were fought, the victors would rule and the vanquished would become subject. But the gods brought it to pass that each side erected a trophy, claiming that they had

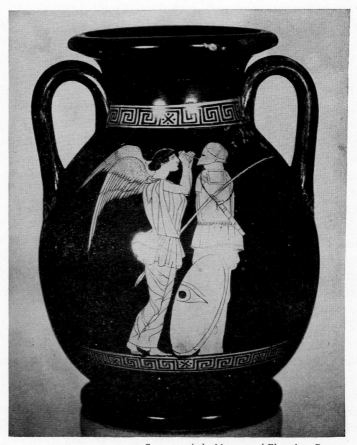

Courtesy of the Museum of Fine Arts, Boston

FIGURE 125. NIKE, OR VICTORY, SETTING UP A TROPHY. Attic red-figured pelike. Sixth century B.C. The trophy consisted of the armor of a defeated enemy draped on a wooden pole and erected at the turning point of battle.

been victorious, and neither side was able to prevent the other from erecting it. Each side, claiming victory, gave back the dead under truce, and each side, as though acknowledging defeat, received them back under like conditions. And though each side claimed to have conquered, neither of them, either in territory, state, or government, appeared to have any greater advantage than before the battle took place. Indecision and confusion became greater in Greece after the battle than before.

THE RISE OF MACEDON

Philip II. Union was closer to the Greek states than they realized, but its coming was to be both unexpected and unwelcome. To go back a little, in 368 B.C., three years after the Battle of Leuctra, the Thebans, in the course of a successful expedition to the north, took the young prince, Philip, back to Thebes as a hostage, to guarantee the good behavior of Macedon. For three years he remained in Thebes, where he was treated with the respect due his rank. There he learned much of Theban military science, of Greek culture, of Greek political institutions, and above all of the fatal lack of unity among the Greek states. This information he was soon to put to effective use.

The Character of Philip. In 359 B.C., at the age of twenty-four, he became Philip II of Macedon. During the twenty-three years of his reign, he undertook to strengthen and enrich his kingdom by whatever means that might best be done. He was a man of great political judgment, of high military genius, and of inexhaustible patience. He could be diplomatic, friendly, harsh, or unscrupulous, as occasion demanded. The force of arms and judicious bribery were alike made to serve his purpose.

The Extension of Philip's Power. By building up his army along the lines that he had learned from the efficient military system in Thebes, and by vigorously working the gold mines in the neighborhood of the Macedonian city of Philippi, he gained the resources, both military and economic, with which

[447]

to extend his ambitious projects. Every movement of dissension among the Greeks and every instance of internal strife in a powerful state such as Athens was seized upon by Philip to consolidate his power, first in Macedonia and later in Greece proper. Amphipolis, the city whose capture by the Spartans had caused the banishment of Thucydides more than half a century before, fell into the hands of Philip, and in 356 B.C., the year of the birth of his son Alexander, he captured Pydna and Potidæa. For some eight years Philip proceeded with his plans, meeting no serious obstacle, for the Athenians, his logical opponents, were either too deeply engrossed with other problems or too blind to the menace against their own interests to offer serious opposition to him.

The Opposition of Demosthenes. However, in 351 B.C., the orator Demosthenes, then thirty-two years of age, arose in the Athenian Assembly, and in a speech which has come to be called the *First Philippic,* denounced Philip and sought to rouse the Athenians to a sense of the peril that threatened them in the north. But, in spite of the unremitting opposition of Demosthenes and the anti-Macedonian party, Philip was able to further his plans, playing one state against another and taking advantage of the treachery of cities and parties in Greece. It was the dream of Demosthenes that Athens should again become a great imperialistic power, but the hope was an idle one, for the stern qualities of the fifth-century Athenians had disappeared and the wars of the city were now fought with mercenaries. In addition, there were men in the city who honestly believed that the best policy for Athens was an alliance with Philip, which would leave them free to carry on their commerce.

The Battle of Chæronea (*338* B.C.). Philip completed his conquests in the region around Macedonia by the capture through treachery of Olynthus, which brought the whole Chalcidic peninsula into his hands. Shortly thereafter, at the invitation of the Amphictyonic Council, the governing body of a religious and political league embracing many of the Greek states, which was at war with Phocis, Philip came through the Pass of Thermopylæ, where the Persians had destroyed Leonidas and his three hundred Spartans more than a century before, in 480 B.C. This first entry of Philip into central Greece occurred in 346–345 B.C., and a year or two later, after an interval during which he again engaged in war in the north, he once more entered Greece at the invitation of the Council. At length, after these demonstrations of Philip's power, Demosthenes aroused to a hasty union those Greek cities that were not in sympathy with the Amphictyonic Council; the effort came too late; and a Macedonian victory at the important Battle of Chæronea, near Thebes, in 338 B.C., gave Philip control of all the states of Greece. Quickly he consolidated his position. A congress was called at Corinth to form a new league of Greece, with nominal autonomy for all states. The pretence of freedom was an idle gesture, for Philip had no thought of relinquishing the power to dictate, which is the negation of liberty. At his own insistence he was elected general, and it was proposed to undertake a joint expedition of all Greece against Persia, in order that Hellas might thus be united in devotion to a common cause. The death of Philip two years later delayed that project for the moment.

The Significance of the Macedonian Victory. There has been much argument as to whether Greek liberty perished at Chæronea. Demosthenes and many thousands like him, who refused to recognize the Macedonians as Hellenes but identified them rather as semi-civilized barbarians, would have said without question that it did. But a new order of government was inevitably approaching. The Greek city-states had shown themselves lamentably incapable of working out any reconciliation between their fanatical love of local independence and a larger unity, in which safety might have been found. It is more reasonable, therefore, to look on Chæronea, as on Ægospotami, Leuctra, and Mantinea, as a battle which shifted the leadership to other hands within Greece. Liberty

[449]

was already languishing in Hellas before the shock of Chæronea.

The Death of Philip II. In 336 B.C., Philip was assassinated and was succeeded by his son, Alexander, who quickly became known as Alexander the Great. Macedon did not disintegrate when Philip II died, because he had by various means built up a powerful nation to bequeath to his son. In estimating the career of Philip, some large measure of the subsequent achievements of Alexander the Great must be credited to the shrewd statecraft of his father, on whose foundation Alexander built. It is also well to remember that in spite of the unquestioned duplicity with which Philip conducted some of his foreign relations, the principal source of information about the Macedonian king is the bitterly antagonistic series of speeches of his great opponent Demosthenes.

Alexander the Great (336–323 B.C.). Alexander early showed the precocity that was to abide with him through his brief dynamic career. He had a romantic and vivid imagination, and was filled with admiration for the Homeric hero Achilles, whose valor he took as the model of his own conduct. The tutor and companion of the young Alexander was the philosopher Aristotle.

Alexander's first years on the throne were not unaccompanied by threats against the stability of his nation. Thrace to the east, Illyria to the west, and Greece to the south all hailed the death of the seasoned Philip and the accession of his young son as a splendid opportunity to free themselves from the yoke of Macedon. Alexander, however, was quite capable of defending his territories. Rapid victorious expeditions against the three revolting areas brought them back within his power.

Shortly thereafter, a false report of his death was followed by the open revolt of Thebes, which was quickly suppressed by Alexander, who arrived in person, and, as an example to the rest of Greece, razed the city. Jealous Greek neighbors joined with Alexander at this time in wreaking a fearful vengeance on Thebes. Thousands of citizens were slaughtered, and others were sold into slavery. Only the temples of the gods and the house of Pindar were spared by Alexander as a gesture of his veneration for Greek religion and his respect for Greek letters.

The Expedition to Asia. Meanwhile, the mind of the young king was turning to the campaign of eastern conquest which his father had planned, and by 334 B.C., Alexander was ready to cross into Asia on the expedition against Persia, where he was to spend the remaining eleven years of his life on an unparalleled pilgrimage of conquest, settlement, and organization, which he hoped might result in a new world empire, united by willing cooperation of Greeks and Asiatics for common ends. The military accomplishments of the energetic Alexander cannot be told adequately in a few pages, but in limited space the most satisfactory account of his progress may be gained by describing the events in chronological order.

The Battle at the River Granicus (334 B.C.). When Alexander left Greece in 334 B.C., he took with him some thirty thousand foot soldiers and five thousand cavalry, and turned his back on Europe with the confidence of a man to whom success alone was possible. On reaching the site of Troy, Alexander paid his devotions to the heroes of the Homeric poems—Protesilaus, the first Greek to leap ashore, Achilles, his ideal hero, and Patroclus, the companion of Achilles. With these rites performed, he moved forward with his army to face the advancing Persians. The first of four major battles was fought at the River Granicus, near the Hellespont, where Alexander was successful against a force of approximately equal numbers. He then proceeded down the coast of Asia Minor, reducing as he went the once Greek cities of Miletus and Halicarnassus. At each city he was obliged to undertake vigorous and systematic siege operations before effecting a capture, and the months slipped by during the campaigns.

The Gordian Knot. The winter of 333 B.C. was spent in Asia Minor, and during that time Alexander went to Gordium to attempt to untie the Gordian knot which fastened the yoke to the chariot of Gordius, for an oracle said that the man who

[451]

loosened it should rule Asia. Failing in his attempt, Alexander drew his sword, and cut the knot. It is an incident which, with peculiar naïveté, is frequently told to illustrate the vigorous purpose of Alexander, and yet it indicates neither manual skill nor political sagacity, but only impetuosity. It was an attitude that served him well enough while the tides of fortune ran in his favor.

The Battle of Issus (*333* B.C.) In the fall of 333 B.C., in a narrow pass between the mountains and the sea, the Battle of Issus was fought, the second major battle of Alexander's expedition. Alexander himself led the cavalry to the attack, and the result was a disordered rout of the enemy, rather than a battle. As the Greeks pressed on toward the place where Darius had taken his stand, the Persian king turned and fled, abandoning his mother, wife, and children to Alexander, who treated them with a respect which was seldom observed by conquerors at that time, and which indicates very clearly the purpose of ultimate reconciliation that he cherished. A city, one of the many founded in the east by Alexander, was established on the site of the Battle of Issus to commemorate the victory.

The Siege of Tyre (*332* B.C.), *and the Founding of Alexandria* (*331* B.C.). In 332 B.C., Alexander captured the city of Tyre after an exceedingly difficult siege of several months, and reduced the fortress of Gaza, further to the south. During the same year, he had taken Egypt, without resistance, for the latter country had already been reduced by force to membership in the Persian Empire. He remained in Egypt until the spring of 331 B.C., making plans to set up a permanent government there, and in particular attending personally to the founding and street planning of the new seaport Alexandria, which, with rare judgment, he marked out to be the commercial successor to the city of Tyre.

The Battle of Gaugamela (*331* B.C.). Alexander spent considerable time in Egypt, busied with the organization of the country. His eyes, however, were on the east, rather than on the south or west, and, consequently, early in 331 B.C., he came back to Tyre, whence, after a brief interval, he marched toward Babylon with forces, both of infantry and cavalry, considerably larger than those with which he had originally crossed from Europe. He was now freely enlisting Persian soldiers in his army. He met with no opposition either at the Euphrates or the Tigris, doubtless much to his surprise. At Gaugamela he came upon a Persian army of prodigious numbers. There the third important battle against his enemies was fought and won. Darius again sought safety in flight to the interior, and for a time Alexander allowed him to escape. Instead of pursuing him, he turned to the south and took, one after another, the great cities of Babylon, Susa, and Persepolis, with their fabulous accumulation of treasure.

In the spring of 330 B.C., he was at length ready to press on to Ecbatana, where Darius had taken up his quarters. By the time Alexander reached that city, Darius had fled, and when Alexander did come upon the king, it was to find him already slain by his own treacherous attendants. Again Alexander showed his tact and generosity by sending the body of the king back to Persepolis to be interred with the honor due to a Persian monarch.

The Battle of the Hydaspes River Against King Porus (326 B.C.). The unquenchable energy of Alexander was carrying him far into the interior, beyond the furthest penetration of his Greek predecessors, and it was to bring him into armed conflict with tribes and kings that can have been but shadowy names to him when he left Macedon on his campaign of conquest. The circumstances of the moment were now guiding his movements, and it was the pursuit of one of the assassins of Darius that led him next into Hyrcania. This was in 330 B.C., and the following four years found him moving relentlessly on to Afghanistan, over the Hindu Kush mountains, and finally through the Khyber Pass into India.

Everywhere vast territories fell into his hands, for the countless hordes of the east were no match for the hardened and disciplined army that Alexander led. The rapid recital of these

[453]

penetrations gives little idea of the enormous geographical difficulties that hampered even the most brilliant military strategy during the four years from 330 to 326 B.C. No great armies have since succeeded in approaching those regions over the same routes. In 326 B.C., on the Hydaspes River in India,

Photograph by Alinari

FIGURE 126. LION HUNT FROM THE SO-CALLED ALEXANDER SARCOPHAGUS. Fourth century B.C. Istanbul.

he fought against King Porus the last and greatest of his four pitched battles. Here, too, he was successful.

Alexander Turns Homeward. The zeal of Alexander was still strong for conquest and exploration, but his Macedonian soldiers began to rebel against the continuation of the Asiatic campaign. For eight years they had been away from their

[454]

homes, and so far beyond the known limits of geography had they penetrated, that they thought that they were already close to the Ocean Stream that bounded their flat earth. Alexander was obliged to hearken to their words, and the long journey homeward began. He chose a route that took him along the shore of the Indian Ocean, where the ravages of desert and sun took great toll of his men. In 324 B.C., he reached Susa again, leaving the story of his exploration and conquest in the confused traditions of the east and in many a geographical name, such as Samarkand and Khandahar.

Death of Alexander (*323* B.C.). Toward the end of 324 B.C., Alexander left Susa and proceeded to Babylon, where he received the ambassadors of many western states, to whose apprehensive ears news of his conquests had come. Alexander's immediate plan appears to have been to lead an expedition to Arabia and the Persian Gulf in order to establish trade routes between India and Egypt. It is the same strategic territory that is now served by the Suez Canal. That purpose was never to be realized, for in the summer of 323 B.C., thirteen years after ascending the throne, he died at Babylon. He was thirty-three years of age. Whether he would have succeeded, had he lived, in duplicating his great Asiatic conquests in the new fields of northern Africa, Sicily, and Italy can never be told. The time was not far distant when the tide was to turn, and even the kingdom of Alexander was to fall a prey to Rome.

Significance of Alexander's Conquests. Alexander combined the qualities of energy, ambition, and military genius with the opportunity for conquest, which he was quick to seize. A tireless nature and a virile curiosity drove him on to further and further goals. He accompanied his military exploits with consistent efforts to consolidate his conquests by permanent organization, to which end he established many cities throughout Asia and Africa, some of which exist today. He cherished also the greater aim, though it met with but indifferent success, of having the Greeks and Asiatics assimilated into a single people.

[455]

Alexander's active career belongs to the closing years of the fourth century, for the date of his death is taken as the dividing line between that period and the Hellenistic Age. As a background for the study of Greek civilization, the enormous expansion of his years of conquest is probably more important in opening fields of new endeavor and in enlarging the limited sphere of activity that was characteristic of Greek art and artists through the earlier classical centuries, than in the actual contributions to civilization which he made during his military campaigns.

Thus, while the year 323 B.C. is not as immediately significant as were the years 480 B.C. and 404 B.C., which marked the divisions between the archaic period and the fifth century, and between the fifth century and the fourth century, the tremendous extension of the Greek language and of Greek culture through the campaigns of Alexander was directly responsible for taking away from Athens and centering in other cities the schools of art and letters during the Hellenistic Period. The career of Alexander therefore affected the future age rather more than it did the fourth century.

CHAPTER XXVI

THE SCULPTURE OF THE FOURTH CENTURY (404–323 B.C.)

INDIVIDUALISM IN ART

The Background of Fourth-Century Art. The inspiration of archaic art had been endeavor and experiment; of fifth-century art, religion and the submergence of the individual in the state. In the fourth century, experiment was clearly unnecessary, since technical proficiency had long since been attained and showed no signs of waning. In attempting to judge the significance of fourth-century art, the most important historical circumstance to be borne in mind is the defeat of Athens and the fall of her Empire in 404 B.C. After that, the impersonal quality of fifth-century art quickly gave place to the individualism characteristic of the work of the fourth century.

The Causes of Individualism. It is not difficult to see why the individual citizen should now have been compelled to rely on his own resources, rather than finding his old satisfaction in the communal life of his state. When an Athenian in the fifth century, obeying the adjuration of Pericles in his *Funeral Speech,* fixed his eyes on the beauty of Athens and became filled with a sense of the greatness of her institutions, he might well have felt that the glorification of the state was sufficient compensation for the submergence of his own personality. In the fourth century, however, he had no such solace. He could reflect only in sorrow on the lost leadership of a once great city, and inevitably he turned for comfort to his own soul.

[457]

FIGURE 127. MARBLE HEAD FROM CHIOS. Fourth century B.C. Portions of the hair on either side were made separately and later attached. The repose and individualism of the fourth century are evident in this figure.

Nor was the movement toward individualism confined to Athens, for in various ways the same trend may be observed in the other states of Greece. The individual assumed a new importance, and that importance quickly showed itself in art.

Courtesy of the Metropolitan Museum of Art

FIGURE 128. MARBLE RELIEF FROM RHODES. Fourth century B.C. The figure of the youthful horseman and his mount both reflect the individualism of the period.

sonal than national. Though the types of the gods changed more slowly, because of religious conservatism, yet even in the motivation of the religious offerings was more often per-Dedications were more freely made by private citizens, and statues of the deities there is an unmistakably finite quality that differentiates the work of a fourth-century artist from the remote dignity of a god sculptured by Pheidias.

Even more significant, however, was the choice of subjects. Personality and allegory found a place, and the statues began to portray momentary human emotions. Such a relief as that of the young athlete riding a horse (Figure 128) has the quality of a substantive statue, designed to be understood without immediate relation to its environment; this quality was absent in similar themes that are a part of the Panathenaic Procession on the Ionic frieze of the Parthenon.

Portraiture is also a type of individualized art appropriate to the fourth century and later. It could not well have flourished in the atmosphere of the previous age, in which the community meant so much and the individual so little. It was not that the earliest artists were unable to cope with portraiture. The statues of Pericles and the portrayal by Pheidias of his own countenance on the shield of the Athena Parthenos testify to their skill in that field. Yet, in each case, exact portraiture was only an incidental objective. The little gold likeness of Pheidias was looked upon as blasphemy, and the face of Pericles, while recognizable as the great leader, was idealized into the concept of statesman and general in the same way as a contemporary statue of Zeus or Athena was modeled to convey the divine attributes of a deity. The artist of the fifth century regarded his skill as a means to convey his thought, but never to be used merely for copying a visible object, animate or inanimate.

The Eirene and Plutus of Cephisodotus. For many reasons, the group of Eirene and Plutus, or Peace and Wealth, by Cephisodotus (Figure 129), affords an appropriate example of the transition from the art of the fifth to that of the fourth century. Cephisodotus was apparently the father or elder brother of Praxiteles, and his work, as illustrated by this statue, indicates how he carried the technique that he learned in the fifth century over into a subject that was characteristic of the fourth century. In certain details of execution, notably in the rendering of the drapery, which falls over one slightly bent

[460]

knee, the statue owes much to fifth-century inspiration. The introduction of symbolism by the allegorical representation of the child Plutus, or Wealth, held safe on the arm of Eirene,

Courtesy of University Prints

FIGURE 129. EIRENE AND PLUTUS, OR PEACE AND WEALTH, BY CEPHISODOTUS. Roman copy of a Greek original of the early fourth century B.C. Glyptothek, Munich. This is one of the best-known fourth-century statues of adult and child.

or Peace, belongs essentially to the fourth century, and points in particular to the dearly bought lesson of the recently concluded Peloponnesian War.

[461]

Though the motif of an adult and child was known in art as early as the archaic period, it was only in the fourth century that the theme was made the most prominent part of a major group. In the statue by Cephisodotus the Goddess of Peace gazes on the infant Plutus with maternal tenderness; the fleeting expression on her face has been called forth by some chance act of the child, and it may vanish as quickly. There is nothing of the eternal impersonality of a deity, which by its very nature must avoid an expression of the moment. The popularity of this and similar groups indicates the degree to which the people of Greece had changed in thought and taste during a few short years. It is interesting to note that Aristophanes also dealt with an economic theme and the importance of the god of wealth in his comedy, the *Plutus,* which was presented in 388 B.C., though the literary treatment of allegory differs sharply from that of Cephisodotus in his statue.

The Three Chief Sculptors of the Fourth Century. In the fourth century, there were three principal sculptors, Praxiteles, Scopas, and Lysippus, whose works very largely illustrate the contributions of that age to art, just as the qualities of fifth-century art could be observed in the work of Myron, Pheidias, and Polycleitus.

PRAXITELES

With Praxiteles the individualistic qualities of the fourth century appear most clearly, although he was still sufficiently under the influence of Hellenic restraint to exclude from his work the exaggerated and the undignified. His ability to represent all human emotions is beyond controversy, yet he chose to confine his studies to the softer and more reflective moods.

The Statue of Hermes and Dionysus. The best known statue of Praxiteles is that of Hermes holding the child Dionysus on his arm (Figure 130). It was found in 1877 in the Heræum at Olympia, where Pausanias, the traveler of the

[462]

second century after Christ, tells of seeing it. Hence the identification seems complete. Fortunately, the statue had fallen in the soft mud, and for that reason the face of Hermes is quite unmarred. It is sculptured in beautiful Parian marble.

Photograph by Alinari

FIGURE 130. THE GOD HERMES HOLDING THE INFANT DIONYSUS, BY PRAXITELES. Fourth century B.C. Olympia. The group represents a scene of momentary interest.

In the Hermes group, Praxiteles has continued the theme of adult and child that was introduced by Cephisodotus. The god is standing quietly, even indolently, holding up in one hand something, perhaps a bunch of grapes, for the amusement

[463]

of the child. He is looking off into space with a mildly reflective expression on his face. The body of Hermes is carved with the gentle graceful curve so characteristic of the artist that it has been called the Praxitelean curve. The infant Dionysus is created with less skill, for the form of the body resembles that of a miniature adult rather than of a child. The proper representation of children's figures is an accomplishment of the Hellenistic Period, which is to follow. In this individualized figure of Hermes, modeled on the type of the young athletic Athenian rather than on the impersonal and abstract conception of a god, Praxiteles has bridged the gap between god and man.

The Controversy About the Statue. When the statue was first found, there was an insistent opinion that it was not an original work of Praxiteles, but a good Roman copy that was seen by Pausanias. Within recent years the same controversy has arisen again. If the statue is an actual work of Praxiteles, then it is the single identified authentic work of one of the six great sculptors of the classical period which can be studied directly and not through later copies. The statue has some defects, both of conception and workmanship, which may, according to the differing opinion of scholars, be attributed either to the fact that it is a Roman copy or to the limitations of Praxiteles himself. When Praxiteles introduced sentimentalism into his figures, he thereby renounced for himself and his successors some measure of the strength of fifth-century work. Consequently, in the eyes of certain critics the statues of Praxiteles suffer from too great delicacy of execution and too much gentleness, if not weakness, of countenance. It should be added that in antiquity the Hermes was not considered one of the best works of Praxiteles, and it will be well, in estimating the heated controversy on the authenticity of the statue, to remember that, as with the Homeric poems, the intrinsic qualities of the work remain quite unchanged, whatever may be the conclusions of scholars.

The Aphrodite of Cnidus. A work of Praxiteles, more

[464]

famous in antiquity, is the Aphrodite of Cnidus, of which the best Roman copy is now preserved in the Vatican Museum (Figure 131). The statue shows the same poise, flow of line,

Photograph by Alinari

FIGURE 131. APHRODITE OF CNIDUS BY PRAXITELES. Roman copy of a Greek original of the fourth century B.C. Vatican. The characteristic S-curve of Praxiteles is evident.

[465]

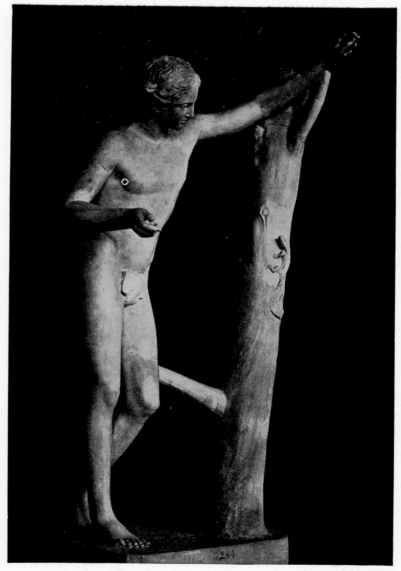

Photograph by Alinari

FIGURE 132. APOLLO SAUROCTONUS, OR APOLLO THE LIZARD-SLAYER.
Roman copy of a Greek original of the fourth century B.C. Vatican.
This figure might more appropriately be named "The Boy Watching a
Lizard."

[466]

qualities of carving, and Praxitelean curve as the Hermes group. The face again bears an expression of quiet youthful innocence rather than of strong emotion. Pliny, the Roman critic, tells an anecdote to illustrate the esteem in which the statue was held at Cnidus.

King Nicomedes later wished to buy it from the Cnidians, offering to pay the entire debt of the state, which was enormous. But they rightly preferred to endure any suffering rather than part with it, for by that statue Praxiteles spread the fame of Cnidus.

The popularity of the Aphrodite of Cnidus led to the frequent copying or adaptation of this statue in Roman times, often, as will be noted later, in the less tasteful manner of the Græco-Roman Age.

The Apollo Sauroctonus and Other Statues of Praxiteles. Praxiteles was a prolific sculptor, and many of his statues have become well known through Roman copies. The Marble Faun, celebrated by Hawthorne, is a copy of a work by Praxiteles, and it is known that he produced also statues of Eros, of Satyrs, and of Dionysus. His Apollo Sauroctonus, or lizard-slayer, was frequently copied in antiquity (Figure 132). The statue shows a boy, or the young god, supporting himself against a tree on which a lizard is climbing. The characteristic curve of the body is maintained, and one hand is extended to strike the lizard, according to the interpretation of those who first named the statue. The Praxitelean curve has, however, here degenerated from the quiet repose of the Hermes into a weak and slothful posture, so that the youth is scarcely energetic enough to kill the lizard. He watches it in complete indolence, and the uplifted hand is simply a variation of the pose, without the significance, of the raised arm of the god in the group of Hermes and Dionysus.

Qualities of Praxitelean Art. Grace, elegance, facility of execution, the easy curve, and the pensive expression are characteristic of Praxiteles. With his successors these elements

[467]

were to destroy the quality of permanence which the magnificent impersonal restraint of the fifth century had created. Yet the work of Praxiteles has been held in high esteem both in antiquity and in modern times.

Scopas

The Delineation of Emotion Under Stress. Scopas is the second artist of the fourth century to be described, although in date it is impossible to say whether he preceded or followed Praxiteles. Neither artist was directly influenced by the other, but rather each was in his own way working out in art the individualism of fourth-century society. Praxiteles had introduced quiet and restful emotion into his statues. Scopas reproduced intense, strained, passionate moods. Unfortunately, the archæological evidence, either by way of original statues or probable copies, on which to reconstruct an estimate of Scopas' artistic qualities, is small. Nevertheless, where evidence is available, the distinctive contribution of Scopas is clear even on casual examination.

The Career of Scopas. Certain activities of Scopas are known from literary accounts, and through them some significant dates may be assigned to him. He worked on the rebuilding and decoration of the Temple of Athena Alea at Tegea in the Peloponnese, after it had been burned in 395 B.C., nine years after the destruction of the Long Walls of Athens. In the excavations about this temple certain ancient Greek heads, made of local marble, were found, which are of the school of Scopas and marked with the influence of his technique. The heads are tilted up and turned slightly to the side. It requires but little imagination to fill out the remainder of the statues, showing hands clenched and eyes turned to Heaven in an agony of terror, surprise, or anguish.

Some of the technical devices by which Scopas attained his effects can also be analyzed. The eyes are set more deeply in the head and are looking upward. The proportion of length to breadth of the eyes is reduced, and the lower lid is turned up. The mouth is usually half open. Even the most casual study of Scopas and his school reveals the intensity and emotion of these works in contrast alike with the dispassionate severity of the sculpture of the fifth century and with the mood of calm reflection that Praxiteles, as well as some other contemporary artists, were able to impart to their statues.

The Mausoleum at Halicarnassus. Some years may have elapsed after the burning of the temple at Tegea in 395 B.C. before Scopas actually worked on its restoration. In any case, the statues from that temple must represent the efforts of his earlier years, for it is known also that he worked on the Mausoleum at Halicarnassus, the tomb of King Mausolus, which was started by his wife, Artemisia, after his death, about 353 B.C. In the absence of readily identifiable works of Scopas, either in original form or through

Photograph by the British Museum

FIGURE 133. KING MAUSOLUS. Fourth century B.C. A portrait of the king for whom the Mausoleum was built at Halicarnassus.

[469]

Roman copies, the sculptures of the Mausoleum merit very careful study, for the acknowledged association of Scopas with them conveys some information about the art of the time. Thus, in the proud kingly figure of Mausolus (Figure 133), there is a new quality, for Hellenic art has here been adapted to the portrayal of a definitely foreign type.

In the sweep and curve of the body of the charioteer from the smaller frieze of the Mausoleum (Figure 134), the intensity of purpose characteristic of the technique of Scopas presents a striking contrast with the repose of the Charioteer of Delphi, which was made early in the fifth century. So far as the figures from the Mausoleum may be understood to represent the emotional intensity of Scopas, he appears in his maturity to have moderated somewhat the passionate anguish that was described in connection with the Tegea heads in favor of a more quiet melancholy.

Qualities of Scopaic Art. If subjective opinion is to determine the relative dates of Praxiteles and Scopas, there is, in the exaggerated feeling of the latter, more suggestion of the lengths to which some of the Hellenistic artists were presently to go, and for that reason he may be regarded as coming closer, both in time and sympathy, to this later work. The variety of his interests is further attested by the titles of some of his works that have not survived. Most distinctive among these was a group of three figures representing Eros, Himeros, and Pothos, or Passion, Desire, and Yearning. The composition must have belonged to his later years, when he felt sufficient surety of touch to attempt to differentiate these three similar emotions in the countenances of three different figures.

LYSIPPUS

Portraits of Alexander the Great. The last great artist of the fourth century is Lysippus. The fact that he was the favorite portrait sculptor of Alexander the Great fixes the date of his activity as the later years of the fourth century and the

Photograph by the British Museum

FIGURE 134. CHARIOTEER. Fourth century B.C. This figure of the charioteer driving his team was taken from the small frieze of the Mausoleum. The sculptor has been peculiarly successful in suggesting rapid motion. Note the different conception of the subject from the Charioteer of Delphi, Figure 84.

[471]

beginning of the Hellenistic Period. The extant portraits of Alexander that may be traced to an original work of Lysippus indicate the manner in which the sculptor has sought to embody the power and determination of a world conqueror in a figure which at the same time purports to be a realistic likeness of an individual. Many later portraits of Alexander also owed their origin to the works of Lysippus, but it is very difficult to assign them to particular sculptors or schools with any degree of certainty.

The Apoxyomenus. Lysippus was a native of Sicyon, in the Peloponnese, and he there established a school of sculptors who were especially interested in athletic types. The essential qualities of his style may be seen in his best known work, that of an athlete scraping the encrusted oil and sand from his body with a strigil (Figure 135). The statue, which is known from various Roman copies, is usually referred to by its Greek name, the Apoxyomenus, or the youth using a strigil.

Lysippus, working in the same athletic tradition as his fifth-century colleague Polycleitus, has, however, modified the heavy set figures characteristic of the earlier sculptor, by increasing the total height of the body in relation to the length of the head. The ancient critics observed that he was not intent upon imitating the exact proportions of nature, but rather on studying the laws of perspective and pose in order to produce a certain desired effect when the finished statue was displayed. Lysippus rendered the hair in a lively manner; he made the heads of his statues small and the body muscles lean and hard. The technical execution of his work was exceedingly careful, with the smallest details worked out with extreme delicacy.

The Extension of Symbolism. Lysippus definitely abandoned the fifth-century practice of idealizing the features of his portrait heads, and though he did not intentionally exaggerate defects in his passion for realism, he did not on the other hand obscure whatever deficiencies he saw. To these qualities should be added the further development of sym-

[472]

FIGURE 135. THE APOXYOMENUS, OR YOUTH USING A STRIGIL, BY LYSIPPUS. Roman copy of a Greek original of the fourth century B.C. Vatican. Compare this figure with the heavier athletic type of Polycleitus, Figure 96.

bolism, which had appeared at the beginning of the fourth century in such a group as the Eirene and Plutus by Cephisodotus. This trait is illustrated in Lysippus' statue of Kairos, or Opportunity. The various descriptions of the statue, or allusions to it in verse and prose, indicate the approximate form that it must have taken. It portrayed a youth with winged feet, possibly resting on a ball, and with a razor in his hand to signify the keenness of opportunity. A tuft of hair grew from his brow, but his head was bald behind, suggesting that Time must be seized by the forelock, for, once gone, it is hard to recapture. The inept statue of Kairos, which, perhaps fortunately, has not been preserved, illustrates the decadence that followed on the abandonment of the impersonal fifth-century reserve and the introduction of sentiment and allegory in the work of the fourth-century artists.

Of the fifteen hundred statues, mostly in bronze, which Lysippus is said to have made, no certain original has been preserved. The metal proved too useful for the commercial and military needs of the following centuries, when many inspired works were melted down. For that reason it is very difficult to form objective estimates of the excellence of Lysippus' art, although the evidence of his popularity with the people of his own time and the conclusions that can be drawn from the Roman copies of the Apoxyomenus and of other statues of his school are sufficient to differentiate his purpose and his technique from that of his predecessors.

GRAVE STELÆ AND SARCOPHAGI

The beautiful reliefs with which the Greeks marked the graves of their dead were not confined to any single locality or to any one period. Because of the similarity of form they took, they afford the opportunity to study the development of Greek art in a restricted field through three or more centuries. A stele evidently intended to mark the grave of a young girl shows her with two pigeons that were her pets in life. A more

[474]

Photograph by Alinari

FIGURE 136. GRAVE STELE OF HEGESO. Fifth century B.C. This stele from the Dipylon Cemetery outside the city walls of Athens is characteristic of funeral monuments of the region.

[475]

famous stele is that which is identified by an accompanying inscription as the funeral monument of a woman named Hegeso (Figure 136).

Many of the stelæ bear inscriptions that permit of precise dating and identification with known historical incidents. Such a one is the monument of Dexileos, who is shown on horseback striking down an enemy. Dexileos was killed in the Corinthian War of 394 B.C. A characteristic style of gravestone shows the figure of the person commemorated in a calm and sober attitude, but usually with the full features of health, surrounded by sorrowing members of his family, whose faces reveal the lines and emaciation of grief. The essential Hellenic restraint of emotion is always felt in the representations of death.

CHAPTER XXVII

LITERATURE IN THE FOURTH CENTURY: ORATORY AND MIDDLE COMEDY

THE ORATORS

The study of human conduct in situations of difficulty and doubt, that supplied the plots of the tragedies, gave place in the fourth century to the systematic writings of the philosophers. Similarly, the recording of movements of national significance, which had attracted Herodotus and Thucydides, was superseded after the fall of Athens by the more personal and immediate problems of the orators.

The Beginnings of Oratory. Though formal oratory reached its most significant development during the fourth century, its origins go back to a much earlier time. In the epic poems of Homer, the vividness of the narrative depends in no small measure on the large place of direct discourse, or speech, and there are also splendid metrical orations in the poems, such as that in which Odysseus addresses Achilles, attempting to persuade him to return to the Greek army. The oratory of the epics is, however, part of a larger literary device, rather than a specific theme in itself. As a literary form, oratory may be said to have commenced as soon as men began to speak persuasively to their fellows in the Assembly or the law courts.

A Transitional Stage. Yet even if this definition is accepted, it is clear that there was an intermediate stage when men used all their ingenuity to compose effective speeches, before the characteristic and formalized stage of Attic oratory was

[477]

reached. It will be recalled, for instance, that when Solon, prior to his archonship in 594 B.C., wished to stir the Athenian people to the conquest of Salamis, he resorted to verse, in the absence of a developed art of oratory. In the fifth century, Pericles delivered addresses before the Athenians, which, for dignity, beauty of language, and above all for persuasiveness, may well have surpassed the formal compositions of the Attic orators of the fourth century.

No speech of Pericles has been preserved. We can come no nearer to his eloquence than the speeches that Thucydides wrote and attributed to him, or than a chance metaphor of poignant feeling, such as the one that Aristotle quotes from a *Funeral Oration* delivered over the Athenian dead, in which Pericles compares the city that has lost her young men in war to "the year that has been bereft of its spring." But it seems not unnatural that the oratory of Pericles should excel that of Demosthenes a century later, for Pericles was a man of larger vision and mental caliber, and was engaged with nobler issues than any that confronted Athens after his time.

Pericles spoke as a statesman. He would have scorned the name of orator, for, before his death, there was growing up in Athens a group of men whose task it was to teach legal and political eloquence for use in the law courts or the Assembly, a profession which to Pericles would have seemed a debasement of the art of public speaking. In the Athenian courts, however, each man was originally obliged to conduct his own case, and hence litigants turned to professional speechwrights, who composed an argument of prosecution or defense, as the occasion demanded, for memorization and delivery by the client.

The Canon of Ten Attic Orators. In the Hellenistic Period, the scholars of the Alexandrian Library drew up a Canon of Ten Attic Orators consisting of Antiphon, Andocides, Lysias, Isæus, Isocrates, Demosthenes, Æschines, Hypereides, Lycurgus, and Deinarchus. All the orators of the Canon lived and worked in Athens, though not all had been born there. The

[478]

age of their activity was from the late fifth to the late fourth century. Three distinctive types of oratory were developed. These were forensic, political, and epideictic oratory. By *forensic* oratory is meant the type of speech intended for delivery in the law courts; *political* oratory refers to the speeches in the Assembly; *epideictic* oratory refers to the formal oration pronounced in eulogy of the dead, or in exposition of some general principle, such as the *Panegyricus* of Isocrates, in which he urged Greek unity against Persia.

The orators took their profession seriously, evolving meticulous rules of construction and arrangement which were rigid in their exactions. The essential place of the orators in the society of Athens may readily be understood without insisting on the intricacies of their art, which in many instances were trivial and pedantic.

Antiphon and Andocides. The two earliest orators of the Canon were both active in the fifth century, and both were involved in the political movements that shook Athens during the Peloponnesian War. Antiphon, the older of the two, took part in the brief oligarchic revolution of 411 B.C.; while Andocides was arrested on the charge of complicity in the mutilation of the Hermæ on the night before the great expedition sailed against Syracuse in 415 B.C.

In the growth of oratory, the chief importance of Antiphon lies in the tetralogies that he wrote, not for presentation in specific cases, but as models. They were composed of alternating speeches of prosecutor and defendant upon a fictitious case and were written in a very stiff, set manner. The speeches of Andocides, on the other hand, were definitely related to his own political troubles in the city, but his place in the history of oratory is not high. He was less formalized than Antiphon, but there is little evidence of consistent and sustained mental capacity in his extant works, nor did he develop a good, convincing style.

Lysias (440–380 B.C.). The first of the Attic orators to achieve a distinctive place for the excellence of his prose was

[479]

Lysias. He was born of a Sicilian family, resident in Attica. His father, Cephalus, was a wealthy manufacturer of arms, a man of cultured interests, and a friend of Socrates. He had taken up his residence in Attica with the necessarily limited political status of a *metic,* or resident alien. Lysias and his brother Polemarchus received their training in rhetoric from the Sicilian teacher Tisias, with whom they both studied in Italy.

The two brothers returned to Athens during the turmoil of 411 B.C., but their political disability as metics debarred them from public life, although Lysias kept alive his intellectual interests by the composition of speeches and the delivery of lectures, while he pursued a lucrative business in armaments. During the reign of terror in 403 B.C., the Thirty Tyrants plotted the execution of wealthy metics without trial in order to confiscate their property. Both Lysias and Polemarchus were arrested, and the latter was put to death. On the restoration of the democracy, Lysias sought a just revenge against Eratosthenes, one of the guilty Tyrants, for his brother's death.

The Oration "Against Eratosthenes." The speech, *Against Eratosthenes,* which deals with this prosecution, is the single extant legal oration that Lysias himself delivered. It is remarkable not only for the clarity of style but for the interesting details of ancient life and customs that occur in it, such as the incidents surrounding the arrest of Polemarchus, and the description of the interior of the house where he was imprisoned for a time. The speech opens in a somewhat formal and rhetorical style, with a carefully balanced sentence structure.

There seems to me, gentlemen of the jury, to be no difficulty in commencing my accusation, but rather in reaching an end of what I have to say. So great in enormity and so many in number are the wrongs that my opponents have committed, that if one were to resort to falsehood, he could not accuse them of deeds more vile, nor if one wished to tell the truth, could he accomplish the whole

[480]

tale of iniquity. Inevitably the accuser would be worn out with speech, or time would fail him.

The speech is of considerable length, and of great interest for the student of politics and social life, as well as of formal oratory. It closes with the customary appeal to the judges for a favorable decision. "I shall now bring my accusation to an end; you have heard, you have seen, you have suffered, you have the facts; now render your verdict."

The Adaptation of the Style of Oratory to the Client. As a public speechwright Lysias succeeded in adapting his compositions to the individual character of his different clients as no other writer had been able to do. Thucydides had composed speeches for the characters in his *History,* causing Athenian, Spartan, and Corinthian generals, Melian ambassadors, and private citizens all to speak in the same difficult and academic style. Antiphon and Andocides left the mark of their own personalities on everything that they wrote. Lysias, however, both in phraseology and in the selection of material could adapt a speech to the wealthy businessman, the querulous invalid, the farmer improperly accused of impiety, or whatever other character the occasion might demand. With all his variations of style, he wrote in a simple, direct, and concise manner that won the admiration of ancient literary critics.

Isæus and Isocrates. Isæus represents the type of orator who employed his talents exclusively in the law courts, for all his extant speeches deal with inheritances. He was minute and accurate in his arguments, but the skillful advocate showed too clearly through all his utterances, arousing suspicion in the minds of his hearers even when he was most sincere.

Isocrates was a much more versatile man than Isæus and ranks high in the history of Attic oratory. He was born in 436 B.C. and died in 338 B.C. Thus his long life of ninety-eight years carried him from the days before the outbreak of the Peloponnesian War down to the Battle of Chæronea and made him a contemporary of both Pericles and Alexander the Great.

He made no public appearance himself, for a weak voice and diffident manner deterred him; but he established a school of rhetoric that quickly made him the most distinguished teacher in Greece and afforded him the opportunity to influence many of the literary, political, and military figures of the fourth century, who came to him for instruction.

Isocrates also indulged in the sophistic practice of writing difficult speeches in praise of unpopular things. The speech *On Busiris,* written in praise of an Egyptian king who sacrificed strangers to Zeus and the oration *On Helen,* lauding a literary character who was by that time considered the primal cause of all the woes of the Greeks and Trojans, illustrate the type of encomium that he affected. The political pamphlet was further developed by him, as illustrated in the *Panegyricus,* an appeal to Athens and Sparta to unite against Persia. It is the most important work of Isocrates. Not only is it an essay of considerable length, showing in its style and its content the toil that the author expended on it, but the speech reveals the manner in which, toward the end of the fourth century, the minds of some men were turning away from the separate city-state idea that had so long dominated Greek thinking, and were seeking instead some form of political union. Toward the end of his life, in 342 B.C., Isocrates wrote the *Panathenaicus,* a eulogy of Athens, which also affords a good example of epideictic oratory.

Demosthenes (384–322 B.C.). Unquestionably the ablest representative of formal Attic oratory was Demosthenes. He owes his distinction not alone to his power and eloquence of delivery, and to the organization of his speeches, but even more to the passionate conviction that lay behind them. Difficulties about his inheritance led him to overcome his defects of enunciation and to secure a legal training, so that he might recover his rights. In 363 B.C., he won his point in the law courts, and with it the scanty remnants of his estate, whereupon he turned to a career of speech writing.

The speeches of Demosthenes, of which a great number have

been preserved, may be divided into private and public orations. The former are rich as source material for a study of ancient law, finance, private economics, and family relations, as well as for an estimate of his literary style; but inevitably the orations dealing with politics command greater interest, for in some respects the foreign policy of Athens during the fourth century reads like a biography of Demosthenes.

The "Philippics" and the "Olynthiacs." In 359 B.C., Philip II ascended the throne of Macedon and commenced the systematic policy of expansion that was to bring all Greece under his control. Demosthenes recognized the danger to Athens, and for more than thirty years vigorously upheld the cause of the anti-Macedonian party in the city. In six speeches are collected the principal indictments that Demosthenes hurled against Philip. These are the *First Philippic,* delivered in 351 B.C., the *First, Second,* and *Third Olynthiacs,* all delivered in 349 B.C., the *Second Philippic,* which belongs to 344 B.C., and the *Third Philippic,* delivered in 341 B.C. In 388 B.C. the Battle of Chæronea was fought, resulting in victory for Philip. With that disaster the cause of Demosthenes was lost.

The Oration "On the Crown." In 330 B.C. Demosthenes delivered the longest, most eloquent, and most intricately composed speech of his career. This speech has been preserved under the title *On the Crown.* For the purposes of literary criticism, the circumstances leading up to the oration are less important than a recognition of the fact that Demosthenes within this single speech reviews and defends his own public policy and position in the state during the years that he stood as the great opponent of Philip and the threat of Macedonian encroachment.

All the skill and resource of a great pleader are present in the speech. Here one will find virulent and sometimes scurrilous attacks on Demosthenes' great political opponent Æschines, ardent defense of the integrity of his friends, impassioned pleading for a renewed spirit of patriotism in the name of the Athenians who died in defense of Greek freedom

[483]

in the Persian Wars a century and a half before, dispassionate appraisals of the duty of statesmanship, a moving description of the quiet courage with which the threat of disaster was met by Athens, and many other themes of intense feeling.

Though Demosthenes was technically successful in his defense, it is evident that the speech was delivered by a man whose effective political career had come to an end. For this reason among others the oration *On the Crown* appeals more strongly to the specialist on ancient oratory than to the admirer of the vitality of Greek achievement.

The Close of Demosthenes' Career. In 324 B.C., Demosthenes became involved in an unfortunate bribery affair in connection with Harpalus, an officer of Alexander the Great. For a time he went into exile. In 322 B.C., the year following the death of Alexander, Demosthenes saw an opportunity to free Athens from Macedonian authority; but Antipater, the Macedonian general, quickly quelled the attempt, and Demosthenes ended his life with poison to escape arrest. There can be no doubt of the power that Demosthenes wielded through his eloquence, but the wisdom of his purpose and the soundness of his judgment are not so clear. He was trying to rouse fourth-century Athenians to regain the imperial position that their forefathers had held a century before, and his cause was lost from the outset. He failed to see that the day of the city-state had passed, and by the very earnestness of his advocacy he stood in the way of any enlightened movement toward coöperative unity.

Æschines (389–320 B.C.). The public career of Demosthenes was intimately associated with that of Æschines, his contemporary and great opponent. Æschines, if we may believe the testimony of Demosthenes, had worked his way from humble origin, up through various occupations demeaning in the sight of a noble-born Athenian, such as usher in a school, minor actor, and clerk of the Assembly, into a commanding position in Athenian politics. In public life his policy varied from time to time. In 348 B.C., the year following the delivery of Demosthenes' three *Olynthiacs,* Æschines denounced Philip, although

[484]

in general he favored Athenian cooperation with Macedon, and was a member of various embassies which treated with Philip.

Much of the prejudice against Æschines has arisen from the vilification heaped upon him by Demosthenes, who, in turn, wins a more ready sympathy because of his sincere attachment to the cause of a free and revitalized Athens. That Æschines accepted handsome donations from Philip is, however, a regrettable commentary upon him as well as on the civic morality of the time.

Of the three extant speeches of Æschines, the most important is the oration *Against Ctesiphon,* delivered in 330 B.C. This speech is an indictment against Ctesiphon for proposing the award of a crown to Demosthenes. It takes the form of a lengthy and able, though not always scrupulously honest, review of the foreign policy of Athens during the previous generation, especially as Æschines and

Courtesy of the Metropolitan Museum of Art

FIGURE 137. AESCHINES. Roman copy of a Greek original.

Demosthenes urged their contrary policies. It is to this speech that Demosthenes replied in his oration *On the Crown.* Æschines was inferior to Demosthenes in his eloquence, his

[485]

thought, and in the disinterestedness of his pleas. Nevertheless, he stands high among Greek orators, although his reputation is lessened by inevitable comparison with his abler opponent.

Hypereides, Lycurgus, and Deinarchus. The three remaining orators of the Canon were all associated in one way or another with the political policies of Demosthenes and Æschines. They are not of great importance, either for the intrinsic value of their orations or for their influence on the political life of the fourth century. Only the unpredictable taste of the Alexandrian scholars, who included them in the Canon, has saved them from a deserved oblivion. For the sake of completeness their names are added—Hypereides, Lycurgus, and Deinarchus.

MIDDLE COMEDY

The Transition. During the fourth century, a new form of comedy arose, which, for convenience, is called Middle Comedy. Although one feels peculiarly helpless in trying to describe a type of literature of which not a single complete example has been preserved, unless the later plays of Aristophanes be included in this division, the nature of the change from the characteristic political satire of Old Comedy, and the reasons for it, can be readily understood. During the fifth century, while Athens was still a free state and democratic government afforded liberty of conduct to the citizens, Old Comedy, with its sharp, personal, political satire, flourished, for the Athenians could enjoy laughing at themselves and their institutions. But after the destruction of the city by the Spartans and the fall of the democracy in 404 B.C., there was small pleasure to be found in jesting at institutions that were now under foreign domination. Consequently, the personal and political features of comedy were abandoned, and in their place appeared Middle Comedy, with a mythological travesty, a burlesque of the dining table, a literary parody, or a satire on current life as the basis of the plot. Thus the writers adapted themselves quickly to the change in public psychology.

The Nature of Middle Comedy. The known facts about Middle Comedy may be briefly set down. Some eight hundred plays were familiar to Athenæus, who in the third century after Christ wrote his discursive treatment of the *Philosophers at Dinner,* with extended quotations from the comic poets, a very large proportion of which were given over to long lists of fishes, wines, and other foods. These details, together with the characterization of the ubiquitous parasite, or professional diner-out, appear to have amused the devotees of Middle Comedy. The lack of originality in Middle Comedy is further indicated by the free use of mythological or literary parody. The themes that in the fifth century had been employed in tragedy were treated in farcical manner by the writers of Middle Comedy, who also took delight in introducing such literary figures as Sappho, Archilochus, Hesiod, or Plato in ridiculous scenes.

The plots, none of which have great dramatic value, were centered about trades and professions of the city, as can be concluded from known titles, such as the *Perfume Dealer,* the *Doll Maker,* the *Shepherd,* or the *Jeweler.* The anagnorisis, or recognition scene, which was used in tragedy as early as the time of Æschylus, was frequently an important element in a play of Middle Comedy, where confusion of identity played a large part. Comedies of character, featuring the avaricious, the irate, or the meddlesome man, occur both in Middle and New Comedy, which succeeds it and is often very difficult to differentiate from it.

The Writers of Middle Comedy. The names of nearly two score writers of Middle Comedy are known. Of these the most noteworthy are Antiphanes, Alexis, Diphilus, and Philemon. The industry of the poets is attested by the tradition that each of the first two mentioned wrote about two hundred comedies. The great number of plays that belong to Middle Comedy, and especially the large quantity assigned to a single writer—such as Alexis, who is said to have composed two hundred and forty-five comedies—is perhaps the strongest

[487]

indication of the triviality of the themes. Whereas the riotous humor of Old Comedy provided a vehicle for serious philosophy and deep conviction, the clever, witty themes of Middle Comedy flowed from personal vivacity and little else.

The Athenians were still wounded and bewildered by the destruction of their Empire, and Middle Comedy provided relaxation for a moment. It was, however, an unnatural poetic invention of a century that was to find its more appropriate outlet in the prose of oratory, and its more mature intellectual development in the writings of the philosophers. The characteristics of Diphilus and Philemon can be studied, not only in extant fragments, but in the complete Latin plays of Plautus and Terence, which were translated or adapted from original works of these writers of Greek Middle Comedy.

One other phase of comedy remains; that is, New Comedy, which flourished after the death of Alexander the Great. In the discussion of Alexandrian literature, the characteristics of New Comedy will be explained.

CHAPTER XXVIII

THE HUMANISTIC PHILOSOPHERS:
PLATO AND ARISTOTLE

The Place of Philosophy in the Fourth Century. The keen thought and vigorous debate which characterized the daily activities of Socrates and, to a lesser extent, of the sophists during the fifth century would have found no more permanent record than did the speeches of Pericles, if the philosophers of a later period had not undertaken the task of systematizing and recording what had gone before. Plato and Aristotle, the two men who in the fourth century were the most active in preserving this wealth of philosophical material in their writings, had at their disposal not only the thoughtful analysis of ethical conduct that grew out of the conversations of Socrates, but also the entire body of thinking on the problems of human conduct, that had been developed in all the preceding centuries of Greek writing, and that was now a part of the rich Hellenic heritage.

Furthermore, humanistic philosophy, as a literary form, came into being at a peculiarly appropriate time. Accordingly, Plato and Aristotle merit study not only because of their place in Greek literature, but also because of the significance of their efforts in seeking to comprehend the life and thought of Athens in the century following the highest peak of the city's attainment. Philosophy in its fourth-century manifestation may be attributed to the political circumstances of the age, for Plato and Aristotle, who could no longer look with pride on a great and free city, took refuge in cities of their own mental creation. In the *Republic* of Plato and in the *Politics* of Aristotle are found the origins of the philosophic and literary utopias of subsequent times, such as More's *Utopia,* or Hobbes's *Leviathan.* The ideal state was a type of literary creation that evolved out of the troubled and depressing conditions of the age in which it was written.

PLATO

Life of Plato. Aristocles, a young Athenian who was born in 428 B.C. or 427 B.C., is known to the world by the name of Plato. The epithet means "broad" in Greek, and it was attached to him by his fellows with quizzical humor to indicate the breadth of his shoulders. By the time of his birth, the great plague had already devastated the city, Pericles had died, Aristophanes was proclaiming the doctrine of the old conservatism in his comedies, Socrates was a familiar figure in the streets of the city, and Sophocles and Euripides had still a score of years in which to write and work.

The aristocratic young Plato was trained in the studies suited to his age, so far as the troubled state of affairs permitted, and he early showed interest and remarkable talent in drama and lyric poetry. He was born too late, however, to become a dramatist. Even Euripides, who was born in 480 B.C., the year of the Battle of Salamis, was as much a sceptic and philosopher as a poet. By the time of the fall of Athens in 404 B.C., Plato, then in his early twenties, had become devoted to the teachings of Socrates, and he forsook his poetic pursuits, leaving only a few epigrams of peculiarly lucid beauty as an indication of what the world lost in poetry when he chose to devote himself exclusively to philosophy. Some reflections of his dramatic talent may still be traced in the superlative skill with which he has delineated the characters of his dialogues, especially in the *Republic.*

Plato was also a mathematician of distinction and gave a large place to mathematical studies in the Academy that he

[490]

founded, believing that sound judgments on philosophical problems were possible only in the minds of men who had learned to think clearly and logically.

The Place of Socrates in Plato's Dialogues. The unjust execution of Socrates in 399 B.C. laid on his pupil, Plato, the self-imposed task of vindicating the memory of his master, with the result that all the extended writings of Plato, except the *Apology*—and they have survived intact—are cast in the form of conversations or dialogues, in which the exponent of philosophy, ethics, religion, politics, or morality is almost always Socrates. In the early and later dialogues alike, it is Socrates who dominates the scene. The Hellenic instinct to choose and abide by a single theme, coupled with a more than human devotion to one master, has bound the creations of Plato indissolubly to the personality of Socrates. Only three or four times in all the body of literature that flowed from Plato's pen is his own name mentioned, and then in but casual fashion.

Plato's Travels. Plato traveled extensively after the death of Socrates, stopping at Megara, Egypt, southern Italy, and Sicily. He visited the court of the tyrants of Syracuse three times, in 388 B.C., when Dionysius I was reigning, and again in 367 B.C. and 360 B.C., under the rule of Dionysius II, each time apparently with the fixed purpose of putting into actual operation the philosophic principles of government that he treated fully in his *Republic*. The latter years of his life were spent in Athens teaching in the Academy, which he founded. He died in 347 B.C., at the age of eighty.

His writings. More than forty extant dialogues and thirteen letters are attributed to Plato, although the list accepted as authentic is considerably shorter. The works that have, with few exceptions, been admitted by scholars as genuine follow in alphabetical order: *Apology, Charmides, Cratylus, Critias, Crito, Euthydemus, Euthyphro, Gorgias, Hippias Minor, Ion, Laches, Laws, Lysis, Menexenus, Meno, Parmenides, Phædo, Phædrus, Philebus, Protagoras, Republic, Sophist, Statesman, Symposium, Theætetus, Timæus.*

[491]

Difficulties of Dating the Dialogues. It is practically impossible to construct a convincing account of the chronology of the dialogues. The genius of Plato appears to have sprung to birth in all its power, for neither in philosophic depth nor in literary style is there discernible any consecutive growth within the dialogues to differentiate those of his youth from those of his old age. The practice of introducing into the same dialogues historical interlocutors who are chronologically impossible adds to the difficulty of dating. Some observations about certain of the works can, however, be made.

The Trial and Death of Socrates. One group of dialogues is directly concerned with the death of Socrates, namely, the *Apology, Crito, Euthyphro, Gorgias,* and *Phædo.* The *Apology,* which alone of the works is cast as continuous discourse rather than in the form of a dialogue, contains the defense of Socrates in the law court, and takes the form of a justification of his whole life. The *Crito* contains an explanation of Socrates' refusal to escape from prison in disobedience to the laws; the *Euthyphro* discusses the meaning of "piety," and the manner in which its violation by the citizens of Athens has led to the condemnation of Socrates; the *Gorgias* contains a bitter attack on the political chicanery of Athens; and the *Phædo,* which is devoted in the main to a discussion of the immortality of the soul, ends with one of the most beautiful and solemn passages of the world's prose literature, in which the story of the death of Socrates is told.

The executioner, who has himself been moved to tears by the nobility of his prisoner, has just handed the cup of hemlock to Socrates. The story continues in the words of Phædo, who was present:

And as he spoke he put the cup to his lips, and calmly and with dignity drank the contents. Most of us up to that time had been able fairly well to restrain our tears, but when we saw him drink and observed that he had drained the cup, we could do so no longer, and in spite of myself the tears fell unquenched, so that I covered my face and wept for my own sorrow as I thought of the companion of whom I should now be bereft. Then Socrates rebuked us for our unrestraint, and we stayed our tears.

He walked about until he said that his legs were heavy, and then lay down on his back, for so the jailer had bidden him. The man who had administered the poison touched him, and after a time looked to his feet and his legs. Then pressing his foot very hard he asked if he felt it. Socrates replied that he did not, and next the man made the same trial on his calves. And working his way up in this manner, the jailer showed us that he was growing cold and stiff. Socrates then touched his own body, and said that when it reached his heart he would be gone. When the region about his groin had already grown cold, he uncovered his face, for it had been covered, and spoke, and these were the last words that he uttered: "Crito," he said, "I owe a cock to Asclepius; see that it is paid, and do not fail me." "It shall be done," said Crito. "Is there anything else?" Socrates made no reply to this question, but after a short time there was a movement, and the jailer uncovered his face, and his eyes were fixed. Crito, observing this, closed his mouth and his eyes.

This was the end, Echecrates, of our friend, a man, as I should say, who was the best, the wisest, and the justest, of all those whom I have ever known.

The Search for Truth. In spite of the impossibility of reducing the dialogues of Plato to any single theme, some of the basic concepts of his thinking can be set forth. The search for ultimate truth was common to all philosophers. The early physical philosophers of the sixth century had found reality in physical things: Thales in water, Heracleitus in fire. With the sophists and with Socrates the quest had turned to human needs, and from Socrates, Plato had inherited the ethical problem of determining the ultimate end of life, or the final good for man.

Virtue and Knowledge. In the numerous dialogues the object of inquiry is the proper relation of man to pleasure, restraint, judgment, and wisdom, and as a common thread of the diverse arguments there emerges the basic philosophic conclusion of Plato that virtue comes from knowledge and is inseparable from it. Thus it follows that no one can really sin against knowledge, for when he has departed from virtue he has thereby departed from knowledge. If the function of a pilot is to steer a true course, in the moment that he departs from the channel and piles his ship on the rocks, he has ceased by definition to be a pilot. Not all persons, Plato contends, can appreciate the true good for man any more than the untrained individual can appreciate the real worth of music or art, and hence the trained man, or philosopher, is the only sound judge of ultimate human values.

The "Republic." The problem of the *Republic* is the search for justice, which Plato felt could be most easily discerned in an ideal state, that would show the individual writ large. That there may be no room for subjective error of evaluation, and to discredit the current sophistic contention that honesty and justice are to be cultivated for personal ends, Plato sets up two hypothetical cases. On the one hand, he pictures a man who is a complete scoundrel, but who goes through life with the reputation for honesty and probity, until in death he is honored and revered by the citizens; on the other hand, he describes an honest and upright man, who by some evil chance passes his life with a reputation for rascality and goes dishonored to his grave. Having set up these extreme examples, Plato undertakes by a thoroughgoing examination of the psychology of the soul, whose function it is to direct aright the constituent parts of man, to prove that justice is still the only proper pursuit.

To vindicate this highly ethical and apparently paradoxical position, Plato took in the end a very practical attitude. Maintaining that it is the function of the soul to nourish justice, he undertook first to discover the nature of justice. Then, because man is a social animal and because the quality of justice may be more readily understood if it can be studied in a community rather than in the individual, he set up an ideal state, the

Republic, in which he examined the workings of justice. Through long and detailed search he reached the conclusion that justice was to be found in a due order; that is, in the appropriate allocation of duties to the various members of the state.

In the *Republic,* Plato divided the people into three classes, in whose harmonious cooperation he found the demonstration of justice. The classes are (1) the sustaining class, consisting of farmers and craftsmen, who supply the necessaries of life, (2) the defending class, consisting of warriors, whose duty it is to protect the state from aggression, and (3) the ruling class, whose function it is to direct the destinies of the community. This highest class constitutes the guardians, or philosopher-kings.

When Plato had defined the classes in the state, he applied his philosophy to the individual man. Corresponding to the first and lowest sustaining class, there is the base part of man's being, which embraces physical sensation and personal desires. Though it is base, it maintains the body for a higher purpose. The second, or warrior, class of the state is paralleled by the active part of man's nature, which Plato describes as the spirit. It is the impulsive and sometimes irrational will of man. The final ruling class of the state corresponds to the reason or wisdom of man, which orders the body aright.

The Practical Application. Plato's treatment of justice was essentially practical in spite of what may seem to be vague comparisons. Since he no longer can feel that the gods will intervene immediately to reward the good and punish the wicked, he is offering as an alternative a workable philosophy of life which he believes will serve in a world of free will. In modern society also, thoughtful man is confronted with the same problem when he realizes that all too often virtue goes unrewarded and vice unpunished; he is fortunate if, with Plato, he can discover a satisfying basis of decent behavior by attaining harmony within himself. This is true both of man's relation to his fellow man and of the proper ordering of the

[495]

three conflicting elements within his own soul—the base, the spirited, and the wise. The very presentation of this principle and, still more, the thoughtful argument in support of it, predicate a degree of mature judgment to which modern society does not generally attain.

The Doctrine of Ideas. The Platonic theory of ideas has played a large part in philosophic thought. It will be well to bear in mind the fact that "idea" is a transliteration, rather than a translation, of a Greek word and should therefore be interpreted in the somewhat technical manner that is here attempted. Plato pointed out that the error of the early physical philosophers lay in seeking reality in concrete form, for, he claimed, the abiding and unchanging reality can be found only in an abstract concept of the soul. Thus any material object, such as a table or chair, even if apparently flawless, has some defect. Yet the very recognition of that defect is possible only because somewhere in the abode of the gods the perfect idea, or form, of a table or chair exists and is understood by man. To cite an illustration that Plato did not use, it is simple to understand that the geometric conception of a circle is something more perfect than any physical drawing of a circle ever can be. In the same way, the law of gravity is more real than any visible physical manifestation of the law, and the idea of beauty, or courage, or justice, more real than any number of specific illustrations of those qualities. Thus Plato builds up two worlds, a world of ideas, and a less real, though corresponding, world of physical facts. He holds that man can never attain more than partial knowledge of truth in this life, because he is clogged by the weight of the physical body placed in a world of physical facts. Only when the soul is freed from the flesh can it aspire to perfect knowledge in the world of ideas.

The Myth of the Cave. Having stated the doctrine of the restriction of human knowledge imposed by the body, Plato seeks, as he does on other similar occasions, to argue by the device of allegory, or myth, a conviction that eludes demonstrable proof. Thus one can scarcely fail to make the appropriate application to the problems of human learning that are implicit in the myth of the prisoners in the cave, who see only shadows of the realities of life, and from whose number a single one is at length brought to the light of earth. The myth, in part, is told thus:

Next, I said, observe in this way the state of our own nature in the matter of knowledge and ignorance. Suppose a number of men are living in an underground cave, with an entrance turned toward the light and extending the entire length of the cave, and that they have lived in this place since childhood, with their legs and necks so fastened that they can look only straight ahead and are prevented by the bonds from turning their heads about. Suppose further that a fire is blazing at some distance above and behind them; and that between the fire and the prisoners there is an elevated road, along which a low wall is built like the railing in front of magicians, above which they display their works of wonder.

Socrates goes on to sketch a situation wherein passers-by walk beside the wall, carrying all manner of objects; they have their shadows reflected on the wall before the prisoners in the cave, and their voices are echoed back from the wall in front of them, until the prisoners, with no experience in their lives but shadows and echoes, look upon such reflections of reality as truth. In the same manner, men on earth do not comprehend the real truth, but only shadows and echoes of it. Furthermore, man is confused and resistant if he is led toward truth, even as a prisoner from the cave would be confused if he were led to the light. The allegory continues:

Imagine now, I said, that the prisoners are freed from their bonds and cured of their illusion. If one of them is loosed and compelled to stand up suddenly and turn his neck about and walk up and look upon the light, he will suffer in every act, and because of the glare he will be unable to distinguish even those things of which he previously saw the shadows. What then do you think

[497]

he will say, if someone tells him that in his former state he was looking on illusions, whereas now he is closer to reality, and being turned more toward truth, he sees more clearly? Do you not suppose that he will be confused, and think that the shadows, which he saw before, are more true than the things that are now pointed out to him?

In like manner a person who has lived in ignorance of philosophy will be impatient and incredulous of truth when it is shown to him. As the prisoner from the cave is brought into the light of the sun, he will at first be able to distinguish shadows more easily than the objects themselves, and only by degrees, after looking in turn on reflections in the water, on visible objects, and on the moon and stars by night, will he be able to look upon the sun itself. Such a prisoner, having come to a knowledge of reality, will look back with compassion on those who are left in ignorance in the cave, and will now have but small regard for those who once had great skill in observing shadows and catching the echo of a voice.

But suppose that he returned again to the darkness of the cave. His true knowledge would incapacitate him for a life among the shadows, and he would be received with derision by his old associates:

It would be said of him that he had gone up to the light and had come back with the loss of his eyes, and that it was not worth while making the effort to ascend. And if anyone tried to free another prisoner and take him up, would they not kill him if they could lay hold of him?

Through the myth of the cave Plato makes clear his conviction that man is imprisoned in his physical body. The ascent of the prisoner to the sun is an allegory of the struggle of the human mind to attain philosophic wisdom.

It is the belief of Plato, which he expresses again and again, that the pursuit of wisdom is the true path to the attainment of virtue and justice, the end toward which man is con-

[498]

stantly striving. Plato recognized the truth that must be relearned by every thoughtful man, namely, that the process of seeking philosophic wisdom must be its own reward and that the attainment of complete wisdom or virtue is something that will forever elude man's grasp.

ARISTOTLE

Life of Aristotle. The second great philosopher of the fourth century was Aristotle, who was born at Stagira in Macedonia about 384 B.C., when Plato was some forty-three years of age. He was the son of Nicomachus, the court physician of the Macedonian king, and he early absorbed the intellectual atmosphere of his home. At the age of seventeen, he went to Athens, where he studied first with Isocrates and later at the Academy with Plato. By this time Plato was well past middle life, and Aristotle found himself striking out on new paths of philosophy that sometimes diverged sharply from the teachings of his master, though he always thought and spoke of him with respect. So long as philosophic speculation was a vital force, it was inevitable that each generation should modify the concepts of the preceding one. Plato had deliberately obscured the palimpsest that represented the superimposition of his own vigorous thought on the principles that he inherited from Socrates. Between Plato and Aristotle there is no such artificial barrier to stand in the way of a separate evaluation of the work of the two men.

On the death of Plato in 347 B.C., Aristotle went to the court of Hermeias, a petty tyrant in Asia, only to leave that position to become the tutor of the twelve-year-old Alexander of Macedon in 344 B.C. Nine years later, in 335 B.C., at the age of forty-nine, he returned to Athens to establish the Lyceum, a school in which he delivered his lectures during *peripatoi,* or "promenades," with his students, thus giving a name to the Peripatetic school of philosophy. This method of instruction precluded both the dialectic, or question-and-answer technique of Socrates, and the lecture method of the modern classroom. The death of Alexander in 323 B.C. stirred such violent anti-Macedonian passions in Athens, that, in view of his former association with Alexander, Aristotle withdrew to Chalcis, lest, as he said with his mind on the martyrdom of Socrates, "the Athenians should sin twice against philosophy." He died there in the following year. Thus within a few months of one another three of the most prominent figures of the fourth century met their deaths: Alexander in 323 B.C., Demosthenes in 322 B.C., and Aristotle in 322 B.C.

Aristotle's Contact with Alexander. The association of Aristotle with Alexander, which continued long after the relationship of tutor and pupil had ended, had one important result in aiding the scholarly pursuits of the philosopher, for Alexander was able to make available from his distant marches large quantities of botanical and biological specimens for detailed study and classification. Doubtless the interest of Aristotle in scientific research had early been enkindled by his father, who was a physician, and his study of scientific specimens influenced his philosophic attitude, for he shows very clearly the marks of the collector and the compiler. Through this discipline he became a more practical thinker than Plato.

The Exoteric and Esoteric Lectures. Aristotle was highly praised by ancient critics for the graceful and eloquent style of his *exoteric* lectures, that is, popular discourses. None of these, unfortunately, has survived, although it is known that they dealt with friendship, justice, exhortations to philosophy, and similar matters. His extant works, which are preserved in considerable volume, were written in a particularly elliptical, crabbed, and awkward style, perhaps as notes for the detailed courses addressed to his students in the Lyceum. These were called *esoteric* lectures, as opposed to the popular, or exoteric, discourses. What the esoteric lectures lack in literary grace, they compensate for in diversity of subject and depth of thought.

Aristotle's Breadth of Interest. Aristotle came late enough

[500]

in the history of Greek thought to profit by all the efforts of his predecessors, including Plato, who had built up the intellectual heritage which Greece was to bequeath to the world. His amazing versatility may best be demonstrated by listing his works with a word of explanation about the contents of each. The *Organon,* or "Instrument," is a study in logic; the *History of Animals,* together with some allied treatises, deals with his observations in natural science; the essay *Concerning the Sky* is, as the name suggests, a study of astronomy; the *Physics* treats not only of matter but also of causes. More humanistic works include *Concerning the Soul,* a psychological study, and the *Metaphysics,* so named because it was placed by the editor after the *Physics.* The *Metaphysics* deals with the desire of man for knowledge, and with the nature of knowledge and of the things known. The *Nicomachean Ethics* contains a search for the final good, with a definition of human happiness. In the field of government there is preserved the *Politics,* a study of justice as practiced by man in his environment, and the *Constitution of Athens,* a papyrus document of disputed authenticity, discovered in 1885. On literature, we have the *Rhetoric* in three books, the *Letters,* the *Poems,* and the *Poetics.* The debt of literary critics to the cogent observations of Aristotle contained in his *Poetics* was made clear in connection with the discussion of the development of Greek tragedy.

Modification of Plato's Doctrine of Ideas. Aristotle found it necessary to postulate some modifications of the Platonic theory of ideas before he could accept it. He insisted that Plato had erred in teaching that there were two distinct worlds, one of ideas and a corresponding one of concrete objects. He was willing to concede that an idea could exist, but he found that existence in the visible object and not apart from it.

The Teleological Theory. Thus Aristotle substituted the teleological theory of completed purpose for the static teaching of Plato. For instance, he could not agree that at any given moment a plant, or an animal, or a child could be defined as an entity, for after an interval of time the leaves of the plant would have changed or the hair of the child might have grown or been cut, thus changing the definition. The only possibility of arriving at a concept of reality, therefore, is to include the whole process of growth and decay, from the seed to the completed whole and thence to disintegration. This is the idea which embraces the end, or purpose, fulfilled by each object in its span of existence, for the teleological explanation of any principle depends on an understanding of the "end," or *telos*.

Various extensions of the theory are possible. A completed statue is, for instance, capable of definition only when the idea in the mind of the artist is translated into the material of the marble, and the end is accomplished. Aristotle was always practical enough to contemplate the implications of his philosophy in the light of human experience, and he was ready to explain the imperfections, whether of a statue or of a human character, by the intractability of the material available.

The Highest Good. Two or three passages from the *Nicomachean Ethics* will indicate the method by which Aristotle tries to discover the primary good, which man seeks for its own sake and not as a step toward something else. The treatise opens thus:

Every act and every pursuit, every action and every choice, seems to be directed toward some good. Consequently the good has been well defined as that toward which all things are directed. But a difference appears in the various ends that are sought. Sometimes the ends are activities, and sometimes they are the consequences that follow the activities. Where the consequences lie beyond the activities, then the resulting products are more important than the activities.

It is clear that Aristotle, with his practical mind, is assessing the completed product above the action that necessarily precedes it, and it is an easy step from the practical illustration to the application of his reasoning to human conduct. Just as the completed Parthenon is more important than the science of architecture in the minds of Ictinus and Callicrates, whose genius would remain sterile unless translated into results, so the proper ethical conduct of man is more important than the theory of education that brings it to pass.

After pointing out that there are a variety of ends sought by different sciences, as health is the end sought by the science of medicine, a ship by the science of shipbuilding, victory by the science of strategy, and wealth by the science of economics, he makes clear the fact that some ends, and consequently some sciences, are subordinate to others. But the supreme end, or good, must by definition be subordinate to nothing else. This idea is developed in the following quotations, all taken from the *Ethics,* though they do not form a single consecutive passage:

If then there is an end in practical matters which we seek for itself alone, and all other things for the sake of this, and if it is not true that we seek each thing for the sake of something else, for this would go on to infinity and render the whole inquiry empty and vain, it is clear that this end would be the good, and the best.

The highest good appears to have finality. Consequently, if there is a single complete end, this would be what we are seeking, and if more than one, then the most complete of these.

Happiness appears to be most completely this thing. We invariably choose happiness for itself and never for something else. Honor, pleasure, intelligence, and every excellence we choose, both for their own sake, for we would wish to have each of them even though nothing else came of it, but also for the sake of happiness, because we suppose that we will be happy through these qualities. But no one chooses happiness for the sake of these others, nor for the sake of anything else.

So happiness appears as something complete and sufficient unto itself, the end of everything that is done.

The Application of the Theory. Yet if happiness is the final end of activity, it must still be shown how the attainment of happiness by man will result in his highest good. This Aristotle finds in the fulfillment of the appropriate idea, or function, of each existing entity, animate or inanimate.

Aristotle ventures the assertion that the proper function of man is "an activity of the soul in accordance with virtue, or at least not apart from it, in a complete life." The definition is not specific, for so subjective an idea is really indefinable, but Aristotle attempts to clarify his meaning by elaborating the Doctrine of the Mean and pointing out that virtue will be found in choosing always the middle course between two extremes, as courage lies somewhere between cowardice and foolhardiness. He decides that human virtue is a sort of activity of the soul that adequately meets any situation with which man must cope. One has a feeling, nevertheless, that his ultimate conclusion still leaves the whole problem of moral conduct unsolved. Once again the value of his argument lies in the process of endeavor that it provokes; it is the end that defies capture. Although his definition of the *summum bonum*, or highest good, as the conduct best suiting a given situation, is tantalizingly vague, he is in reality seeking to discover the noblest way of life. Aristotle, even more than Plato, felt the impulse to map out a path of conduct that would justify the choice of a good life in existing society.

The Pursuit of Excellence, or Areté. In the writings of the philosophers, both Plato and Aristotle, there is a recurring treatment of that human virtue, which is described as *areté*. This concept did not originate with the philosophers. It was a quality of man himself, recognized in the virtues of the Homeric heroes, and constantly changing its meaning with the growth of humanism and intellectualism through the subsequent centuries.

The appreciation of areté depends on the recognition of a certain perfection inherent in every living creature, and, for that matter, in every inanimate object as well, as has been suggested above. It is a challenging doctrine, and its exposition commences with deceptive ease. The virtue, or function, or areté of a mattock is to prepare the soil for planting, of an ox to turn the sod, of an eye to see, of an ear to hear. What then is the areté of man? It is small wonder that this question defied a ready answer, for it poses the whole problem of human conduct.

Yet it was a query that would not be stilled, and the answers that were propounded, specifically or by implication, by a succession of Greek writers—Hesiod, Pindar, the dramatists, Plato, and Aristotle—suggest the pattern of clear thinking in the development of Greek humanism. Courage in battle, health, athletic prowess, the acquisition of money, or fame, or knowledge were put forward from time to time as the embodiment of areté. It was with the humanistic philosophers that areté took on its noblest aspect. Man was always central to Greek thought, and areté came ultimately to imply the finest conduct, moral, spiritual, and ethical, of the complete man, transcending his function and duty as soldier or juryman, sailor or poet, and manifesting itself in man himself. It is a tenuous concept, difficult of comprehension and, to the minds of some, inadequate in that it fails to provide adequately for the place of religion as a guide of conduct beyond the limits of human power. But it was a powerful idea, noble in conception, and capable of continuous growth.

Estimate of Aristotle. Aristotle was a more practical and realistic philosopher than was Plato. Plato planned an imagined society in which government should be conducted by the philosopher-kings, and then with perfect good faith attempted to launch that theory of government by moral suasion on the hard-headed tyrant of Syracuse. Aristotle, on the other hand, was much more disposed to pause from time to time in the development of his social or political philosophy and to ask himself how his theories would actually work in the society of his time.

It is well-nigh impossible to exaggerate the influence wielded by either man on the world's thought, although through the Middle Ages and until the time of the Renaissance it was

[505]

Aristotle who was the guide of all European study, and only later was the more mellow wisdom of Plato rediscovered. Curiously enough, when the mediæval universities of Europe adopted Aristotle as their universal and infallible textbook, they used his philosophy for deductive rather than for inductive reasoning. In other words, from the body of Aristotelian knowledge they deduced their own concepts of life. It was an approach that would have been distasteful in the extreme to Aristotle. Even today there are few fields of human interest, from painting to astronomy, or from literary criticism to the science of government, which one can essay to study deeply without being obliged to pay heed to the pertinent observations of Aristotle.

In leaving Plato and Aristotle with a treatment somewhat briefer in compass than that devoted to Greek arts and crafts, it must not be supposed that the relative importance of the two is necessarily to be thus evaluated. The attention devoted to a single brief treatise of Aristotle, the *Poetics,* in connection with Greek drama affords an indication of the wealth of provocative wisdom that lies embedded in his work. This is true in quite as large measure of Plato. Yet an attempt to present even in brief space a picture of all the philosophic inquiries of these two men, ranging from women's suffrage to the censorship of literature, and from the parts of animals to the analysis of rhetorical figures, would be futile. Proportion would be obscured by mass, for a study in any detail of the humanistic philosophy of the fourth century demands its own exclusive treatment.

It is, however, not too much to hope that something of the method and purpose of each philosopher may be grasped by the illustrative examples that have been given, and that the profound influence that they exercised on their successors, not only on such groups as the Neo-Platonists but on the systematic thinking of academicians and theologians, may be inferred from the history of scholarship.

[506]

OTHER HUMANISTIC PHILOSOPHIES

The Wide Influence of Socrates. The preeminent contributions of Plato and Aristotle to the furtherance of philosophy in the more or less direct tradition of Socrates must not lead to the supposition that humanistic philosophy, or the study of man and his problems, was studied only in the Academy and the Lyceum. So inclusive an intellect as that of Socrates inevitably left innumerable aspects of philosophy to be pursued by later men, and in a sense every school of philosophy through the remaining classical ages, both in Greece and Rome, owed something to the mind of Socrates. Yet practical considerations render it preferable to leave any treatment of such teachings as Stoicism and Epicureanism to the centuries of the Christian era and to the Roman scene in which they were most actively pursued.

The Cynics and Cyrenaics. Other more or less formally organized schools, in addition to those of Plato and Aristotle, grew up as a direct result of the teaching of Socrates. Among these the Cynics, founded by Antisthenes, and the Cyrenaics, founded by Aristippus, should be briefly defined as to their purpose and thought. The Cynics, impressed by the doctrine that virtue and knowledge were, if not identical, at least inseparable, founded their thinking on this principle, but with the added conviction that external possessions and the opinions of others were of no consequence. They deliberately cultivated a social and intellectual isolation that amounted to boorishness, and their philosophy became essentially negative. Diogenes the Cynic, who lived in a tub, was representative of the attitude of rejection of all physical possessions and comforts. He was indifferent to everything except virtue, and he took satisfaction in outraging the opinions of the city. In the pursuit of the form of their philosophy, Diogenes and his fellow Cynics lost much of the substance of the Socratic teaching that they had undertaken to perpetuate.

The Cyrenaics likewise commenced with the idea of culti-

[507]

vating virtue, as Socrates had taught it, but the emphasis of their teaching very quickly turned to the happiness that results from virtue, and in time the philosophy of the school became frankly a pursuit of happiness as an end in itself. The Cyrenaics were, however, saved from the decadence of complete self-indulgence by the recognition, at least on the part of some of them, that Hellenic restraint was a necessary accompaniment of true happiness, and further that intellectual and moral happiness might be cultivated no less intensely than the satisfaction of immediate physical appetites.

Important though the Cynic and Cyrenaic schools, not to mention the group of Megarics founded by Euclid, were in the history of humanistic philosophy, none of them produced men of the mental capacity of Plato or Aristotle, and consequently their place in the history of Greek civilization is less significant.

CHAPTER XXIX

GREEK HISTORY
FROM 323 B.C. TO 330 A.D.

THE HELLENISTIC PERIOD (323–146 B.C.)

The Problem of Later Greek History. To determine the exact point at which a civilization begins to decline involves a large element of subjective reasoning, and there would be little agreement upon any date assigned. Nonetheless, it is clear that the vigor of experimentation that marked the archaic age, the flowering of genius in the fifth century, and the creation of new, though more individualized, types in the fourth century are the evidences of a civilization more original and vital than that which existed in Greek lands during the six centuries and longer that make up the Hellenistic and Græco-Roman Periods. After the death of Alexander the Great, and more particularly after the establishment of Roman power, the Greeks lost their capacity for creative achievement and began more and more to solace themselves with the memory of the past. A few of the significant historical events of these later times must, however, be sketched, in order to arrive at some understanding of the type of society in which Greek art and letters continued to be produced.

The Influence of Alexander's Conquests. The most important historical movement of the closing years of the fourth century had been associated with the military campaigns of Alexander the Great, who in the thirteen years of his reign, from 336 B.C. to 323 B.C., had carried the arms and language of

[509]

Greece far into the eastern kingdoms of Asia and south to the ancient land of Egypt. The rise of Macedon under Philip and Alexander had brought about the political eclipse of Athens, as well as of the other states of Greece, and it had served to transfer the leadership in art and literature from Athens to the more distant Greek cities, especially those in Asia Minor and Egypt. The ancient world entered upon this new heritage after the death of Alexander in 323 B.C., and the period that is known as the Hellenistic Age ensued.

Revolt Against Macedon. The historical development of the next two centuries is better known from the Roman point of view than from the Greek, though it must remain our primary task to trace the relationship of Athens and of the other city-states of Greece to Rome, their eventual conqueror, as well as to one another. When news reached Athens of the death of Alexander, Demosthenes, with the active support of the orator Hypereides, immediately commenced an agitation to throw off the Macedonian yoke. He succeeded by his eloquence and his energy in uniting in the attempt many of the Greek states, already eager for revolt, although the conservative and wealthy element of Athens, led by Phocion and Demades, earnestly desired peace.

The commander of the united Greek forces was a competent general, named Leosthenes, who, with a body of combined mercenary and Athenian troops, occupied Thermopylæ, in order to block the advance of the Macedonian soldiers. Meanwhile, the Athenians hastily assembled a fleet of two hundred and forty ships, a larger naval armament than they had mustered at any time since the Peloponnesian War. The Macedonian general Antipater, who could equip himself with only one hundred and ten vessels and an inferior land force, was defeated in battle and took refuge in the town of Lamia in southern Thessaly. However, Leosthenes was killed, and with his loss the military advantage of the Athenians waned. The siege of Lamia was presently lifted, and Antipater made his way back to Macedon. In the following year the Macedonians gained the ascendancy at sea, and the Greek states hastened to make separate treaties with Antipater. Thus ended the Lamian War and the abortive attempt of the Greeks to free themselves from Macedon. It was following this debacle that Demosthenes ended his own life to escape surrender to Antipater.

The Division of Alexander's Empire. The part played by Antipater in suppressing the uprising calls for some explanation of the government, after the death of Alexander, of the great dominions subjugated by him. It had been his ambition to weld together a world empire, but neither time nor genius had sufficed for the consolidation of his conquests, and the years between 323 B.C. and 301 B.C. were filled with the plots of rival Macedonian generals, who sought their own aggrandizement. For a time Antigonus, one of the commanders of Alexander's army, strove to continue the vast empire under his personal rule, but it was quickly evident that no one man could do so. The result was that Alexander's empire was divided into three more or less natural areas, Macedon, Egypt, and Asia, or the eastern kingdom of the Seleucidæ.

The Diadochi. The rulers of the three new kingdoms are called the *Diadochi,* or "Successors," of Alexander. Macedon, which extended its sway over the rest of Greece, was ruled by Cassander, the son of Antipater, until his death in 289 B.C. Macedon was then claimed by Demetrius, son of Antigonus, a claim that was subsequently made good by his son Antigonus Gonatas. From this descent the later kings of Macedon came to be known as the Antigonids. Egypt remained in the power of Ptolemy, who had long been governor of that province, or kingdom. It is from this date that the Ptolemaic dynasty, which includes the famous Cleopatra, begins. The third division of the empire occupied the eastern areas of Alexander's conquest, and after 281 B.C. the empire of Lysimachus in Thrace and Asia Minor was absorbed into this kingdom. Its ruler was Seleucus, and his successors were called the Seleucidæ.

The Achæan and Ætolian Leagues. During this same

period, the separate city-states of Greece began seriously to experiment with the idea of federal unions, and two groups, the Achæan League in the Peloponnese and the Ætolian League in northern Greece, came into existence. By common consent the different communities allied themselves together for mutual advantage and protection. It will be observed that the federal leagues developed in those regions of Greece that had played little part in the political life of the fifth and fourth centuries. With less pride in the past and less intense feeling about the old type of city-state, they were the more ready to venture on new paths of union. In view of the great strength of local loyalties, it is a remarkable accomplishment that the Greeks were able to work out in these two leagues some measure of federal union, with common counsels prevailing in economic matters, in foreign negotiations, and in the conduct of war. The birth of the Leagues is indicative of the inevitable movement toward larger administrative units. That they did not effect the political salvation of Greece was perhaps due to the fact that they came too late. First Macedon, and later Rome, were rising too rapidly, and these powers imposed their will on states that had grown weary of the struggle and weak through their own individual folly.

The patterns of these federal alliances were carefully studied by the founding fathers of America, and although the Greeks were indifferently successful in unions formed too late in their history, their efforts were not without influence in the framing of our own constitution.

The Growth of Rome. Finally, one must take account of Rome. According to tradition, in 753 B.C., twenty-three years after the accepted date of the first Olympic games in Greece, a tiny city on the Tiber had been founded, and for more than two centuries was ruled by kings. In 509 B.C., the same year in which Cleisthenes was striving to set up a democratic government in Athens, the kings were driven from Rome and the Republic was established. Through the following centuries Rome extended her power step by step over the other cities and states of the Italian peninsula, until she inevitably came in contact with the Greek colonies that had been founded in southern Italy and Sicily from the eighth to the sixth centuries.

Pyrrhus. In 324 B.C., Rome had refrained from sending ambassadors to greet Alexander at Babylon. This was because she was occupied with her own military problems in Italy, already showing thereby the vigor that was destined to make her the conqueror of the whole Mediterranean area. The death of Alexander delayed a test of strength between Macedon and Rome. But a generation later, in 281 B.C., Pyrrhus of Epirus, a distant kinsman of Alexander, invaded southern Italy with 25,000 men on the invitation of the people of Tarentum, a Greek colony located on the southern coast of Italy, which was hard-pressed by Rome. For six years, Pyrrhus fought with varying success against the Romans in Italy and the Carthaginians in Sicily. Had he met with loyal and consistent support from the Greeks of Magna Græcia, he might have won for them their freedom; but, as it was, in 275 B.C., disillusioned by the response that he had received, he returned to Epirus. Three years later Rome conquered Tarentum and extended her enforced federation to the foot of the peninsula.

The Punic Wars. The destiny of Rome was now to carry her to conquests beyond the borders of Italy, and for over a hundred years she was engaged in foreign campaigns, of which the most celebrated were the three wars against Carthage, her great Phœnician rival in Africa. These were the First Punic War (264–241 B.C.), the Second Punic War (218–201 B.C.), and the Third Punic War (153–146 B.C.). The Third Punic War ended with the destruction of Carthage in which the city suffered in 146 B.C. a demolition as complete as that effected by modern systematic bombing. The same date is taken as the end of the Hellenistic Period in Greece. The reason for adopting it will presently be observed.

The Clash of Greek and Roman Interests. However, to turn back to the Second Punic War (218–201 B.C.), it was then that Rome and Greece definitely clashed for the first time, although

Roman expeditions for the suppression of piracy in Illyria had led to both trouble and alliances with Greek states some years before. The invasion of Italy by Hannibal, the Carthaginian, suggested to Philip V, the king of Macedon, that he might strike a blow at the power of Rome, which had been encroaching on his territory. The result was the First Macedonian War (215–204 B.C.), which dragged on in desultory fashion for a decade. This war was for Rome only an aggravating incident within the scope of the much more important struggle against Carthage. No decisive results followed, except the determination of Rome to extend her sway to the east and over the dominions of Macedon when occasion presented itself. Twice again in the next forty years or thereabouts Macedon and Rome came to armed conflict.

The Romans hoped that the other Greek states would rise at the opportunity to throw off the Macedonian yoke, but the once vigorous communities looked listlessly upon the struggles, which now seemed strangely unrelated to their own destinies. In 194 B.C., following a Roman victory over Macedon, the "liberation of Greece" was proclaimed by the Roman general Flamininus, and ostensibly effected by the withdrawal of Roman troops from the country. For the moment it served the purpose of Rome that the free states of Greece should balance a too powerful Macedon. But the liberation was not followed by the expected harmony between Rome and the communities of southern Greece.

The Roman Conquest of Greece. Philip V of Macedon aided the Romans against the Ætolians, but it was an unequal alliance and the Macedonian king cherished a growing resentment against the Romans for the humiliations that were successively visited upon him as Rome expanded to the east, modifying boundaries, casting down and setting up potentates at will, and constantly thwarting the ambitions of Macedon. In 179 B.C., Philip died, and was succeeded by his son, Perseus, who began even more vigorously than his father to cement alliances with neighboring states and to recreate in his Macedonian subjects

[514]

the will to revive the glories of that kingdom as they had existed under Alexander the Great. The Roman Senate presently took action, and in a brief war, ending with the victory of the Romans under L. Æmilius Paullus at Pydna in southeastern Macedonia in 168 B.C., Macedon was finally and completely defeated. The effort of Rome to establish representative forms of government in the Macedonian states is one of the little known but most interesting experiments in ancient political history. The project, however, failed of success, and for twenty-two years, confusion, divided authority, and discontent disturbed the country. In 146 B.C., following an unsuccessful attempt of the Macedonians to restore the monarchy, the Roman Senate constituted Macedon a province of the Empire.

The Destruction of Corinth (146 B.C.). Meanwhile, the attempt of Rome to balance the remaining states of Greece against Macedon, or to harmonize the antagonisms of the Achæan and Ætolian Leagues, had not brought happy results. Despite their leagues, rivalries among various cities were constantly leading to quarrels and appeals to Rome. In general, Rome was content that internal discord should prevent any single state from rising to a predominant position. But following the victory of Paullus at Pydna in 168 B.C., the manifest anti-Roman sentiment in Greece seemed to demand action. It was at this time that Rome removed from Achæa, the name now given to the Roman province comprising the greater part of Greece, a thousand distinguished hostages, including the historian Polybius. The Greeks, however, continued their hostile political activities, and a commission headed by L. Mummius was sent out from Rome with instructions to make a final settlement in Greece. This was done in 146 B.C. and was marked by the burning of the city of Corinth to the ground.

The Status of Greece. A Roman governor was now established in Macedon, and the city-states of Greece, though left in nominal independence, were subject to his jurisdiction. This is the settlement that marks the close of the Hellenistic Period in Greek history. It is a sorry picture to see Athens and Sparta,

[515]

Corinth, Thebes, and Macedon, whose destinies have been followed through all their vicissitudes of government, through the trial of the Persian Wars, the Age of Pericles, the Peloponnesian War, and the successive hegemonies of Sparta, Thebes, and Macedon, reduced at length to minor communities in a world empire. The city-states, forgetting their own Greek motto, "Moderation in all things," had loved their separate independence too ardently to retain it.

THE GRÆCO-ROMAN PERIOD (146 B.C.–330 A.D.)

The Dates of the Period. The sack of Corinth in 146 B.C., which marked the end of the Hellenistic Period, was followed by a renewed attempt on the part of Rome to have the Greek people govern themselves so far as they were able. The essential features of the following period, which stretches for five centuries, from the subjugation of Greece in 146 B.C. to the establishment of Constantinople in 330 A.D., with a consequent division of the dominions of Rome into an eastern and a western empire, are quickly told. It is a time in which the control of policy and the stimulus to endeavor alike emanated from Rome. The alliances that were made and the wars that were fought were but a part of the larger progress of Rome, and the Greeks, with disheartening consistency, at Pharsalus, Philippi, and elsewhere supported the losing side, to their cost. Yet it is with justice that the age is described as Græco-Roman, for the more powerful and vigorous Romans remained indebted for the refinements of life to the Greeks, whom they had subjugated. Both in the intangible influence of the achievements of the classical centuries and in the contemporary pursuit of art, literature, and philosophy, Hellas continued to impose her culture on the ancient world.

Political Division in the Greek Cities. Following the active assumption of authority by Rome in 146 B.C., the Roman governor of Macedon exercised a general oversight over the other states of Greece, supplying troops to maintain order where

[516]

necessary and rigorously suppressing any incipient federations that might cause trouble to Rome. In the various cities political divisions among the Greeks themselves arose. This was indeed no new experience in their national history, but the motivation was no longer the same, for now the wealthier classes, especially those with lands, realized that the continued enjoyment of their privileged position depended on maintaining friendship with Rome, and they grew to be a party favorable to Roman rule. To some extent patriotism became a matter of economics, and personal self-interest dictated the political convictions of the Greeks.

Trouble with Rome. The old zest for local independence, however, continued to animate many of the Greek people, who cherished the constant hope that they might yet shake off the power of Rome. But the governor of Macedon was now too alert and the opportunities were too few for the establishment of formal federal groups, such as the Achæan League, with the result that the restless discontent of the different cities found expression in their readiness to associate themselves with any leader who raised arms against Rome. Consequently, when the long-continued trouble visited on the Romans by Mithridates, an Oriental king, whose power had rapidly expanded in Asia Minor, led to an open rupture between him and Rome, many Greeks sided with Mithridates. The course of the war, known as the First Mithridatic War, which lasted from 88 B.C. to 84 B.C., need not be recalled, but one result of the disturbance is important. The Roman commander who brought the war to a close was the notorious Sulla. He proceeded to restore order in Asia by the arrest and execution of all prominent supporters of Mithridates as well as by requiring enormous reparations, and some of that severity he turned also on the rebellious cities of Greece. The military exactions of Sulla, coming close upon the economic exhaustion of protracted warfare, brought the major part of Hellas to the verge of ruin.

Economic Depression in Greece. Other factors also contributed to the decline of the country. The extension of Roman

[517]

power in the eastern Mediterranean opened up direct trade routes between the far east and Rome, with a consequent decline in the commerce of once wealthy cities, such as Corinth, which had grown rich by the trans-shipment of goods across the isthmus. Meanwhile, Roman military officers, administrative officials, traders, and capitalists, under one pretext or another, imposed an enormous financial strain on the resources of Greece. Pirates, too, preyed on Hellenic shipping, although, be it said to the credit of Rome, piracy was very largely suppressed by the vigorous action of Pompey in 67 B.C.

The Battle of Pharsalus (49 B.C.). Meanwhile, rivalries in Roman politics were coming to a head with unhappy consequences for Greece. When the Roman generals Pompey and Julius Cæsar reached an open break, the Greek cities, with unfortunate judgment, supported the cause of Pompey. The decisive battle was fought at Pharsalus in Greece in 49 B.C., resulting in a victory for Cæsar. The strain of the levies of both armies prior to the conflict had been severe, and Hellas was once again impoverished. Cæsar took no vengeance on the Greek cities for their support of his opponent, and on the whole the country was treated with consideration by him, so far as he was able to spare a thought at all for the fate of Greece in his extraordinarily busy life. The Battles of Philippi and Actium were still to be fought in Greek territory. But before that, on the Ides of March, 44 B.C., Julius Cæsar was assassinated in Rome, and the struggle for control of the government passed to other hands. For thirteen years, until in 31 B.C. the victory of Octavianus over Antony and Cleopatra at Actium gave him an effective control over the state, Rome and her dominions were torn by anarchy and bloodshed.

The Battle of Philippi (42 B.C.). In the interval, however, the same Octavianus, the grandnephew and adopted son of Julius Cæsar, united with Mark Antony and Lepidus to form the Second Triumvirate. They were opposed principally by Sextus Pompeius, the son of the great Pompey who had met defeat at Pharsalus, and by Brutus and Cassius. It was against

[518]

the latter two that Antony and Octavianus set out from Brundisium in the autumn of 42 B.C. They crossed to the western coast of Greece, and the two armies met at Philippi in eastern Macedonia, where for the second time the quarrels of Rome were fought out on Greek soil. The fighting was at first indecisive, and for a time it looked as if the campaign might be prolonged, but Brutus, who had been left alone by the suicide of Cassius, presently risked another encounter and was decisively defeated.

The Influence of Antony. Octavianus and Antony were now the two most powerful figures in the ancient world. Unfortunately for Greece, in the division of authority that followed, Octavianus elected to return to Italy, while to the rapacious Antony was entrusted the task of restoring Roman authority in the east and in Greece. From the Hellenic cities he exacted repeated contributions to finance his wars. For nearly a decade Antony was engaged in various eastern localities, including Armenia and Alexandria, where he fell a victim to the wiles and charms of Cleopatra. During the same period, Octavianus was consolidating his position in Rome.

The Battle of Actium (31 B.C.). For some time it had been growing increasingly obvious that a final test of strength between Octavianus and Antony could not be indefinitely delayed, but it was not until 32 B.C. that the Roman Senate, at the instigation of Octavianus, deprived Antony of his eastern command and opened war on Cleopatra. At this time, Antony was in Greece, and both from the forced contributions of the Greek cities and from the liberal donations of Cleopatra, he was better supplied with money, troops, and ships than was Octavianus. However, he delayed action for months, until Octavianus, by the simple expedient of sending his fleet out to blockade Antony's ships at Actium on the west coast of Greece, kept the encounter away from home. There in September, 31 B.C., the Battle of Actium was fought, resulting in a victory for Octavianus, and the flight of Antony and Cleopatra to Egypt, where in the following year they ended their lives by suicide.

[519]

Greece herself was now prostrate, exhausted with long years of internal strife, stupid politics, and heartless exactions. One of the first acts of Octavianus after his victory at Actium was the relief of the Greeks from actual starvation.

The Emergence of Augustus. With the death of Antony and Cleopatra and the capture of Alexandria in the summer of 30 B.C., Octavianus became the undisputed ruler of Rome, and the ancient world for the first time in two centuries could look for some measure of peace. In 27 B.C., Octavianus "restored the Republic to the Senate and the people," receiving back from them the essential powers of an emperor. The settlement with the Senate of 27 B.C. was a very important constitutional measure, from which dates the power of the first of the Roman emperors. From this year by decree of the Senate Octavianus received and bore the name of Augustus. For the next three hundred years and more the fate of Greece was bound up with the history of the Roman emperors. A Roman proconsul, with his seat of government at Corinth, ruled the province of Achæa.

The Attitude of the Greeks. A curious and yet comprehensible lethargy laid hold of Greece at this time. The Hellenes presented the appearance of a people whose energies had been burned out in the swift flight of genius. Even in the Hellenistic Period the Greeks had so far lost their taste for fighting that they employed mercenary troops in their own wars, and hence it is not surprising that they did not seek careers in the Roman legions. The Romans no longer had any fear of organized revolt in Greece, and they actually looked with favor on any measures of union that were adopted, for their own administrative task might thereby be made easier. But the Greeks evolved no significant federations. They began rather to live upon the glories of their past, and since the Romans frankly admired Hellenic culture, the Greeks sought to emphasize and profit by the differences between themselves and their conquerors. In time an industry grew out of their cultivation of the Hellenic qualities, particularly as they were able to instruct Romans who sought an education in their

[520]

schools. The once imperialistic city of Athens became little more than a university town.

Visitation Between Greece and Italy. In some few places, notably at Patræ and Corinth, the Greek merchants grew prosperous by catering to the taste of the wealthy Romans, especially in foods, marble, and objects of art. In general, however, commerce languished in Greece, and, lacking money themselves, the Greeks sought consolation by frowning on the poor taste that the Romans displayed in flaunting their wealth. Many Romans came to Greece in search of health or culture, or to perform administrative duties. Among them such Roman citizens as Cicero, Vergil, and Horace were numbered. In turn, a great many Greeks went to Rome and to other communities in Italy to teach or trade or supply the demand of the market for paintings or sculptures. Local patriotism, however, precluded the employment of many Greeks in the Roman civil service.

The Interest of Later Emperors in Greece. Different Roman emperors came in contact with Greece, and the resulting incidents are of varying degrees of importance. Tiberius and Claudius, each in turn, made changes in the Roman senatorial control of the Greek provinces. In another generation, the conceited and vainglorious Nero was emperor of Rome, and during 67 A.D. and 68 A.D., he undertook an extensive tour of Greece, visiting the various national festivals, where he gave personal demonstrations of his mediocre talents in art and letters. The astute Greeks applauded him vociferously wherever he went, and he rewarded their flattery by gifts of local political freedom and exemption from taxation, though he nullified the value of his favors by the indiscriminate confiscation of art treasures that caught his fancy.

Hadrian in Greece. The next important imperial visit to Greece did not take place until the accession of Hadrian in the second century after Christ. During the years 123 A.D. to 126 A.D., Hadrian was occupied in an extensive tour of the Greek-speaking lands of the eastern half of his Empire.

Hadrian was an emperor of very different character from Nero. He was a man of wide culture and of genuine sympathy with Hellenic achievements, and consequently he sought to confer

FIGURE 138. ARCH OF HADRIAN. The arch was erected by the Roman emperor Hadrian in the second century A.D. to mark the dividing line between the ancient city of Athens and the extensions made through his benefactions. The temple seen beyond the arch is the Olympieum.

[522]

on Greece such relief as he could. Aqueducts, public works, and monuments were erected in many Greek communities at his behest, and he extended relief from tribute and arrears of taxation with a more discriminating hand, and consequently with more permanence, than Nero had done. He did something also to foster national sentiment and to encourage the organization of an internal Pan-Hellenic Congress, meeting at Athens. The Arch of Hadrian still stands in Athens as a memorial to his visit. Nevertheless, his association with Greece is only an incident in the long story of Greek dependence on Roman initiative.

The Invasions of Greece. Toward the end of the second Christian century, Greece was threatened by invasion from the north. A wild tribe actually penetrated into central Greece, where it was repelled by the local states. The hand of Rome was loosening, and the danger of external attack was thereby increased. In the middle of the third century, in 253 A.D., the northerners again made a determined attack on Greece, but this time the Macedonian town of Thessalonica turned them back. A few years later, the Goths, who were eventually to descend on western Europe, penetrated into the Greek peninsula, though they were unable to establish permanent settlements.

The Founding of Constantinople (330 A.D.); the End of Ancient Greek History. With the mention of the northern tribes, and particularly of the Goths, we are verging on mediæval history. One will think of other racial groups that in the following centuries invaded Greece, of the Longbeards and Vandals and Avars, even of Otto de la Roche and his fellows, who came in the time of the Crusades. For present purposes, however, the story of Greek history must be brought to a close in the fourth Christian century. The Roman Empire had grown too unwieldy for management from a single city on the Tiber, and consequently the Emperor Constantine gave directions that Byzantium, a city that had been founded by Megara in 660 B.C. during the great period of organized Greek colonization, should be enlarged and converted into the new capital of the Eastern Roman Empire. On May 11, 330 A.D., Byzantium was inaugurated as the seat of government and given the name of New Rome, or Constantinople, a name that the city bore until the present century, when it became first Stamboul, and now Istanbul. From that date a mingling of Greek, Latin, and Christian interests was to lead the peoples of Greece into paths far removed from those of classical culture.

ALEXANDRIAN LITERATURE
(323–146 B.C.)

The Patronage of Literature at Alexandria. During the Hellenistic Age, from 323 B.C. to 146 B.C., the center of literary, as well as of artistic, activity passed from Athens. Although important schools of Hellenistic art flourished at a half dozen different sites in Asia Minor and Africa, literature was fostered so largely at Alexandria, the city founded by Alexander himself in 331 B.C., that the writings of the age are described more frequently as Alexandrian than as Hellenistic. The years of Alexandrian literature are, however, the same as those of the Hellenistic Age. The accumulation of academic resources at Alexandria was without parallel in the ancient world. The first king of Egypt, Ptolemy Soter, who assumed the rule after the death of Alexander and the partition of the empire he had founded, proved to be a tyrant with a scholarly ambition to foster letters at his court. He invited the most distinguished literary men of the time to make their homes in Alexandria, and many of them came.

The Alexandrian Library. In addition, Ptolemy commenced to gather together a huge collection of manuscripts, which, during the next three centuries, through the patronage of successive Ptolemies, grew into a great library estimated to have contained 700,000 texts, embracing the works of all the distinguished writers of antiquity. The Library was burned in 47 B.C. It was rebuilt, a great collection was again assembled in it, and the Library flourished for centuries. The story has long persisted that following the successful siege of Alexandria by the Mohammedan general Amrou in 642 A.D., the Library was again destroyed and the manuscripts distributed to the city baths for fuel by order of the Caliph, but the details of this tale are not now generally accepted. It is, nevertheless, tantalizing to reflect that some of the lost tragedies of Æschylus, Sophocles, and Euripides, known now only by name or allusion, were probably extant in that great but ill-fated collection that existed for nearly seven hundred years of the Christian era.

The Artificiality of Alexandrian Literature. In the Alexandrian Period, an appropriate building with beautiful grounds was provided to house not only the texts, but also the scholars who were invited to Alexandria to continue and further the traditions of Greek letters. Unfortunately, it was to become evident to posterity that more than papyri and buildings and patronage was necessary to continue a great literature. The scholarship of the Alexandrian writers was above reproach. Simply to cite the names of the librarians who in turn assumed the leadership of the learned community, Zenodotus, Callimachus, Eratosthenes, Apollonius of Rhodes, Aristophanes of Byzantium, and Aristarchus, is sufficient warrant of their learning.

The efforts of the Alexandrians were, however, turned too often to tedious scholarly pursuits. Men busied themselves in compiling lists of the notable writers of the classical age, such as the Canon of Ten Attic Orators, the Canon of Nine Lyric Poets, or the list of the Seven Sages of Antiquity, in writing commentaries on Homer, or dividing the histories of Herodotus and Thucydides into books, rather than in writing enthusiastically and with original ideas, in prose or poetry, in the spirit of the men whom they studied. The genius of the creative centuries of Greek civilization had given place to great learning, pedantry, and reflection unrelated to life. It is a fault that is not entirely absent from modern scholarship, for the meticulous and exact evaluation of past achievement leaves too little zest for the creation of new forms of literature at any time. When the Alexandrians did write poetry, they wrote, with the possible

[526]

exception of Theocritus, in the academic style of men who had learned the rules and sought a topic, and not because they were possessed of the divine madness that Plato said must lay hold of the poet. They wrote, in short, because they wanted to be honored as scholars and authors, and not because they had anything of importance to say.

The Librarians. Three of the Alexandrian librarians, Zenodotus, who was born in 310 B.C., Aristophanes of Byzantium, who was active about 200 B.C., and Aristarchus, who flourished about 160 B.C., were grammarians and Homeric critics, who achieved little of independent literary value. A fourth librarian, Eratosthenes, was a man of encyclopædic knowledge, whose writings touched on such diverse fields as geography, poetry, physics, philosophy, mathematics, and chronology. He was an honest scientist, but the greater part of his work has been lost, and the literary quality of his writings cannot have been high. Two other librarians remain to be discussed, Callimachus and Apollonius of Rhodes.

Callimachus. Callimachus was born in Cyrene about 310 B.C., and educated in Athens. He taught school in Alexandria, and spent the latter half of his life in connection with the Alexandrian Library, first as a scholar under the patronage of Ptolemy Philadelphus, and later as librarian. He died about 240 B.C. A man of great learning and industry, he was nevertheless one of the most artificial, and hence one of the most characteristic, of all the Alexandrians. His *Lock of Berenice's Hair* is among the best known of his poems, largely because the Alexandrian stiffness has been perpetuated in Alexander Pope's English adaptation of the poem, *The Rape of the Lock*. The theme, which is treated with mock seriousness, is the deification of a lock of hair dedicated by Berenice for the safe return from war of her husband Ptolemy.

The Writings of Callimachus. It is from his *Epigrams,* of which more than three score have been preserved in the *Greek Anthology,* that we can form the best estimate of the poetic gifts of Callimachus and credit him with at least a few verses of rare beauty of feeling. His lament on the death of his old friend and fellow poet, Heraclitus of Halicarnassus, is among his most graceful efforts, and it has become part of the English poetic heritage through William Cory's beautiful verse translation. The poem tells, with a restraint and clarity worthy of the best classical period, of the bitter grief of Callimachus on learning of his friend's death, of his recollection of their long conversations together, and finally, referring to the verses of Heraclitus as "nightingales," closes with a beautiful apostrophe to the immortality of poetry.

> They told me, Heraclitus, they told me you were dead,
> They brought me bitter news to hear and bitter tears to shed.
> I wept, as I remembered, how often you and I
> Had tired the sun with talking and sent him down the sky.
>
> And now that thou art lying, my dear old Carian guest,
> A handful of grey ashes, long long ago at rest,
> Still are thy pleasant voices, thy nightingales, awake;
> For Death, he taketh all away, but them he cannot take.

The lament for the sailor lost at sea is likewise characteristic of the epitaphs of Callimachus:

Would that man had never made swift ships, for then we should not be weeping for Sopolis, the son of Diocleides. But now his body is cast upon the sea, and we pass by only a name upon a cenotaph.

The Revival of the Epic. The literary prestige of Callimachus, who had pronounced "a big book a big evil," had turned the minds of the Alexandrian scholars to the composition of brief hymns, epigrams, or at most miniature epics. Signs of revolt, however, presently appeared. A Cretan poet, Rhianus, treated an historical theme at some length. His subject was the struggle of the Messenians to free themselves from Sparta. Rhianus entitled his epic the *Messenians,* and wrote it from the point of view of a Messenian sympathizer.

[528]

Apollonius Rhodius. More important was the venture of Apollonius, who wrote an epic recounting the voyage of Jason and the Argonauts in search of the Golden Fleece. The poem was commenced while he was living in Alexandria, but, in irritation at the ridicule which he encountered in that city, Apollonius withdrew to Rhodes, where he was received with enthusiasm, and there finished his work. Accordingly, it is as Apollonius Rhodius that he is commonly known. After the death of Callimachus and Eratosthenes, Apollonius was recalled to Alexandria, where he became librarian.

The "Argonautica." In the *Argonautica,* Apollonius deliberately undertook to write an epic that, both in style and length, should compare with the Homeric poems. Since the *Argonautica* consists of four books, totaling about six thousand verses, Apollonius amply demonstrated his capacity for sustained epic narrative. Nor is the poem hopelessly weak and insipid. He had in the story of Jason and his comrades a good theme, and he dealt with it as competently as any man of his period could do. He tells of the assembling of the Argonauts for their voyage, of Orpheus who sang to them of the infancy of Greece and of the world, of the launching of the Argo, and of the adventures of the heroes. He brings in the beautiful myth of Hylas, who, having gone ashore to draw water, was snatched away by the nymphs of the spring, and tells how Heracles left the expedition to search for his beloved Hylas. He recounts also in epic manner a series of adventures that were met as the ship sailed on. The boxing match, the punishment of Phineus, who was tortured by eternal old age for betraying the will of Zeus, the rescue of the sons of Phrixus, and the near approach to Prometheus chained on the Scythian rock, a story that Æschylus had treated in the *Prometheus Bound,* are also included.

The principal part of the tale, however, is the account of Medea's love for Jason, which leads her not only to use her magic powers to enable him to slay the sleepless dragon and escape with the Golden Fleece, but even to kill her own brother

[529]

in the haste of flight. Medea, in spite of the introduction of conventional savagery to accomplish her purpose, is not the wicked sorceress that Euripides had depicted in his play, the *Medea.* She is, rather, a maiden who, as Phineus had prophesied, has become so enraptured of Jason through the arts of Aphrodite that she is inexorably drawn to him and away from her father, even though she is torn with anguish of soul for the pain she is causing.

After the Argonauts have left Colchis with the Golden Fleece and with Medea, Apollonius describes their further course in tedious detail. His great weakness lies in yielding to the temptation of the scholar to include every incident that legend records, in order to make a pedantic parade of his learning. The achievement of Apollonius was great, but his work lacked vitality, for he was looking to the past and he had lost the spirit of intellectual adventure without which progress is impossible.

Theocritus. Theocritus, who was active about 285 B.C., was the greatest of the Alexandrian poets, both for the originality of his thought and the effectiveness of his composition. He was not one of the librarians, and possibly his escape from the arid routine of scholarship enabled him to write on a new theme with the freshness of a true poet. The biographical details concerning Theocritus are exceedingly meager. Apparently he was born in Syracuse but went at an early age to the island of Cos, the summer home of the Ptolemies, where he came in contact with the Alexandrian rulers. Subsequently he spent some time in Alexandria under the patronage of one of the Ptolemies. From internal evidence there is also good reason to believe that he had personal knowledge of the countryside of Italy.

The Pastoral Poetry of Theocritus. The great original contribution of Theocritus to Greek letters was his development of pastoral poetry. Thirty *Idyls,* or little poems, in all have been preserved. Some of these are colored by the artificial themes and techniques of the Alexandrian School, some reflect a mood of comedy, but others, in sufficient quantity to assure

[530]

their author an important place in the history of literature, are marked by the simplicity and originality of scenes from rustic life.

The songs of the shepherds, their contests for the prize of a lamb, a kid, or a carved bowl, their sentimental poems, and the gifts and devices by which they sought the favor of a loved one; the lament for the dead shepherd, with the fancy that all nature, animate and inanimate, joins in the mourning—all these Theocritus celebrates. No one before had sung in so simple a manner of the beauty of everyday things. As a consequence, in his themes of the countryside there appears the outlook on life that prompted the artists of the *genre* school of sculpture, who worked during the same period, to select similar subjects. Theocritus thus started a type of poetry that was to be imitated and continued by Vergil, Sannazaro, Mantuan, Petrarch, Sainte-Beuve, Spenser, Cowper, and Wordsworth, to mention but a few names.

The Death of Daphnis. The first *Idyl* in the collection is at once the most typical and perhaps the most charmingly pastoral in mood. A shepherd, Thyrsis, meets a goatherd, and they exchange compliments on their skill in piping. Presently Thyrsis consents, for the gift of a carved wooden cup, which is described in poetic detail, to sing the song of Daphnis, the shepherd who dies for the sake of love.

THYRSIS AND THE GOATHERD

THYRSIS

> A sweet thing, goatherd, is a tree's whisper,
> And sweet, too, is the pine
> That murmureth softly by yon spring:
> And of like sweetness is thy piping:
> After Pan alone shall thy piping be acclaim'd.

GOATHERD

> More sweetly, shepherd, doth thy singing
> Fall upon my ears
> Than sound of the echoing rivulet
> That tumbleth from the rock above.

[531]

THYRSIS

    Now by the Nymphs I pray thee, goatherd,
    Come sit thee by the tamarisks
    On this gentle slope,
    And gently pipe for me.

    The goatherd is prevailed upon to sing and with incomparable effectiveness he describes in verse the intricate artistry of the carven ivy bowl which he pledges as a prize.

THE IVY BOWL

    And round about the bowl's lip
    Entwineth ivy from above,
    Ivy mark'd by helichryse:
    And the helichryse, bright with saffron fruit,
    Twisteth with grace
    Among the ivy-leaves.

    Within the bowl a maid is carv'd,
    The cunning craftsmanship of gods,
    Bedight with robe and band.
    And by her either side two lovers stand;
    Fair of flowing hair are they;
    With rival words they vie
    And seek her love;
    But all untouchèd is her mind,
    For now to one, now to the other,
    For an instant's span
    A laughing glance she turns;
    And they, eyes lack-luster'd by the weight of love,
    Contend in vain for her.

    And by these swains within the cup
    An agèd fisher is engrav'd,
    And near to him a jagged rock;
    Upon this rock with eager craft
    The fisher draws his spreading net,
    Like to one who toileth mightily,
    As he would throw.
    Yea, the old man fishes,
    Thou wouldst vow, with every nerve drawn taut;

For on his neck the sinews strain,
And lo, the greybeard's strength
Is as the strength of youth.

And still within the cup at slight remove
From the weather'd figure of the fisherman
Is fashioned clear a vineyard's slope,
Rich with ripe-cluster'd grapes.
And on the hedge there sits a little lad,
Set to watch the fruit.
Round about are foxes two:
One creeps with stealth along the rows
And preyeth on the grapes,
The other layeth cunning siege
To the wallet of the lad
And voweth that he will not cease
Until he spoileth him
Of all his food.

But the lad with mind intent upon his weaving
Plaiteth a locust-cage
With fitted reeds;
Naught careth he for wallet
Nor for the vineyard's fruit,
For all his joy
Is in his chosen task.

And all about the goblet
Curves the acanthus leaf,
A sight of varied loveliness.
A wondrous piece of work it is
To lift the heart of man.

Theocritus, Idyl I, verses 1–56, extracts
Translated by H. N. Couch

The ivy bowl serves a dual purpose. Not only does it enable the poet to describe the imaginative *genre* scenes of his fancy but it affords also a setting for the graceful description of art in verse.

The Syracusan Women. Theocritus found place among his *Idyls* for topics other than the pastoral. *Idyl XV,* for instance,

[533]

affords an excellent example of the humorous character sketch, which was to be developed, especially by Herondas, into his *Mimes,* or mimic-pieces. In this *Idyl* Theocritus, with rollicking good humor, tells how Gorgo, a Syracusan woman, calls on a fellow Syracusan, Praxinoë, living in Alexandria, so that they may go together to see the festival of Adonis. The dialogue is vigorous, of a homespun frankness, and fresh with the reality of middle class life in antiquity. The two women gossip in an amiably ill-bred manner about their clothes, their homes, the servants, and their husbands, hastily trying to divert the attention of Praxinoë's child who shows evidence of understanding too much. The idle chatter of every age is inherent in their speech. Presently they go forth to the festival where the lament for Adonis, a beautiful and dignified hymn, is sung.

The Hylas Legend. One more idyl of Theocritus, the thirteenth, may be briefly described for the pretty myth that it recalls. In it is told the story of the snatching away of Hylas and the grief of Heracles, the same theme that Apollonius Rhodius had dealt with in one incident of the *Argonautica.* A few verses follow.

And Hylas, the fair-haired youth, had gone forth to bear back water for the meal of Heracles and the stout Telamon. And straightway he beheld a spring in a little hollow, and many a shrub grew about it. And within the water the Nymphs were leading the dance, sleepless Nymphs, dread goddesses to the country-folk, even Eunice, and Malis, and Nycheia, whose glance was the glance of Spring. And when Hylas held forth his vessel to dip it into the pool, all the Nymphs seized him by the arm, for love of the Argive lad stirred the tender breast of each. Then headlong he fell into the dark water, as when a star falls from the Heavens into the sea. But the Nymphs took the weeping lad upon their knees, and comforted him with soft words.

Moschus and Bion. Two other poets, Moschus and Bion, carried forward certain of the poetic traditions of Theocritus, especially the *Lament.* Moschus wrote a *Lament for Bion,*

[534]

and Bion, a *Lament for Adonis*. In the latter poem the idea of mountains, streams, and flowers weeping for the dead Adonis is very effectively treated. It was Theocritus who first intro-duced allegory into pastoral poetry, and the practice was carried still further by Moschus and Bion. Many will feel that by this bequest to later pastoral verse they have not served the cause of literature well.

The Mime. The character sketch, usually of a humorous nature, which was observed in the *Syracusan Women* of Theocritus, was further developed by Herondas, Theophrastus, and by the writers of New Comedy. Herondas of Cos, who lived from about 300 B.C. to about 250 B.C., wrote *Mimes,* or "Imitations," in which something of the quality of contempo-rary *genre* sculpture may again be detected. He delighted to portray vulgar, even base, characters, engaged in the most trivial pursuits. The gossiping of women and the scolding of servants, so common in the *Mimes,* remind one of the similar scene in the *Syracusan Women* of Theocritus.

The third *Mime* of Herondas will serve to illustrate this type of literature. The poem is called the *Schoolmaster,* and it pic-tures an outraged mother, Metrotime, who brings her worthless son, Cottalus, to the schoolmaster, Lampriscus, and urges the latter to thrash her son "until his wicked life hangs only from his lips. For he has destroyed my roof by gambling there, not with knuckle-bones, but using coins." Lampriscus undertakes to beat the boy, who, however, escapes with a jeer, pursued by the threats of his mother, who will go home and tell "the old man," so that the boy may be brought back, tied by the feet, and soundly beaten, while the Muses of the schoolroom, whom he hates, look down on him. The *Mimes* of Herondas were written in the *scazon,* or limping iambic meter, which Hippo-nax had used for vituperative verse in the archaic age.

Theophrastus. A more versatile writer, Theophrastus, is noteworthy for his contributions to the same type of literature. His life extended from 372 B.C. to 287 B.C. He was born in Lesbos, but after the death of Aristotle in 322 B.C., he settled

[535]

in Athens, where he became a distinguished philosopher and teacher. Though some of his observations on philosophy and botany have been preserved, it is through his treatise called the *Characters* that he is chiefly known. This work belongs in the tradition of Herondas and New Comedy, for it consists of a collection of some thirty brief essays, each describing a typical man, such as the tactless man, the avaricious man, or the stupid man. Theophrastus' judgment of human nature was keen, and he has succeeded in observing and recording universal traits, which have given his essays a certain perennial interest, although the literary quality is not the highest.

NEW COMEDY

Menander. Comedy, which has already been treated under Old Comedy during the fifth century and Middle Comedy during the fourth century, reaches its final phase as New Comedy in the Hellenistic Period. Something of its nature has already been indicated in the references to the character sketches of Theocritus, Herondas, and Theophrastus, but fortunately it is possible to judge New Comedy directly from the fairly long consecutive passages of a few plays of Menander discovered among the papyri, as well as from a very large number of shorter scattered fragments.

Menander was born in Athens in 342 B.C. and died in 291 B.C., at the age of fifty-one. Though he was associated in various ways with the public men of his time, it is as a writer of comedies of manners that he is known. In antiquity he was extravagantly admired for his style, his wit, and especially for his fidelity to human nature in his plot portrayals. Modern taste has apparently changed, for it is difficult, on reading the extant portions of his plays, to believe that he deserves as high a place in literature as was accorded to him in ancient times. It will be remembered that Archilochus and Mimnermus were also more highly regarded in antiquity than at present, and the reason is probably to be sought in the sense of reality with

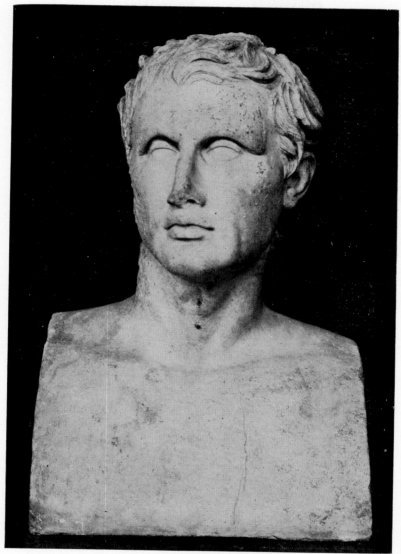

FIGURE 139. MENANDER. Græco-Roman Period. Idealization of type in portraiture has by this time yielded to a larger measure of individualism in the features.

[537]

which each of these men looked on his immediate environment.

The Plays of Menander. Several of the comedies of Menander may be mentioned and identified. The *Arbitrants* is most nearly complete. It is a comedy of intrigue, unknown identity, domestic misunderstanding, and ultimate recognition. The anagnorisis, or recognition scene, in this play is effected through the mechanical means of trinkets or birth-tokens left with a child exposed in infancy, a device which was to become increasingly common. The *Girl from Samos,* the *Girl with Bobbed Hair,* and the *Heros,* likewise, deal largely with domestic intrigue, confusion, and jealousy, though in some passages a fine note of pathos and unselfishness is struck. Of the *Countryman* a fragment has been preserved, which gives us an indication of one type of scene that amused the audience. It represents a youth, who comes into the house and finds preparations in progress for his own wedding, in which he has no desire to take part, and who leaves the scene hastily.

The trivial and momentary qualities of the plots of New Comedy represent the final stage of this type of literature, and contrast sharply with the political satire and the moral conviction of Old Comedy as it flourished a century or more earlier.

Subsequent Influence of Alexandrian Literature. It would not be correct to assume that Alexandrian literature was the major influence on Roman letters, for the indebtedness of Vergil to Homer, of Horace to Sappho and Alcæus, and of Cicero to Plato is too well known to leave any doubt of the direct influence of the greatest of the Greek writers on the literary figures of Rome. Nevertheless, the literary forms of the Alexandrian Age held a peculiar fascination for many of the young Roman poets, and the Alexandrian source of the early reading and study of Vergil and Catullus and many others can be readily detected. This is revealed in the themes of poetry, in the erotic element, and again in the long, tedious, and pedantic parade of learning, which tempts Vergil, for instance, in his youthful efforts to include elaborate mythological allusions, lists of flowers, or tales of intrigue.

The attention to form, even the interest in detail, may have served a useful purpose at one stage of Roman poetic endeavor. The vigor of Roman literature, however, as seen in the mature work of Vergil and in the poems of strong personal conviction of Catullus and his fellows, depended on an intellectual and emotional growth that quickly superseded the stultifying formalism that continued devotion to Alexandrian models would have produced in Latin poetry.

CHAPTER XXXI

HELLENISTIC AND GRÆCO-ROMAN SCULPTURE

The Hellenistic Period (323–146 b.c.)

The Meaning of the Hellenistic Period. The literature of the Hellenistic Age was described in connection with its association with Alexander and the Alexandrian Library. During the same period, art developed along lines which, as has already been seen in the field of literature, can be characterized as *Hellenistic.* This term, as opposed to *Hellenic,* signifies a civilization in which peoples who may not have had long generations of Greek ancestry behind them were seeking to act and think like Hellenes, or Greeks. The campaigns of Alexander had carried Greek culture far into Asia and Africa, and people on those continents seized avidly on the Greek spirit in art, or on the peculiarly vigorous and expressive Greek language as a vehicle for the conveyance of their thoughts, though their parents may have known little or nothing of Greece. Similarly, even in Athens and in the other ancient cities of Greece proper, revivalism dominated endeavor, producing a self-conscious Hellenism. By such an explanation, Hellenistic art and literature are neither praised nor disparaged. The achievements in that age must be judged by their inherent qualities.

The Centers of Hellenistic Art. During the Hellenistic Age, the most active centers of art were no longer to be found in Greece proper. The exhaustion of war and the resulting political confusion among the city-states were not conducive to sustained creative effort. It was rather in Asia Minor, Egypt, and on the islands, in such cities as Pergamum, Ephesus, Tralles, Delos, and Rhodes, that significant artistic work was now to be sought, for in these places ample funds to foster the arts were available from governments and individuals, while comparative political peace was assured to the artists. The geographical location of the art centers makes it clear that the penetration of Alexander into the remote interior of Asia did not result in the establishment of schools of art in those regions. Instead, it was in the coastal cities of Asia Minor, which were Greek in origin, and which in the archaic period had developed a vigorous Hellenic civilization even in advance of Athens and the other cities of the Greek mainland, that art, especially sculpture, was again actively pursued.

Travel Among the Hellenistic Artists. Although the artists of the new age were not deficient in technical skill, it was difficult for them to strike out on original paths. In the very nature of things, aspiring artists visited Athens, Delphi, and Olympia, where the choicest creations of the past were dedicated. Here they were forced to the discouraging conclusion that original efforts were no longer possible in the different fields developed by such artists as Pheidias, Polycleitus, or Ictinus. The constant travel of the young artists of the Hellenistic Period, both to the older centers of Greek art and among the communities where their fellows were working, quickly produced a similarity of technique and purpose, which was reflected in the qualities common to all Hellenistic sculpture.

Realism. A further result of the study of techniques perfected by the earlier artists was the tendency of some of the sculptors of the Hellenistic schools to turn to realism as a still unexplored field. The portrayal of realistic types was already to some extent familiar. It may be seen in the momentary expression of the faces of the statues of Cephisodotus and Praxiteles, and in the intense emotion delineated by Scopas. In the Hellenistic Age, however, the fine restraint of feeling

[541]

FIGURE 140. APOLLO BELVEDERE. Hellenistic Period. Vatican. The free and romantic pose is characteristic of the period.

[542]

that had characterized the earlier ages of Greece was relaxed, and the artists began to introduce into their works the garish, the elaborate, and the tasteless, provided only that it appealed to the emotions. It would, however, be unfair to assume that such qualities were present in all Hellenistic works, for if that were true, this art could scarcely command our attention at all. In spite of a certain amount of artificiality, there is much that is dignified and fine in the Hellenistic Period.

The Apollo Belvedere. Furthermore, realism in art may mean no more than the absence of allegory or idealization. Thus the Apollo Belvedere (Figure 140), which is a statue of definitely Hellenistic qualities, is a good example of realism in that the artist has tried to picture the young god, without idealization, exactly as a contemporary youth. It is not realistic in the very common, but less desirable, sense of seeking a sensational or exaggerated pose. There is no suggestion of symbolism or distortion. The Apollo Belvedere is simply a trifle theatrical and self-conscious. It lacks the permanent qualities of a fifth-century statue of a god; in fact, it would have been virtually impossible for the artist who was reared in the atmosphere of more immediate human interest to have created the remote and abiding type of a century before, even in the unlikely event that he had wished to do so.

The Dying Gaul. The Dying Gaul, or more properly the Dying Galatian (Figure 141), is an example of the Hellenistic manner of handling a subject and pose very similar to those of the figure of the wounded warrior on the eastern pediment of the Temple of Aphæa at Ægina, which dates about 480 B.C. (see Figure 85). Consequently, one can study in the Ægina figure the method by which an artist working in the archaic age expressed the anguish of a wounded warrior, and compare this with the way in which it was done by a later artist, with all the devices of a developed technique at hand. Some will think that in the figure from Ægina there is a rugged honesty of purpose, which is lost in the Dying Gaul by the very abundance of technical devices available to create the illusion of

[543]

pain, as, for instance, the representation of blood flowing from the wound. If that be one's reaction, he will feel that he has in these two statues examples of the ascent and the descent of Greek art. The Dying Gaul also illustrates the interest of the Hellenistic artists in foreign peoples and their success in rendering the features of races that were not Hellenic, for the statue was made at Pergamum to celebrate the victory of King

Photograph by Alinari

FIGURE 141. DYING GAUL. Hellenistic Period. Capitoline Museum, Rome. The pose of this figure affords a more realistic rendering of the theme that was treated in the Archaic Age in the Dying Warrior from the Temple of Aphæa, Figure 85.

Attalus I, who reigned from 241 B.C. to 197 B.C., over the Galatian marauders from the north.

The Gaul and His Wife. The well-known statue of the Gaul who has slain his wife and is about to slay himself, so that they may both escape capture, shows a magnificent contrast between the intense vigor of the Gaul and the limp body of his dead wife. This statue and also the figure of the Scythian sharpening his knife for the punishment of Marsyas belong to the same school of art as the Dying Gaul, and like

[544]

it illustrate the preoccupation of the Hellenistic artists with foreign types. The great Pergamene Altar is an architectural monument of the Hellenistic Age. Its larger and smaller friezes represent the Battle of the Gods and Giants and symbolize the conflict between the Pergamenes and Galatians in the same way as such scenes had been used by the artists of the early fifth century to recall the struggle of the Greeks and the Persians.

Eclecticism. Realism in art was the inevitable result of individualism. Another element of Hellenistic art already mentioned—the dependence on the inspiration of the past—is shown by the large place of eclecticism. *Eclecticism* means the selection by the artist of different features characteristic of earlier sculptors, and the incorporation of these in his own productions. Thus in a single eclectic statue of the Hellenistic Period it may be possible to pick out the heavy, square-cut head first found on the statues of Polycleitus, the Praxitelean curve of the body, and the spare, hard surface of Lysippus.

The Nike of Samothrace. The Nike of Samothrace (Figure 142) is a well-known and well-executed piece of Hellenistic art, in which eclecticism is notably present. The winged figure of Victory is a type that first occurred in the archaic period, when the sculptors were still working with the problem of transition from full front to profile aspects of the body; it was fully developed as a type in the Nike of Pæonius in 425 B.C.; it is seen in the figures on the balustrade of the Temple of Athena Nike in Athens; and, finally, in the statue at Samothrace it appears again in a Hellenistic rendering. A close study of various parts of the Nike of Samothrace will reveal qualities developed in the fourth century by Scopas, Praxiteles, and Lysippus, for the very emotion of victory recalls Scopas; the curve of the body is Praxitelean; and the precision and accuracy of carving bespeak Lysippus. The statue is accordingly an eclectic work, made by an unknown sculptor who had studied the methods of his predecessors.

The Aphrodite of Melos. The Aphrodite of Melos, or the

[545]

Photograph by Alinari

FIGURE 142. NIKE, OR VICTORY, OF SAMOTHRACE. Hellenistic Period.
Louvre. The use of diaphanous drapery, the curve of the body, and
various other attributes mark this as a late statue utilizing earlier
techniques.

[546]

Venus de Milo, to give it a better known name (Figure 143), is a statue of very wide celebrity, which was discovered under dramatic circumstances on the island of Melos, and has been the subject of considerable subsequent controversy regarding its date and its place in the history of art. The statue was made in two parts, the upper and nude portion being of finer marble than the lower half. This statue, too, is an eclectic work, showing in the heavy folds of drapery the characteristics of fifth-century art, but the rendering of the head and the curve of the body are features that surely owe their origin to the example of Praxiteles. The statue should be dated in the third century before Christ, that is, in the first half of the Hellenistic Period. It is remarkably well preserved and has long been one of the admired possessions of the Louvre in Paris.

Portraiture. It was natural that portraiture should occupy an increasingly important place in Hellenistic art, for such a field afforded an outlet for the delineation of immediate and realistic features. It is this quality that characterizes the Hellenistic statues of the poets and the orators (see Figure 137); excellent likenesses, as they obviously are, they offer a striking contrast to the idealized fifth-century portrait of Pericles (Figure 47), which shows not so much the individual man as the typical statesman and general. Conversely, the Hellenistic artists were not markedly successful in carving statues of the gods, though some figures of deities were attempted. The religious life of the age was not sufficiently composed to allow for the creation of abiding and impersonal types, such as Pheidias had sculptured.

Genre Sculpture. Still another contribution of the Hellenistic Age to originality of conception was the development of *genre* statuary, the field which, with portraiture, is the most original in the period. In the *genre* groups, the artists completely abandoned the old heroic, mythological, and historical types, and produced instead scenes of family life, of the farmyard, or of childhood, in which no significance is to be read beyond

[547]

FIGURE 143. APHRODITE OF MELOS. Hellenistic
Period. Louvre. This statue incorporates various
techniques of earlier periods.

the picture itself. Naturally, in such art realism was likely to run rampant, and scenes like the old and haggard shepherdess, the drunken man, the fish-seller, or the old, bent peasant woman with her market basket became common. The well-known humorous group of the boy struggling with a goose almost as large as himself, which was made during this age by Boëthos, illustrates the casual choice of subject matter by the artists of the *genre* school, and also the more successful, as well as the more frequent, rendering of children's forms.

Qualities of Hellenistic Art. In summarizing the characteristics of the art of the Hellenistic Period, the emergence of portraiture and *genre* sculpture as two significant features should be emphasized. It will be observed also that the geographical area over which Greek art was spread was now much wider than at any previous time, and that the active centers had moved away from the Greek mainland, although they were still largely confined to the cities of Asia Minor that were predominantly Greek in population.

While technical capacity actually increased in the Hellenistic Age, there was a decline in the inherent excellence of the work. The genius of the people had diminished since the fifth century, and it is not to be expected that technical skill will of itself produce great art any more than mechanical facilities for printing will produce great literature. It will also be noted that, though the names of many Hellenistic artists are known, it has not been possible or desirable to attempt to identify specific men with continuing principles of art, as, for instance, it was possible to identify the works of Myron by the torsion of the body, or those of Scopas by the intensity of the facial expression. This situation is a natural outcome of the pre-emption of practically every distinctive type by the earlier artists, as well as the greater frequency of travel which quickly familiarized the Hellenistic sculptors with the work of many schools. They were faced with the inevitable alternative between yielding in some measure to the influence of their predecessors and groping for originality; when they adopted the latter course, it is small wonder that they departed at times from the sensitivity of Greek art in its finest manifestation.

THE GRÆCO-ROMAN PERIOD (146 B.C.–330 A.D.)

The Environment of Græco-Roman Art. Certain definite characteristics that may be associated with the artistic productions of the Græco-Roman Period are the natural outgrowth of the time and circumstances under which they were created. Rome, rather than Athens or the Hellenistic cities, became the center of artistic activity. The art of the period was Roman in two respects; first, it was largely produced in Italy, and second, it belonged to the era of Roman ascendancy. On the other hand, the workmen, or craftsmen, or artists, by whichever term one may choose to call them, were usually Greeks who sought a livelihood in supplying the Roman market, and in that respect the art was Greek. Although the Roman conquest of Greece did not destroy the manual dexterity of the artists, it did deaden their spiritual sensitivity, and the untrammeled freedom of earlier centuries was no longer to be seen.

Furthermore, the demand for objects of art now came largely from newly enriched Roman families, who cultivated a taste for Greek art because it was the fashion. The result was twofold. In the first place, original Greek statues were plundered and brought to Rome by traveling officials, among whom Nero has already been mentioned; in the second place, Greek artists made copies and adaptations of the works of Myron and Pheidias, Cephisodotus and Praxiteles, to be sold in the Roman market. In fact, it will be well to repeat at this point what was emphasized in an earlier chapter, namely, that many famous statues of the fifth and fourth centuries, such as the Tyrannicides of Critius and Nesiotes, the Discobolus of Myron, the Doryphorus and the Amazon of Polycleitus, the Apoxyomenus of Lysippus, and the Aphrodite of Cnidus by Praxiteles, are in each case known to us only through Roman copies.

[550]

FIGURE 144. VENUS GENETRIX. Græco-Roman Period. Louvre.
Note the artistic qualities of earlier centuries.

In the same connection it will be wise to recall also that it is time and convention that have accustomed us to look on the gleaming white surfaces of statuary, whether of ancient or modern marble, or in the collections of casts that many museums display. To an ancient Greek such unadorned works would have seemed inexpressibly bad. He painted his statues; the drapery reflected the rich colors of the day, the flesh was tinted, the eyes according to Plato the most beautiful part of the body, received peculiarly careful attention, the hair was colored with lifelike detail.

It is small wonder that such statues, when, greater than life size, they represented deities, assumed more than human beauty in the eyes of the beholders. If we must content ourselves with studying form rather than color or the completed concept (and it would be a bold man who would suggest the painting of the Venus de Milo at this date), at least we should refrain from praising the austere beauty of white marble as if it were so intended by the Greeks.

The Venus Genetrix. It is possible to determine in many cases the inspiration of particular statues or groups of the Græco-Roman Period, even though they may not be specifically identified copies of any Greek original. For instance, the statue of Venus Genetrix (Figure 144) presumably made by Arcesilaus about the middle of the first century before Christ, is clearly modeled after the fifth-century tradition and may owe its origin, together with many another Græco-Roman statue of similar style, to the Aphrodite of the Gardens, sculptured by Alcamenes, a contemporary of Pheidias, who made the figures of the west pediment on the Temple of Zeus at Olympia. Thus a statue of the Venus Genetrix type reveals qualities of diaphanous drapery and a curve of the body that suggest the finest techniques of the classical centuries. It is, however, the work of an artist of the Græco-Roman Age, who has made a successful adaptation of a fifth-century type.

Other Adaptations of the Aphrodite Type. It is clear also that a considerable number of Roman statues of Venus, such

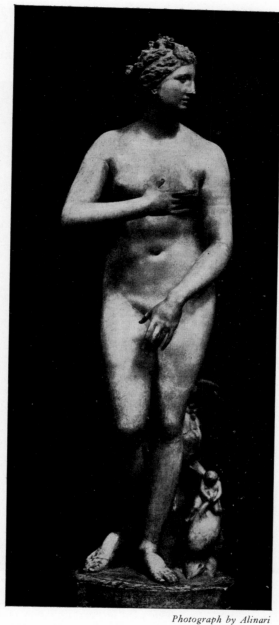

FIGURE 145. VENUS OF THE MEDICI. Græco-Roman Period. Uffizi, Florence.

as the Capitoline Venus, or the Venus of the Medici (Figure 145), were inspired by the Aphrodite of Cnidus, made by

Photograph by Alinari

FIGURE 146. ARCHAISTIC STATUE OF ATHENA. Græco-Roman Period. National Museum, Naples. The self-conscious imitation of an archaic pose is evident. For a true archaic statue, compare Figure 40.

[554]

Praxiteles in the fourth century. The Græco-Roman artists have, however, conceded so much to their own conception of the goddess, or to the taste of the Roman public, that the resulting statues should, in many cases, be regarded as adaptations rather than as copies of the Praxitelean masterpiece. The impersonal beauty of the Cnidian Aphrodite of Praxiteles (see Figure 131), in comparison with the affected attitude of the Græco-Roman adaptations of the type, indicates how definitely the spirit of art has declined in the interval. In the Aphrodite of Cnidus the copyist endeavored to reproduce as faithfully as he could the spirit of the original, while the Medicean Venus is a Roman adaptation, in which the decadent conceptions of the time predominate.

Archaizing Statues. Another pursuit of the Græco-Roman artists was the creation of archaized, or archaistic, statues. These were figures or groups in which the artist deliberately sought to imitate the stiff archaic creations of the sixth century. The goddess Athena (Figure 146) was a subject that lent itself to archaistic treatment, for the artists had before them the draped female figures of the early centuries on which to base their efforts. An archaistic Athena, however, indicates not only the resemblance to the Acropolis Maidens, but also the inevitable differences of a later age. The law of frontality has been disregarded, the archaic smile omitted; the countenance has the individualized composure of a Roman matron, and the lines of drapery betray an uninspired hardness.

Mythological Scenes in Sculpture. The return to earlier models was apparently fostered by a Greek named Pasiteles, who was admitted to Roman citizenship in 87 B.C. No works of Pasiteles are extant, but something is known of his life, his versatile talents—which were used to create works of art in gold, silver, and ivory, as well as in marble—and especially of the school of artists that he founded. His successors made statues or groups in the heavy, square style that had been developed by Polycleitus in the fifth century, and their choice of subject matter illustrates still another interest of the Græco-

Roman Period, namely, Greek mythological or literary themes. Thus a group consisting of the children of Agamemnon, Orestes and Electra, who slew their mother Clytemnestra, recalls the literary treatment of those characters by Æschylus, Sophocles, and Euripides three hundred years before, a span of time that had already made the subject an ancient one for the Græco-Roman artists. The group of Orestes with Pylades, the friend of his exile, and that of Ajax holding the body of the slain Patroclus, while he looks defiantly on the Trojans (Figure 31), a theme familiar from the *Iliad,* belong to the same period and have the same inspiration.

The Laocoön Group. The Laocoön Group was sculptured by three Rhodian artists, Agesander, Polydorus, and Athenodorus, who were active about 40 b.c. It shows the punishment that descended upon the Trojan priest and his two sons because of the aspersions that he cast on the Wooden Horse before Troy, and again indicates the preoccupation of the artists of the Græco-Roman Period with subjects drawn from Greek mythology. It illustrates other qualities also, many of which are undesirable. The group is a study in stark realism, in which the artists have sought both by choice of subject and by every technical device at their command to portray a scene of human anguish. They have shown a deficient sense of balance in the disparity in size between the father and the two sons, and in the lack of harmony in the rendering of the facial expressions.

The Laocoön Group, which is somewhat less than life size, was discovered in the early sixteenth century, just when an interest in Greek civilization was being reborn in Europe, and, lacking an adequate background of comparative studies in Hellenic art, scholars heaped on the composition a quite undeserved measure of praise. It was extensively, and rather poorly, restored after its discovery in the sixteenth century. The description of the attack of the serpents on Laocoön and his sons that Vergil has written (*Æneid II,* 37–61, 212–224) is of particular interest in the study of Gæco-Roman art, because the *Æneid* was composed about the same time that the group

[556]

was made and it is a fair assumption that one influenced the other.

The Farnese Bull. Little need be said about the Farnese Bull

Photograph by Alinari

FIGURE 147. THE FARNESE BULL. Græco-Roman Period. Naples. The elaborate combination of realistic and allegorical figures marks the closing period of Greek art.

(Figure 147) except to point out the same pursuit of an elaborate theatrical pose, which was to be observed in the Laocoön Group. The Farnese Bull, also a product of the first century

[557]

before Christ, was made by two brothers, Apollonius and Tauriscus, at Tralles in Asia Minor, whence a flourishing export trade in statues was carried on with Rome.

Portraiture. Portraiture, once firmly established in the Hellenistic Period, continued to be cultivated in the Græco-Roman Age. It was natural that the wealthy Romans, with their material interests, should wish to have sculptured portraits of themselves, and the completely faithful rendering of life may be observed in the marble and bronze heads of this age. Portraiture and the historical relief sculpture of the style preserved on Trajan's Column in Rome came to be distinctive types of Roman art in which the debt to Greece was tenuous in the extreme, if not entirely absent. Symbolism, allegory, and idealism have given place to historical accuracy, devoted to a narrative purpose. With the emergence of a definitely Roman type of art, we may, therefore, conclude our description of Greek archæology and art.

CHAPTER XXXII

THE CLOSE OF GREEK LETTERS

The Absence of New Literary Forms. In the Græco-Roman Period, there were few new types of literature peculiar to the age alone, in the way that lyric poetry was distinctive of the archaic age or oratory of the fourth century. The reason for the lack of originality is to be found first, in the exhaustion of Greek genius, which is to be observed also in contemporary history and art, and second, in the fact that, during the intense years of the classical period, the Greek writers had successively discovered and developed almost every type of literature that has since been employed in Western civilization. Epic, lyric, tragedy, comedy, history, oratory, philosophy, the novel, in turn occupied the center of Greek literary thought, and satire alone appears to be a new form that was evolved by the authors of either Græco-Roman or Roman days. The writers of the age were, in short, confronted with the same problem as the sculptors, who discovered to their chagrin that almost every technique had been exploited by their predecessors. In this situation, however, where the search for novelty defied human genius, the writers made less intense efforts to attain originality than did the contemporary artists.

The very considerable body of Greek writing of the Græco-Roman Period may best be treated, therefore, by discussing as many of the authors as their individual merits warrant. In doing so, it will not be difficult to observe wherein their works are a logical and appropriate outcome of their age and environment, even though they contributed no new forms to literature.

[559]

Polybius. Polybius of Megalopolis, who lived from 210 B.C. to 128 B.C., was definitely related to the political vicissitudes of his city, and his life work typifies the dependence of Greek genius on Roman policy. The city of Megalopolis had been founded as an artificial center of the Arcadian states when Epaminondas was leading his Thebans against the Spartans in the years following his victory at Leuctra in 371 B.C. About the middle of the third century before Christ, this city had joined the Achæan League, and the family of Polybius was prominently associated with the fortunes of that alliance. In 168 B.C., the year of the Battle of Pydna, the Achæan League was destroyed by Rome, and one thousand Achæans, among whom Polybius was included, were taken to Rome as hostages. Polybius, with the patronage and active assistance of the leading literary men of Rome, studied the methods and policies of the makers of the new world empire, until he became a more enthusiastic apologist for the Roman conquest than the Romans themselves. It was the history of the expansion of Rome that Polybius undertook to record. Five of the forty scholarly books that he wrote are still extant. They are exceedingly useful as source material on Roman history, but in style they are the extraordinarily dull product of an industrious scholar who lacked all literary and artistic sense.

The Historians of the Græco-Roman Period. A number of other historians, notably Josephus, Arrian, Appian, Cassius Dio, and Diodorus Siculus, in various ways typify the current interest in recording past events rather than living actively in the present or looking with confidence to the future. The situation was inevitable among Greek scholars who were dominated by Rome, for, having lost the power to sway history, they could only record it. The Jewish Josephus, a native of Jerusalem, who lived from 37 A.D. to 94 A.D., acquired Greek for the specific purpose of making his history of the revolt and suppression of the Jews between 66 A.D. and 70 A.D. more widely available to readers who knew no Hebrew. His decision may be compared to that of Joseph Conrad, whose native tongue was Polish, but

[560]

who chose to write his sea stories in English in order to appeal to a wider audience. The history of Josephus is a scholarly production, but as a literary work it betrays the hand of one to whom Greek was an alien tongue. In addition to his *History of the Jewish War,* Josephus wrote a later book, the *Early History of Judæa,* also in Greek.

The New Testament. In a similar way, the Greek language, modified with the passing of the centuries but rich and powerful in the vocabulary of moral discourse, became the means for the spread of the New Testament writings. It would not be appropriate in a work of this nature to venture into the linguistic controversy of New Testament Greek. Some scholars have explained the peculiarities of the style and phraseology of the New Testament as the work of Jews who thought in Aramaic but composed in Greek, while others have contended that the Gospels were originally written in Aramaic and later translated into Greek. The fact remains that it was through the widely understood language of Greece that the message of Christianity was conveyed to the Roman world.

Probably no book or books have been translated into so many languages and dialects in the last two thousand years as have the books of the New Testament. They have become cherished by many millions of people who know no language but their own. Yet it was the Greek language that was the original means of preserving and disseminating the books of scripture.

There are other and more philosophic aspects of association between the culture of ancient Greece and the subsequent growth of the Christian religion. The doctrines of moral suasion, the exaltation of righteousness for its own sake, the creation of a kingdom of the spirit that should transcend temporal power—all these concepts, that were to become so powerfully shaped in the teachings of the church, had been slowly taking form in the minds of men during the period of the development of the Greek dramas and, more particularly, in the humanistic and moral dialogues of Plato.

Recognizing the place of Greek culture and thought and

[561]

language in the transmission of Christian teaching to the world, a modern scholar has written: "The Christian Church was the last great creative achievement of the classical culture." (W. R. Inge, *The Legacy of Greece.*)

Arrian. The past achievements of Greece, as well as of Rome, found men in the new age to record them. One of these was Arrian, of Nicomedia, who lived from 95 A.D. to 175 A.D. He published in seven books a work entitled the *Anabasis of Alexander the Great,* which covered the years of Alexander's reign from 336 B.C. to 323 B.C. Though Arrian displays industry and scholarship on every page, he was dealing with the life of a man who lived four centuries before his own time, and contemporary accuracy must not be expected. Arrian also had philosophic interests. He was a disciple of Epictetus, the Stoic philosopher, and after the fashion of Plato and Xenophon, who commemorated the life of Socrates, he, too, wrote of the teachings of his master. Other works from his pen, such as his essays *On Tactics* and *On Hunting,* owe their origin to the example of the popular works of Xenophon, while his book *On India* is, in style and in the use of the Ionic dialect, clearly modeled on Herodotus. The career of Arrian, marked as it is by the imitation of his literary predecessors, reminds one of similar backward glances of the eclectic sculptors of the same period, who incorporated in their statues qualities peculiar to Polycleitus, Praxiteles, Lysippus, and others.

Appian. In spite, however, of the interests of Josephus or Arrian in the history of their own people, it was essentially the empire of Rome that provided the inspiration for the Greek writers of history. Appian, of Alexandria, whose period coincides with that of Arrian, wrote in twenty-four books an extended *History of Rome,* dealing with the entire period from the early myths down to the reign of Trajan. Only part of the work has survived, but it is sufficient to enable us to form an estimate of his ability and his style. He includes a great deal of compiled or statistical information, but his arrangement is confused and the form undistinguished. The most arresting thing about him is again the fact that an Alexandrian Greek should have taken the history of conquering Rome as the subject of his literary efforts.

Cassius Dio, Diodorus Siculus, and Strabo. The great expansion of the Roman Empire over the ancient world seemed to turn the minds of the historians to themes embracing the history of many centuries. The old Hellenic restraint that had suggested to Herodotus a subject limited to the few years of the Persian Wars and to Thucydides the space of twenty-seven years occupied by the Peloponnesian War gave place to the expansive spirit of men who were now content with a literary canvas no less restricted in time than in geography. Such a man was Cassius Dio, of Nicæa in Bithynia, who migrated to Rome, where he pursued his historical work toward the end of the second Christian century. He took the history of Rome as his theme and dealt with the period extending from the mythical traditions of Æneas to 229 A.D., in a colossal work of eighty books; of these, some twenty-five, covering the important years, 68 B.C. to 47 A.D., have come down as a valuable source of Roman history. Other parts survive in abridged form.

Diodorus Siculus, an earlier writer who was active about 40 B.C., had already undertaken the still more enormous task of compiling a universal history in forty books, of which fifteen are extant. There are other writers too of the Græco-Roman Period whose works verged on history. Strabo, a native of the Pontic regions in Asia Minor, who was born about 60 B.C., is chiefly remembered for his geographical studies of various countries in Europe, Asia, and Africa, though it should not be forgotten that he wrote a Roman history, now lost, of the years following the period covered by Polybius. These books are of great value in the study of history, for they have preserved the evidence of many sources that have since been lost. Needless to say, they are of little importance for their literary style.

Plutarch. In dealing with Plutarch, who was born at Chæronea in Bœotia about 50 A.D., we depart somewhat from a historian in the strict sense, though we gain in return a much

[563]

more interesting and important character. Plutarch was educated in Athens, and, although he knew Rome from repeated
visits, he preferred to remain a Greek and live his life in the
tiny Bœotian town of Chæronea. Nevertheless, few men illustrate the necessary relationship between Greece and Rome
more clearly than does Plutarch in his distinguished work, the
Parallel Lives of famous Greek and Roman generals and statesmen. In the reasoned moderation with which he accepted the
new order imposed by the Roman Empire, still retaining his
loyalty to the Greek city-state, and especially in the energy and
skill with which he devoted himself to his writing, there is
much to suggest the single-minded pursuit of a great theme
that was characteristic of his Hellenic predecessors four centuries before his own time.

In composing the *Parallel Lives,* Plutarch chose his characters
in pairs, one from either nation as they appeared to him to
have qualities in common; Demosthenes and Cicero represent
political orators, Alexander the Great and Julius Cæsar conquering rulers. Of each man he wrote a biographical sketch,
which he did not hesitate to dramatize by the introduction of
uncritical anecdotes, and followed his discussion with a comparison of the characters of the two men, especially as they
reflected national qualities.

A brief passage from the *Life of Pericles* by Plutarch will
illustrate the manner in which he wrote. It describes the argument offered by Pericles for diverting to the adornment of
Athens the funds contributed by the allied states of the Delian
Confederacy for defense against the Persians.

Pericles used to say to the people that they owed no explanation
to the allies regarding the money, so long as they bore the brunt of
war on behalf of the others and kept the barbarians at a distance;
for the allies contributed not a horse, nor a ship, nor a soldier, but
only money; and money belongs not to those who give it, but to
those who receive it, if they provide that for which they accept it.
Consequently, when the city has adequately prepared herself for

the exigencies of war, it is only right that she should then turn her surplus resources to those things which, when brought to pass, will reflect everlasting glory on her; and further, the abundance of wealth will, even in the process of attaining the ends, bring into being all manner of manifest activity and varied needs, which will stimulate every act, rouse every hand, and benefit practically the entire city, which thus is not only beautified, but at the same time sustained out of her own resources.

It is true that Plutarch introduces illustrative anecdotes very freely into his work, but if he may be censured as an uncritical historian, he was not a dishonest one, and his biographical sketches contain an exceedingly useful volume of information, especially about the personalities and private lives of his characters. He was more deeply interested in human problems than in objective history, as one may observe in his second major work, the *Moralia,* a collection of some eighty essays or studies on a variety of topics, but all characterized by a common tone of moral suasion.

Literary Criticism. In addition to the historians and historical biographers, a considerable group of literary critics were also writing voluminously at this time. Dionysius of Halicarnassus, who flourished toward the end of the first century before Christ, wrote a history of early Rome, but he is more commonly remembered as a critic, whose ambition it was by scholarship and industry to achieve and to teach others the mastery of Greek prose composition that was the natural endowment of the writers of the fifth century. In this ambition he was far from successful. Two of his more important essays are *On the Arrangement of Words* and *On the Ancient Orators.*

Diogenes Lærtius, who worked about the middle of the third Christian century, wrote a useful treatise on the *Lives of the Philosophers,* discussing in ten volumes the development of philosophy from the early physical philosophers of Asia Minor and southern Italy down to Epicurus, although he did not maintain a strictly chronological order.

[565]

Other studies on prose style were made at the same time. One essay *On Style* has been attributed to Demetrius of Phalerum, while another treatise of considerable importance for those interested in the development of the grand style is the work entitled *On the Sublime,* which is attributed to Longinus. The essay is written with remarkable appreciation of the finest achievements of the classical Greek writers, and with a penetrating sense of the basic qualities of training and character that must lie behind any literature of real value. The author sharply criticizes unthinking facility of speech, that does not rest on knowledge, and commends Hellenic restraint.

The sublime lies closer to danger when it is unaccompanied by knowledge but is abandoned to impulse alone and to ignorant self-assurance; for while it often stands in need of the spur, so also does it of the rein. Thus Demosthenes indicates that in the common lot of human life, the greatest thing is good fortune, but good judgment, which stands second, is not far inferior to it; for the lack of good judgment contributes to the complete ruin of good fortune.

In another passage, he speaks again of high-mindedness as an indispensable prerequisite to eloquent and effective speech.

The first quality, namely an exalted mind, holds a place above all others. Consequently, though this is a gift rather than something to be acquired, we must so far as possible nurture our own souls toward sublimity, so that they may ever become great with noble purpose. "In what manner?" you will say. I have written thus elsewhere: "Sublimity is the reflection of high-mindedness."

Pausanias. A Lydian Greek, Pausanias, who traveled widely over Greek lands about 150 A.D., has left an exceedingly valuable record of his visits. His *Tour of Greece* was written in antiquity for the practical purpose of guiding those with an historical, archæological, or literary interest who were traveling in the country, and it has proved also of inestimable value to modern archæologists. Into ten books he has crowded an

[566]

incredible amount of information about Attica, Corinthia, Messenia, Elis, Arcadia, Bœotia, and Phocis. He has not only described the topography of these lands and the fortifications and buildings of the cities, but has copied inscriptions and delved into the mythology and traditions of the sites that he covered. When archæologists are working on a site for which they are so fortunate as to have a description by Pausanias, his work becomes an indispensable manual for the excavators. For the reconstruction of many pieces of sculpture of the fifth and fourth centuries, known only through Roman copies, we are indebted for further details to the precise descriptions of Pausanias, who himself saw and appraised the originals.

Of the two groups of the Tyrannicides in Athens, he says:

Not far away stand Harmodius and Aristogeiton, who slew Hipparchus. The reason why this happened and the manner in which they did it has been told by others. Of the statues, one pair represents the craft of Critius, while Antenor made the older pair. When Xerxes seized Athens after the Athenians abandoned the citadel, he carried off the earlier statues, but, later, Antiochus sent them back to the Athenians.

Pausanias also describes the sculptures of the Parthenon. The brief, but accurate, detail of his account may be judged by his description of the pediments and of the colossal chryselephantine statue of the Athena Parthenos by Pheidias that stood within the temple.

In the temple which they name the Parthenon, all the sculptures in the part called the eagle [pediment] at the entrance have to do with the birth of Athena, while those at the back refer to the strife of Athena and Poseidon for sovereignty over the land. The cult statue itself has been made of ivory and gold. In the middle of the helmet there rests a figure of the Sphinx—the reference to the Sphinx I shall explain when my narrative reaches Bœotia—and on either side of the helmet griffins have been fashioned. The statue of Athena is standing upright, and she wears a chiton that reaches to her feet, while on her breast the head of Medusa is represented in ivory. In one hand she holds a figure of Nike about four cubits high, and in the other a spear, while at her feet there lies a shield, and near her spear a serpent; this serpent is, presumably, Erichthonius. On the base of the statue the birth of Pandora has been carved.

The interest of Pausanias in mythology is indicated by his promise to deal with the story of the Sphinx in its appropriate setting at Thebes in Bœotia.

Perhaps the most striking correlation of Pausanias with archæological research has to do with the Hermes of Praxiteles. In describing the Temple of Hera at Olympia, Pausanias remarked that within it there was "a Hermes in marble, bearing the infant Dionysus, the work of Praxiteles." When the Heræum was excavated, the archæologists, with the text of Pausanias before them, enjoyed the incomparable satisfaction of finding the statue buried in the soft soil formed by the dissolution of the mud-brick walls, at the precise point where Pausanias had seen it more than seventeen centuries earlier.

Philosophy and Rhetoric. With the whole body of earlier Greek writing before them, those who pursued literature in the Græco-Roman Period turned to a wide variety of adaptations of previous types. Philosophy and rhetoric flourished, although the names of the writers are scarcely important enough to demand anything more than mention and identification with their works. Dio Chrysostom, or Dio the Golden-tongued, who is known also from his birthplace as Dio of Prusa, was born about 40 A.D. He fell a victim to the absurd practice of writing artificially in praise of difficult things, and composed essays eulogizing such creatures as the parrot and the gnat. It will be remembered that the orator Isocrates did the same thing in the fourth century, when he wrote in praise of Busiris, the Egyptian king who slaughtered his guests. Dio Chrysostom does, however, deserve credit for more commendable pursuits, especially for his inspirational addresses on moral questions and for his contribution to the development of fiction through his story called the *Hunter,* or the *Eubœan Tale.* It is a pretty sketch dealing with the simplicity of country life in comparison with the excesses of the city.

Herodes Atticus, a wealthy Greek who is remembered by archæologists for his rebuilding of the marble stadium in Athens, lived from 100 to 175 A.D. He prided himself on his facile oratory, in which he developed a smooth, flowing, and carefully composed style.

To the philosophic or sophistic group, although of distinctly greater merit than the rest, belonged the Roman emperor, Marcus Aurelius, who lived from 121 to 180 A.D. He recorded his daily meditations in a work of twelve books, which bears the revealing title *To Himself.* The noble stoic reflections of the emperor win for the work a place in literature, although the style is that of a man who acquired the Greek tongue late in life.

Natural History, the Epic, Romance, and Mythology. Natural history was represented in the Græco-Roman Period by Oppian's poem *On Fishing,* written between 177 and 180 A.D., in a somewhat overelaborate style, but with remarkable scientific accuracy. The epic was again taken up by Quintus Smyrnæus, who flourished about 380 A.D. and who wrote of the period following the *Iliad* of Homer. Nonnus of Panopolis in Egypt, whose period of activity lies about a generation later, wrote an epic of the god Dionysus, an enormously long and tedious composition in forty-eight books. In contrast and with vastly greater genius, Musæus told in three hundred and forty-three graceful verses the story of the love of Leander, the youth who swam each night from Abydus across the Hellespont to Sestus to be with the maiden Hero. The theme was known from Alexandrian times and was frequently repeated by the Roman poets as well as by the Elizabethan dramatists. Babrius in the third century after Christ turned the fables of Æsop into verse.

The "Greek Anthology." Meleager, who was writing about

[569]

50 B.C., represents the remote geographical regions in which Greek letters were fostered, for he came originally from Gadara in Syria and lived also in Tyre and Cos. He was the first man to collect an anthology of poetry, including in his *Garland* the works of some forty poets from Sappho in the sixth century before Christ down to writers of his own time. He himself composed a preface to the *Garland,* of which some verses are extant, associating each poet with a different flower. A number of Meleager's own epigrams have been preserved—graceful, sensuous, and exotic lines suggestive of his eastern ancestry.

The *Garland* of Meleager introduced the practice of assembling an anthology of brief poems, and the further history of that type of collection may be briefly sketched. The *Garland* itself has not been preserved intact, but many of the poems that Meleager brought together were taken over by later compilers. In the reign of Hadrian, Strato of Sardis collected an *Anthology* of love poems, and, in the sixth century after Christ, the Byzantine poet Agathias brought together a more universal collection arranged by subject matter. Four centuries later, that is, in the tenth century after Christ, Cephalas of Byzantium, or Constantinople, compiled a collection, which has come to be called the *Palatine Anthology.* Cephalas expanded his choice from the forty poets selected by Meleager to some three hundred and twenty, arranging his material by subject matter. In the fourteenth Christian century, Planudes, a monk of Constantinople, in a burst of modernism, modified the *Palatine Anthology* by discarding many of the poems collected by Cephalas and substituting later ones. The *Palatine Anthology,* of which the manuscript has fortunately survived, remains, however, the more important collection.

The poems of the *Anthology,* which are usually brief and range over the field of epigram, ode, idyl, and elegy, constitute an extraordinarily important source for the study of the development of the Greek language as well as of the tastes of different ages, for they cover a period of nearly nineteen cen-

[570]

turies, extending from the seventh century before Christ to the twelfth Christian century. Naturally, the quality of the work varies greatly with the different authors and periods.

The Close of the Period. It is difficult to know at just what point Græco-Roman literature comes to a close. We have already mentioned a number of writers, such as Quintus Smyrnæus and Agathias, whose dates fall long after the founding of Constantinople in 330 A.D., the point at which we chose to conclude the story of Greek history. The Greek language never ceased to be used, but a further study of literature would quickly lead into the Byzantine Period. Rather than trying to determine, therefore, who should be accounted the last of the writers of Græco-Roman literature, we shall turn finally to one form of writing and one author, who, amid the great mass of recorders and imitators, may lay claim to some measure of originality.

Lucian. Lucian of Samosata, a Syrian Greek, who lived during the second century after Christ, from about 125 A.D. to about 200 A.D., wrote in the field of fiction. He traveled widely, first through the cities of Asia Minor, where he acquired a facility in the use of the Greek language that later enabled him to write a remarkably easy and pure Greek style, and later in southern Italy, Sicily, and in Gaul. Much of his life he spent in the free intellectual atmosphere of Athens, although he afterwards accepted a civil service appointment from the Roman government and carried on his work in Egypt. Rhetoric and philosophy engaged the attention of Lucian, whose writings became more and more prolific. He took up again the dialogue as a literary form, and, with a clever combination of wit and satire, drove home his points. From his *Dialogues of the Dead,* in which he represents those who have passed to Hades conversing with the gods about the folly of mortals, as well as from his *Dialogues of the Gods* and his *Dialogues of the Sea Gods,* we are able to judge of the wit, the brilliance, the philosophy, and the sincerity of Lucian, hiding behind his satiric attacks on gods and men alike.

[571]

Two dialogues from the *Dialogues of the Dead* are quoted in translation. The first represents a conversation between Hermes, who, in his capacity as *psychopompos,* or "spirit-guide," conducted the souls of those who had died to the River Styx, and Charon, the ferryman of the dead. Hermes and Charon are straightening out their accounts, and the dialogue is a satire on the omnipresent commercialism of the age.

HERMES

> Ferryman, let's reckon up what you owe me now, if that suits you. It will obviate any quarrel about these matters later.

CHARON

> All right, Hermes. It's better to have these things understood. It saves trouble.

HERMES

> I provided one anchor, which you ordered, at a cost of five drachmæ.

CHARON

> That's a high price you mention.

HERMES

> Yes, by Hades, but it's only what I had to pay! And then there was a rowlock at two obols.

CHARON

> All right, put down five drachmæ and two obols.

HERMES

> And a darning needle for the sail; I paid five obols for that.

CHARON

> Put that down, too.

HERMES

> Then there was wax to caulk up the holes of the boat, and nails and string to mend the upper part. All that cost two drachmæ.

CHARON
Well, you paid all they were worth!

HERMES
That's the lot, unless something has escaped us in the reckoning. Now when will you pay me?

CHARON
I can't do it just now, Hermes. If a plague or a war sends a lot of passengers along together, I'll be able to make a bit by cheating on the fares.

HERMES [*ruefully*]
So all I can do is pray for the worst, so I can get my money.

CHARON
That's about it, Hermes. Very few passengers come to us now. It's because of the peace.

HERMES
It's better so, even though my pay is slow. But, Charon, do you remember the old-timers—how they used to come in? They were real men, all of them—covered with blood and wounds! Nowadays a man is poisoned by his slave or his wife, or he eats too much fancy food. They're a pale, insipid lot, compared with those others. It seems to me that most of them come here through plotting over money.

CHARON
Yes, money is in demand.

HERMES
That's right, and I wouldn't seem to be far out if I insisted on getting what you owe me either.

The second dialogue is a satire on the human disposition to shift blame. Æacus, a chamberlain in the halls of the dead, acts as a sort of moderator, while Protesilaus, the warrior who first leapt ashore and was the first to be slain when the Greeks came to Troy, attacks in turn Helen, Menelaus, and Paris as the cause of his death. In the end he accepts his destiny as part of Fate.

AEACUS

Here, Protesilaus, what's the idea of attacking and choking Helen?

PROTESILAUS

Because it was on her account that I died, Aeacus, leaving my home half-finished and my bride a widow.

AEACUS

I think Menelaus was to blame for leading you all to Troy for the sake of such a woman as Helen.

PROTESILAUS

Right you are! He's the one to blame.

MENELAUS

Not at all, my dear fellow! It would be more reasonable to blame Paris. He broke all the laws of hospitality and ran away with my wife. He really deserves choking, and that not only by you, but by all the Greeks and barbarians. He brought death to enough of them.

PROTESILAUS

That's better. Now, Paris, you scoundrel, I'll never let you out of my clutches!

PARIS

Oh, Protesilaus, you're wronging me—a member of the same craft as yourself. I am a lover, too; I owe allegiance to the same god as yourself. You know how that god drives us wherever he chooses, regardless of our wishes. You can't fight against him.

PROTESILAUS

Well said! I only wish I could lay hold of Eros, the god of love.

AEACUS

Just a moment! I should like to speak in defense of

[574]

Eros. He will perhaps admit that he was responsible for Paris falling in love, but as for your death, Protesilaus, he will claim that you were alone responsible. You forgot all about your new-wed bride, and as soon as you reached Troyland, you fell in love with glory, and with a mixture of bravado and stupidity you leapt out before all the rest. That is what caused your death.

PROTESILAUS

And now if you don't mind, Aeacus, I'll set the record straight on my own behalf. I was not to blame: it was Fate. That is how it was spun out from the very beginning.

AEACUS

Precisely! Why then blame these gentlemen?

Lucian's dialogues and satires are rich with the lore of learning from the classical centuries of Greece, but by the combination of serious philosophy and mocking ridicule of human frailties he escaped the dreariness of the self-conscious critic. Much of the sparkling brilliance of Greece abides in this late writer.

The Novel. The romantic novel, or fiction, had its roots in times earlier than Lucian, and it was to have a long history after him. Xenophon's idealized biography of the education of a prince, the *Cyropædia,* written in the fourth century before Christ, has something of fiction about it; the *Milesian Tales* of Aristotle's time are fanciful stories; and the *Hunter* of Dio Chrysostom, written in the first century after Christ, uses the same method again. Longus of Lesbos, a man of uncertain date though later than Lucian, wrote perhaps the best Greek fiction, in the real sense of the word. His work was a romance of the countryside, called *Daphnis and Chloe.* Yet for originality and genius, Lucian ranks above all other writers who used the Greek language during the Græco-Roman Period.

In a very real sense the inheritance of the modern world from ancient Greece has been the theme of this entire book,

[575]

even though parallels and influences have not invariably been pointed out. Yet the reader who has mastered the details of the Doric Order of architecture will look with a new understanding on the austere beauty of the Lincoln Memorial in Washington; and a study of the principles of drama, which Aristotle discussed with painstaking exactitude, will carry its own reward as one detects the universal qualities of tragedy in such a novel as Emily Bronte's *Wuthering Heights* or in a modern sociological play.

The Greeks had an exceptional capacity for expressing in words or in art the heart of problems common to all mankind. Thus, if one chooses to work from the modern scene to antiquity, the brutality of a secret police organization in a totalitarian country of the twentieth century will instantly summon a picure of the Krypteia in Sparta, a ceremony of commemoration at the Tomb of the Unknown Soldier will recall the Funeral Oration of Pericles, the powerful words of a statesman summoning a nation to duty will awaken memories of Demosthenes addressing the Athenian Assembly.

To attempt to list each parallel would at once provoke tedium, and, what is more serious, it would reduce to specific instances principles that are universal and, therefore, timeless. It would, in short, destroy in the minds of the student the very qualities of Greek thought that he will wish to retain. The student who has come to understand the achievement of Greece will be forever alert to make his own discoveries of the persistence of Greek ideas in the modern world. It is in this manner that he can most effectively relate learning to life, which is the end of all true education. To learn facts alone from an ancient culture would be a barren reward of effort; to acquire a sense of intellectual curiosity is to gain a possession forever.

REFERENCES AND BIBLIOGRAPHY

REFERENCES

The sources of the more important translated extracts are here in-dicated. Whenever the translator of an extract has not been iden-tified in the text, the version is that of the author of this book.

CHAPTER I

Description of Ithaca, *Odyssey* IV. 605–608; the snowstorm, *Iliad* XII. 278–286.

CHAPTER III

The nine seasons of King Minos' reign, *Odyssey* XIX. 178–179; the baleful signs, *Iliad* VI. 168.

CHAPTER V

The palace of Alcinous, *Odyssey* VII. 84–89; the palace of Mene-laus, *ibid*. IV. 71–75; the wrath of Achilles, *Iliad* I. 1–7; Helen on the walls, *ibid*. III. 121–158; the campfires of the Trojans, *ibid*. VIII. 553–565; the simile of the bees, *ibid*. II. 86–93; the simile of the sea and the cornfield, *ibid*. II. 144–149; the simile of the birds, the leaves, the flowers, and the flies, *ibid*. II. 459–473; the simile of the lazy ass, *ibid*. XI. 558–569; the parting of Hector and Andromache, *ibid*. VI. 359–496 (extracts); the Helen of the *Odyssey, Odyssey* IV. 74–266 (extracts); Odysseus and the Cyclops, *ibid*. IX. 364–367, 369–370, 395–412, 413–414; the story of Nausicaa, *ibid*. VI. 25–30, 68–70, 160–163, 226–233; VII. 311–314; VIII. 454–468; Circe and the com-rades of Odysseus, *ibid*. X. 234–238; Odysseus and Irus, *ibid*. XVIII. 10, 90–100; *Hymn to Hermes* III. 10–16, 260–268; *Batrachomyo-machia* 9–16.

CHAPTER VI

The reply of Callicratidas, Xenophon, *Hellenica* I. vi. 32; the news of Leuctra in Sparta, Xenophon, *ibid*. VI. iv. 16.

REFERENCES

Chapter VII

The criticism of the laws of Dracon, Plutarch *Life of Solon* XVII;
Aristotle *Rhetoric* II. 23. 29 (1400*b*); Solon's reply to his critics,
Diogenes Laertius *Lives of Eminent Philosophers* I. 49, *Solon*.

Chapter IX

The extracts from the lyric poets, unless otherwise stated, are
numbered according to the arrangement of the following volumes
of the Loeb Classical Library: J. M. Edmonds, Editor, *Elegy and
Iambus,* 2 volumes, Cambridge: Harvard University Press, 1931;
and J. M. Edmonds, Editor, *Lyra Græca,* 3 volumes, Cambridge:
Harvard University Press, 1922–1927. The translations, however,
have been taken from a variety of sources or made by the author
for the present book.

The good and the bad wives, Hesiod *Works and Days* 702–705;
the sparing tongue, *ibid.* 719–720; the martial ode, *Elegy and
Iambus,* Vol. I, Callinus 1.1–4; the exhortation to battle, *ibid.*
Tyrtæus 10.1–6; the Salamis ode, *ibid.* Solon 1–2; the purpose of
Solon, *ibid.* Solon 5; the address to Cyrnus, *ibid.* Theognis 19–23;
the pursuit of pleasure, *ibid.* Mimnermus 1.1–2; the prayer for
death at sixty years, *ibid.* Mimnermus 11; the prayer for death at
eighty years, *ibid.* Solon 20; the lampoon on the Lerians, *ibid.*
Phocylides 1; the lampoon on the Milesians, *ibid.* Demodocus 1;
the ship of state, *Lyra Græca,* Vol. I, Alcæus 37.1–5; the Hymn to
Aphrodite, *ibid.* Sappho 1; the ode to Cleïs, *ibid.* Sappho 130; the
evening star, *ibid.* Sappho 149; the drinking song, *ibid.* Vol. II,
Anacreon 76; the love poem, *ibid.* Anacreon 48; the ode on drinking, *Elegy and Iambus,* Vol. II, *Anacreontics* 21; the abandoned
shield, *ibid.* Archilochus 6; the soldier's spear, *ibid.* Archilochus 2;
the apostrophe to the soul, *ibid.* Archilochus 66; the two days of a
woman's life, Hiller-Crusius, Editors, *Anthologia Lyrica* (Leipzig:
Teubner, 1913), Hipponax 11; the extravagant woman, *ibid.*
Semonides 7.57–70; the quiet of nature, *Lyra Græca,* Vol. I, Alcman
36; the praise of Athens, Pindar *Fragment* 76; the ode to Megacles,
Pindar *Pythian Odes* VII; the ode to Psaumis, *ibid. Olympian Odes*
IV; the epitaph on the soldiers who died in the Persian Wars, *Lyra
Græca,* Vol. II, Simonides of Ceos 127; the epitaph on the Spartans
who died at Thermopylæ, *ibid.* Simonides of Ceos 119; Danaë and
Perseus in the chest, *ibid.* Simonides of Ceos 27; the scolion to the

tyrannicides, *ibid*. Vol. III, *Attic Scolia* 10; the *Swallow Song, ibid*. *Folk Songs* 20.

CHAPTER X

The one god, *Elegy and Iambus,* Vol. I, Xenophanes 23; the challenge to anthropomorphism, *ibid*. Xenophanes 14–16; the continuity of art, Hippocrates *Aphorisms* I. 1; the physician's oath, Hippocrates *The Oath*.

CHAPTER XI

Themistocles and the Seriphian, Plutarch *Life of Themistocles* XVIII. 3.

CHAPTER XII

Babylonian marriage customs, Herodotus I. 196; the ancient medical clinic, *ibid*. I. 197; the Thracians on birth and death, *ibid*. V. 4; the Persians on infant mortality, *ibid*. I. 136; the Persian use of wine, *ibid*. I. 133; the origin of language, *ibid*. II. 2.

CHAPTER XIV

The definition of tragedy, Aristotle *Poetics* VI (1449*b*).

CHAPTER XV

The epitaph of Aeschylus, Athenæus *Deipnosophistæ* XIV. 627*c*; the beacon fire, Aeschylus *Agamemnon* 281–316; the purple tapestry, *ibid*. 905–911, 956–957; the sea of purple, *ibid*. 958–962; Cassandra's foreknowledge of the murder, *ibid*. 1107–1111, 1125–1129; Cassandra's prayer for vengeance, *ibid*. 1323–1326; the murder of Agamemnon, *ibid*. 1343–1346; the boast of Clytemnestra, *ibid*. 1672–1673; Orestes' vision of the Furies, Aeschylus *Choephori* 1057–1062.

CHAPTER XVI

The curse of Oedipus on the slayer, Sophocles *Oedipus Tyrannus* 233–251; the charge of Teiresias against Oedipus, *ibid*. 350–353; Iocasta's disclosure of the past oracle, *ibid*. 707–724; Oedipus' perturbation, *ibid*. 744–745; the dispatch of the maidservant, *ibid*. 945–949; the withdrawal of Iocasta, *ibid*. 1068–1072.

CHAPTER XVII

The soliloquy of Medea's nurse, Euripides *Medea* 1–8; the invective of Medea, *ibid*. 248–266; Medea's tirade against Jason, *ibid*.

`488–495; the instructions to the children, *ibid.* 969–975; Medea's re-solve to slay her children, *ibid.* 1236–1240.

CHAPTER XX

The statue of Olympian Zeus, *Iliad* I. 528–530; Quintilian *Institutio Oratoria* XII. x.9; Lucian *On Sacrifices* 11.

CHAPTER XXI

The magnificence of the arms of Achilles, *Iliad.* XIX. 12–15.

CHAPTER XXII

News of the Battle of Aegospotami in Athens, Xenophon *Hellenica* II. ii.3–6.

CHAPTER XXIII

The capture of Amphipolis, Thucydides IV. 106. 3; the exile of Thucydides, *ibid.* V. 26. 5; the siege of Platæa, *ibid.* II. 4. 2–4; the Funeral Speech of Pericles, *ibid.* II. 34–46 (extracts).

The burdens of Xanthias, Aristophanes *Frogs* 21–30; Dionysus in Charon's skiff, *ibid.* 197–207; the two innkeepers, *ibid.* 549–573; the pretended recitation of poetry, *ibid.* 659; the weighing of the verses, *ibid.* 1382–1383; the swearing of the tongue, *ibid.* 1471.

CHAPTER XXV

The aftermath of the Battle of Mantinea, Xenophon, *Hellenica* VII. v. 26–27.

CHAPTER XXVI

The Aphrodite of Cnidus, Pliny *Natural History* XXXVI. 21.

CHAPTER XXVII

The oration of Lysias *Against Eratosthenes;* peroration, § 100.

CHAPTER XXVIII

The death of Socrates, Plato *Phædo* 117c–118a; the myth of the cave, Plato *Republic* 514a–514b, 515c–515d, 517a.

The highest good, Aristotle *Nicomachean Ethics* 1094a, 1097a–1097b.

CHAPTER XXX

The ode to Heraclitus, *Greek Anthology* VII. 80; the drowned sailor, *ibid*. VII. 271; the death of Daphnis, Theocritus, *Idyl* I, 1–56 (extracts); the Hylas legend, *ibid*. XIII.

CHAPTER XXXII

Pericles on the expenditure of funds, Plutarch *Life of Pericles* XII. 3–4; knowledge and facility of speech, Longinus *On the Sublime* II. 2–3; high-mindedness and eloquence, *ibid*. IX. 1–2; the statues of Harmodius and Aristogeiton, Pausanias I. 8. 5; the statue of Athena Parthenos, *ibid*. I. 24. 5–7; the dialogue of Hermes and Charon, Lucian *Dialogues of the Dead* IV; the problem of Protesilaus, *ibid*. XIX.

SELECTED BIBLIOGRAPHY

The preparation of a second edition of this book has afforded an opportunity to review the list of books in the selected bibliography and to make a considerable number of changes. The original principle, however, has been maintained, namely, to suggest a limited number of volumes, accompanied by a brief estimate of the content and nature of each, which are best calculated to serve the practical needs of students. Many excellent books have been excluded because, either by reason of their specialization or purpose, they seemed to form a less satisfactory complement to the present work. The standard handbooks and lexicons have not been included, nor has modernity been the only consideration. Lists of recommended supplementary reading call for constant revision in the light of continuing scholarship.

Bassett, Samuel Eliot, *The Poetry of Homer*. Berkeley: University of California Press, 1938. A series of eight lectures which may be advantageously read after some familiarity with the content of the Homeric poems has been gained.

Beazley, J. D., *Potter and Painter in Ancient Athens*. London: Oxford University Press, 1946. A humanistic treatment of an important branch of Greek art. Exhaustive scholarship does not interfere with clarity of presentation.

Botsford, George Willis, *Hellenic History,* revised and rewritten by Charles Alexander Robinson, Jr., Third Edition. New York: The Macmillan Company, 1950. Contains a noteworthy series of new maps. Especially illuminating and valuable for the historical and economic problems of the Hellenistic Period. Well illustrated.

SELECTED BIBLIOGRAPHY

Bowra, C. M., *Early Greek Elegists*. Cambridge: Harvard University Press, 1938. A series of six lectures, which afford a brilliant picture of a comparatively limited field. Not too technical for the average reader.

Burn, A. R., *Pericles and Athens*. New York: The Macmillan Company, 1949. A new treatment of an old theme: subjective appraisals are added to a careful and full assemblage of the pertinent information on the life of Athens at its most brilliant epoch.

Burnet, John, *Early Greek Philosophy*. London: A. and C. Black, Ltd., 1930. A very satisfactory standard book on the early philosophers of Greece from Thales to Leucippus.

Calhoun, George M., *The Business Life of Ancient Athens*. Chicago: University of Chicago Press, 1926. A series of sketches on banking, capitalism, the shipping trade, merchandising, mining, and so forth; designed to afford a picture of the personality and practice of the ancient Greek man of business.

Cambridge Ancient History, edited by J. B. Bury, S. A. Cook, F. E. Adcock, M. P. Charlesworth, and N. H. Baynes; 12 volumes; 5 volumes of plates prepared by C. T. Seltman. New York: The Macmillan Company, 1923–1939. The work of many hands. The most exhaustive studies of different problems and periods of Greek history available in English.

Carpenter, Rhys, *Folk Tale, Fiction, and Saga in the Homeric Epics*. Berkeley: University of California Press, 1946. A novel approach to some old problems of Homeric criticism, presented with persuasive arguments. Interesting sociological implications.

——, *The Esthetic Basis of Greek Art of the Fifth and Fourth Centuries B.C.* Bryn Mawr: Bryn Mawr College Press, 1921. A study of Greek art based especially on sculpture and architecture. Nontechnical, but closely reasoned.

Casson, Stanley, *The Technique of Early Greek Sculpture*. Oxford: Clarendon Press, 1933. An exhaustive study of the methods employed by the Greeks in making their bronze and marble statues. The technical conclusions are applied in turn to an interpretation of the motives and methods of the artists.

Dickens, Guy, *Hellenistic Sculpture,* Second Edition. Oxford: Clarendon Press, 1920. A brief treatment of the general field of Hellenistic sculpture, together with studies of the different centers of art. Illuminating for the culture of the late period.

Dickinson, G. Lowes, *The Greek View of Life.* New York: Doubleday, Doran & Company, Inc., 1930. A subjective appraisal of the Greek attitude toward religion, the state, the individual, and artistic appreciation, based essentially on ancient literary sources. May well be read at any stage of the study of Greek civilization.

Dinsmoor, W. B., *The Architecture of Ancient Greece.* London: Batsford, 1950. Exact knowledge and imaginative application of evidence to the reconstruction of ancient buildings affords the basis of an appreciation of Greek temple planning and construction.

Evans, Sir Arthur, *The Palace of Minos at Knossos,* 4 volumes. New York: The Macmillan Company, 1921–1935. A monumental work on the excavations at Cnossus, richly illustrated and abounding in detail. The student new to the field will be well advised to use these volumes for reference in conjunction with his reading of some of the briefer handbooks on Crete.

Finley, J. H., Jr., *Thucydides.* Cambridge: Harvard University Press, 1942. A well-organized study of the mentality and philosophy of the Greek historian with a careful evaluation of his work.

Flickinger, Roy C., *The Greek Theater and Its Drama,* Fourth Edition. Chicago: University of Chicago Press, 1938. An exhaustive treatment, amply documented, of the technical problems of the Greek theater and stagecraft as well as of the development of Greek drama. Useful for detailed study or reference.

Gardiner, E. Norman, *Athletics of the Ancient World.* Oxford:

Clarendon Press, 1930. A brief account of athletics in antiquity, the history of their development, and the form in which various games and exercises were practiced. Well illustrated and presented in a manner comprehensible and interesting to the general reader.

Gardner, Ernest Arthur, *A Handbook of Greek Sculpture,* Second Edition. New York: The Macmillan Company, 1924. A standard handbook, highly detailed. The illustrations, which are less frequent than might be desired for the very inclusive text, are nevertheless conveniently arranged throughout the book for observation in connection with the reading.

Gardner, Percy, *A History of Ancient Coinage, 700–300 B. C.* Oxford: Clarendon Press, 1918. A consecutive history of the development of coinage. Contains instructive chapters on various economic and historical aspects of Greek coinage.

Grundy, G. B., *The Great Persian War and Its Preliminaries; A Study of the Evidence, Literary and Topographical.* London: John Murray, 1901. Discusses the Persian Wars according to Herodotus and other pertinent sources. Useful for detailed studies of political and strategic problems.

Hamilton, Edith, *The Great Age of Greek Literature.* New York: W. W. Norton & Company, Inc., 1942. A pleasing literary study of the Greek attitude toward life and letters, with modern parallels; separate chapters on many of the more important writers; illustrated by quotations from Greek, Biblical, and English literary sources.

Harvey, Sir Paul, Editor, *The Oxford Companion to Classical Literature.* Oxford: Clarendon Press, 1937. A comprehensive handbook with brief explanations of a wide variety of literary themes and characters. Conveniently arranged in alphabetical order after the fashion of a short classical encyclopædia.

Hasebroek, Johannes, *Trade and Politics in Ancient Greece,* translated by L. M. Fraser and D. C. MacGregor. London: George Bell and Sons, Ltd., 1933. A survey of ancient Greek commerce and economics, with particular emphasis on the relation of the state to the problems of trade and money. A sound and well-documented study.

Henderson, B. W., *The Great War Between Athens and Sparta.* London: Macmillan & Co., Ltd., 1927. An excellent detailed study of the policies and strategy of the Athenians and Spartans in the Peloponnesian War, affording also valuable criticism of Thucydides as an historian.

Highet, Gilbert, *The Classical Tradition.* New York: Oxford University Press, 1949. This book, written in subjective manner, traces the influence of classical studies on European and American culture. An interesting study of comparative literature, based on broad and liberal scholarship.

Jaeger, Werner, *Paideia,* translated by Gilbert Highet, 3 volumes. New York: Oxford University Press, 1939–45. A detailed study of the philosophy of education in Greece considered in its broadest implications; penetrating judgments of Homer, Plato, and Aristotle are of particular interest.

Kitto, H. D. F., *Greek Tragedy,* Second Edition. London: Methuen & Co., Ltd., 1950. This book contains much that is new in organization and evaluation; rich in comparative allusions and personal judgments.

Lawrence, A. W., *Later Greek Sculpture and Its Influence on East and West.* London: Jonathan Cape, Ltd., 1927. An interesting attempt to trace the growth and form of sculpture after Alexander the Great. Takes account of successive periods and of different localities. Well illustrated.

Livingstone, R. W., *The Greek Genius and Its Meaning to Us,* Second Edition. Oxford: Clarendon Press, 1924. An understanding book, written by a humanist trained in the best classical tradition, on the qualities that have rendered the culture of ancient Greece significant to the modern world.

———, Editor, *The Legacy of Greece.* Oxford: Clarendon Press, 1922. A series of essays by different scholars on such fields as religion, philosophy, medicine, and politics. Authoritative and detailed in treatment, though adapted for supplementary rather than primary study.

——, *The Pageant of Greece.* Oxford: Clarendon Press, 1923. Extended translated passages of ancient Greek literature from the successive fields, such as epic, tragedy, history, and so forth, interspersed with very useful, subjective criticisms.

Lord, John King, Editor, *Atlas of the Geography and History of the Ancient World.* New York: Benj. H. Sanborn & Co., 1902. A useful collection of maps of classical lands in color, adequately indexed.

McClees, H., and Alexander, C., *The Daily Life of the Greeks and Romans,* Sixth Edition. New York: Metropolitan Museum of Art, 1941. A study of the problems and activities inherent in every society as they applied to classical antiquity.

Murray, Gilbert, *The Rise of the Greek Epic,* Third Edition. Oxford: Clarendon Press, 1924. This book, which grew out of a series of lectures delivered at Harvard University, deals with much more than the limited field indicated by the title. Some knowledge of Greek history and literature is predicated.

Nilsson, M. P., *Greek Piety,* translated by H. J. Rose. Oxford: Clarendon Press, 1948. Author and translator alike have worked long in the field of Greek religion. A scholarly study from a somewhat abstract point of view.

——, *Homer and Mycenæ.* London: Methuen & Co., Ltd., 1933. Contains a wide variety of topics relating to both the literary and archæological aspects of the subject. Useful for the elucidation of problems that arise from the Homeric poems in relation to their ancient setting.

The Oxford Book of Greek Verse in Translation, edited by T. F. Higham and C. M. Bowra. Oxford: Clarendon Press, 1938. The passages have been selected with care to illustrate the principal surviving forms of Greek literature. The translations are in general of high merit.

Oxford Classical Dictionary, edited by M. Cary and others. Oxford: Clarendon Press, 1949. A very full and useful volume, with brief scholarly essays on a wide variety of classical topics.

Pendlebury, J. D. S., *The Archæology of Crete, An Introduction.* London: Methuen & Co., Ltd., 1939. A very complete and useful handbook. Deals with the Minoan civilization chronologically and in the various divisions of art and culture. Well illustrated and documented.

Richter, Gisela M. A., *The Sculpture and Sculptors of the Greeks,* Third Edition. New Haven: Yale University Press, 1941. A careful discussion of the problems connected with Greek sculpture as well as of the individual artists. The numerous illustrations, grouped at the back, should be consulted constantly as reference is made to them in the text.

Robertson, D. S., *A Handbook of Greek and Roman Architecture,* Second Edition. Cambridge: The University Press, 1943. A chronological treatment of the technical problems of Greek and Roman architecture. The tables, indicating such things as the location and dates of Greek temples, constitute a valuable source of reference.

Rogers, Arthur Kenyon, *A Student's History of Philosophy,* Third Edition. New York: The Macmillan Company, 1936. Contains a survey of philosophy from ancient to modern times. The chapters on the Greek philosophers are brief, but lucid in exposition. Recommended for rapid review.

Rose, H. J., *A Handbook of Greek Mythology.* New York: E. P. Dutton & Co., Inc., 1928. A study in very considerable detail of the history of Greek mythology, the early stories of the beginnings of things, the genealogies of the gods, as well as the sagas and legends of Greek lands. Thoroughly documented; useful for reference.

Rostovtzeff, M., *A History of the Ancient World,* translated by J. D. Duff, Second Edition, 2 volumes. Oxford: Clarendon Press, 1933. Greek history is considered in its relation to wide movements in the ancient world. The work is a useful corrective to the tendency to study Greece as an isolated entity.

SELECTED BIBLIOGRAPHY

Seltman, Charles T., *Athens, Its History and Coinage Before the Persian Invasion*. Cambridge: The University Press, 1924. A fascinating treatment of the times of the Eupatridæ, Solon, and the tyranny in Athens. The book abounds in numismatic detail.

——, *Masterpieces of Greek Coinage*. Oxford: Cassirer, 1949. Greek coins considered as works of ancient art. The historical associations and relations are kept in constant review.

Shorey, Paul, *What Plato Said*. Chicago: University of Chicago Press, 1933. The dialogues of Plato are examined in order, and a running commentary on the thought and purpose of the philosopher is offered. Abundant cross references.

Smith, A. H., *The Sculptures of the Parthenon*. London: British Museum, 1910. A large folio of plates illustrating the sculptures of the Parthenon. A very useful and detailed introduction and commentary are included.

Tozer, H. F., *A History of Ancient Geography,* Second Edition. With additional notes by M. Cary. Cambridge: The University Press, 1935. A detailed study of ancient physical geography, with chapters on the geographical implications of historical events, such as the growth of colonization and the campaigns of Alexander the Great. The geographical knowledge of Herodotus and other ancient authors is examined.

Ure, P. N., *The Origin of Tyranny*. Cambridge: The University Press, 1922. Many controversial problems in political history during the period of the settlement of Greece are presented in cogent style. A useful supplement to the pages of orthodox Greek history.

Wace, A. J. B., *Mycenæ, An Archæological History and Guide*. Princeton: Princeton University Press, 1949. A recent treatment of the most important site of Mycenæan culture by a man of long personal acquaintance with the scene.

Weller, Charles Heald, *Athens and Its Monuments*. New York: The Macmillan Company, 1913. A brief and consecutive account of the topography of the principal archæological remains in Athens. Well arranged and illustrated.

Whibley, Leonard, Editor, *A Companion to Greek Studies,* Fourth Edition. Cambridge: The University Press, 1931. The technical and detailed aspects of many fields of Greek studies, literary, archæological, philosophical, and historical, prepared by different scholars. An exceedingly useful book of reference; not for general reading.

Wright, Wilmer Cave, *A Short History of Greek Literature.* New York: American Book Company, 1907. A consecutive history of the development of Greek literature from the earliest days to the time of Julian.

Zimmern, Alfred, *The Greek Commonwealth: Politics and Economics in Fifth-Century Athens,* Fifth Edition. Oxford: Clarendon Press, 1931. One of the best subjective books on the Athenian state; deals with such problems as climate, geography, industrial and agricultural life, and the attitude of the citizens.

INDEX

The pronunciation has been indicated only for unfamiliar names and words. It will be useful to recall that in virtually all cases Greek *ch* is hard; thus *Achilles* and *Chryses* are pronounced *aki'l lēs* and *krī' sēs*. In dealing with vowel sounds consistency has sometimes been sacrificed to established usage.

It will also be noted that the Greek, rather than the English, syllabic divisions are used.

INDEX

[596]

INDEX

Artemis, 8, 260, 290
Artemisia (ar te mis' ia), 469
Artemisium, Cape (ar te mis' ium), 217
Aryballos (*see* Vases, shapes)
Asclepius (as clē' pius), 203
Ascra (as' cra), 159
Ashlar masonry, 68
Aspasia (as pā' sia), 199
Assembly (*see also* Athens, government) :
  in Homer, 116
  in Macedon, 117
Assinarus River (as si nar' us), 400
Assyria, 207
Astragalus (*see* Temples)
Astyanax (astī' anax), 89
Athena, 27, 87, 101–102
  in art, 372–373
  statues of :
    archaistic, 554, 555
    Lemnian, 343
    Mourning, 358–359
    Parthenos (par' the nos), 284, 344–345, 567–568
    Promachos (pro' ma kos), 343, 344
  temples (*see also* Parthenon) :
    of Athena Alea, at Tegea (a' le a, Te' je a), 468
    of Athena Nike (nī' kē), 318–319, 358
Athenæus (athe nē' us), *Philosophers at Dinner,* 487
Athenian Empire, 238–239, 398, 457
Athenians :
  autochthonous, 123
  members of the Ionian tribe, 26
Athens :
  government :
    Board of Nine Archons, 124, 131
    Board of Ten Generals (*Strategoi*), 140, 212–213, 240–241, 401
    Council of Five Hundred, 140
    Council of Five Thousand, 140–141
    Council of Four Hundred, 132
    Court of the Areopagus, 128, 131, 240
    democracy, 118–119, 137–138, 140, 239–240

Athens (*Cont.*) :
  government (*Cont.*) :
    early forms of, 123–125
    Ecclesia, 131, 140
    Eupatridæ, rule of, 124
    kingship, 116, 124–125
    law courts, 478, 479
    payment for service, 240–241
  history :
    aids Ionian Revolt, 208–209
    early fifth century, 234–244
    Funeral Speech of Pericles, 457
    Peloponnesian War, 394–405
    Pentacontaëtia, 233–234
    rebuilding of walls, 234–235, 442–443
    under Peisistratus, 132–138
    under the Thirty Tyrants, 405
Athenodorus (athenō dō' rus), 556
Athletics (*see also* Games *and* Sports) :
  athletes, types in archaic sculpture, 144–146
  overemphasis on, 191
Athos, 261
  canal, 216
  wreck of Persian fleet at, 210, 216
Atlas, 338, 339
Atomic theory, 200–201
Atreus (ā' treūs), 260
  Treasury of, 72–75
Attalus I (at' tal us), 544
Attica, size of, 3
Augustine, Saint, 83
Augustus (*see* Octavianus)
Aulis, 260
Axioms of Hesiod, 160

B

Babrius (bā' brius), 569
Babylon, 226, 227, 453
Babylonia, 207
  marriage market at, 228–229
Bacchæ of Euripides, 283
Bacchylides (ba kil' i dēs), 163
Barbarians, 449
  definition of, 27
Barbotine ware (bar' bō tēn), 54
Bassæ (bas' sē), Temple at, 298, 319
Batrachomyomachia (ba' tra kō mi ō ma' kia), 108–109
Batter (*see* Temples)

[597]

INDEX

[598]

INDEX

INDEX

Dialogues of the Sea Gods (*see* Lucian)

Diazoma (*see* Theater)

Dictæan Cave (dic tē' an), 60

Didactic epic, 158–159

Die cutting, 143, 391–392

Dio Chrysostom (kri' sos tom), *Eubœan Tale,* or *Hunter,* 568–569

Diodorus Siculus (dio dō' rus, si' cu lus), 560, 563

Diogenes Laertius (dio' ge nēs la er' tius), *Lives of the Philosophers,* 565

Diogenes the Cynic, 508

Diomedes (dio mē' dēs), 81

Dionysiac festivals, 246–247

Dionysius I (dio ny' sius), 491

Dionysius II, 491

Dionysius of Halicarnassus:
   On the Ancient Orators, 565
   On the Arrangement of Words, 565

Dionysus (dio nī' sus):
   epic of Nonnus, 569
   god of comedy, 416
   god of tragedy, 246, 422
   in the *Frogs* of Aristophanes, 422–428
   Theater of, 36, 323, 324, 326
   worship of, 247

Diphilus (di' phil us), 487–488

Dipteral (*see* Temples)

Dipylon (di' pi lon) Cemetery, 364, 369, 475

Dirce (dir' sē), 11

Discobolus (dis co' bo lus), 280, 340–342

Dithyrambs (di' thē rambs), 246, 247, 322–323

Doctrine of Ideas, Aristotle's criticism of, 501 (*see also* Plato)

Doctrine of the Mean, 252–253, 504 (*see also* Aristotle)

Doll Maker (*see* Middle Comedy)

Dorian migrations, 9

Dorians, 26, 115

Doric order (*see* Architecture)

Dorus, 26

Doryphorus (dory' phorus), 280, 355, 356, 357

Dracon (drā' con), 128, 129, 132, 143

Drama:
   audience, 253
   definition of, 248
   technical terms and conventions, 253–256, 288
      anagnorisis (anag nō' ri sis), 255–256
      ananke (an ang' kē), 254
      hamartia (ha mar tī' a), 254
      hubris (hu' bris), 254, 255
      peripeteia (peri pe tī' a), 255, 256
      tragic hero, 253–254
      trilogy and tetralogy, 248–249, 259–260, 263–266

Dramatic festivals, 246–247

Dramatists, Attic:
   relative ages of, 257
   same theme in, 266

Dromos (drō' mos), 74

Dying Gaul, 543–544
   compared with Fallen Warrior from Ægina, 336, 543

E

Earring, Nike, 382–383

Earth, air, fire, and water, philosophic concepts, 197

Ecbatana (ec ba' ta na), 453

Ecclesia (ec clēs' ia), 131

Ecclesiazusæ of Aristophanes, 418, 428–429

Eccyclema (*see* Theater)

Echinus (*see* Temples)

Eclecticism in art, 545

Egypt:
   art of, 14
   association of Alexander with, 452, 455, 511, 525–526
   bronze casting, 154–155
   culture of, 40, 43–44, 57
   visited by Herodotus, 227

Egyptian portrait plaques (*see* Painting)

Eirene and Plutus (ī rē' nē, plu' tus), statue of, 460–462, 463

Ekecheiria (e ke kī ri' a), 33

Eleatic (ē le a' tic) school, 190–193

Electra:
   of Euripides, 266, 283
   of Sophocles, 266, 271

[601]

INDEX

INDEX

[604]

INDEX

INDEX

INDEX

Philemon (phi lē′ mon), 487–488

Philip II of Macedon, 19, 441, 447, 483–485
  career and character, 447
  elected general of Greece, 449
  hostage of Thebes, 447
  opposed by Demosthenes, 448

Philip V, 514

Philippics (*see* Demosthenes)

Philoctetes of Sophocles, 271, 280

Philosophers at Dinner (*see* Athenæus)

Phocians, 217

Phocion, 510

Phocylides (pho si′ li dēs), 169

Phœnician Women of Euripides, 283

Phœnicians, 39, 228
  alphabet, 15
  culture, 40
  trade, 15

Phrynichus (phri′ ni kus), 209, 249
  Phœnician Women, 249
  Sack of Miletus, 209, 249

Phye (phī′ ē), story of, 133–134

Physical philosophers, 185–205

Physics of Aristotle, 501

Pinax (*see* Vases, shapes)

Pindar, 163, 177–181
  house spared by Alexander the Great, 178, 451
  ode to Megacles, 179
  ode to Psaumis, 179–180
  poems of victory, 177–178
  position in antiquity, 178
  praise of Athens, 18, 178–179
  Pythian odes, 35

Piracy, 65, 514, 518

Piræus (pi rē′ us), 212
  battle at, 405
  defense of, 236
  rebuilding of Long Walls, 442–443

Pillars of Heracles, 115, 228

Pirithous (pir i′ tho us), 339

Pittacus (pit′ ta cus), 167, 170

Pity and terror, 251–253 (*see also* Catharsis)

Plague:
  at Athens, 396, 421–422
  at Thebes, 274

Plant designs (*see* Vases, decorative motifs)

Planudes (pla nu′ des), 570

Platæa (pla tē′ a), 397
  Battle of, 220–222, 234, 236
    Æschylus fights in, 258
  joins Athens at Marathon, 212, 214
  siege of, 408–410

Plato, 490–499
  Academy of, 491, 508
  association with Socrates, 438–439, 490–491
    trial and death of Socrates, 492–493
  career, 490–491
  dating of dialogues, 492
  Doctrine of Ideas, 496
  influenced by Pythagoreans, 196
  myth of the cave, 496–499
  philosophic concepts, 493, 496–499
  travestied in Middle Comedy, 487
  works:
    Apology, 439, 491, 492
    Charmides (kar′ mi dēs), 491
    Cratylus (cra′ ti lus), 491
    Critias (cri′ ti as), 491
    Crito (crī′ to), 491, 492
    Euthydemus (eu thi dē′ mus), 491, 492
    Euthyphro (eu′ thi phrō), 491, 492
    Gorgias (gor′ ji as), 491, 492
    Hippias Minor (hip′ pi as), 491
    Ion (ī′ on), 491
    Laches (lā′ kes), 491
    Laws, 491
    Lysis (lī′ sis), 491
    Menexenus (me ne′ xen us), 491
    Meno (mē′ no), 491
    Parmenides (par men′ i dēs), 491
    Phædo (phē′ do), 491, 492
    Phædrus (phē′ drus), 491
    Philebus (phi lē′ bus), 491
    Protagoras (pro ta′ goras), 491
    Republic, 490, 491, 494–499
    Sophist, 491
    Statesman, 491
    Symposium, 491
    Theætetus (the ē tē′ tus), 491
    Timæus (ti mē′ us), 491

Plautus, 488

Plutarch, 243, 563–565
  Moralia, 565

[614]

INDEX

INDEX

INDEX

Vases (*Cont.*) :
  painters and potters (*Cont.*) :
    Execias (ex ē' ki as), 370
    Hieron (hi' er on), 372
    Nicosthenes (ni cos' the nēs), 370
    Pan Painter, 374
  shapes :
    alabastron (ala bas' tron), 364
    amphora (am' pho ra), 370
    aryballos (ari bal' los), 366, 370, 371
    crater, 373
    cup in shape of cow's hoof, 376–377
    cylix (sī' lix), 370, 375
    fish plates, 376
    hydria (hī' dri a), 183
    lekythos (le' ki thos), 364, 372, 374, 375
    Little Master, 376, 378
    œnochoë (ē no' ko ē), 366, 368
    pyxis (pi' xis), 365, 375
    rhyton (rhī' ton), 374–375
    scyphus (skī' phus), 366
    variety of, 370, 374–376
  steatite, 56–57
  technique :
    Attic black-figured, 370
    Attic red-figured, 372
    relief line, 371
    use of slip, 367
Venus (*see also* Aphrodite) :
  Capitoline, 554
  Genetrix, 551, 552
  of the Medici, 554, 555
Vergil, 521, 531
  Æneid, 109, 556
Virtue, philosophic concept, 493–494
Volo, funeral stelæ, 378

W

Walls, Athenian, 235–236 (*see also* Fortifications)
Wars :
  Lamian (lā' mi an), 510–511
  Messenian (mes sēn' i an), 165
  Peloponnesian, 19, 394–405
  Persian, 206–224
  Trojan, 81, 109
Wasps of Aristophanes, 418, 428–429
Water, basic reality, 187–188

Weaving, implements of, 385–386
Wine, a Persian use of, 230–231
Wolf, *Prolegomena ad Homerum,* 80
Wood :
  opæ, 303, 305–306
  revolving forms of Solon, 132
  use of, 303, 305–306, 308–309
Wooden Horse, 109
Wordsworth, 531
Wrath of Achilles, 81
Writing, early evidence of, 40, 58–60

X

Xanthias (xan' thi as), 422–427
Xenophanes (xen o' pha nēs), 190–191
  challenge to anthromorphism, 191
  moral censures of, 191, 195–196
Xenophon (xen' o phon), 16, 403, 413–416, 438–439, 441
  career, 413–414
  estimate of, 415–416
  evidence on Socrates, 414, 415, 438
  works :
    Anabasis (an a' ba sis), 414–415, 441
    Apology, 415
    Constitution of Sparta, 415
    Cyropædia (sī ro pē dī' a), 415, 575
    Hellenica (hel le' ni ca), 414, 445
    Hiero (hi' er o), 415
    Memorabilia (me mor a bi' li a), 415
    Œconomicus (ē co no' mi cus), 415
    Symposium, 415
Xerxes (xer' xēs), 215–221, 331
  at Salamis, 219
  at Thermopylæ, 217
Xuthus (xu' thus), 26

Z

Zeno (zē' no), 190, 192–193
Zenodotus (ze no' do tus), 526
Zeugitæ (zeū' gi tē), 131
Zeus (zeūs), 28, 32, 34, 36, 82, 87, 92, 335
  of Pheidias, 280
  statue from Artemisium, 333, 335–336
  Temple of, 336–340
Zoster, 16